The Sports Immortals

Jimmy Brown

Joe Namath

Johnny Unitas

Bobby Orr   Pele

A.J. Foyt

Muhammad Ali   Joe Frazier

Kareem Abdul-Jabbar

Rod Laver

Wilt Chamberlain

The Sports Immortals

A Rutledge Book

Published by Prentice-Hall, Inc.
Englewood Cliffs, New Jersey

by THE ASSOCIATED PRESS SPORTS STAFF

Supervising Editor: Will Grimsley
Photo Editor: Thomas V. diLustro

Project Director: *Keith Fuller*
Editor-in-Chief: *Dan Perkes*
Supervising Editor: *Will Grimsley*
Photo Editor: *Thomas V. diLustro*
Manuscript Editor: *Ben Olan*

Authors: Ralph Bernstein, Hal Bock, Bloys Britt, Tom Emory, Earl Gerheim, Bob Green, Will Grimsley, Dick Joyce, Jerry Liska, Bruce Lowitt, Geoffrey Miller, Charles Morey, Hubert Mizell, Herschel Nissenson, Ben Olan, Eric Prewitt, Ken Rappoport, Mike Rathet, Ron Roach, Bert Rosenthal, Alex Sachare, Ed Schuyler, Jr., Jack Simms, Karol Stonger, Ben Thomas, George Vecsey

Pictures were made by the staff photographers of The Associated Press and its member newspapers except for color photos of Johnny Unitas and Rod Laver, which are by Ken Regan, and of Bobby Hull, by Melchior Di Giacomo.

Associated Press.
 The sports immortals.

 "A Rutledge book."
 1. Sports—Biography. I. Grimsley, Will, ed.
II. Title.
GV697.A1A64   796'.092'2 [B]   72-6900
ISBN 0-13-837740-5

Contents

Introduction

These pages tell the stories of 50 of the greatest athletes in the history of modern sports.

They were chosen by the sports staff of the Associated Press, men and women whose careers and professional standing are based on their ability to record with accuracy, objectivity, flavor and dimension the achievements and failures of the world's athletes. These staffers demonstrate this ability every day in the stories you read in the pages of your newspaper and hear broadcast both on the networks and on your local station.

Even so, choosing immortals is a task that leads to long, reasoned debate, hot bursts of argument and a great deal of name juggling. After all, even in ancient Greece there was argument about the proper ranking of the mythological immortals of Mount Olympus. When the job entails writing a book about real people instead of simply cataloging the make-believe population of a mountain, exercising a high degree of judgment, knowledge and sensitivity is absolutely essential.

As it applies to athletes, the dictionary definition of an *immortal*—"one who has enduring fame"—isn't much help. So we just had to go ahead and confer upon ourselves a certain omniscience as to which athletes, living and dead, have earned a place here.

We think there is no doubt that the men and women whose careers make up these pages belong in them. They are athletes whose names will live on as long as modern games are played.

All of them have some of the same qualities: determination, pride, both natural and developed skill. Many of them display generosity and largeness of spirit and unwavering physical and moral courage. Yet they are all individuals, from all kinds of backgrounds; they are rich, poor, hot-tempered, mild-mannered, courteous, arrogant.

The greatest single thing binding them together is a mysterious quality that makes them live in the mind of the observer or reader. They are people who are reflected in life as an ordinary person is reflected in a magnifying mirror.

And yet the perceptive, knowledgeable reader will sense the pangs that accompanied the inclusion of some athletes at the expense of others. This was required by the nature of the book. Not only is it limited to 50 great athletes, it also must encompass every era of modern sports, including the present one.

You are entitled to wonder, as we did, whether Dick Butkus is more immortal than Tom Harmon or Don Hutson in football or whether Hank Aaron really deserves a place on Mount Olympus above Rogers Hornsby or Stan Musial or why Glenn Cunningham, the miler who overcame badly burned legs to become a world champion, could not be included. What about Cornelius Warmerdam, Don Budge, Lou Gehrig and Tris Speaker, Oscar Robertson, Sid Luckman and Ernie Nevers?

There is no denying that they were great—even immortal—but the effort in this book is to represent each sport and each era with the athletes who cast the largest shadows.

You may also wonder why there were no coaches or managers included. What about Knute Rockne, Vince Lombardi, Casey Stengel, Connie Mack? The answer is simply that this volume is limited to those who won their greatest fame playing. Having considered these things, see whether you would rule out any athlete included in this book. Whom would you eliminate?

Would it be Satchel Paige, the best baseball pitcher who ever lived? Would it be Paavo Nurmi or Jesse Owens or Red Grange? What about Johnny Weissmuller, the most renowned swimming champion of all time, or Babe Didrikson Zaharias, the greatest woman athlete in history? Perhaps it should be Ted Williams, Joe DiMaggio, Sammy Baugh or Joe Louis or, in more recent years, Joe Namath, Muhammad Ali or Arnold Palmer?

No, in each era these names tower. Certainly in years to come, new immortals will rise and push some of them into the background; that is inevitable. Twenty years from now, a similar volume would have to exclude some of them in order to include immortals now just toddlers.

That makes those left out here or those to be omitted in the future no less great. Each of us—and surely this includes every reader—would have liked to include someone who is immortal to him, if only within a more limited circle than this book encompasses.

My Uncle Verne was a tall, gangly, curly-haired boy who grew up on a farm in north Texas. In the 1920s, he went away to college at Texas A&M. They laughed when he went out for football in his bib overalls and work shoes. In his senior year, he was all-Southwest Conference in football, basketball and baseball, and he was the offensive star of the East-West game in San Francisco.

Many years later, at East Texas State College, where he was head coach, the athletic dormitory was named after him. I guess the time will come, if it hasn't already, when a boy showing up at East Texas for the first time will look up at the name on the dorm and wonder who in the world was J. V. Sikes.

In my mind, he is a sports immortal—the kind of man against whom you measure other immortals. I know a lot of men who would agree with me, including men who have offered their friendship for no better quality of my own than the fact that J. V. Sikes was my uncle.

It's that indefinable quality of living on in the minds of others that really makes men immortal. The athletes in this book have that quality, for reasons that are mostly good.

You can learn quite a few homely lessons from their careers. You realize the worth of toil and perseverance and the strength that come from being generous and the wealth and fame that come from being strong.

And maybe another value of the book is that as you read, you will be reminded of your own Uncle Verne, who—like hundreds of other great athletes—didn't make these chapters but whose life rubbed off on yours and perhaps made yours a little more worthwhile and who lives on eternally in your mind.

Bob Johnson
General Sports Editor
The Associated Press

The Early Pioneers

Imagination leads us to believe that most of the sophisticated pastimes existing today—individual and team—trace their ancestry back to primitive days when the only argument over style was the fit of a loincloth. A caveman once picked up a crooked limb and, en route home to dinner, fed his boredom by using it to belt loose stones. As he neared his abode, one of the missiles fell into a smoking cauldron. The caveman was fascinated. He told his friends. A contest ensued. Thus golf was born. Later a group chose up sides and began trying to hit rocks through each other at a fixed target. Out of it came a crude form of hockey.

There were races in the woods, jumping and vaulting contests. Men grappled and slugged it out with fists to establish physical superiority. They sewed cloth into round balls and batted them back and forth with paddles carved from wood. From such activities emerged tennis, badminton, squash and other racket sports.

Baseball was the outgrowth of a popular English schoolboy game named "rounders," which New Englanders later played as "town ball," but the sport's inventor is generally recognized as Abner Doubleday and the year and place of its birth as 1839 in Cooperstown, New York. Football traces its ancestry to soccer—played in England in the eleventh century—but the American version came into being in the 1870s, with Harvard, Princeton, Rutgers and Canada's McGill University breaking the ground. Golf probably goes back to the caveman, or almost certainly to the shepherds at the time of Christ, but its cradle rests at St. Andrews, Scotland. Prize-fighting is one of the most primitive of sports. The horse is said to be perhaps 4 million years old, and Italy has an automobile relic at Torino dated 1837. The ages of various sports differ widely.

The early pioneers in all athletic endeavors, however, were a hardy breed. Their playing areas were often atrocious in condition, with none of the manicured carpets—real or synthetic—produced in later years. Most of them were veritable iron men who plied their trade largely for the fun and the glory of the game with a pittance for pay.

Prize fighters fought bare-knuckled in the early days, sometimes on a river barge or in an obscure barn away from the eyes of the law. The great John L. Sullivan needed 75 rounds to batter Jake Kilrain into submission in a slugging marathon that lasted 2 hours, 16 minutes in a clearing near Richburg, Mississippi, in 1892. Baseball pitchers didn't have the luxury of working with three days' rest. Iron-man Joe McGinnity pitched and won doubleheaders. He once had a season record of 35–8. Old Cy Young pitched 7,377 innings in a 22-year career that lasted until he was 41 years old, and he won a phenomenal 511 games. There were no specialists in football, only all-purpose performers, playing every minute of 90 minutes in the late 1890s. Pudge Heffelfinger, an immortal at Yale, was one of the first professionals. He received $500 for playing a game for the Allegheny Athletic Association. Another time he fielded a team whose pay was "double train fare."

It was from such sturdy stock as these that sports produced some of the greatest all-time stars, including Jim Thorpe, the tragedy-plagued Sac and Fox Indian whom many regarded as the greatest all-around athlete who ever lived; Ty Cobb, whose slashing spikes and potent bat made baseball history; Walter Johnson, who threw bullets instead of baseballs; Red Grange, the fabled Galloping Ghost of the gridiron, and the indefatigable Finn, Paavo Nurmi, whose name forever will be synonymous with long-distance running. Improved diets and changing techniques brought forth a newer breed of athlete who made old records obsolete, but the names of the pioneers and their exploits could never be crushed.

Red Grange
The Galloping Ghost

The autumn wind still whistles shrilly through cavernous Memorial Stadium at the University of Illinois, as if in perpetual tribute to college football's legendary Galloping Ghost.

It was at the dedication of Memorial Stadium, an imposing landmark on the flat plains surrounding Champaign, Illinois, that Halfback Harold ("Red") Grange slashed, whirled and spun phantomlike for the most fabulous 12 minutes in college gridiron history.

Against Fielding H. ("Hurry Up") Yost's proud Michigan team, on a sultry October 18, 1924, Grange streaked 95 yards for a touchdown on the opening kickoff and then darted from scrimmage for three more stunning touchdown runs of 67, 56 and 44 yards before leaving the field with three minutes remaining in the first quarter. In the second half, he scored a fifth TD on a 12-yard run just for good measure.

Almost one year later to the month, October 31, 1925, the Illini Thunderbolt in his senior season made Eastern skeptics complete believers, in a game against a great Pennsylvania team. Before a partisan crowd of 63,000 that expected to see a Midwestern myth disintegrated, Grange swivel-hipped to three touchdowns, the first a 60-yard scoring run the first time he carried.

Football has grown much more sophisticated, specialized and intricate since Grange —a picture of grace, balance and speed—was the epitome of gridiron greatness, a Golden Twenties' athletic peer of Babe Ruth's, Jack Dempsey's, Bobby Jones's and Bill Tilden's. Grange, whose magic name turned pro football from an ugly duckling to a present-day gilded and plush bird of paradise, will be remembered as long as football is played in America.

Even by latter-day standards in an era of two-platoon football, Grange's three-season Illini record of 31 touchdowns and 3,637 rushing yards remained impressive. The flame-thatched star also piled up 643 yards passing when the air game still was young. He was credited with luring 738,555 spectators to Illini games.

No football player since has quite given the game the same charisma or left the same electrifying memories as did Grange, whose jersey number, 77, became symbolic of an all-time superstar.

During his high school, college and professional career, Grange carried the ball 4,013 times for 33,820 yards, averaging 8.4 yards per try over a period of 18 seasons. Contrary to some football folklore, Grange was not an accidental find by the wily Illini coach Bob Zuppke. He had scored 74 touchdowns at Wheaton High School, enough to attract any intelligent college coach.

Grange was born in modest circumstances June 13, 1903, in the village of Wheaton, Illinois. His father was the town's police chief. His mother, who was sickly, died while Harold was still a young boy. Grange became disheartened by the death of his mother, the family's lack of money and the dullness of small-town life. He wanted to quit rather than enter high school, but his father gave him a stern lecture and young Harold continued his schooling, finding an outlet for his frustrations in sports.

He was a superb athlete in football, basketball and track, but it was football that he liked best. Soon stories about his gridiron skills circulated in high school coaching circles throughout the state. College coaches and scouts swarmed to Wheaton to see the ball-carrying whiz who was averaging five touchdowns a game.

A devoted admirer of Zuppke, Grange naturally gravitated to Illinois. With 200 players reporting for the freshman team, Grange lost his nerve and decided to return home. But Zuppke insisted that he stay and assigned him to the seventh team. Within a week he was number one in the lineup. His collegiate career had begun.

During the summer Grange hauled 200-pound blocks of ice to help build his physique. That's how he became known as the "Illinois Iceman."

Before and after his phenomenal junior season performance against Michigan, Grange was a heroic ballcarrier whose swift elusiveness and amazing change of pace gave him a wraith-like quality that defied and frustrated would-be tacklers. He became the Galloping Ghost in

Red recorded the most fabulous 12 minutes in college football.

Above: Close-up of Illinois' gridiron star. Right: Grange starts for enemy goal line. It's the Illini versus Michigan. Right, below: Red has turned professional. Here, he is on the bench with Curly Lambeau.

newspaper write-ups of his broken field running.

Grange played his first college varsity game in 1923 against Nebraska, scoring three touchdowns on runs of 35, 65 and 12 yards in a 24–7 victory over the Cornhuskers. He also had a 3-touchdown game in a 29–27 loss to Northwestern and finished his sophomore year with 12 touchdowns in 6 games.

The following season, the Michigan student newspaper contended of Grange: "All he can do is run," to which caustic Zuppke retorted: "All Galli-Curci [great operatic star of the era] can do is sing."

The epic 1924 game brought Michigan to Champaign with Wolverine coach Yost confidently predicting: "Every time Grange takes the ball, there will be eleven hard, clean tackling Michigan men headed for him at the same time. We have made special preparations for Grange."

On hand for the Memorial Stadium dedication—"The House That Grange Built"—was the largest crowd—67,000—ever at a Midwest game. With auto travel rare, fans poured in by special trains from all directions. Pregame tension on the field was spiced by an innovation of the sly Zuppke's. The Old Dutchman, noting the unseasonably warm weather, told a coaching aide: "See if anything in the rule book says we got to wear stockings."

The assistant found there wasn't such a rule, and Zup ordered his players to strip off their heavy wool stockings. When the Illini trotted on the field after the pregame pep talk, Yost was flustered by the bare-legged foe, particularly Grange. The Wolverine coach protested to the officials, who could find no objection in the rule book. They also checked, at Yost's insistence, the Illini players' legs for grease but found none.

Finally, Michigan kicked off, Capt. Herb Steger's boot floating into Grange's arms on the Illini five-yard line. The Redhead loped down the middle, darted to the right and then reversed to the left sideline and sped clear on a 95-yard touchdown run.

Michigan failed to advance on the ensuing kickoff and punted to the Illini 33. Grange got the first call, circling Michigan's left end and then floating easily behind his interference to break open on a second touchdown run.

A few minutes later, Illinois again had possession. A plunge by Earl Britton, Grange's superb blocker, moved the ball to the Illini 44.

Again the ball was snapped to Grange, who squirted through Michigan's left side and this time raced 56 yards for his third touchdown with less than seven minutes played.

Another exchange of punts put Illinois on Michigan's 44. Once more Grange exploded to his right, cut back and eluded the entire Michigan defense on his fourth touchdown run with three minutes still left in the historic first quarter.

"I'm so tired, I can hardly stand up," the panting Grange told Illini quarterback Harry Hall. "Better get me out of here."

As Grange trotted to the bench, the crowd thundered an ovation that lasted five minutes. The Redhead returned in the second half and scored his fifth touchdown on a 12-yard burst and then tossed a 20-yard scoring pass to Marion Leonard as the Illini wrapped up a 39–14 victory over a completely demoralized Michigan team.

Legend often credits Grange with scoring five touchdowns on the only five times he carried the ball in that epic game. Actually, he carried 21 times for a total of 409 yards in three quarters of play. He also completed six passes for another 64 yards and held the ball for Britton's conversion attempts.

Ironically, Illinois failed to capture the Big Ten title that 1924 season. Against A. A. Stagg's then-powerful University of Chicago, Grange raced for three touchdowns on runs of 80, 35 and 25 yards, but the Illini wou d end up in a 21–21 tie with the Maroons. Grange was racked up the following week in a 20–7 loss to Minnesota and Chicago took the championship.

Against Pennsylvania in the 1925 game that more than silenced Eastern doubters of Grange's greatness, Zuppke learned from scouting reports that powerful Penn overshifted its defense when the opposing offense shifted into an unbalanced line.

Later, Grange, leading a life of pleasant retirement in his Indian Lake Estates, Florida, home, recalled: "Zuppke decided the only way we could gain was to shift right and run left, or vice versa."

Grange, who played quarterback his senior season, explained: "My instructions as quarterback were to shift strong side on the first two plays and run fullback Britton into the strong side. They nearly killed him.

"But on the third play, strong right, I carried the ball to my left—sixty yards for a touchdown. There was no one there. This happened throughout the game. They just kept overshifting on us."

Grange sent Eastern writers groping for adjectives as he ripped through Penn for two more touchdowns, one for 60 yards, the third for 35, as he carried 36 times and gained 363 yards in a 24–2 upset of the mighty Red and Blue club.

Grange also recounted that his immortal 1924 game against Michigan stemmed from Zuppke's strategy of having Old 77 cut back on end sweeps from the Illini unbalanced line.

"That was the first game in which I suddenly turned in and back on end runs," said Grange. "At any rate, Michigan was fooled. Maybe they were thinking more about our bare legs than the game. Overall incidentally, my college success was due in great measure to Earl Britton, one of the finest blocking backs who ever played football. On one of my runs against Michigan, I saw Britton go down making one block; then bounce up in time to take out another man and finally clear away a third tackler."

The day after Grange completed his collegiate career against Ohio State, November 21, 1925, the famed Redhead became pro football's first $100,000-a-year player. He signed a contract with the then-struggling Chicago Bears, stipulating a gate percentage and other benefits with a $100,000 guarantee.

Up until then, Bear owner–coach–player George Halas, himself an Illini football star, and the rest of the infant National Football League were playing for peanuts before pitifully small crowds.

On Sunday, November 22, Grange signed the contract in the morning and that afernoon sat on the Bear bench as the Bears defeated the Green Bay Packers 21–0.

The next Thursday, Thanksgiving Day, Grange made his professional debut against the arch-rival Chicago Cardinals. Instead of the usual Turkey Day crowd of less than 14,000, a capacity 36,000 packed Wrigley Field, lured by the magic of Grange's prowess. Unfortunately, the Cardinals' Paddy Driscoll consistently punted away from Grange and the game ended in a disappointing scoreless tie.

On Sunday, November 29, a crowd of 28,000 appeared at Wrigley Field as the Bears edged the Columbus (Ohio) Tigers, 14–13, with

Joining in some horseplay with Jim Thorpe and his sons.

Grange hammering out 140 rushing yards in swirling snow.

Then began a Bear tour, with Grange the big attraction, that hit a climax with a crowd of 65,000 at the Polo Grounds where the Bears whipped the New York Giants 19–7.

A lucrative but ill-fated switch by Grange occurred in 1926 when the heralded promoter C. C. ("Cash and Carry") Pyle organized a short-lived rival pro league with Grange signing with the New York Yankee club.

In 1927, the new league folded, but Pyle was given a New York franchise in the National Football League with Grange on the roster as the big gate lure. Early in the season, Red twisted his right knee—he was on crutches for six months and missed the entire 1928 season.

When Grange's personal contract with Pyle expired, he rejoined the Bears in 1929 to begin a six-season stint in which defense became his forte. The 6-foot, 185-pound star was voted into pro football's Hall of Fame as a charter member in 1963. He was a four-time all-NFL halfback.

At his peak, Grange was twice summoned to Hollywood to star in football films *One Minute to Play* and *The Galloping Ghost*. He retired from pro football in 1935.

Grange participated in the National Football League's first title play-off game in 1933 and always regarded the Bears' 23–21 triumph over the New York Giants as one of the greatest championship games of all time.

"The winner's share was something like two hundred forty dollars a man and the losers were very happy with one hundred forty dollars apiece," said Grange. "I earned more than my expected one hundred thousand dollars on that Chicago Bear 1925 tour when I first turned pro. But we played seventeen games between December second and February first—including eight in eleven days, and there wasn't a bone in my body that didn't ache like the devil."

After quitting football, Grange had a financially successful career in football broadcasting, sales promotion and insurance. Still trim after having reached 60, the Galloping Ghost retired with his wife to a sprawling, gleaming white ranch house in Florida.

"My routine these so-called Golden Years is to have breakfast and then if I feel like doing nothing, that's what I do," said Grange. "If I feel like work, I can take out my boat on our fifteen-square-mile lake and fish. Or, if I want to work harder, I can play golf. The conversation in this lovely Florida community is 'What's your latest golf score?' or 'What are the grandchildren doing?'

"No one cares what you were. It's what you are that counts here."

JERRY LISKA

Ty Cobb
Every Man an Enemy

On May 15, 1912, in a game in New York, the short-tempered left fielder of the Detroit Tigers was being heckled by a fan. Finally, as the abuse continued, the 25-year-old Ty Cobb charged the bleachers and began swinging at his tormenter.

As a result, American League president Ban Johnson suspended Cobb indefinitely. The fiery Cobb had few friends among his teammates, but the Tigers decided to go on strike until Cobb was reinstated. They felt their chances of winning were slight without their star player, who had hit .420 the previous year.

The strike lasted one day. To avoid paying a $5,000 forfeit, the Detroit club fielded a team of semipros, sandlotters and students from Philadelphia's St. Joseph's College; they were trounced by the Athletics, 24–2. Cobb himself finally urged the Tigers to end their walkout. They did, but Johnson fined nearly every Detroit player $100, while Cobb was assessed $50 and given a 10-day suspension.

That was Tyrus Raymond Cobb. Peaceful moments were few and far between when the battling Georgia Peach was around. If ever there was a ballplayer who wanted and fought for every edge he could get, it was Cobb.

Reminiscing with a Detroit writer long after his retirement, Cobb recalled the idiosyncrasies of other players, such as Eddie Collins, who would remove his chewing gum from his mouth after two strikes and stick it on top of his cap. Cobb said he never had any nervous habits, but the writer reminded him that whenever he reached first base, he always kicked the bag a couple of times.

Cobb smiled slyly. "I wanted the other side to think as you did," he said, "but that wasn't an absent-minded habit at all. It was really a percentage trick. With my long lead and pitchers trying to pick me off, I needed every advantage. By kicking the sack a couple of inches closer to second base, I had the edge when a good, quick pick-off move almost got me going back to first base."

Ty Cobb lived for the edge. He acknowledged that some others had more talent but boasted he had more determination and dedication. He practiced bunting and sliding by the hour. He hunted with heavy boots during the winter to keep his legs—the legs that stole a record 892 bases—in shape. He put lead weights in his spiked shoes during spring training so that on opening day, when he removed them, he'd feel light as a feather. A daring base runner, often scoring from second base and sometimes from first on an infield out, he slid high and hard, mastering the fade-away and hook slides. Others could hit the ball farther, run faster, field better, throw better, but no one cast more fear into the hearts of rival pitchers, catchers and fielders.

"Don't let anyone tell you I was a dirty player," Cobb said 30 years after his retirement. "When you're out on those base paths, you've got to protect yourself. The base paths belonged to me, the runner. The rules gave me the right. I always went into a bag full speed, feet first. I had sharp spikes on my shoes. If the baseman stood where he had no business to be and got hurt, that was his fault."

Until he died in 1961 at the age of 74, Cobb insisted that he "wasn't nearly as rough as everyone said" and that he spiked only two or three opponents deliberately. And he staunchly insisted that Frank ("Home Run") Baker of the Philadelphia Athletics wasn't one of them.

That incident—Cobb spiked third baseman Baker during an important game in 1910—caused a furor, with loyal Philadelphia fans threatening to lynch Cobb.

"Pictures show I couldn't have done it deliberately," Cobb protested, "and Baker didn't lose an inning, but I got thirteen threatening letters. One of the nuts threatened to shoot me from a window outside the park."

Cobb could be many things, including cruel and sadistic, but no one ever questioned his gameness. He not only played the next time the Tigers came to Philadelphia, but he put on a display of hitting, running and fielding that was truly magnificent.

To some, such as New York catcher Fred Hofmann, it was a mark of distinction to be spiked by Cobb.

Whether playing as a kid (bottom row, far left in team picture) or with the Tigers, Cobb maintained, "I've got to be first all the time—first in everything."

The first time Hofmann caught against Detroit, he snarled as Cobb stepped into the batter's box, "So this is the great Georgia Peach."

Cobb stepped out. "Listen, busher," he warned, "I'm going to get on, and when I do I'm coming around."

Cobb singled, swiped second and tried to score on a ground ball to short. The throw had him beaten from New York to Detroit and Hofmann got set to apply the tag. Cobb left the ground. Hofmann's chest protector went one way, a shin guard another way, the ball a third way. Hofmann lay in the dirt, his thigh cut. This is the way he remembered it:

"Cobb got up, stepped over me onto the plate, brushed his dust off on me, looked down and said, 'Yes, you fresh busher, that was the great Georgia Peach.' "

And great was the word. Cobb's record 4,191 hits and .367 lifetime batting average in a 24-year career—22 with the Tigers and 2 with the Athletics—may stand forever. He was not a natural hitter, but the 6-foot 1-inch, 175-pounder developed a closed stance—feet together, bat choked slightly, hands apart for better bat control—that enabled him to drop the top (left) hand down to swing away or slide the bottom hand up to push the ball where he wanted.

Because of his batting style, Cobb was not a long-ball hitter. He hit 118 home runs, never more than 12 in one season, and reached that level only twice. But since he could do pretty much what he wanted on the baseball field, it was suspected he could have become a home run hitter if he'd swung for the fences as Babe Ruth did.

In 1925, a St. Louis writer was talking about Ruth's home runs before a game at Sportsman's Park. Harry Heilmann, Detroit's great right fielder, needled Cobb, then the Tigers' 38-year-old playing manager, about hitting to left field so often (Cobb was a left-handed hitter). Cobb didn't say much; his bat spoke for him. That day he hit two singles, a double and three home runs. The next day he hit two more homers, plus two doubles, which landed high on the right field wall, barely missing home run territory.

The record book is Cobb territory. Besides his 4,191 hits and .367 lifetime average, he played the most games (3,033), scored 2,244 runs, led the American League in batting 9 straight times (1907–1915) and 12 times in 13

years, led the league in hits 8 times and set the record for most triples, 297. His nine straight league-leading averages were .350, .324, .377, .385, .420, .410, .390, .368 and .369.

Indeed, he hit .371 the following year, but Cleveland's Tris Speaker batted .386. Cobb was the champion again the next three years, though, hitting .383, .382, and .384. And although he didn't win any more batting crowns, his averages for the rest of his career were .334, .389, .401, .340, .338, .378, .339, .357 and .323, the last at the age of 41.

This was quite an achievement for the young man from Narrows, Banks County, Georgia, who flunked his first baseball test by hitting only .237 for Augusta of the Sally League in 1904 and dropped a fly ball with the same team the following year because he tried to catch it one-handed while eating popcorn with the other hand. Cobb went on to poll 222 of 226 votes to lead the first five all-time stars who made it to baseball's Hall of Fame in 1936. His spiked shoes were Cooperstown's first memento. Cobb was first then, just as he was first—had to be first—in almost everything else. That second year at Augusta he returned to his hotel after a game to find roommate Nap Rucker, a pitcher who had been driven from the mound earlier, taking a bath. There were no showers in the minor league park. Cobb, only 18 at the time, grumbled that he should have had first crack at the tub.

"You mean," asked Rucker, "that you wanted to be first today?"

"I mean," answered Cobb, "that I've got to be first all the time—first in everything."

When the Augusta team sold him to Detroit for $750 later that season, he was only a fair hitter, knew nothing about sliding and was a poor judge of fly balls. But he learned, perhaps because his schoolmaster–state senator father had told Ty after he had been sold by Augusta in 1904, "Don't come home a failure."

Cobb broke into the majors on August 30, 1905, at Detroit's Bennett Field. The sharp-featured, mean-eyed rookie launched his brilliant career with a two-run double off New York's Jack Chesbro, who had won 41 games during the previous year. From that point on, every game was a matter of life and death as Cobb scrapped with teammates, umpires and fans, anything to win.

"I don't blame any ballplayer who looks at the records Cobb set and refuses to believe

them," said Ray Schalk, a Hall of Fame catcher with the Chicago White Sox. "If I hadn't played against that devil I wouldn't believe them myself. Most of the time, it was hard to believe the things you actually saw him do."

Cobb asked no quarter and gave none. Most of the time, his legs were covered with scars, cuts and bruises. But nothing fazed him.

"I was their enemy," Cobb said. "If any player had learned I could be scared, I would have lasted two years in the league, not twenty-four."

St. Louis catcher Lou Criger once bragged that Cobb would be a "dead pigeon" if he tried to run on him. That afternoon, after reaching first base, Cobb called time and informed Criger he would steal second, third and home. He did, too, and stole two other bases that day.

"I recall a day," Grantland Rice, the famed sportswriter once said, "when Cobb played with each leg a mass of raw flesh. He had a temperature of one hundred and three and the doctors ordered him to bed for several days, but he got three hits, stole three bases and won the game.

Afterward, he collapsed at the bench and was revived by a hypodermic injection of strychnine."

Cobb had to be fighting somebody, it seemed. He brawled in a hotel room with Buck Herzog of the New York Giants and under the stands with umpire Billy Evans. Early in his career he picked a fight with a powerful, good-natured Detroit catcher named Germany Schmidt. Not until Cobb, 50 pounds lighter, tore into him would Schmidt retaliate. When he did, he almost killed Cobb, but Ty came back for more. Finally, his teammates, most of whom hated Cobb, pulled Schmidt off him.

Other teams, of course, hated Cobb, too. In 1910, the St. Louis Browns tried to give Cleveland's Napoleon Lajoie the batting title by having rookie third baseman Red Corriden play so far back that Lajoie beat out seven bunts on the final day of the season to hit .384 for the season. Cobb hit .385.

Cobb selected the game of September 30, 1907, as his greatest thrill. That was the year the Tigers won the first of three straight pennants. They took a half-game lead over

Cobb swung from the left side, compiling a record 4,191 hits, a .367 lifetime average. He led the league in batting 9 straight times, 12 times in 13 years.

Philadelphia on September 28 by beating the Athletics. It rained the next day and a double-header was scheduled for September 30.

A crowd of 30,000 packed Columbia Park, home of the Athletics, and the home team took a 7–1 lead after five innings. The Tigers scored four runs in the seventh, but the A's got one back and led 8–5. Detroit made it 8–6 in the eighth and Cobb hit a two-run homer in the ninth to tie the score.

In the eleventh, Cobb doubled home a run, but the A's retied it 9–9. After 17 innings, the game was halted by darkness. The second game was never played and the Tigers won the pennant.

"Ty Cobb has been unequaled," said Charles A. Comiskey, owner of the Chicago White Sox. "Until Ty came into the American League it was a case of one team against another. But after a while, everybody was trying to beat Cobb."

Said Babe Ruth, "Cobb was in a class by himself everywhere but on defense," even though he once threw out three players at first base from right field in a single game.

Cobb once was in a class by himself when it came to outfoxing the Babe, too. While a playing manager of the Tigers (1921–26), he ordered an intentional walk to Ruth. The pitcher fired a strike down the middle. Cobb raced in from the outfield and yelled at the pitcher. The next pitch was another strike. Cobb, fuming, rushed in again and, loudly enough for all to hear, said he was fining the pitcher and catcher $100 each. He then brought in a new battery. Same result—for strike three. Cobb had planned the entire episode to confuse Ruth. After his two years with Philadelphia, Cobb retired a wealthy man, thanks to shrewd investments. And, while he was thrifty, he could be generous, too. He gave financial assistance to a former minor league manager who had helped him become a big leaguer. He contributed to a medical center in Royston, Georgia, in his father's name. He established and endowed an educational foundation but insisted

that students seeking a college education make it through their freshman year before becoming eligible for Cobb's assistance.

But he always insisted that he'd "cut the heart out of my best friend if he ever tried to block the road. When the right of way belonged to me, I took it—spikes first."

If he mellowed in later years, the old fire wasn't far beneath the surface. Once, chatting with Grantland Rice and Nig Clarke, a former catcher, Clarke told how he'd been able to fool umpires with a quick tag at the plate.

"Ty," he said, "I can remember at least five times an umpire called you out when I didn't tag you."

Cobb erupted. "You so-and-so," he stormed, "you cost me five runs."

HERSCHEL NISSENSON

Far left: The Cobbs: Herschel; Jimmie; Ty, Sr.; Beverly; Ty, Jr., and Shirley in back. Left: Cobb in 1928, his last season in pro ball. Below: Babe Ruth pats the characteristically thin-haired head of Cobb.

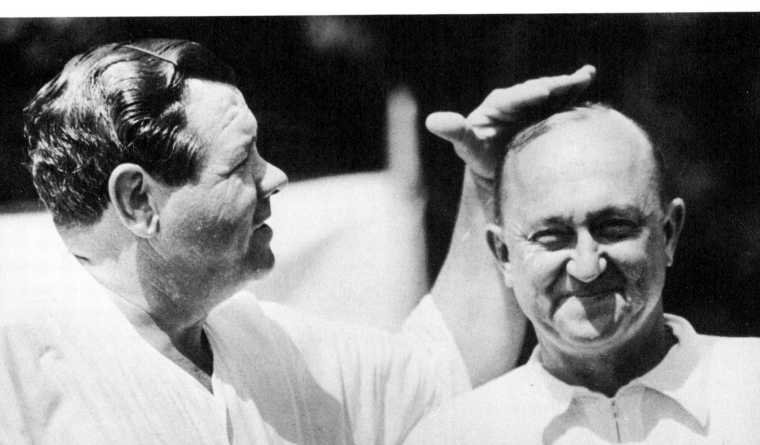

Paavo Nurmi
The Flying Finn

Beside the path that leads up to the Olympic Stadium in Helsinki is a statue of a runner in action. It is a study in classic movement, the long stride and rippling muscles captured in bronze, the arms crooked, the left leg trailing with instep parallel to the ground.

The runner, of course, is Paavo Nurmi, Finland's hero of the twenties, who became a legend in track and field. He won 10 Olympic gold medals—7 individual and 3 team—and set 21 world records in a career spanning a little more than a decade. Contemporary critics and later sports historians have without exception called him the greatest distance runner of all time.

The statue stands high on its base, silhouetted against the sky. It is an idealized sculpture, symbolic and worthy of Nurmi's titanic achievements, but possibly it does not quite suggest him as he really was. Those who saw him run do not recall him as a great stylist. He is described as being barrel-chested and as running with his head upright. Some say that he just shuffled along with one arm held across his chest or sometimes with both arms hanging limply at his sides. What really mattered was that he reached the finish line ahead.

No other runner has ever dominated the sport of his generation as Nurmi did. He set world marks for everything from 1,500 to 20,000 meters. He held the record for 6 miles for 18 years, and his time for 10 miles stood unchallenged for 17 years. He once set two world records—in the 1,500 and 5,000—in less than an hour. In the 1924 Olympics, he won four individual golds.

If he is remembered as holding one arm across his chest as he ran, that was probably when he was carrying a stopwatch. He did this not only in training but in important competitive races as well. He would keep the watch in his hand, timing his progress to the last second, and then toss it away as he began his final lap. This symbolizes one aspect of Nurmi's importance in track-and-field history—he was the first long-distance runner who planned his races scientifically. Until he dominated the scene, long-distance performers were content to jog for most of the race and concentrate all their efforts on the last lap or two. The great Finn set new standards of approach. The last 40 years or more can be called the post-Nurmi period of long-distance running.

Nurmi was born at Abo, near Turku, on June 13, 1897, the eldest of five children in a poor, well-disciplined family. When he was 12 years old, his father died. To keep her children fed and clothed, his mother went to work as a cleaner. Paavo also had to become a wage-earner, first running errands for a shopkeeper and then working as an apprentice mechanic.

While his father was alive, the boy belonged to a youth club and is said to have shown exceptional promise as a runner.

Then came World War I and Nurmi became a soldier. He didn't allow that to interfere with his progress. In the dark northern mornings, long before the sun came up, he used to leave his camp and stride for miles along icy country roads, returning in time for reveille. Still working alone and in secret, he continued his buildup, convinced that he would become a great long-distance runner.

When peace returned and the 1920 Olympics at Antwerp were imminent, Nurmi got down to serious mathematical planning. He kept hundreds of notes in a file, recording his lap times and those of other runners, and calculated how much patience would be needed at this point, how much extra effort at that point.

At Antwerp, Nurmi was 23 years old, in the peak of physical condition but still inexperienced in world competition. He lost one race, quickly profited from his mistakes and won another. The legend of Nurmi had begun.

During the next three years he stayed at home in Finland, still working out his race plans in advance and planning to run faster. In June, 1921, he set his first world records—30:40.2 for 10,000 meters and 28:41.2 for six miles, both at one stroke. In September, 1922, he set a mark of 14:35.2 for 5,000 meters. In August, 1923, he added two more records—3:52.6 for 1,500 meters and 4:10.4 for the mile.

And so Nurmi came to the 1924 Olympics

Nurmi takes the lead in 1924 Olympics.

in Paris. No other runner has ever dominated an Olympics so completely. He won the 1,500 meters, the 5,000 meters, the cross-country and the 3,000-meter team race, collecting two additional gold medals as a victorious team member in the last two events. The world talked of him as a superman. He was called "the Flying Finn," "the Phantom Finn," "Peerless Paavo." But for Nurmi those Olympics were clouded by a bitter disappointment—they wouldn't let him run in the 10,000 meters. Nobody had any doubt that if Nurmi had competed in the 10,000, he would have won it.

The drama of those 1924 Olympics began months in advance. At one time it appeared doubtful that Nurmi would be fit to run at all. On Easter, running in a cross-country club event over the still icy Finnish roads, he slipped and badly injured a knee. For almost two months Nurmi could not bend his leg and did no running at all. When he finally got going again, his times were depressingly slow. Ville Ritola, who was living in the United States, came home for the Finnish Olympic trials and defeated Nurmi in both the 5,000 and 10,000 meters.

Meanwhile, the Finns had been angered by the announcement of the Olympic schedule, which placed the 1,500- and 5,000-meter finals on the same day, a mere 55 minutes apart. They thought it had been deliberately arranged to prevent the same man from winning both races and to ensure that the gold medals would be distributed more evenly.

After his failure in the Finnish trials, Nurmi stepped up his training and regained his form. His preparations for the Olympics reached a climax at a meet in Helsinki in June, a little more than two weeks before the start of the Games in Paris. What Nurmi did that day is still held by many to be the most incredible feat in the whole history of track and field.

At Nurmi's request the program at Helsinki was arranged exactly on the proposed Olympic pattern, with the 1,500 meters first and the 5,000 meters starting 55 minutes later.

Some who were there said that Nurmi looked angry before he started running. He meant to show them. He set off in the 1,500 meters at a furious pace and covered the first lap in 57.3; then he ran on with machinelike consistency to lower his own world record, finishing in 3:52.6. In the 5,000 meters, he said that his aim was to break the 15 minute mark.

Again he started with a fast lap, and again he finished in world-record time—14:28.4.

Two world records in less than an hour!

So much for the supposed international conspiracy to stop Nurmi's winning too many gold medals in Paris. But then came another blow, this time from his own countrymen. He was not entered for the 10,000 meters. Even the Finns apparently did not appreciate his amazing potential. They told him it would be better if Ritola won the 10,000 meters for Finland and allowed him to conserve his energies for that formidable doubleheader, the 1,500 and 5,000.

While the Finnish team was cheering Ritola to his fine victory, Nurmi was nowhere to be seen. The story was told afterwards—and neither Nurmi nor anyone else ever denied it—that he went off to a training ground, ran his own private 10,000 meters and, without removing the top of his track suit, clocked 29:58.0—25 seconds faster than Ritola.

The doubleheader came three days later. There were no world records this time, but Nurmi ran fast enough to pocket both gold medals, as everyone knew he would.

In the 1,500 meters, he made Olympic history by running with a stopwatch in his hand. In training he had aimed at a steady pace of 60 seconds per lap, reaching the 1,000-meter mark in exactly two-and-a-half minutes. This time he was not quite accurate in his timing and passed the 1,000 meters in 2:30.1.

After he had tossed the watch aside at the bell and started on the last lap, he looked over his shoulder and found that he had no need to worry, for his rivals were all showing signs of fatigue. Nurmi ran round the track on his own and won in 3:53.6, one second outside his world mark.

Ritola was the only man to offer Nurmi any real competition in the 5,000. They pulled out so far ahead of their rivals that it became a two-man race long before the finish. Some said that Nurmi ran well within himself and that if he had pressed harder on the last two laps, he might have bettered his world mark of 14:28.2. Instead, he kept comfortably ahead of Ritola, striding ahead of him down the straight and clocking 4:31.2.

The great man's next triumph was in the 10,000-meter cross-country, one of the most grueling races ever staged in the history of the modern Olympics. It was run on a cruelly hot day—so hot that out of 39 starters only 15 reached the finish line. Quite a difference from the crisp cold of the North in which Nurmi was used to running!

The Colombes Stadium that day began to look like the Coliseum in Rome in the heyday of the Emperor Vespasian. Some runners staggered into the stadium, groped their way drunkenly toward the finish line and collapsed. One man, dazed and half-blinded, turned the wrong way inside the stadium, ran straight into a wall and fell insensible with blood streaming from his head. Another was stricken by sunstroke and was seriously ill in a hospital for several days afterward.

But these gruesome scenes did not disturb Nurmi. He had reached the stadium, looking as cool as an iceberg, two minutes before anyone else, and had run nonchalantly round the track to win in complete comfort.

That meant two more gold medals for Nurmi—one as the individual winner and one as a member of the winning Finnish team. He collected two more in similar style in the 3,000-meter team race on the final day of the Games.

So ended Nurmi's incredible Olympics of 1924. It was not the end of his achievements—he had more gold medals and more world records to come—but his powers were taken so much for granted after Paris that his victories had a touch of anticlimax.

His mile record, which he had set in Helsinki before the games, stood for eight years. No other man has held the mark for so long.

At the 1928 Olympics in Amsterdam, Nurmi, now 31, widened his horizons and entered the 3,000-meter steeplechase in addition to the 5,000- and 10,000-meter runs. As things turned out, however, he was a little past his peak. He won the 10,000 meters on the opening day in 30:18.8, more than 12 seconds outside his world record but recapturing the Olympic title eight years after first winning it. No other Olympic competitor has ever spread two 10,000-meter golds over an eight-year span. But that was Nurmi's only gold medal this time. He finished second to Ritola in the 5,000 and second to another Finn, Toivo Loukola, in the steeplechase.

Although Nurmi's star was dimming somewhat with age, he continued to set records. Two months after the Amsterdam Games, he ran 11 miles 1,648 yards in one hour and bettered a mark that had stood for 15 years. Two years later he set a world record for the 20,000 meters, running it in 1:04:38.4. These achievements were consistent with the normal pattern of aging runners who turn to longer distances. More remarkable was a race in July, 1931, when, at the age of 34, he clocked a time of 8:59.5 for the two miles—a record he had never before held.

Nurmi planned to crown his Olympic career by winning the marathon at Los Angeles in 1932. That would have been his fourth Olympics, and victory in the marathon would have brought his total of gold medals to 11. It was not to be. In a sensational inquiry just before the 1932 games began, Nurmi was disqualified because of alleged irregularities in expenses paid to him in Germany three years before.

Under the conditions of the present, a man of Nurmi's phenomenal talents might have yielded to commercial pressures and turned professional. As it was, the ruling that he had infringed upon the Olympic code upset him bitterly. The iron man, who had seldom betrayed any sign of emotion during his remarkable years of world mastery, was in tears.

"If I did something wrong, why did they wait three years before taking action?" he asked. "Why turn on me now, when my heart bleeds to end my career by winning the marathon?"

Nurmi won his last race at the Finnish national championships in 1933, when he was 36. Entered as a "national amateur," he won the 1,500 meters in 3:55.8. When he began his long career, that time would have been a world record; now it was more than six seconds outside the world mark. But for the proud Finnish crowd who watched him, it was a glorious farewell.

When the Olympics were staged in Helsinki in 1952, Nurmi was officially forgiven and had the honor of carrying the Olympic torch into the stadium.

The European championships were held at the Helsinki stadium in 1971, and officials wanted Nurmi to be present at the opening ceremony. Age 74 and in poor health, he was unable to attend. But a new generation of athletes and fans passed by his statue each day and his legend lived on. In all probability, it will still be there a hundred years from now and sportsmen will still point to it and say, "That man was the greatest long-distance runner of all time."

GEOFFREY MILLER

Jim Thorpe
Son of Triumph and Tragedy

Superlatives best describe James Francis Thorpe, generally conceded the title of greatest all-around athlete the world has ever known. He was a phenomenon at any sport he tried. An Olympic Games decathlon and pentathlon winner, all-American football player, professional football star, major league baseball player, boxer, wrestler, swimmer, a golfer who scored in the 70s, a bowler who rolled in the 200s, his versatility was exceeded by his fantastic ability. Thorpe indeed was a legendary figure in the world of sports. He was, as one writer so aptly phrased it, "the fictional Frank Merriwell come to life." Probably there never was an athlete who could do so many things so well.

Jim Thorpe was born in a one-room cabin in Prague, Oklahoma, in 1888, one of twin boys. His father was half Irish and half Indian, his mother a mixture of French and Indian. He was named Wa-Tho-Huck, meaning Bright Path in the language of the Sac and the Fox. He shot his first deer at the age of 10, rode horses, trapped bears and hiked as much as 30 miles a day. He was the great grandson of Chief Black Hawk, a brave warrior in the days of the fight against the white invasion of Indian territory.

Thorpe probably is best remembered for the 1912 Olympic Games at Stockholm, Sweden, in which the bushy-haired Indian swamped the pick of the world's athletes in the decathlon and pentathlon. He set a point total that stood as a record for 20 years. The powerful, agile athlete was so superior in running, hurdling, high jumping, pole vaulting and the weight events that he presented almost no contest. His marks in most of the events were exceeded later, but in the early 1900s, nobody could come close to the fabled Indian. His performances were considered even more exceptional because of his lack of training habits. There were some who said that the lean 185-pounder was inclined to be lazy. Thorpe described it as relaxed. Sports to him were fun, and he refused to take games and events seriously, never showing any sign that the pressures of competition affected him. He came home from the Stockholm Olympic Games a hero. One year later, in 1913, Thorpe's amateur sports world blew up in his face. It was disclosed that the spectacular Indian had played baseball three years earlier for pay, thus branding him as a professional.

All Thorpe's Olympic medals were taken away. The marks he set in winning every event in the pentathlon, four victories and no worse than a fourth place in the other six events of the decathlon, were expunged from the books. All he had left were some personal gifts and the words of the Swedish king, who had said to Thorpe, "Sir, you are the greatest athlete in the world."

Thorpe admitted to the charges of professionalism, although it was quite evident that at the time he played baseball for $15 a week at Rocky Mount, North Carolina, he was not aware of the damage he was doing to his amateur status. The Indian from the plains of the Southwest knew so little about amateur codes that he used his own name at Rocky Mount. There were scores of college athletes doing the same thing, but they participated under assumed names, a common practice in those days. Thorpe tried to explain his position to the Amateur Athletic Union: "I did not play for the money," he wrote. "I was not very wise in the ways of the world and did not realize this was wrong. I hope I will be partly excused by the fact I was simply an Indian schoolboy and did not know I was doing wrong, because I was doing what many other college men had done, except they did not use their own names."

The AAU, adhering to its strict rules and principles, found Thorpe guilty and stripped him of his records, removed his name from the roll of Olympic victors and directed him to return all the prizes he had collected in Sweden. There were a few who felt that the AAU action was one of courage; the reaction around the world of most people, however, was one of anger. One of America's leading sportswriters, the late Damon Runyon, wrote at the time: "This league [in which Thorpe played baseball] . . . lived long enough to furnish a means of destruction for the career as an amateur of the greatest athlete of all time. It develops that down South where Thorpe played, and among

He was truly a phenomenon, the world's greatest all-around athlete, but football always was his first love. He kicked, blocked, had an amazing change of pace and ran with blinding speed.

The Sac and Fox Indian excelled in kicking field goals.

his friends and associates, there was no secret of the fact he played baseball for money. They did not know that there was any particular harm in it. During the Olympic Games, Southern newspapers printed stories and pictures of the great Indian, lauding his prowess and constantly referring to his baseball connections in the Carolinas, and no hint of this reached the ears of the AAU authorities?" The AAU reportedly never answered Runyon but stuck by its decisions. Thorpe's prizes were wrapped and sent back to Sweden.

Next to his Olympic fame, Thorpe was known best for his football skills. Twice he was selected an all-American by Walter Camp after performing gridiron miracles for a little school in Central Pennsylvania known as Carlisle Indian Institute. Carlisle wasn't exactly a college but rather a preparatory school that had no classes above the twelfth grade. The pupils were older than boys in a regular prep school, some of them in their twenties.

Thorpe was 19 when he left the reservation to pursue a career as an electrician. He discovered Carlisle had no course in electricity and settled for one in tailoring. It was during a football game between the tailoring class and the carpentering class that Thorpe's magnificent athletic ability first was noticed. An assistant coach watched the lithe Indian slice through the line and nail a runner before he could get moving. The coach was impressed with Thorpe's blocking, running and kicking skills. He suggested that the young man report to Glenn S. Warner, the Carlisle football coach, who was to become one of the game's coaching immortals.

The first time that Warner saw Thorpe on a football field was an event he never forgot. One of the coach's favorite practice maneuvers was to have a ballcarrier run from one goal line to the other through a gauntlet of linemen and backs spaced about five feet apart. No one had ever gone the distance—until Jim Thorpe. As the story goes, Thorpe made it from goal line to goal line, infuriating Warner, who screamed, "This is tackling practice." He ordered Thorpe to try it again as the embarrassed team members took their places. The result was the same. "Nobody tackles Jim," Thorpe told Warner as he handed the coach the ball.

Thorpe was used sparingly in 1907, his first year on the Carlisle varsity. He finally got his chance at Franklin Field in Philadelphia against Pennsylvania. Shortly after the opening kickoff, Carlisle back Albert Payne was injured. Thorpe came in and on the second play carried 75 yards for a touchdown. Carlisle beat Penn, 26–6. The Indians defeated Harvard, Minnesota and Chicago among the college football giants of 1907, losing only to Princeton. Warner is reported as listing the 1907 Carlisle team as the greatest he ever coached. In 1908, Thorpe was the starting halfback from the first scrimmage. He scored the touchdown that tied an unbeaten Penn team and kicked three field goals in a 12–5 triumph over Penn State. Carlisle won 10, lost 2 and tied 1 that season as Thorpe made Walter Camp's third-team all-American.

The football season of 1908 was Thorpe's last for Carlisle until 1911. He left school after the 1909 track-and-field season and didn't return until the fall of 1911. It was during these two years that Thorpe played baseball at Rocky Mount. Before he left Carlisle, however, the 6-foot 2-inch Indian made his first mark in track and field. Warner also was track coach at Carlisle, and he discovered Thorpe's prowess in that sport quite by accident. The coach was watching his high jumpers practice one day when Thorpe stopped to take a look. When none of the jumpers could clear 5 feet 9 inches, Thorpe asked permission to give it a try. The team members snickered. Thorpe, attired in overalls and sneakers, made it with plenty to spare. Warner sent for the Indian the next day and informed him that in a track suit and with proper shoes he would jump 6 feet. It was the beginning of the career that was to carry Thorpe to international fame and to the depths of despair.

Warner discovered that Thorpe not only could high jump with the best of his day, but could also run, hurdle, pole vault and handle the shot put, discus and hammer with standout ability. He was virtually a one-man track team. Warner scheduled meets with the best track-and-field teams in the East. Against a powerful 45-man Lafayette College squad, Carlisle entered five men, including Thorpe, who proceeded to win the pole vault, high jump, low hurdles, shot put and broad jump and finish second in the 100-yard dash. Carlisle won the meet over the stunned Lafayettes, 71–31. Later, Warner added three performers and took an 8-man team to Syracuse, where Carlisle outscored the strong Orange by a single point. Thorpe took five firsts, one second and two

thirds. Against an even stronger Harvard team, Thorpe competed in eight events and won all eight.

After a two-year hiatus, Thorpe returned to Carlisle for the football season of 1911. He came back at the insistence of Warner and was rewarded for a spectacular season by being named to Camp's all-American team. That year, against Harvard, which dominated football in the early 1900s the way such teams as Notre Dame, Texas, Oklahoma and Nebraska were to do in later years, he played what most experts felt was his greatest game. Coach Percy Haughton's Harvards were unbeaten in eight games when they met Carlisle and Thorpe before a packed stadium of 25,000 at Cambridge, Massachusetts. The Ivy Leaguers were so confident that they started their second team and quickly scored a first-period touchdown, kicking the conversion for a 6–0 lead (touchdowns counted five points then). Thorpe wasn't doing much running because of sore legs, but he still managed to kick field goals of 23, 43 and 37 yards to give Carlisle a 9–6 half-time lead.

The crimson-jersied legions of Harvard, infuriated at trailing little Carlisle, marched to a touchdown, conversion and a field goal to go ahead 15–9. Now, Thorpe wanted the ball. His legs encased in bandages, the powerful Indian tore the bigger and heavier Harvard line to shreds. He took the ball nine straight times. On his ninth carry, Thorpe ripped across the Harvard team's goal line to tie the score at 15. It appeared that the great game would end in an unsatisfying tie. Big Jim would have none of that. He helped Carlisle drive to the Harvard 43-yard line in the late minutes of the fourth quarter. "I'll kick one," Thorpe told his quarterback. "But you've already kicked three," the quarterback replied. "So I'll kick another," said Thorpe. He did, from just inside the 50-yard line, clinching an 18–15 Carlisle victory in which he had scored all the points.

It has been said that Thorpe on the football field did everything but blow up the ball. The Army team of 1912, which included a cadet by the name of Dwight Eisenhower, probably would attest to that statement. Eisenhower, later to lead the victorious Allied Forces in the greatest war in history and to serve his country as president, often recalled that meeting with Thorpe. "He was the greatest football man I've ever seen." Army that fall afternoon had geared its defense to stop Thorpe. It didn't help. At the start of the second half, the fabulous Indian took the kickoff and returned 90 yards for what appeared to be a touchdown. The run, however, was nullified by a penalty against Carlisle. Army kicked off again. The unbelievable Thorpe merely ran 95 yards through the clutching West Point defenders to touch the ball down again in the end zone. Thorpe laughed as he handed the ball to the referee and then said to his teammates, "That's the longest run I've ever made—one hundred and eighty-five yards for a touchdown." Final score: Carlisle 27, Army 7.

Carlisle with Thorpe as captain won 12 games that year, lost 1 and tied 1. Thorpe scored 25 of his team's 60 touchdowns and kicked goals for a total of 198 points. Years later, when asked about his greatest football thrills, Thorpe answered, "Thrills were mostly hard work for me. That's what I remember most about them. But I did get a kick out of running back two straight kickoffs for touchdowns against Army in 1912 and kicking four field goals to beat Harvard eighteen to fifteen in 1911."

If Thorpe had any weakness in football, it was his tendency to relax. Warner said that his great player was lazy. Once, in a tight game, the opposition threw a forward pass into Thorpe's defensive area. Thorpe made no effort to knock it down but watched as an opposing end caught it on the fingertips for a touchdown. "Thorpe," Warner screamed, "why didn't you knock it down?"

The Indian replied, "Coach, I didn't think he could reach it," and flashed a big grin. In college, during his 15-year career in professional football and during his baseball career, Thorpe was never injured seriously enough to leave a game. He was durable as well as strong and swift.

Arthur Daley, a columnist with *The New York Times*, once described Thorpe's football ability. "As a runner, Thorpe had blinding speed, an astonishing change of pace, a stiff-arm that shattered defenders and a snaky twist of the hips that shed tacklers. He could sweep the ends, slash off tackle or splinter the center of a line. He passed well in an era when there was little passing. He was a phenomenon as a kicker—punts, placements or drop kicks. He blocked beautifully. His one flaw as a football player was that he'd occasionally not put out to his fullest ability."

After leaving Carlisle, Thorpe played professional football with the Canton Bulldogs and spent his summers in baseball. He started out with John McGraw's New York Giants and also played for the Cincinnati Reds and Boston Braves before winding up, in 1928, his diamond career in Akron, Ohio, at the age of 40. Baseball was the only game that Thorpe never overwhelmed. He was a spectacular fielder, maybe the fastest and most reckless player ever to play the game, but he had trouble hitting the curve ball. He always claimed he could have hit the curve but that McGraw hampered his style. "If McGraw had only left me alone," he said many years after his baseball career was history. "It wasn't the curves that bothered me so much as it was his way of telling me when to swing and when to take one."

Thorpe reported to the Giants' spring training camp at Marlin Springs, Texas, in 1913, and there was conflict with the manager almost from the first day. It was a clash of two stubborn men, two dominant personalities. There was the day that Thorpe reported to the ball park five minutes before a game. McGraw told him to get out on time. Thorpe snapped back, "I can hit, can't I? I can throw, can't I? I can run, can't I? What do you want to do, see me sweat?"

McGraw barked, "Yeah! I want to see you sweat." McGraw never liked Thorpe, and the feeling was mutual.

The big blowup between Thorpe and McGraw came early in the season. The Giants had lost a tough game and Thorpe became fed up with his role as a pinch hitter and bench-warmer. He and McGraw had harsh words, Thorpe charging the manager with being "a little wind trying to blow hard" and McGraw shouting "Indian" at Thorpe. They almost came to blows, and McGraw dropped Thorpe to the Giants' Milwaukee farm team. Thorpe always believed that had he broken into the major league with any other manager, his exploits on the diamond would have matched his achievements in other sports.

Thorpe spent most of the 1914 season with Milwaukee. The next year he was sent to Harrisburg, Pennsylvania. McGraw wanted to waive the Indian, but Thorpe's untapped baseball potential and gate-appeal foiled that maneuver. McGraw and Thorpe finally parted, early in the 1919 season. Thorpe had been smoldering with resentment because McGraw preferred a youngster by the name of Red Murray to the Indian. One day, McGraw told Thorpe to pinch-hit for Murray, and Thorpe shouted, "Why don't you let Murray hit? He can do much better for you than I can." Thorpe batted but just waved his bat at three pitches. McGraw fired Thorpe, who went to the Boston Braves and hit .327 in 60 games, once going seven for seven in pinch-hitting roles.

Thorpe liked baseball, but football was his first love. While he was battling with McGraw and the Giants, Thorpe, in 1915, accepted an offer of $500 a game to coach and play for the Canton Bulldogs. In 1920, the American Football Association was organized, and Thorpe was appointed president. The league included such teams as the Bulldogs, the Staleys, the Cleveland Indians, the Dayton Triangles, the Akron Professionals, the Massillon Tigers, the Chicago Cardinals and a number of others. Thorpe played for several teams in the league, including Canton, the Oorang Indians in LaRue, Ohio, the Rock Island Independents and finally the New York Football Giants. With the Giants, the old problem, refusal to get into proper playing condition, caused his release. Thorpe hung on with various teams until 1929, when, at the age of 41, he finally played his last football in a game between the Cardinals and the Bears.

Thorpe had been careless with his money, and by 1930 with his second wife and four children to support, he was in financial trouble. When the Depression struck the nation, Thorpe tried a variety of jobs—painting, acting and finally working with a shovel at four dollars a day. A newspaper reporter took a picture of America's greatest all-time athlete wielding a pick and shovel. In 1932, Thorpe was invited by Charles Curtis, then vice-president of the United States, to sit in the presidential box at the Olympics in Los Angeles. Thorpe received a mighty ovation from the crowd. Then, except for an occasional note in the newspapers, Thorpe was forgotten. During World War II, he served with the Merchant Marine. A number of efforts were made to get his Olympic medals restored, but the AAU would never back down on that 1913 decision.

Thorpe's last hurrah came in 1950, when the Associated Press conducted a poll that brought Thorpe recognition as the greatest athlete of the first half of the twentieth century. He was also voted, in a poll of the nation's sportswriters, as the outstanding football player

Thorpe with sons Phil and Bill.

of the first 50 years of this century. The wonderful Sac and Fox was the only double winner in the series of votes. Thorpe in the poll on "greatest athlete" finished far ahead of baseball's Babe Ruth, the runner-up in the balloting. Fighter Jack Dempsey, another national hero, was third, with Ty Cobb, the famed Georgia Peach of baseball, fourth. The voters were asked to name their first, second and third choices for the supreme athlete of them all. Points were scored on a 3-2-1 basis. Thorpe compiled 875; Ruth, 539; Dempsey, 246; Cobb, 148. As the greatest football player of the first half-century, Thorpe outpolled the Galloping Ghost of Illinois, Red Grange, and Georgia's Charley Trippi.

Thorpe died, in 1953, of a heart attack at the age of 64, in the modest trailer in which he lived with his third wife. He left his mark, nevertheless, as the greatest all-around athlete his country had ever known. The legend of Jim Thorpe won't die, not until someone can truthfully say he has punted a football 90 yards, kicked a field goal 79 or run 185 yards for a touchdown on two consecutive plays. Until then, the big Indian's eminence in sports can't be questioned.

RALPH BERNSTEIN

33

Walter Johnson
The Fastest Fastball

"The great thing about Walter Johnson was that even though you knew a fastball was coming, it didn't help," Ty Cobb, the greatest hitter of all, recalled many years after both had retired. "You never had to worry about a curve or any change of pace. Just speed, raw speed, blinding speed, too much speed."

All that speed and, for the most part, a poor team behind him. In Johnson's 21 seasons (1907-1927), the Washington Senators managed to play .500 ball only 10 times. Twice they finished last in the American League, five times seventh, twice sixth, once fifth. In 1924 and 1925, the hard-throwing (hardest-throwing, they say) right-hander pitched in his only two World Series.

In such circumstances, the raw-boned, 6-foot 1-inch, 200-pound farmboy from Humboldt, Kansas, had to be great to establish the records he did—he pitched 113 shutouts, he struck out 3,508 batters, he pitched 5,924 innings, he started 666 games, he hurled 531 complete games. He led the league in complete games seven years in a row. He struck out more than 200 batters seven years in succession. He pitched 56 consecutive scoreless innings in 1913, still the American League record and the major league mark until 1968.

He led the leagues in shutouts for three seasons and tied for the honor four other times. He led the league's pitchers in winning percentage six times and in fielding three times. He was the top strike-out pitcher in the league 12 times.

He did it all with a blazing sidearm fastball, a nickel curve that probably wasn't worth more than two cents and an even temperament that prevented him from ever throwing at a batter (well, just once, perhaps) or arguing with an umpire.

Blinding speed made Johnson live with the fear of maiming a hitter. He fired a knockdown pitch only once in his life. Egged on by his teammates, he took dead aim at Frank ("Home Run") Baker, who dropped out of the way just in time. Johnson turned pale.

"I'm not ashamed to admit that I used to blink my eyes when I first saw Johnson's speed," said former umpire Billy Evans. "He was unbelievably fast. On dark days, players used to hope the game would be over before they had to face him again."

In 1915, Cleveland's Ray Chapman, who was killed by a pitch from New York's Carl Mays in 1920, took one of Johnson's burners and listened to Evans intone, "Strike two!" Chapman headed for the bench. "That's only strike two," shouted Evans.

"I know it," said Chapman. "You can have the next one. It won't do me any good."

Johnson, according to teammate Al Schacht, was "the only pitcher I ever saw who would throw a ball out of the game if he found it scuffed or roughed up in any spot. Other pitchers would try to keep such a ball in play so that they could cheat a bit with it. Scuffed baseballs will sail and are twice as difficult to follow as one on which the cover is smooth. Walter was always afraid of hitting somebody. He knew that with his speed, it could be fatal."

Although Cobb struck out often enough against Johnson, he took advantage of the blaze-baller's good nature and stubbornness—Johnson insisted on throwing his nothing curve with two strikes on the batter—crowding the plate, knowing that Walter would keep the ball outside in such a situation.

Eddie Collins, another great hitter, used to take two strikes and wait for the so-called curve. "It's the only way I can hit him," he confessed.

The arm that whistled its way to a record 416 American League triumphs—Cy Young won many of his 511 in the National League before the turn of the century—was discovered by a traveling cigar salesman, whose name has been lost to history, in Weiser, Idaho, where Johnson was working for the local telephone company for $75 a month and pitching semi-pro ball. The salesman flooded the Detroit Tigers with letters about the 19-year-old phenomenon, prompting the following conversation between owner Bill Yawkey and Frank Navin, his partner.

Navin: "Who is this guy?"

Yawkey: "A friend of mine. He's a cigar

Records prove it: fireballer Walter Johnson was a baseball great.

salesman and he gets around the country a lot. He knows baseball, too."

Navin: "If he knows so much about baseball, what's he doing peddling cigars?"

The letter was stuffed away in Navin's desk and forgotten. Meanwhile, the cigar salesman turned his attention to the Senators and bombarded manager Joe Cantillon with stories about his discovery. Cantillon finally dispatched Cliff Blankenship, an injured catcher, to take a look at Clyde Milan, an outfielder playing in Witchita, Kansas, and then detour up to Idaho for a peek at Johnson.

Was there ever a better scouting trip? Johnson became one of the original five inductees into baseball's Hall of Fame, and Milan was Washington's center fielder for the next 14 years. Both became managers of the Senators. Blankenship saw Johnson lose a 1 to 0 game on a twelfth-inning error, but he knew that the cigar salesman was right when he wrote to Cantillon:

> *You better come out here and get this pitcher. He throws a ball so fast nobody can see it, and he strikes out everybody. His control is so good that the catcher just holds up his glove, shuts his eyes, then picks the ball, which comes to him looking like a little white bullet, out of the pocket.*
>
> *He's a big, 19-year-old fellow like I told you before, and if you don't hurry up someone will sign him and he will be the best pitcher that ever lived. He throws faster than Addie Joss or Amos Rusie ever did, and his control is better than Christy Mathewson's. He knows where he's throwing because if he didn't there would be dead bodies strewn all over Idaho. So you'd better hurry, Joe, or you'll be sorry.*

Blankenship, impressed, whipped out a $100 bill as a bonus and offered Johnson $350 a month to join the Senators for the rest of the 1907 season. Before his father would sign a makeshift contract on a piece of wrapping paper, Johnson wanted to know about expenses to Washington and a return trip home if he failed.

Johnson never returned home. He settled in the rolling Maryland countryside, not far from the nation's capital, and became the only baseball immortal for whom an educational institution was named—Walter Johnson High School in Bethesda, Maryland.

Signed and sealed for Washington—a Seattle scout was en route to sign him at the time—Johnson left the Snake River Valley League of Idaho for the American League. In August of 1907, Walter Perry Johnson, three months shy of his twentieth birthday, made his major league debut against the pennant-bound Detroit Tigers. He led until the eighth inning, when Cobb beat out a bunt, sped to third on another bunt—they did things like that in those days—and scored the winning run. Johnson left for a pinch hitter after allowing six hits, three of them bunts.

More than twenty years after his retirement, the Senators invited all those who had seen Johnson's first game to sit in a special section. More than 8,000 bulled their way in. On that August day in 1907, exactly 2,841 spectators had been in the ball park, but it had become a mark of distinction in Washington to say you saw Walter Johnson pitch his first major league game.

Johnson had only a 5–9 record that season, followed by 14–14 in 1908 and—believe it or not—13–25 with the last-place Senators in 1909, although he surrendered only 247 hits in 297 innings. Then things started to pick up, and for the next ten seasons Johnson went 25–17, 25–13, 32–12, 36–7, 28–18, 27–13, 25–20, 23–16, 23–13 and 20–14. In that fabulous campaign of 1913, the first of his two Most Valuable Player seasons, Johnson hurled 12 shutouts and 5 one-hitters, had winning streaks of 10, 11 and 14 games, tossed his 56 consecutive scoreless innings (from the second inning, April 10, to the fourth inning, May 14) and recorded the lowest earned run average ever for a 300-inning pitcher—1.14—a record that stood until Bob Gibson came along with 1.12 in 1968.

The previous year, 1912, Johnson reeled off 16 victories in a row, a feat matched in the American League by Smoky Joe Wood, Lefty Grove and Schoolboy Rowe. Johnson, however, was the only one to do it with a team that wasn't a pennant winner.

Johnson was an easy, rapid worker, and his sweeping sidearm motion didn't put much strain on his rubber arm. In 1908, he pitched an incredible three shutouts in four days against New York. On Friday, September 6, he blanked the Highlanders—they weren't the Yankees yet—3–0. On Saturday he did it again, 6–0. Sunday was an off-day because of the blue laws in New York. The Highlanders couldn't believe it when they saw Johnson warming up for the first game of a Monday doubleheader. Final score: 4–0. Baseball lore has it that Johnson disappeared when Cantillon was looking for a second-game hurler.

That season, Johnson received the princely salary of $2,700. When he followed up his brilliant 1912 and 1913 seasons with 28 victories in 1914—96–37 over those three years—he asked for a raise over the $12,000 level to which he had risen. A combination of a letter from the Senators stating that he hadn't been worth his 1914 wages because he won only 28 games and an offer of $16,000 plus a $10,000 bonus for signing from the Chicago club of the new Federal League had Johnson thinking seriously about jumping.

Canny club executive Clark Griffith kept Johnson with the Senators by playing on the pitcher's love for his wife—Washington was home to the former Hazel Lee Roberts, daughter of a Nevada congressman—and by pulling strings to match the Federal League's offer. He managed to talk the Senators' board of directors into meeting the $16,000 salary, but the $10,000 bonus was something else.

They didn't call Griffith "the Old Fox" without reason. Griffith was turned down when Ban Johnson, with whom he'd helped found the American League, refused to contribute league funds. So Griffith went to Charles Comiskey, owner of the Chicago White Sox. He asked Comiskey—one noted penny-pincher to another —how he'd like to have Johnson firing that smoke on the north side of town and drawing all those paying fans away from the White Sox on the south side. Comiskey's answer was a $10,000 check. Johnson used it to pay off a brother's debt.

Johnson also had money problems with his employers in 1911 and missed the opening game. He had asked for a raise from $4,500 to $9,000 after winning 25 games in 1910. The parties compromised at $7,000, two days after the season got under way.

Johnson's first opening-day assignment, in 1910—he missed in 1908 because of mastoid surgery and in 1909 with a heavy cold—was also the first presidential opener. President William Howard Taft, a former catcher from Cincinnati, threw out the first ball and then sat back to watch Sir Walter shut out the Philadelphia Athletics, 3–0, on one measly hit, a

Late honors: Johnson in 1935 being presented with silver bowl by the Washington sportswriters. At his left, Clark Griffith, then president of the club.

Johnson coaching.

37

wind-blown double by Home Run Baker. Six more times Johnson inaugurated a new season with a shutout, pitching, in all, 14 presidential openers.

Sixteen years later, on April 13, 1926, at the advanced baseball age of 38, he hooked up with Philadelphia's Eddie Rommel and won a 15-inning duel 1–0, one of his 34 1–0 victories.

One of those squeakers was Johnson's only no-hitter, on July 1, 1920, at Boston's Fenway Park. It would have been a perfect game but for an error by second baseman Bucky Harris, who was disconsolate. "Goodness gracious, Bucky," said Johnson, a nonswearer, nonsmoker and nondrinker, "forget it." Johnson had forgotten it because Harris also singled home the game's only run.

Harris was managing the Senators when Johnson finally made it to a World Series in 1924. In 1923, they had finished 24 games behind the Yankees. In 1924, they won out by a mere two games. Johnson—who else?—was Harris's choice to pitch the opener. The New York Giants beat the veteran flamethrower, 4–3, in 12 innings, although Johnson struck out 12 of them for what was then a Series record. In his second start, in game five, the Giants beat him again, 6–2. Was the great Johnson to pitch his heart out all those years and never know the taste of a Series triumph?

Lady Luck had written the right script, though. In the seventh and final game, the Senators rallied for two runs in the eighth inning to tie the game 3–3. Out of the bullpen, before a hometown Washington crowd, came the great Johnson. His fastball again resembling that "little white bullet" of yesteryear, he struck out five in four innings and, when Earl McNeely's grounder took that famed bad hop over the head of third baseman Fred Lindstrom, was the winning pitcher.

The script was reversed in 1925. Johnson beat the Pittsburgh Pirates, 4–1, in the opener and shut them out on six hits in game four, 4–0. In the seventh game, this time at Forbes Field, Johnson was beaten 9–7, even though he had held leads of 4–0 and 6–3. Ban Johnson, president of the American League, fired off a telegram to Harris, berating him for staying with Johnson. "You have sacrificed a world's championship, which the American League should have won, to maudlin sentiment."

Answered Harris: "No man is going to tell me that when I need a pitcher in a pinch, Walter Johnson isn't the man for me. I'll go down the line with him until they carry either of us off the field."

Harris went down the line with Johnson to a 15–16 record in 1926—and then his words came true. They carried Walter off the field in spring training of 1927. His leg had been broken by a line drive off the bat of teammate Joe Judge. Managing to appear in only 18 games that season, Johnson finished with a 5–6 record and only 48 strike-outs in 108 innings. That was his swan song.

Victim of influenza in the spring of 1928, Johnson lost 35 pounds, and Griffith, by now the Washington owner, arranged for him to become manager at Newark. In 1929, he succeeded Harris as manager of the Senators for four seasons and piloted the Cleveland Indians from June of 1933 until he was released in August of 1935. The managerial years weren't happy ones for Johnson, even though all the clubs he headed for a full season had winning records, except for Washington in his first season. He lost the patience he had shown even when pitching for poor teams, and he became, according to his critics, surly, cold and aloof. One reason for the change in his disposition may have been the death of his wife in 1930 at the age of 36, leaving him with five children ranging in age from 5 to 15.

His managing days done, Johnson retired to his Maryland farm, where he raised cattle and foxhounds. "He really loved dogs," said his son, Eddie. "He'd open the bedroom window and listen to the hounds baying and he could tell you which hound was leading."

As a gentleman farmer, Johnson's public appearances were few. In 1936, he reenacted George Washington's feat of hurling a silver dollar across the Potomac (a fastball, no doubt). He spent a year as the Senators' play-by-play radio announcer, he lost a close race for Congress in 1940 and during World War II he put on his uniform to pitch to Babe Ruth at Yankee Stadium. A capacity crowd of 70,000 bought a considerable number of bonds that day.

Paralyzed by a brain tumor in April of 1946, Walter Johnson died on December 10, a nice guy who didn't finish last.

HERSCHEL NISSENSON

The
Golden
Era

With the end of World War I in 1918, tensions of the world snapped. In order to forget the killings, destruction and international hatreds that marked the conflict, everyone was an easy target for any type of diversion. The world entered upon a mad and uninhibited age. Ladies sheared their locks and affected something called the windblown bob. They raised their dresses to their knees and applied mascara, lipstick and rouge by the layers. With prohibition the law, it was smart to frequent speakeasies. Harvard students gulped goldfish out of ladies' shoes. The Charleston was the dance craze. Dance marathons and six-day bicycle races jammed the big arenas, such as Madison Square Garden. It was the period of flagpole sitters, fly-by-night promoters and around-the-clock high jinks. Money was plentiful. Spirits were gay. It was only natural that this mood would find an outlet in sports.

The decade of the twenties fed this hunger for excitement with the most fabulous collection of athletic giants ever assembled into a single generation. In baseball, there was Babe Ruth, an incongruous figure of a man with a beer-barrel belly and pipestem legs who lobbed baseballs into the bleachers with an ease and regularity that sent crowds into hysterics. Bob Jones, playing with wooden-shafted clubs, was the round-cheeked wonder of golf. Tennis was ruled by a gaunt, lantern-jawed Philadelphian named Big Bill Tilden and a frozen-faced machine with an eyeshade, Helen Wills Moody. Jack Dempsey was heavyweight champion of the boxing world. Johnny Weissmuller was undisputed king of swimming, and a dimpled Norwegian named Sonja Henie, with her flashing skates, had mothers putting skates on their daughters before they were out of the crib. A raw-boned Texas girl, Babe Didrikson, awed galleries with her feats in all sports.

To record the deeds of these titans of sport, the country produced a special breed of word makers. There was Grantland Rice, a courtly essayist from the South who often composed poems to his athletic heroes and who conceived such lasting phrases as "The Four Horsemen" (Notre Dame backfield) and the "Seven Blocks of Granite" (Fordham line). Damon Runyon lent a brisk, staccato style. Westbrook Pegler tempered the period with a laconic, jaundiced approach. Ernest Hemingway turned from sportswriting to the role of leading contemporary author. Paul Gallico wearied of the sports beat and hied off to Hollywood. All left an imprint, leading latter-day observers to wonder—did the writers glorify the men or did the men glorify the writers? They called it "the Golden Era" and "the Age of Wonderful Nonsense." The feats indeed were great, the prose always purple.

The majesty of the era was reflected in a poll conducted in 1951 to determine the greatest athletes of the first half-century. The poll, taken among the nation's sportswriters and sports broadcasters, was dominated by personalities of "the Golden Era." Dempsey, the Manassa Mauler, was the number-one fighter. Tilden topped the tennis players. Jim Thorpe, a pioneer whose career overlapped the twenties, was the best all-around athlete and the number-one football player. Babe Ruth was an overwhelming choice in baseball. Babe Didrikson Zaharias was number one among the women. They lived in an age that may never be duplicated, but they all measured up to the times.

Babe Ruth
Savior of Baseball

In deepest center field at Yankee Stadium stands a monument to Babe Ruth, the man acclaimed the greatest slugger of them all. Every ball park should have one because the big fellow with the booming bat, the booming voice and the booming way of life saved baseball by restoring public confidence in the national pastime at a time when the sport was staggering from the effects of the Black Sox scandal.

"Why that big, wild, old son-of-a-gun used to bring out the worst language in me," an American League pitcher, who had often been victimized by Babe Ruth's explosive bat, once said, "but I guess he was just about the greatest thing that ever came to the game. I guess you'd say that Babe Ruth is baseball."

By raising his own home run record from a previously undreamed-of 29 in 1919 to an astounding 54 in 1920, the Babe changed baseball from a black mark to a shining star. He not only saved the sport, he made the New York Yankees baseball's dominant team—a reign that lasted into the early 1960s—and he was the reason the Yankees moved out of the Polo Grounds, which they shared with the Giants, in 1923 to their own spanking new stadium just across the Harlem River in the Bronx, truly "the House That Ruth Built."

His popularity spread to baseball-mad Japan, as well, where the Bambino played first base in the rain with a Japanese parasol over his shoulder during a 1934 exhibition tour, where a plaque in front of Osaka's huge Koshien Stadium commemorates the visit of "Beibu Rusu"; where the annual baseball day to promote the game among children is called "Babe Ruth Day" and where a list of the most famous personalities in Japan over a 40-year period contained all Japanese names except one—Babe Ruth. So popular did the Babe become that Japanese soldiers shouted at American troops during World War II what they thought was the supreme insult—"To hell with Babe Ruth."

The face of baseball changed on January 3, 1920, when the financially troubled Boston Red Sox, for whom Ruth spent five seasons as a top-flight pitcher and sometimes outfielder, sold the Babe to the Yankees for $125,000 and a $350,000 mortgage on Boston's Fenway Park. Ruth went on to become the top gate attraction in baseball history, and he did it by hitting 714 home runs—most of them towering shots—including his legendary 60 in 1927. Had Roger Maris hit 70 instead of his asterisked 61, he could not have replaced Babe Ruth as the Sultan of Swat.

But the Babe was more than just a slugger. He was an outstanding left-handed pitcher who won 23 games for the Red Sox in 1916, 24 in 1917, compiled a 94–46 career record and a 2.28 earned run average, was 3–0 and 0.87 in World Series competition, won the longest Series game ever played and held the record for most consecutive scoreless innings by a Series pitcher, 29, for more than 40 years. He was a superb outfielder and base runner, too.

But people came to see Babe Ruth swing the bat, and swing it he did, driving in a record 2,209 runs, compiling a .342 lifetime average although aiming for the fences and even striking out a record—at the time—1,330 times. A Ruthian strike-out was almost as grandiose as a Ruthian home run.

Infielders played Ruth so far back he probably could have hit .400 by bunting and spraying the ball around, as Ty Cobb did. "Four hundred, hell, kid," he once snorted, "I could have hit five hundred." And another time he boasted, "Shucks, I coulda hit a six hundred lifetime average easy. But I woulda had to hit them singles. The people were payin' to see me hit them home runs."

"Kid" is what he called younger people. The middle-aged and up were "Doc" to the Babe, who had a terrible memory for names. Asked about a player named Don Heffner, Ruth shot back, "Who?" Heffner had been playing second base for the Yankees for a month. And when Waite Hoyt, a longtime teammate, was traded away from the Yanks and stopped by to say farewell, the Babe told him: "Good luck, kid. Take care of yourself . . . Walter."

Although many Ruthian escapades never made it into print, the Bambino's saga did not lack for stories that became legends. The most

The Babe in pinstripes, 1942, six years before his final appearance in a Yankee uniform. His 714 lifetime home runs is one of baseball's historic records.

famous was the shot he "called" against Charlie Root of the Chicago Cubs in the 1932 World Series, taking two strikes, then waving or pointing his bat in the direction of the center-field bleachers and depositing the next pitch in that very spot.

Hoyt, a star pitcher, once said that if the Babe were sawed in two, half the concessions of Yankee Stadium would flow out. So it was really no surprise when the big fellow came down with a classic case of indigestion during a spring training exhibition tour of the South in 1925. Twelve hot dogs and eight bottles of soda pop was the reported score in the famous "stomachache heard 'round the world." Rushed to New York's St. Vincent's Hospital, Ruth nearly died. For a week, baseball fans around the country followed daily bulletins concerning his condition.

The wonder was that Ruth's ample stomach—he stood 6 feet 2 inches, weighed well over 200 pounds and had a barrel-shaped torso and pipestem legs—did not succumb to overeating sooner. Standard breakfast fare for the Babe, as attested to by Paul Derringer, a pretty good pitcher and eater in his own right, was a Porterhouse steak, four fried eggs and fried potatoes, washed down by a pot of coffee . . . and a pint of bourbon and ginger ale. The Babe also enjoyed the pickled eels Lou Gehrig's mother would bring him whenever the Yankees played a doubleheader in New York. Ruth would send out between games for a quart of chocolate ice cream and eat the two together.

Writer Jimmy Breslin once had the pleasure of witnessing an epicurean performance by the Babe. "In eighteen years of being able to look at things and remember what I have seen," said Breslin, "the only sports legend I ever saw who completely lived up to advance billing was Babe Ruth.

"It was a hot summer afternoon, and the Babe, sweat dripping from his jowls and his shirt stuck to him, came off the eighteenth green at the old Bayside Golf Club in the borough of Queens and stormed into the huge barroom of the club.

" 'Gimme one of them heavens to Betsy drinks you always make for me,' the Babe said in his gravelly voice.

"The bartender put a couple of fistfuls of ice chunks into a big, thick mixing glass and then proceeded to make a Tom Collins that had so much gin in it that the other people at the

bar started to laugh. He served the drink to the Babe just as it was made, right in the mixing glass.

"Ruth said something about how heavens to Betsy hot he was, and then he picked up the glass and opened his mouth, and there went everything. In one shot he swallowed the drink, the orange slice and the rest of the garbage, and the ice chunks, too. He stopped for nothing. There is not a single man I have ever seen in a saloon who does not bring his teeth together a little bit and stop those ice chunks from going in. A man has to have a pipe the size of a trombone to take ice in one shot. But I saw Babe Ruth do it, and whenever somebody tells me about how the Babe used to drink and eat when he was playing ball, I believe every word of it."

George Herman Ruth—"Babe" to the public, "Jidge" to his teammates, "Big Monkey" to opponents—was born on the Baltimore waterfront in 1895 to parents who died when he was very young. The unwanted youngster was in and out of reform school and finally was placed in St. Mary's Industrial School, where he first displayed his athletic ability. He started out as a left-handed catcher but switched to pitching during his final year at St. Mary's.

Jack Dunn, owner of the minor league Baltimore Orioles, offered Big George, as he was known then, $600 for the 1914 season. Ruth arrived at the Orioles' camp tagging at Dunn's heels. That led to the most famous nickname in sports. "Here comes Dunn with his newest babe," the players said.

Perhaps as a result of his own neglected youth, Ruth always had a soft spot for kids. When he became a star he visited them in hospitals and he brought them baseballs and promised to hit home runs for them. More often than not, he came through. To quote Grantland Rice:

"On the night before the famous Yankee–Cub World Series game in Chicago when the Babe called his home run shot, I happened to be in his room.

" 'What are you doing tonight?' I asked.

" 'I'll tell you,' he said, 'if you won't print it. I've got to take an autographed baseball to a sick kid in a Chicago suburb about fifty miles from here. He wrote and asked me to come . . . If you ever print this I'll knock your brains out.'

"This was a trip of a hundred miles . . . to see one ailing youngster."

In 1914, Babe Ruth became a pitcher for the Boston Red Sox and helped pitch them to a pennant in 1918. But it was as a home run hitter that Babe gained enduring fame.

The press loved the Babe, although they had trouble keeping up with him at times. In 1933, Ruth was late for an exhibition game in Nashville, Tennessee, but he still took time to answer the questions of a young local reporter outside the park while his teammates urged him to hurry. The Tennessee newsman was Will Grimsley, one of the editors and contributors to this book.

Ruth advanced to the major leagues as a pitcher with the Red Sox in 1914 winning two of three decisions. A year later he was 18–8 and a full-fledged star. Eight times he hooked up with Washington's Walter Johnson, one of the all-time greats, and won six of them, three by 1–0 scores. In a key game with Detroit, he struck out the Murderers' Row of the day—Bobby Veach, Sam Crawford and Ty Cobb—with the bases loaded. Cobb, in fact, always had trouble hitting the Babe.

But when the Babe began to hit other pitchers, he changed baseball strategy. The big inning became the vogue. Why play for one run when the big fellow could do—or undo—it himself with one swing? When Ruth hit 29 home runs in 1919, his final year with the Red Sox, it was looked upon as a fluke, never to be approached again. Always aware of the dramatic, Ruth didn't wait long to erase that mark. He walloped 54 as a Yankee in 1920, and the Bronx Bombers were born.

Ed Barrow, who managed the Red Sox and later became general manager of the Yankee dynasty, was the man who decided to play Ruth every day in the outfield rather than every fourth or fifth day on the pitcher's mound. It wasn't an easy decision.

"The Babe was as good a left-handed pitcher as I ever saw," Barrow said. "He had everything—speed, control and a good breaking ball. He didn't care whom he pitched against, and half the time he didn't even know.

"When the Red Sox won the pennant in 1918, I went over the Chicago hitters with our club before the first game of the World Series. The Cubs had an outfielder named Leslie Mann, who might hit a long ball and cause you trouble. On the other hand, if you pitched him tight and drove him away from the plate, he wouldn't hurt you. I told Ruth to loosen him up every time he came to bat.

"Mann was a right-handed hitter, a husky chap. There was another outfielder playing with the Cubs at the time, a chunky little fellow, Max Flack, a left-handed batter. The first time Ruth pitched against Flack he cut loose with one that clipped Flack squarely on the forehead. After the inning was over, Ruth came back to the bench all smiles.

" 'Well, manager,' he said to me, 'I sure loosened up that Mann guy all right.' He was the most surprised fellow in the ball park when I told him he hit Flack instead of Mann."

In 14 years with the Yankees, Ruth led or tied for the American League home run title 10 times. His poorest seasons were 1925, when that famous bellyache limited him to 98 games and 25 homers, and 1934, his Yankee swan song, when he hammered out 22 homers at the age of 39.

In February of 1935, angry because he had not been named manager of the Yanks, Ruth asked for his release and signed with the Boston Braves of the National League. He was well past his prime though, and hit only .181 in 28 games, but he managed six home runs and maintained his flair for the dramatic.

Before a game in Pittsburgh, a local writer told manager Pie Traynor of the Pirates that he'd taken Ruth out on the town until 5 A.M. When Ruth showed up at Forbes Field, he was bleary-eyed and short of sleep. "Don't worry about Ruth," said Traynor in going over the Boston hitters.

"I wouldn't say that," said old crony

"Walter" Hoyt, who had become a relief pitcher for the Pirates.

Hoyt was right. The Babe belted three home runs that afternoon, his last Ruthian feat. He retired soon after.

It wasn't the first time they tried that trick on the Babe, somehow overlooking the fact that he could carouse with the best of them and better than most, and still perform magnificently. Years earlier, Ruth and Washington's Goose Goslin burned the midnight oil well into midmorning. Goslin grabbed a quick snooze and went hitless in five at-bats that afternoon. Ruth went to Walter Reed Hospital to autograph baseballs and later hit two home runs and a double.

They weren't smiling in Washington that day, but the Babe once got a chuckle out of Silent Cal Coolidge when the president decided to take in a game at Griffith Stadium. The president was introduced to each of the Yankees for a handshake. Ruth, of course, had to go one better. Sticking out a large hand, he grinned and said, "Geez, it's hot, ain't it, Prez?"

Ruth made $872,000 in salaries during his career—he earned more than $1 million from outside pursuits, such as endorsements, ghost-written stories, barnstorming tours, movies, etc. —and his top figure was $80,000 in 1930. Today's athlete would have to make an estimated $300,000 to take home what Ruth did after taxes. That whopping wage came in the wake of, first, the stock market crash of October, 1929, and second, Ruth's holdout siege in the spring of 1930. A New York writer pointed out that a holdout might not look good during the Depression and said that President Herbert Hoover was making only $75,000. "Yeah," snorted the Babe, "but I had a better year than he did."

Ruth never got his chance to manage. The Yankees passed him by, and he never returned a call from Detroit's Frank Navin, who had permission to talk to him after the 1933 season. Instead, the Detroit job went to Mickey Cochrane.

Ruth turned down a chance to pilot the Yankees' top farm club at Newark in 1935, and a 1938 coaching job with Brooklyn didn't last long.

His final appearance in a baseball uniform was on June 13, 1948, the occasion being the silver anniversary of Yankee Stadium. The Babe was dying of throat cancer and could barely talk. It was a pathetic sight to see him stand at home plate on the pipestem legs that took those little mincing homerun steps around the bases 114 times in regular season and 15 more in World Series. He stood there with a Yankee cap in one hand, a bat in the other and the number 3 on his back that would never again be worn by a Yankee, and in a hoarse voice, he thanked the spectators for their thunderous ovation.

Barely two months later he was dead. His body was viewed by the public first at Yankee Stadium and then at St. Patrick's Cathedral. Finally, the big fellow, who was really nothing more than a big kid himself, was laid to rest in Mount Pleasant, New York, on a steamy summer afternoon.

"Lord," murmured Jumping Joe Dugan, the old Yankee third baseman, "I'd give my right arm for an ice-cold beer."

"So would the Babe," said Waite Hoyt.
HERSCHEL NISSENSON

Left: Before an All-Star Game in New York in 1934 are Al Simmons (White Sox), Lou Gehrig, Ruth and Jimmy Foxx (Athletics). Above: The Yankees' one-two punch—Gehrig and Ruth.

Helen Wills Moody
Queen of Tennis

Helen Wills's words always were as well placed as her serves.

Followers of one of the greatest careers in the history of women's tennis resented the paucity of phrases and on-court animation. They dubbed her "Little Miss Poker Face" and held to public debate her desire for privacy.

Helen's trademark was a tight lip and a steady eye tucked under a green-lined eyeshade. Strictly tennis, not theatrics, thrilled audiences around the globe. As Queen of American tennis in the 1920s, she reigned over seven United States championships and eight Wimbledon titles.

Cast in the role of royalty, in public she was gracious, a smile quick to cross her classic Grecian face, yet aloof. In private she was vivacious, an excellent conversationalist, an artist, a writer, a dress designer, an avid gardener.

One of her rare talkative moments for public consumption came while sequestered in New York City where she was taking time out from tennis to work on one of four mystery books she was eventually to author. When asked whether she would ever write the Great American Novel, her answer reflected her attitude toward attaining all her ambitions:

"I think it's a mistake to talk about a thing, for after a while you feel you've done it."

The well-bred daughter born in 1905 to a Berkeley, California, physician won her first U.S. championship in 1923, at age 17. Her finale was at Wimbledon in 1938.

Helen's father, Clarence, introduced her to the game when, as a youngster, she tagged along with him to the Berkeley Tennis Club. She didn't take to the sport with ease. In fact, many years later she was to say that tennis never had been her life ambition. Nevertheless, the enthusiasm she developed for all pursuits of life paid off, but not until her father had returned from France, where he had served at a military hospital, and she had returned from boarding school at Bishop Hopkins Hall in Burlington, Vermont, in 1919. Her fourteenth-birthday present was her own racket, a junior membership to her father's club and an introduction to one of the most famous nonprofes-

sional coaches William ("Pop") Fuller.

Already she had learned to whip her father, a fair club player, and soon was competing with, and beating, the boys. In the next two years she won the National Junior Girls Championship. At 16 she was ranked number 3 among United States women, and at 17 she took her first singles title at Forest Hills, New York, after winning the doubles the year before.

Serious Helen didn't seem to fit with the lighthearted era of the 1920s. Suzanne Lenglen took the throne of European tennis with theatrics that made her a spectacular, sensational center-court attraction while America's queen ruled with calm. She was impassive, intent, inhibited and amazingly self-controlled. Miss Wills appeared oblivious to critics who chided her for hiding beneath the eyeshade and for appearing on the sacred greens of Wimbledon in a schoolgirl's middy blouse and midcalf pleated skirt.

But she was no less a champion.

In 1923, she was the star of the first Wightman Cup team, a British–American rivalry still going strong. In the first match she conquered Kathleen McKane, 6–2, 7–5, scored another singles victory, then teamed with the famed Molla Mallory for a doubles victory.

The next year, at age 19, she traveled abroad for the first time, in the company of her mother, for the second Wightman Cup match and a crack at Mlle. Lenglen at Wimbledon. Helen lost the two singles matches, her only losses in 18 Cup singles matches in nine years. But with Mrs. Hazel Hotchkiss Wightman, the trophy donor, as her partner, she came back to score the lone U.S. point in doubles.

Wimbledon was somewhat of a disappointment that year, too, although Miss Wills did win the first of her three Wimbledon doubles titles. Suzanne Lenglen, the mademoiselle from Nice, didn't play. The singles title match pitted Helen Wills against Miss McKane. The best of England won, 4–6, 6–4, 6–4, but a composed Helen stayed in Europe, going to France to win the singles and doubles crowns at the Summer Olympics. Then she returned to the United States where she avenged her loss to Miss

Wills's trademark: tight lips, steady eye, green-lined eyeshade.

McKane at Forest Hills, won the doubles with Mrs. Wightman and teamed with Vinnie Richards, the Olympic men's champion, for the mixed doubles title.

While an honor student at the University of California, she not only took up golf as a pastime and added a Phi Beta Kappa key to her growing collection of honors, but she retired the U.S. Championship trophy with her third straight triumph and retained the U.S. doubles title, the third of four she was to take. Her partner was Mary K. Browne, who, a year later, became the first American woman to turn professional.

But two players had yet to cross Helen's path—Suzanne Lenglen and Helen Jacobs. In 1926, she took a six months' leave of absence from the university to pursue art studies in France. She also pursued Mlle. Lenglen, who was reported to be in the south of France.

The match for personal pride rather than prestige finally took place in Cannes, on the French Riviera. Excitement abounded. So did rumors. Some said Miss Wills was guaranteed

$100,000 for movie rights to the match. Others said she was drafted to boost tourism. Still others claimed her opponent was panicked and ready to pull out.

When the flamboyant Frenchwoman and the subdued American took to the courts at the Carlton Club, Mlle. Lenglen took the first set 6–3. Helen held set point at 5–4 in the second set, but Suzanne won that, too, 8–6.

"I never had such a thrill in my life," Miss Wills, still only 21, said later. "It was our only meeting and the greatest match I ever played. Suzanne is just as good as I thought she was."

An appendicitis attack prevented America's ace from defending her United States title later that year. It was the first of several ailments that would curb her activities in years to come. But in 1927, Helen put her physical fitness and powerful forehand to the test. She passed with flying colors, winning the first of three more consecutive U.S. singles championships and taking the first of four straight Wimbledon crowns.

The period between 1927 and 1930 was

Above: Helen in action at Los Angeles. Right: At Wimbledon.

profitable for the prima donna of American tennis. She won three straight French championships and one title each in U.S. doubles and mixed doubles and Wimbledon doubles and mixed doubles. Her 1927 singles triumph at Wimbledon was the first for an American woman in 20 years. In 1928 and 1929, she swept through the French and U.S. national singles without losing a set.

But it was 1933, when she was Mrs. Frederick Moody, bride of a gentleman who had courted her aboard a transoceanic liner, that tennis history was made. She won her sixth Wimbledon championship, despite losing her first set there since 1928, and she finally came face-to-face with Helen Jacobs in the final at Forest Hills. But not before her semifinals opponent, Sarah Palfrey Fabian, handed her her first set loss on an American court since 1926.

There was no doubt that Mrs. Moody would defeat the defending champion who had taken the 1932 title when the Queen abdicated. Miss Jacobs, a few years younger than Mrs. Moody, also was a native of California and a product of Pop Fuller. Miss Jacobs perhaps had greater natural ability than her opponent, and as a result of having lived many years in her shadow, she had a great desire to meet and defeat her.

But Miss Jacobs was never allowed to put her prowess to the full test. She won the first set 8–6 and Mrs. Moody rallied to take the second set 6–3. Miss Jacobs broke the Queen's service in the first game of the final set, then broke it again for a 3–0 lead. Could Mrs. Moody be beaten on a court she had conquered seven times? The question never was answered.

Mrs. Moody made a beeline for the umpire's chair where, without a word to her opponent, she told the official she couldn't continue, donned her sweater and made a dramatic exit. She defaulted. As was her wont, she was wordless to the public. The reason she had walked off was withheld until years later when it was revealed in her autobiography. She had injured her back that spring while lifting rocks in her garden. Heat massages had managed to get her through Wimbledon in the summer, but by early fall at Forest Hills, a back brace was part of her attire in an attempt to cure a sacroiliac condition. She said she had become so dizzy on court that the stadium began swimming.

"My choice was instinctive rather than premeditated," she wrote. "Had I been able to think clearly, I might have chosen to remain.

Animals and often humans, however, prefer to suffer in a quiet, dark place."

Helen Wills Moody never again played at Forest Hills.

The same year that she defaulted, the mysterious Mrs. Moody told the well-known educator and writer of the time William Lyon Phelps that tennis was not her life ambition. Rather, she said, she wanted to achieve success in some field of endeavor that she could steadily develop to the end of her days. Thus she took to the typewriter, writing eventually a total of four mysteries. In 1935, she had her revenge in tennis, beating Miss Jacobs, 6–3, 3–6, 7–5, in the Wimbledon final. Then she busied herself in oil painting. Her still lifes and landscapes, as well as etchings of an earlier era, were the subjects of one-woman shows in New York and exhibitions in London and Paris.

After divorcing her husband in 1937, Mrs. Moody made one final comeback—another Wimbledon triumph over Miss Jacobs in 1938. It wasn't an accurate test of the 32-year-old titlist's skills. Miss Jacobs suffered a sprained heel in the first set and bowed to Mrs. Moody, 6–4, 6–0. After that triumph, Mrs. Moody was asked about the feud between the two Helens.

"In all sports, people like to imagine there is more to a rivalry than merely a match between two players."

That same year she announced she wouldn't compete in the U.S. Championship because of neuritis. In her letter to Forest Hills officials she wrote: "It is with regret that I come to this decision." She also thanked the United States Lawn Tennis Association for "their kind attitude of many years standing, their unselfish interest in tennis which has provided for me, along with other players of the game in the United States, a very happy time in sports."

Helen Wills Moody had said farewell to tennis.

But just as she was harried by news hounds at the height of her career when rumors of romances and movie contracts were rampant, she was in constant demand for comment after she retired to California to become the wife of Aidan Roark, a screenwriter, polo player and official of Santa Anita race track.

In 1943, she suffered broken bones and infection in her right hand attempting to break up a fight between her German shepherd and another dog. She regained use of her hand after surgery but her tennis grip had changed. "I'm

At 17, Helen won her first singles at Forest Hills; in 1927, another of seven U.S. singles titles and the first of eight at Wimbledon. Right: Going to and defending at Wimbledon in 1933.

pleased with my progress," she told newsmen. "And although at my age, I don't yearn for the strenuous play of tournaments, I would enjoy playing some exhibitions."

Approaching 50, nearly two decades after being named Associated Press Athlete of the Year, Helen Wills Moody Roark was still swinging a racket, still full of drive to achieve, still trying to calm the "restless heart" she referred to in Will Durant's book *On the Meaning of Life* in 1932.

But this matron put one question to rest when she reflected on being dubbed "Little Miss Poker Face."

"I always thought it very clever," she said coyly, "although I didn't think it applied and paid no attention to it."

KAROL STONGER

Jack Dempsey
Fists of Cement

America shunned involvement in world politics following World War I, seeking a return to prewar "normalcy." The nation entered the 1920s eager to enjoy an economy unscathed by the problems plaguing postwar Europe. It was an era of marvelous nonsense, and the freewheeling country needed a world heavyweight champion to reflect the times. It found one in Jack Dempsey, a fearsome mauler whose bobbing, weaving, slashing attack captivated the boxing world as no heavyweight king had done since John L. Sullivan. America at first despised Dempsey for not serving in the war but soon learned to idolize him, never forgiving Shakespeare-reading Gene Tunney for winning the title from Dempsey in 1926. Dempsey's bruising style electrified crowds and gave boxing its first million-dollar gate. He was the champion. Ignorant of the meaning of the word *quit*, he battled back with the ferocity of a wounded beast when hurt.

A wild, chaotic defense of his title occurred in 1923 at the New York Polo Grounds when he fought Luis Angel Firpo, the "Wild Bull of the Pampas." A brute of a man, Firpo weighed 216½ pounds, compared to Dempsey's 192½. In the opening seconds of the fight, Firpo brought the crowd to its feet by flooring Dempsey with a sledgehammer right to the head. The champion, visibly shaken, regained his feet and clinched. Dempsey then began slipping Firpo's blows, punishing the Argentine with crushing rights and lefts. He floored Firpo seven times and, even though the neutral-corner rule was in effect, hovered over his fallen opponent each time and battered him the split second his knees left the canvas. Just before the end of the round, Firpo belted Dempsey out of the ring with an overhand right to the jaw. Dempsey landed on a typewriter in the press row and was helped back into the ring by newsmen. Hurt, dazed, barely able to remain upright, Dempsey avoided Firpo's roundhouse swings until the bell.

"I remember that when I came out for the second round, ammonia stinging my nostrils," Dempsey recalled years later, "I saw twenty Firpos. They were everywhere. Every time I saw one, I let him have it. They tell me Firpo went down like a poled steer in the second." He knocked out Firpo at 58 seconds of the second. The wild battle had left the spectators emotionally drained. For all its whirlwind excitement, the bout had lasted slightly less than four minutes.

William Harrison Dempsey was born in 1895 in the sun-baked, rocky mining country of Manassa, Colorado. By the time he reached his teens, Dempsey was doing a full day's work in the mines. Determined to be a fighter, he left the mines and drifted about the West, fighting in the back rooms of saloons for minuscule purses and dreaming of T-bone steaks when doughnuts were all he could afford. He slowly began acquiring the fistic skills. He trained constantly, fought whenever possible, soaked his face in brine to toughen the skin against cuts and chewed wads of gum to strengthen his jaw muscles. It was a grimy existence, riding on brake beams underneath freight cars, sleeping in hobo jungles and searching for odd jobs to earn meal money. But Dempsey was sustained by a deep faith in himself. He had always felt he would become a successful fighter.

While he was toiling in the damp mine shafts, he received a telegram from fight manager Jack ("Doc") Kearns, urging him to come to San Francisco where several bouts awaited. Wary of managers by now, Dempsey agreed to the trip only after Kearns agreed to pay travel expenses. "I'm going to make you the heavyweight champion," Kearns told the lean, hungry Dempsey who stepped off the train in San Francisco. After joining the shrewd and wily Kearns, Dempsey's career began a meteoric rise. Kearns landed matches with several top-ranked heavyweights, and Dempsey beat them all. He won 21 fights in 1918 and scored 17 knockouts, establishing himself as a contender.

On July 4, 1919, a sweltering day, the 187-pound Dempsey met 245-pound Jess Willard for the title. Willard, who had halted aging Jack Johnson for the championship in 1915, had defended his laurels only once and had grown soft. Dempsey, deeply tanned and sporting sev-

54

Fighting pose by the mauler who savaged his way to the top.

eral days' growth of beard, was in superb condition. Dempsey charged out at the bell and began hammering his towering foe with energy-sapping blows. Seven times in that first round Willard crashed to the canvas under Dempsey's relentless onslaught. The Manassa Mauler floored Willard just before the bell, and the referee had counted him out. However, the roar of the crowd had drowned out the sound of the bell when the referee reached seven, saving Willard from a first-round knockout. Dempsey, thinking he had stopped his foe, left the ring and had to be called back by a frantic Kearns.

Kearns had wagered $10,000 at 10-to-1 odds that his fighter would finish the champion in one round. "The bell rang while the referee was counting Jess out, but I left the ring thinking we had won the hundred thousand," Dempsey said later. "I was having a wonderful time thinking of all the automobiles and silk shirts I was going to buy. And then suddenly I was back in the ring and realized I had lost the hundred thousand and the ten thousand, too. I felt mean."

Dempsey, showing arm-weariness after that torrid first round, continued to outclass Willard but could not put the hulking champion down. Finally, just before the bell for the start of the fourth round, Willard's corner threw in the towel. His cheekbone shattered, several teeth broken and his face a crimson mass of cuts and welts, Willard was mute testimony to the savagery of Dempsey's power.

Shortly before his death in 1963, Kearns wrote that he had loaded Dempsey's fists with plaster of paris before the bout but that Jack was not aware of it. Willard concurred and said, "I'm glad Kearns finally admitted it. I've been

In retirement, Dempsey jogs with Max Schmeling and Joe Jacobs.

saying it for forty-five years but nobody would believe me." Dempsey emphatically denied the allegation. Kearns claimed that he had soaked Dempsey's hand bandages in water and then packed them with plaster, telling Jack and a cornerman from Willard's dressing room that it was merely talcum powder. The same method was attempted by newsmen after Kearns aired his claims, but the plaster crumbled instead of hardening. It seems unlikely that Dempsey needed fists encased with plaster in order to defeat Willard. It was simply a case of a fleshy, out-of-shape ring veteran fighting a fierce, rock-hard young man.

Kearns's supposed revelation capped a stormy relationship between him and Dempsey. While Kearns's managerial talents had landed Jack fights that eventually propelled him to the title bout with Willard, the two were constantly at odds. They split up before Dempsey lost his crown. Fight fans thought that time had mellowed the relationship between the two when, in 1950, Dempsey remarked: "I would be a bum today if it weren't for Kearns. I made a million dollars and everything I have I owe to Jack." Ostensibly impressed, Kearns stated that he would "rather hear those words from Dempsey than manage two world champions." However, Kearns probably couldn't resist pumping a dose of controversy into boxing before he died.

Dempsey hadn't gained acceptance by the public by defeating Willard. He was labeled a draft dodger—a charge he was later cleared of in court—and the country wanted to see him defeated. Together with promoter Tex Rickard, Kearns fashioned the first million-dollar gate— $1,626,580 to be exact—when Dempsey defended his title against Georges Carpentier of France in 1921. A handsome, dashing war hero, Carpentier provided little resistance and was knocked out in four rounds.

After a tour of Europe and a trip to Hollywood to make a film, Dempsey's funds were beginning to dwindle, so Kearns began searching for another million-dollar gate. About that time, a group of businessmen in Shelby, Montana, were searching for a promotional theme that would put their town on the map. Why not a world's heavyweight championship fight? They offered Kearns and Dempsey, who was by now a national idol, $300,000 to defend against Tommy Gibbons, a fading gladiator who probably couldn't offer Jack much of a fight. The fight took place on July 4, 1923, and was Dempsey's least-impressive title defense. Gibbons, by running and clinching, managed to last the entire 15 rounds, but lost the decision. Although the bout bankrupted the town's banks, Dempsey and Kearns managed to salvage most of their guarantee. Gibbons, who received some acclaim for lasting the full route with the Manassa Mauler, received nothing. He often had said he would fight Dempsey for nothing just for a crack at the title. And that's what he got.

Dempsey was idle for three years following the Firpo bout. He toured the country fighting exhibitions and enjoying high-spirited America in the Roaring Twenties. Clearly, the inactivity dulled his sharpness. When he defended his title against Tunney before 120,000 fans in Philadelphia in 1926, he was hampered by rust. Tunney, a former marine, had cleared the field of challengers for Dempsey's title, but many did not consider him a worthy contender. Tunney feinted Dempsey dizzy, stung him with rapier-like left jabs and easily outboxed him to a 10-round decision and the title. Dempsey's heart of savage fury hadn't diminished, he just couldn't corner the clever Tunney. When the bout was over, he stood in the ring, his face splotched with purplish bruises and his eyes brimming with tears. Asked by his wife, movie star Estelle Taylor, what had happened, Dempsey replied, "Honey, I just forgot to duck."

No previous heavyweight champion had ever regained the title, but Jack was determined to break the jinx. A year later he was matched with Jack Sharkey to produce a challenger for Tunney's crown. Dempsey was soundly outboxed by Sharkey until the seventh round when some of the Manassa Mauler's body blows strayed below the belt. Forgetting the cardinal rule of boxing to protect oneself at all times, Sharkey dropped his hands and turned to the referee to complain. The sight of Sharkey's naked, unprotected jaw was too tempting for Dempsey, who whipped over a left hook and knocked him cold. When asked about taking advantage of the situation, Dempsey retorted, "What was I supposed to do? Write him a letter?"

More than 100,000 people jammed Chicago's Soldier Field on September 27, 1927. The bout was patterned after their first match, Tunney jabbing and moving while Dempsey plodded forward hoping to land a telling blow. In the seventh round Dempsey rocked Tunney with a left hook to the jaw and pummeled him to the canvas near the ropes with a fusillade of punches. Tunney sat there, glassy-eyed, obviously in trouble and grasping the middle strand of rope. For once, however, Dempsey's aggressive, competitive instinct—the same that had demolished Willard and Firpo—hurt him. Eager to get at his prey, Dempsey stood over Tunney and refused the referee's instruction to go to a neutral corner before the count could begin. Precious seconds elapsed before Dempsey took a neutral corner and the referee started to toll over Tunney. Tunney beat the count but was on the floor almost 17 seconds. It was all the time Gene needed to shake the cobwebs from his brain. Regaining his feet, Tunney kept away from Dempsey and retained his title with a decision. Although Dempsey's supporters claimed that Jack was the first man to regain the heavyweight championship—since Tunney

had been down for more than 10 seconds—the fact was that Dempsey had failed to heed the rules and Tunney was still the champion.

The Battle of the Long Count was a climactic finish to a golden age of boxing during the 1920s. It was not until Joe Louis won the title a decade later that the world would have a heavyweight champion that matched the color and vitality of Dempsey. Tunney, to be sure, was a greater boxer than many would admit. But Dempsey had created a difficult act to follow. Dempsey never disputed Tunney's claim that he didn't need the "long count" to recover from the barrage that dumped him on the canvas. In fact, Jack later said he was glad the bout ended as it did.

"It was the greatest break I ever got," he mused years later. "It was probably time I stopped fighting. I also made a half-million

dollars, and I lost to a nice fellow, a gentleman."

That final clash with Tunney ended Dempsey's boxing career. He attempted a comeback but it was short-lived, and he retired from the ring for good in 1932. A popular hero, Dempsey enjoyed several lucrative business ventures and entered the Coast Guard during World War II as a physical instructor. He had tried to enlist in the army but was rejected for being over age. While on a transport ship in the Pacific, he engaged in one bout that isn't listed in the record books. His opponent was a bully who had once been a sparring partner for Joe Louis. As Dempsey told it:

"This bird was making himself pretty objectionable—bullying other men. One day there was a boxing show and this guy knocked his opponent cold. So, he began to boast that no so-and-so on the ship could lick him. It burned me, but naturally I didn't say anything. Finally, he walked up to me and said, 'How about you? You're a great fighter. You're an ex-champ.' " Dempsey agreed to fight him but had some misgivings as the gloves were being laced on inside the ring.

"I said to myself, 'Are you daffy? Fighting at fifty a fellow about twenty-three or twenty-four?' " The younger man belted Dempsey around in the first round. In the second, Dempsey reached years back into his bag of fistic tricks and knocked his opponent out with a perfectly executed shot to the jaw. For the Coast Guardsmen sitting on the deck in the Pacific that day during World War II, the Manassa Mauler was still champion.

EARL GERHEIM

Above: The famous second fight and the long count that kept the championship for Gene Tunney. Left: Dempsey as a Coast Guard commander on landing craft coming into Okinawa.

Bobby Jones
The Grand Slam

Late on a summer day in 1923, a youthful and disconsolate Robert Tyre Jones sat in the clubhouse at the Inwood Country Club on Long Island. He had yet to win a major golf championship, and he had just finished his final round in the United States Open. It looked as if he would lose again after leading by three strokes with 18 to play.

In his frustration and dismay at the bogey, bogey, double-bogey finish, the 21-year-old Jones was teetering on the brink of deciding to quit competitive golf. His head was down as he told his longtime friend, Atlanta sportswriter O. B. Keeler, "I didn't finish like a champion. I finished like a yellow dog."

Jones didn't know it, but he was only 24 hours away from a victory that was to start him on a succession of triumphs, culminated seven years later in golf's only Grand Slam. Jones rallied from that 5-5-6 finish at Inwood to beat Bobby Cruikshank by two strokes in an 18-hole play-off the next day for the first of his 13 major championships.

Golf emerged from its stuffy, country-club atmosphere when Francis Ouimet defeated Britain's Ted Ray and Harry Vardon in the United States Open at Brookline, Massachusetts, in 1913. But it remained for Bobby Jones to send the sport rocketing to unprecedented popularity. That surge started a decade later at Inwood.

Jones was the typical all-American boy— young, good-looking, clean-cut. He had a flawless style, a grooved swing that became the envy of two continents. Although an amateur, he faced and consistently beat some of the greatest professionals the game has known— Walter Hagen, Gene Sarazen, Tommy Armour, Macdonald Smith, Harry Cooper, Leo Diegel.

Between 1923 and 1930, he amassed 13 national titles—5 U.S. Amateurs, 4 U.S. Opens, 3 British Opens and a single British Amateur. In the last nine years of his career, he played in 12 Open championships—9 American and 3 British—and finished first or second in 11 of them. Jones personally considered this a feat superior to his Grand Slam.

But it is for the Slam that Bobby will forever be remembered. In 1930, he climaxed his career by winning the U.S. Open and Amateur and the British Open and Amateur—an unparalleled sweep of the major championships in a single season. Two months later, on November 17, 1930, he announced his retirement from competitive golf in order to make a series of instructional films. He was only 28, at the peak of his career. Had he continued, it is entirely possible that he could have added another dozen titles to his gaudy collection.

Bobby Jones was born March 17, 1902, not in the golfing tradition. His father, Robert P. Jones, was a good baseball player at the University of Georgia, good enough to get a Brooklyn Dodgers' contract after graduation. But straight-laced Robert Tyre Jones, the grandfather for whom Bobby was named, frowned on such frivolous activities and Bobby's dad pursued a career at law.

Bobby's first memory of golf went back to the summer of 1907, when his family moved to a boardinghouse near the East Lake course in Atlanta. The five-year-old Jones could look out his window and see the rolling fairways and the players whacking away at the ball with their sticks. Looking back on these scenes, Jones later said that he did not remember having had even a wave of inspiration or anything similar—not even when another occupant of the boardinghouse gave him his first club, a sawed-off cleek, and three battered balls.

His mother and father became golf devotees, however, and young Bobby soon was trailing them around the course.

There was no indication, however, that he was cut out for an athletic career. As a child, he had an oversized head and a frail body that was hampered by a digestive ailment. But it didn't stunt his energy. Shortly after he was given his first club, he and some of his playmates improvised a five-hole course in the front yard. They played for hours.

He was six when he won his first tournament, a six-hole event for the neighborhood kids. Bobby's trophy was a three-inch-high silver cup. He proudly displayed it, throughout his life, along with the extravagant trophies he was

Knickered Robert Tyre Jones, Jr., Golfer of the Century.

presented with for his national championships.

Bobby's interest in golf was intensified when a young Scotch professional named Stewart Maiden came to East Lake. Young Bobby dogged the heels of the new pro and soon began trying to copy Maiden's graceful, effortless swing. He succeeded to such a degree that club members soon commented on the similarity of Bobby's swing to Maiden's. Bobby beamed.

In 1911, at the age of nine, he won his first championship, a junior tournament at the Atlanta Athletic Club. At 12, he won two club championships and two invitation tournaments away from home against some of the South's top amateurs. The next year, 1916, he won three more invitation titles and took the Georgia state championship. Southern golf circles began to buzz over the sensational Georgia schoolboy.

Jones was 14 years old and stood 5 feet 4 inches in the late summer of 1916 when he went to the Merion Cricket Club in Philadelphia—a course that was to play a large part in his career—for the National Amateur championship. He created a very considerable stir when he led the first round of qualifying with a 74. He won two matches before losing to the defending champion, Bob Gardner, 5 and 3.

At that time he was noted as being a boy with a perfect swing and a fearsome temper. He raged when he missed a shot and he occasionally threw a club in disgust. He drew sharp criticism from the press. He gradually learned to harness his temper, but he was fated to a series of bitter disappointments before he established himself as the king of golf.

He quickly became a leading golf figure. This was at a time when the amateur game was dominant. In many cases, professionals were looked upon with disdain. The Amateur championship had equal billing with the National Open. Jones won the Southern and other regional titles with regularity. He was widely sought for exhibitions. But when it came to a national event, something always happened to prevent him from winning.

His next National Amateur try was at Oakmont in 1919 when he beat Gardner in an early round and advanced to the final, only to lose to Davison Herron of Pittsburgh, 5 and 4.

The next year, 1920, the 18-year-old Jones won the Southern again and made his first start in the United States Open at Toledo, Ohio. He was only four strokes off the pace at the end

of three rounds but blew up on the last 18 and finished with a 299 total and eighth place behind winner Ted Ray. He won the qualifying medal in the National Amateur later that year but lost to Ouimet in the semifinals at Roslyn, New York.

He made his first trip to England in 1921 as the youngest member of the United States Walker Cup team. He helped the Americans to a team victory. But in the British Amateur at Holyake, he lost in the fourth round.

Back in the United States, he improved to fifth in the American National Open at the Columbia Country Club in Washington, D.C. He was still without a victory, and his jinx followed him to St. Louis where, after two excellent rounds in the U.S. Amateur, he lost to British champion Willie Hunter.

By this time Jones was beginning to worry about his failure to win a major title. He knew he was expected to be a champion—but he wasn't. He was troubled by comments heard in locker rooms: "That Jones boy has everything, but he can't handle it in the clutch." Actually Jones played some of his best golf under pressure, only to run into someone who was having a fabulous round.

Jones had a more philosophical outlook on it.

"Every tournament has somebody's name on it," he once said. "No matter how well you play, the fellow whom the fates have picked will win out. The ball just falls that way." He retained that outlook even when his fortunes changed. He always contended that he won tournaments he shouldn't have and lost some he should have won.

He went to the National Open in Chicago in 1922 and tied for second behind Sarazen. Later in the year at Brookline, in the National Amateur, he was jolted 8 and 7 in the semifinals by the eventual winner, Jess Sweetser.

At that time Jones had entered 11 major tournaments in seven years—and still did not have a title. He had graduated from Georgia Tech and, at the age of 20, was seeking his master's degree at Harvard. He still had time to practice for the National Open at Inwood, however.

He opened with a 71 and was one stroke off the pace. Jones fell another back in the second round, but at the end of three, with 18 holes to go, he led by three strokes. In the final round he began pressing. Instead of playing cautiously, he went for the knockout. He had soared to a 76 and Cruikshank birdied the final hole to tie him.

The play-off the next day seesawed back and forth, and they came to the last hole with the match square.

After Cruikshank hooked his tee shot onto a road, Bobby drove to the short rough on the sun-baked turf. Cruikshank played his second safe, 50 yards short of a lagoon guarding the green. Now it was up to Bobby. He had to decide whether to play it safe or gamble for the victory. He strode to the ball with quick, sure steps, jerked a midiron from his bag, made one quick assessment of the situation and swung. The crowd let out a tremendous roar.

The ball tore some 200 yards through the air, dropped to the green and dribbled six feet past the cup. Cruikshank hit his over the green into a bunker and had to settle for a six and 78. Jones made an easy four for 76 and—at last—was the Open champion of the United States.

Maiden, the Scotch pro from whom Jones had copied his swing, bashed a new straw hat over a neighbor's head. Friends swarmed around the young Georgian, who groped for the clubhouse, too dazed to be elated. Jones said later he did not remember any of it.

"I've won a championship. At last I've won a championship." He said that was his first conscious thought. Later, he said that his morale was wearing so thin at that point that if he hadn't won, he might have been tempted to give up tournament golf.

He was a confident and heavily favored young man when he went to Chicago for the National Amateur later that year. But he was eliminated in the second round.

Bobby had proved he could win, but he hadn't fully shaken that second-place jinx. The National Open in 1924 was at Oakland Hills, near Detroit. Jones used 300 strokes over the long, windswept layout and finished second to a fragile little pro, Cyril Walker. Bobby, however, returned to Merion—the scene of his debut at 14—and scored an impressive 9 and 8 over George Von Elm in the finals of the U.S. Amateur. He lost by a stroke in a play-off with Willie McFarlane in the National Open at Worcester, Massachusetts, in 1925—another second-place finish. But he successfully defended his National Amateur crown at Oakmont, overwhelming Watts Gunn, 8 and 7, in the finals.

He returned to England in 1926. It was a trip he'd looked forward to for five years. He was determined to make the British forget his performance in 1921 when he folded in the Amateur and picked up in the Open. He played well in the Amateur but lost a sixth-round match. Bobby figured in two victories in the Walker Cup matches and then went to the British Open.

It was in a qualifying round at Sunningale that Jones shot what he always considered his finest round in competitive golf. He went around the long, treacherous layout in 66, six under par. He didn't have a five or a two on his card. British golf critics called it the finest round ever shot in the Isles.

The Open itself was something of an anticlimax. Jones won handily with a score of 291. The British promptly forgot the brash youngster of 1921 and took a new Bobby Jones to their hearts. The name was spoken with reverence in the golf-minded islands.

Jones came home to a ticker-tape parade down Broadway. He went on to Scioto at Columbus, Ohio, for the National Open and took

Multiple-flash exposure shows the full arc of swing.

a fat 79 in the second round before rallying to win with a 293. His bid for a sweep of the American titles that year failed in the National Amateur at Baltusrol in New Jersey, where his old rival, Von Elm, beat him in the finals, 2 and 1.

In 1927, he was mixing golf with law books. His studies at Emory University encroached on his golf practice. It showed at Oakmont, in the National Open, where Bobby finished eleventh—the worst ever in that event. But he whipped his game in shape in time to take both the British Open and the U.S. Amateur. He had a record 285 at St. Andrews to win the British Open by six strokes. And he swamped Chick Evans, 8 and 7, in the finals of the National Amateur at Minneapolis.

The next year Bobby was busy with a budding law practice and confined himself to the two major American titles. In the Open at Olympia Fields, near Chicago, he blew an early lead with a final round 77, tied Johnny Farrell at 294 and lost the 36-hole play-off. He retained his amateur title, however, with a one-sided decision over Phillip Perkins at Brae Burn in Massachusetts.

Jones caught up with the pros again in 1929 after they had stopped him two years in a row. He won the National Open at Winged Foot in New York, sinking a spectacular putt

on the seventy-second hole to tie Al Espinosa at 294 and to gain a play-off that he won easily. But Johnny Goodman, then an unknown amateur who later won the Open title, upset him in the first round of the National Amateur at Pebble Beach, California.

Jones, who was long on premonition, was convinced by early spring practices in 1930 that he was headed for an outstanding season. He was hitting the ball better than ever before. He was brimming with confidence. But, he said later, he never dreamed he was heading for the Grand Slam.

As captain of the U.S. Walker Cup team, he was given another shot at the British championships. The British Amateur, the only one that had eluded him, brought him again to the famed old St. Andrews course, a layout he said he learned to love. Bobby squeaked through some early matches and then defeated Roger Wehtered, 7 and 6, in the finals.

A gallery of some 25,000 swarmed over him, shouting, shoving, milling in glee. A cordon of police conveyed him to the clubhouse, nearly a mile away, where Bobby turned to some friends and grinned: "I'd rather have won this tournament than any other in golf."

In the British Open at Holyake, Jones started with rounds of 70 and 72, then faltered.

He closed 74 and 75 for 291 and went to the clubhouse to sweat out the late finishers. Leo Diegel and Macdonald Smith made challenges but fell two strokes back and Jones sailed home with half of his Slam.

Golf enthusiasm in the United States reached a new peak when the game's leading figures gathered at Interlachen in Minneapolis for the U.S. Open. Thousands of fans swarmed along the narrow fairways to see whether the amazing golfer from Georgia could make history. He responded with an opening 71, one stroke off the pace of Smith and Tommy Armour. After 36 holes, Horton Smith led at 142 and Jones was tied for second at 144. At least 10 professionals were in the running. Bobby uncorked a withering 68 in the third round and moved five strokes in front of the field. In the final round he dropped a 40-foot putt on the seventy-second hole for a 75 and a two-stroke victory at 285, winning his third national title of the year.

It was during the second round of that tournament that Jones authored one of the game's most famous shots, the one that came to be known as "the lily pad shot."

On the par-five, 485-yard ninth hole, which has a small pond in front of the green, Jones went for it with his second shot. He half-topped a fairway wood and the ball streaked for the water. It hit on the surface about halfway across, then skipped onto the other side of the pond and hopped up just short of the green. Spectators said it hit a lily pad.

"It looked like a drowned ball for sure," Jones said. "It would have meant a six or a seven and would have cost me the tournament. It was perhaps the luckiest shot I ever played in a championship."

The U.S. Amateur, fourth leg on Bobby's bid for a Grand Slam, was played at Merion, the course that served as a pivotal point for him on at least two other occasions. Jones, at the top of his game, defeated a pair of Canadians, Ross Somerville and Fred Hoblitzel, by identical 5 and 4 margins on the first day. He gained the finals with a 6 and 5 decision over Fay Coleman and 10 and 9 over Jess Sweetser.

Some 18,000 fans turned out for the final match. It was no contest. Jones was unbeatable, and Gene Homans, his opponent, was predictably nervous. Jones won, 8 and 7, for the game's only Slam, closing the book on one of the game's greatest careers on the same course

where he had started his quest for national honors.

He retired two months later, renowned as the greatest player the game had ever seen. However, even after his retirement, he played competitively in the Masters Tournament in Augusta, Georgia, through 1948 but never as a serious contender. His annual appearances were his only return to competition.

Jones was afflicted with a spinal disease in 1948. He was forced to use first one cane and then two canes and finally a wheelchair to move about. Despite his handicap and severe pain, until the last few years of his life he always attended the Masters, the tournament he founded, and draped the green coat over the winner's shoulders. He died on December 18, 1971, at the age of 69.

Keeler, the Atlanta sportswriter who covered all Bobby's major championships, once said about him, "Competitive golf is played mainly on a five-and-a-half-inch course, the space between the ears. This is where Jones excelled."

BOB GREEN

Left: Jones at the Masters in 1934. The Augusta course was largely of his design. Above: 1930 and the sweep of the British Open, the U.S. and British Amateurs and the U.S. Open.

Sonja Henie
Symphony on Silver Skates

They called her "Wonder Child," this Nordic blonde with sparkling brown eyes and dimpled cheeks who grew into the world's leading woman athlete. Her ballet on ice skates captivated two continents, and royalty commanded her performances.

Sonja Henie blended skating with a love of competition and dance into a multimillion dollar career, becoming reputedly the richest athlete of all time. After her amazing triumphs in international competition—10 consecutive world championships through 1936 and Olympic gold medals in 1928, 1932 and 1936—she gave the United States ice-skating fever. Thousands attended her touring ice shows, and mothers brought children to see Sonja perform on the silver screen.

Children yearned for Sonja Henie dolls. They asked Santa Claus for ice skates, just as chubby little Sonja had done while a child in Norway. They tried to imitate the style of Sonja, who cut 40-mile-per-hour figures on ice with the grace of a ballerina.

Children's dreams were Sonja's early goals —gleaming trophies signifying victory and athletic excellence. Miss Henie's trophy room contained 257 accolades, ranging from wine cups to punch bowls. Prominently displayed were her gold medals from international competitions.

America fell in love with Sonja Henie in the 1940s as had Europe in the 1920s and 1930s. Someone once suggested a film biography of Sonja Henie, but the idea was rejected as even Sonja asked, "Who would believe it?"

Her birth followed a spring blizzard on April 8, 1912, in Oslo, the second child of Wilhelm and Selma Henie, who had had a son, Leif, two years earlier.

Sonja, a name suggested by an artist friend, displayed a graceful, competitive nature at an early age. Like many girls all over the world, she dressed up in her mother's old clothes and amused herself by skipping and dancing through the rambling, two-story, gray stone home.

She was given ballet and snow-skiing lessons at the age of four, telling her parents, "I

know what I want to be when I grow up. I shall be a ballet dancer—the best one in the world." In everything, Sonja Henie wanted to be number one.

Wilhelm Henie, a fur merchant able to afford a comfortable life for his family, had won trophies for bicycle racing in his youth. Sonja admired the statues and decided she would have one, too. At five she won a 40-meter footrace when the family vacationed in Grenen, Denmark. Her first athletic reward was a copper medal. At seven, she won a junior skiing competition.

A year later, on her eighth Christmas, Sonja opened packages that included dolls and a toy cooking stove. Brother Leif received a pair of racing ice skates. Sonja also wanted—and had expected—skates, but there were none under the tree.

Tears welled in her eyes and she hurried to her room. Wilhelm rushed downtown, forgetting that stores were closed for the holiday. He told a merchant friend of his dilemma and together they opened a store to get the skates.

Sonja was told that this present had been overlooked. She then ran outside to catch up with Leif, who was on his way to a frozen pond. In much haste, she put on the skates and bounded onto the ice, only to fall in a tumble.

"I had never before had skates on," Sonja recalled. "I was in a terrible hurry and quite confident that all I had to do was just skate and everything would be all right. I took several spills that morning, but even the aches, pains and bruises were joyful to me."

The next day, Leif gave her some basic tips and she stayed upright while her father watched proudly. "She is a born skater," Wilhelm said. "I am going to get her an instructor tomorrow."

Sonja later credited this parental perception for her success. When she came to the United States, her mother was a constant companion, and although Selma Henie could not skate, she made suggestions and approved her daughter's routines.

A sterling-silver letter opener was her next prize, for winning the Norwegian junior figure-

66   *Sonja in 1933 already was dazzling the world with her skating.*

skating championship. She then wanted to compete for the senior championship of Oslo. "Not so fast," cautioned her father. "Your pride and this one bit of success might get the better of you. Take things easy and I will help you."

The 75-pound, nine-year-old girl won the women's championship of Oslo, and that night told her family, "I want to win the world's championship. I want to try for it next year." First, however, there was the Norwegian national championship. Her father allowed her to enter, admitting that defeat might make her less presumptuous. She won at the age of 10, the first of her 11 Norwegian championships.

She was only 12 and called *Das Wunderkind*—"the Wonder Child"—by the press when she competed in her first Olympics in 1924. She finished last but Beatrix Loughran of the United States, the runner-up, noted, "Future aspirants for the world title will have to reckon with Sonja Henie of Norway, already a great performer who has every gift—personality, form, strength, speed and nerve." In 1926, she finished second to Hungary's Helina Jalosi in the world competition. Sonja Henie was never to lose on ice again.

Two events marked her fifteenth year. She saw the famous Russian ballerina Anna Pavlova perform in London, the "Dance of the Dying Swan." Years later she still called Pavlova, the greatest influence in her life. In 1927, she also won her first of 10 consecutive world championships. Because of her youth, she performed in short skirts, a practice later to become common. In those days, though, it would have been shocking attire for an older skater.

The 1928 Olympics were held at St. Moritz, Switzerland, and the 16-year-old Sonja overwhelmed the competition, her unique style of balletlike motion setting a trend for others to follow.

Sonja visited the United States for the first time in 1932, winning her second Olympic gold medal for women's figure skating. After the success at Lake Placid, New York, her parents wondered whether she would seek an unprecedented third gold medal in 1936. "I want to win three Olympics and ten world championships. After that," she added, "I shall go into the movies."

Later she admitted that she had not been serious and that the figures in her boast "just came into my head at the moment."

Sonja was 18 when she performed before

England's King George and Queen Mary. She also appeared before rulers of Sweden, Belgium and, of course, King Haakon VII of Norway, who sent her telegrams and often flowers before her competitions. Although she reportedly never fell during a competition, Sonja once wept with embarrassment when she slipped before a royal family.

Rumors of her intentions to seek a professional career circulated as Sonja competed in the 1936 Olympics in Bavaria. She was awarded 1,760 points for her compulsory school figures—some of the 80 routines every competitor had to master. With her free-skating performance, she ran up nearly 3,000 points, almost 50 more than her nearest rival.

Later that year, in Paris, she won her last world championship, then came to the United States to launch her professional career as "Pavlova of the Silver Blades." Four exhibitions at Madison Square Garden in New York City attracted more than 90,000 persons. She had tea at the White House with President and Mrs. Franklin Delano Roosevelt.

Sonja was not an immediate success in Hollywood. Her initial screen test failed to produce a contract. Determined, she rented a rink in Hollywood and invited sportswriters to the opening show. Darryl F. Zanuck of 20th Century–Fox also attended, and when Sonja's manager informed her of Zanuck's arrival, the unflappable, flaxon-haired Sonja answered, "Sell him a ticket."

Zanuck said later that he had attended the ice show to scout a young male member of the troupe but, "I was electrified by her. There will never be another like her." He offered $10,000 a picture but Sonja demanded $100,000. Negotiations stalled, then she was told Zanuck wanted to see her. "Then let Mr. Zanuck call me," she replied. They agreed to a contract, and her films, starting with *One in a Million*, reportedly grossed $25 million.

"Many dancers are actresses," Sonja said. "They prepare for their acting career by dancing. I have done the same. I do not wish nor intend to ever give up skating. It means too much to me, and I believe it is as beautiful and entertaining to people as dancing. But now I want new experiences, to carry my career another step forward with acting."

Her film career was built around her skating ability. Although she missed "the thrill of competition, the main thing I care for is to skate, no matter for what end. I skate more now than I ever did before, and with greater variety. In working things out for pictures, I have learned new tricks and figures that I did not think possible before. The most important thing for me, though, is that I can at last present to the public my ideas of dancing on skates about which I had dreamed as a child. I firmly believe that skating is not only a sport but also an art closely related to the dance."

Through Sonja Henie, the American public became aware of ice skating. Skating rinks cropped up around the country. The Sonja Henie Junior Olympics Club was formed, and by the end of her first tour, which included 36 performances, the club had 40,000 members. By mail they received pamphlets on skating and other sports, as well as a club button.

Before retiring from public skating in the mid-1950s, Miss Henie, who was naturalized a U.S. citizen in 1941, became a millionairess who married millionaires. She wed sportsman Dan Topping, an owner of the New York Yankees baseball team. The marriage ended in divorce in 1946.

Three years later she married Winthrop Gardiner, Jr., scion of an old New York family. They were divorced in May, 1956, and the following month she married Norwegian shipping magnate Niels Onstad. None of the marriages produced children.

The Onstads lived parts of each year in their $250,000 mansion near Hollywood, an apartment in Switzerland and one in Norway. Her interest in art was furthered by Onstad, and together their collection was valued at about $3 million.

Sonja, who had her legs insured for $260,000 and her trophies for $200,000, also appreciated another kind of ice—diamonds. Onstad once gave her a $2 million diamond necklace for her collection.

The Onstads gave Norway 250 paintings in 1958, housing them in the $3.5 million Hoevikodden Art Center that they had built.

Sonja hadn't skated for five years when, 20 years after her last Hollywood film, *It's a Pleasure*, she began making regular trips to a skating rink in Burbank, California. She drove her Rolls-Royce through morning rush-hour traffic to the rink to skate in privacy, her 5-foot 2½-inch figure still a neat size 8 and weighing about 110 pounds. She never dieted, just kept active with tennis and horseback riding.

"I didn't skate for five years," she said in an interview at the Burbank rink. "Then about six months ago, I came back to it. I don't know why I did. Maybe I will work toward another show. If I get real good, who knows?"

Eugen Mikeler, a former dancing partner, coach and friend since the 1920s, joined Sonja on the ice and said, "Sonja should be an inspiration to all people to go out and be physically active. She has all this fame, all this money. She needs nothing. She could just sit at home and do nothing."

Sonja Henie was just 57 years old when she collapsed during a Paris holiday in 1969. Only those close to her knew she had had leukemia for nine months. Onstad arranged for a hospital plane to take her home to Oslo. She died during the flight on October 12, bringing to an end perhaps the most consistently brilliant career an athlete has ever known.

RON ROACH

Bill Tilden
Court Jouster

In 1969, while a bandy-legged Australian named Rod Laver dominated the world's tennis courts firing left-handed thunderbolts, while the memory of the achievements of such players as Don Budge, Jack Kramer and Pancho Gonzales were still fresh, an international panel of tennis writers was glad to name the greatest player of all time. The runaway winner was Bill Tilden.

A similar poll by the Associated Press in 1951 to determine the greatest athletes of the first half-century placed Tilden solidly atop the tennis division, just as Babe Ruth led the balloting in baseball, Bob Jones in golf and Jack Dempsey in boxing. They were of another era —the period that Westbrook Pegler labeled "The Age of Wonderful Nonsense"—yet they left such an imprint that their names continued to dominate locker-room debates over comparative athletic prowess.

It is true that Tilden came along at a time when tennis superiority was synonymous with all-court technique. It was years later that power took over and the big serve and volley game came into being. Serve, volley, point over. How, some cynics asked, would Tilden, in his long flannel trousers, roaming the back court with mincing steps, fare against the bludgeon attack of the modern court killer?

"You cannot volley the service," Tilden once said. "In any match between the perfect baseline player and the perfect net rusher, I would take the baseliner every time."

Tilden was the master back-court craftsman. A tall, gangling figure, 6 feet 2 inches in height, with long legs and arms, there seemed no corner of the court he could not reach with a stride. Although he preferred the flat drive off both backhand and forehand, he developed spins, chops and slices and destroyed his opponents' timing with devastating changes of pace. He was more than a mere striker of the ball. He was a tactician, an artist. The racket was like a violin in his hands.

Tilden also was a perfectionist. He worked for hours refining his strokes. Once, he decided that his backhand wasn't strong enough, so he quit the circuit and secluded himself for an entire winter. He chopped wood to build his muscles. He hit backhand shots against a practice board day-in and day-out until he felt that the stroke was mastered. Then he came out of hiding and embarked upon the most successful decade of his career.

Tilden learned tennis at an early age, but as a competitor he matured late. He was 27 before he was able to crash through to his first United States championship. He was the first American to win the men's singles at Wimbledon, capturing the first of his three titles in 1920. He put together a string of six straight American championships, and in 1929, at the age of 36, he came back to grab a seventh. He won the National Clay Court crown seven times, six in a row, and the National Indoor and Hard Court. In Davis Cup competition, he won 17 singles matches and lost only 5.

William Tatem Tilden, II, was a frustrated Shakespearean actor who practiced his histrionics before tennis audiences throughout the world. He commanded attention from the moment he strode onto the court—a gaunt, shaggy man with receding hair and a lantern jaw. He was usually draped in white flannels and V-neck cable-stitch sweater, and he carried a half-dozen open-throat Top Flight rackets under his arm. There was a piece of theater in every pose and gesture. Undoubtedly he gained deep satisfaction from the knowledge that he was Mr. Tennis.

He carried on an endless feud with the blue-coated fathers of the game, whom he regarded as "inept and stupid." Once he was suspended for receiving money for an article describing a match in which he had played. But France insisted upon his reinstatement so that he could play in a Davis Cup match in 1929.

Tilden never resorted to childish tantrums and court explosions, such as those that marked many of his prima-donna successors. Such outbursts were below his dignity. Yet he was never predictable. He was always exciting.

In one match, when the crowd began berating him for his casual effort, he walked to the net, picked up his gear and left the court, defaulting without a word. Another time, while playing as a pro, he staged a sit-down strike

Despite a bad knee, Tilden's fluid strokes carried him to victory in a 1930 match against John Millen at Newport, Rhode Island (right). He also won Wimbledon that year.

Although he preferred the flat drive off both backhand and forehand, he developed spins, chops and slices. He was more than a mere striker of the ball. He was a tactician.

until some spectators could be removed from treetops a full block away. He could paralyze a linesman with a withering stare on a controversial call, and when he felt that a bad call was made in his favor, he inevitably responded by throwing the next point. He didn't throw it subtly. The crowd always cheered the obvious gesture and Bill loved it.

Frequently Tilden would stage his own private little dramas. Facing an opponent whom he could polish off handily, he would purposely drop the first two sets in a best-of-five match. An electric charge would spread through the gallery. "Big Bill is down!" The word would drift from court to court, and fans would flock to the Tilden court to witness the upset. Then Tilden would brace himself and run out the match.

Tilden was born February 10, 1893, in Germantown, Pennsylvania, a posh suburb on Philadelphia's Main Line. His father was a wealthy wool merchant, his mother a gifted violinist. It was from her apparently that William inherited his artistic tastes. As a youngster, he was sheltered by his doting parents. He was not allowed to play in the city parks. He had a private tutor until his junior year in high school.

The family belonged to the exclusive Germantown Cricket Club, and it was there, on grass courts, that Bill got his introduction to tennis. His older brother, Herbert, was a good player, but young Bill seemed to be all arms and legs with no coordination whatever. Tennis also was a drudgery to him. He preferred to stay home, read books, listen to music and dream of the theater.

However, through the insistence of Herbert, Bill was thrust into a tennis atmosphere. It was a way of life for Main Liners. Bill was only 8 years old when he entered his first tournament—an event for boys 15 and under—and won it. The triumph failed to light a fire. He remained awkward, ungainly and uninterested.

Germantown was one of the steps on the Eastern grass-court circuit, and Bill constantly was being exposed to first-class tennis and top-flight players. One of these was Mary K. Browne, the U.S. women's singles champion, who one day saw the outsized youngster hitting the ball in practice and was impressed. She asked Tilden to team with her in the national mixed doubles. Tilden was delighted. The two won the title, but there was little glory for the boy from Germantown. It was obvious, everyone said, that Mary K. was carrying her young partner. It made no difference to Tilden. The experience turned his attention to a tennis career. The year was 1913. He was 20 years old.

If Tilden thought he would rocket immediately to the top, he was doomed to disappointment. Success came slowly. It was not until two years later, in 1915, that he first saw his name in the national rankings. Then he was placed in Group 6. He played in his first national championship in 1916, losing to an 18-year-old named Harold Throckmorton.

When World War I broke out, Tilden tried to join the service but failed to pass the physical examination because of flat feet. He served in the Medical Corps and, after the war, entered the University of Pennsylvania where he played on the varsity tennis team but failed to make much of an impression. He devoted most of his spare time to amateur theater work.

Tilden first attracted attention in the 1918 national championships, resuming after the war. Fans flocked courtside to watch the long-legged youngster from Philadelphia with the steaming flat service and the sweeping, graceful strokes. Tilden battled his way into the final where he lost a straight-set decision to R. Lindley Murray, a California left-hander. He then teamed with an apple-cheeked, 15-year-old boy named Vincent Richards to win the men's doubles.

Although Tilden was still an erratic player with an unsure backhand, the American public geared itself for what was to be one of the most intense and thrilling personal rivalries in the history of the game—the Battle of the Bills.

William M. ("Little Bill") Johnston was a thin, frail Californian—5 feet 8½ inches tall, 120 pounds with a ladylike 4½ shoe size—who, although two years younger than Tilden, won the United States championship in 1915 at the age of 20. Despite his slight frame, Little Bill had a devastating forehand that came off his racket face like a gunshot and carried a terrific spin. It was a stroke cultivated on the cement courts around San Francisco and one destined to give Tilden many uncomfortable afternoons.

The dramatic confrontation of the mite-sized Californian with the powerful Western forehand and the gangling, stoop-shouldered Philadelphian came in 1919. Johnston beat Tilden in the clay-court championships, but Tilden won on grass at Newport and in the East–West matches. Then the two swept into the finals of the United States championships at Forest Hills.

Tilden was favored in the match, but the crowd was solidly behind Johnston. Johnston, attacking Tilden's vulnerable backhand and also hitting down the middle to nullify Big Bill's power off both wings, never lost a service, winning 6–4, 6–4, 6–3. It was a humiliating setback for Tilden and resulted in Tilden's going into seclusion to reconstruct his game, particularly his backhand.

By the time 1920 rolled around Big Bill was ready for his revenge. His big test was Wimbledon, the grand dame of tennis championships—that no American man had ever won. Tilden was an alternate on the U.S. Davis Cup team—on which Johnston and Norris Williams were the top singles players—which provided him with plenty of practice on the revered center court on Worple Street.

With Johnston and Williams early victims, Tilden found himself facing Zenzo Shimizu

Tilden as an actor.

of Japan for the right to meet the defending champion, Gerald Patterson of Australia. Against Shimizu, Tilden took a spill that reactivated an old cartilage injury in his left knee. Playing virtually on one foot, he managed to pull out the match despite what he called "an afternoon of acute physical and mental suffering."

The prospect looked grim as he went into the title match against Patterson, but Big Bill pounded away at the Australian's weak backhand. "I remembered it was July third," Tilden recalled later, "and we had a famous holiday to celebrate the next day in the United States. It seemed to me an omen of good luck. In my pocket was a four-leaf clover that had grown under Abraham Lincoln's chair in his garden. How could an American throw down Abraham Lincoln and Uncle Sam on the same day, the day before Independence Day?" Bill won the match going away, 2–6, 6–3, 6–2, 6–4.

Tilden returned home to a successful grass-court campaign that led him again into the final round at Forest Hills. His opponent was his old nemesis, Johnston. The pressure was intense, the excitement electric. The day was cold and cloudy. Everybody was asking, "Does Little Bill Johnston still have Big Bill's number?"

With Tilden leading in the third set, the crowd was distracted by the sputtering of a small plane flying overhead. Suddenly the motor coughed and died, and the plane plummeted earthward, crashing a few hundred yards from the court. For a moment it seemed the crowd would panic. A number broke from their seats to rush to the accident. Tilden and Johnston paused momentarily. The umpire barked, "Let's play!" Fewer than 100 spectators left the stands.

Halfway through the fourth set a flash rainstorm interrupted play. There was further confusion when the tournament referee came onto the court to overrule the umpire on a debated point. Finally, after nearly three hours of stirring tennis, Tilden prevailed, 6–1, 1–6, 7–5, 5–7, 6–3. It was hailed as one of the sport's most historic of matches.

Thus began the Tilden era in tennis. To this national championship he was to add six more—five of them in a row—win additional Wimbledon crowns in 1921 and 1930 and lead the United States through an unbroken string of seven Davis Cup triumphs, ending only when his legs began to falter and his reflexes dull.

The fabulous Tilden carved out his success despite a series of freak illnesses and accidents. In 1921, he was taken sick during the French championships at Paris, and he remained hospitalized until just before Wimbledon, which he won dramatically after losing the first two sets, 2–6 and 1–6, and trailing, 4–5, in the third in his title match against B. I. C. Norton.

In 1922, while playing an exhibition match in Bridgeton, New Jersey, he ran into a wire fence at the back of the court and gashed the middle finger of his right hand. Blood poisoning developed and it appeared that doctors might be forced to amputate his arm. Tilden chose instead to risk amputation of merely the tip of the finger. The gamble paid off and the arm was saved. So was Tilden's career.

In the U.S. championship that same year, Big Bill played what he always considered his greatest match against Johnston in the final. The match had particular significance because each of these great players had two legs on the championship trophy and needed a third to gain possession.

Tilden's strategy was to tax the staying powers of the fragile Johnston, long-bothered by a respiratory ailment. He determined to keep Little Bill on the run from the start, even if it meant losing the first set. Johnston won it, 6–4. Then, puffing, he took the second, 6–3.

Big Bill recalled later that as he hit a shot down the line for an error, giving Johnston the second set, he heard his weary rival sigh under his breath, "Thank God." Describing the prolonged back-court rallies of the match, Tilden said, "Johnston and I play each other from the base line because we fear each other's ground strokes too much to come to the net indiscriminately."

Tilden rallied for the third set, but as tension mounted, Johnston forged into a quick 3–0 lead in the fourth set and had a point for a break at 30–40. Johnston lunged to the net behind a forcing shot and hit a volley at Tilden's feet—a certain winner.

"I spun backward in desperation and, reaching behind me, trap-volleyed the ball," Tilden explained. "It rose over Johnston's head for a clean lob. It was one of the luckiest shots I ever made." The point was too much for Johnston, draining the last of his strength and confidence. Tilden saved the game, reeled off six more in a row to knot the match, then won the final set.

"My God!" a woman spectator was heard to exclaim. "I didn't think I could stand it."

Tilden and Johnston met in the finals of the American championships again in 1923, 1924 and 1925, Tilden always prevailing. But Big Bill, hobbling on a game knee, was finding it increasingly difficult to go five hard sets. And Little Bill, suffering the ravages of a lung ailment, was watching his strength gradually ebb away. He died soon after.

Tilden's winning streak in the nationals was ended in 1926 by one of France's emerging "Four Horsemen," Jean Borotra. The French—Borotra, Henri Cochet, Rene Lacoste and Jacques Brugnon—took over temporary dominance of the sport, winning three straight U.S. titles and six Wimbledons and holding the Davis Cup from 1927 through 1932.

Throughout this period, Tilden continued to court his first love—the theater. He tried his hand at everything from Shakespeare to *Dracula* and *They Got What They Wanted*. He played the title role in Booth Tarkington's *Clarence*, and, in 1942, appeared in his own production, *The Nice Harmons*.

He also fancied himself an author. In addition to instructional books on tennis, *Match*

Play and the Spin on the Ball, The Art of Lawn Tennis, Mixed Doubles and *The Common Sense of Tennis*, he wrote fiction and drama. Many of his stories had a tennis background. None was successful.

In 1931, at the age of 38, Big Bill turned professional and took his show on the road. He was producer, director and star. With a hand-picked cast, he played the big arenas such as Madison Square Garden in New York and the Cow Palace in San Francisco and made whistle-stops in between. He treated customers to the tennis prowess that had made him a king of the court, defeating such players as Karel Kozeluh of Czechoslovakia, Hans Nusslein of Germany, Henri Cochet of France and Americans Vinnie Richards, Bruce Barnes, Lester Stoefen and George Lott. He played every match with a sense of the dramatic and a flair for histrionics.

The gaunt, graying idol of the 1920s came to the end of the competitive trail in 1933 when Ellsworth Vines cashed in his two American titles for a rich pro contract and went on the road with Tilden. Vines won the head-to-head tour, 47 matches to 26, and there was no more applause for a man entering his forties.

"My tennis days are over," Tilden wrote in his reluctant valedictory. "The aged net star, that Patriarch of United States tennis, bids official farewell to international play."

He remained active as an instructor and occasional star at neighborhood clinics in California. In 1951, he emerged from retirement to play in a pro tournament at Cleveland, gaining the quarterfinals before losing to Frank Kovacs. In 1952, he played a charity match in Paris against Henri Cochet.

On June 5, 1953, while making plans to go to Cleveland for another tournament, he was stricken with a heart attack and found dead by the building manager in his modest Hollywood apartment. It was a sad ending—at the age of 60—for a man who had performed before royalty and had himself been a king in his own right. Yet he remained always the mysterious bachelor and loner, admired but never really known by his contemporaries.

"There will never be another Tilden," tennis buffs said. "The only genius the game has ever known," said J. Gilbert Hall. Berkeley Bell, a contemporary, added: "No one ever studied the game like Bill—he had to be the greatest."

WILL GRIMSLEY

Johnny Weissmuller
Olympic Tarzan

History may unduly chronicle Johnny Weissmuller as Tarzan, mighty hero in movie versions of Edgar Rice Burroughs's jungle classics, a prototype of raw masculinity in loincloth, who lived in a tree house with a cute swinger named Jane and a chimp called Cheetah.

The real story of Johnny Weissmuller is much deeper.

A decade before his first swing on a Hollywood vine, Peter John Weissmuller was stroking to athletic glory as a swimmer. He churned to three gold medals in the 1924 Olympic Games at Paris and two more in 1928 competition at Amsterdam.

Weissmuller's incredible cache of 67 world championships and 52 national titles allowed him to share headlines in sports' "Golden Era" of the 1920s with baseball's Ruth, boxing's Dempsey, tennis's Tilden and golfers named Jones and Hagen.

In 10 years John Weissmuller was never beaten.

In 1950, the hulking 6-foot 3-inch son of a poor German immigrant was voted the top swimmer of the first half of the twentieth century in an Associated Press poll. Johnny's endless string of triumphs came at every distance, from 50 yards to a quarter-mile.

This celebrated saga began June 2, 1904, in the coal town of Windber, Pennsylvania. Peter and Elizabeth Weissmuller were emigrating from Austria to the promised land of Chicago. Money ran out en route and Peter gained temporary employment in the mines. It was in Windber that Elizabeth gave birth to a 10-pound son who was to become a double legend in his lifetime.

Eight years later, on a sun-blessed day at Fullerton Beach on Chicago's side of Lake Michigan, young Johnny had his first swim. His mother had saved for a pair of water wings, and with them her tall, stick-thin son romped into the deeper water. Instantly, without instruction, he began swimming.

Johnny had a brother by then. John Peter was a year younger. Peter John liked being called "John" and John Peter became known as "Peter." Fullerton Beach became a second home. They soon challenged "the rocks," a dangerous heap of boulders that was continually thrashed by Lake Michigan's surf.

"Swimming came natural to us, and, like all kids, we yearned for adventure," Johnny recalled in his later years. "If our mother had known, we'd have been lashed with a belt. Sure, it was dangerous, but it was exciting. Youngsters need excitement."

The Weissmullers lived at 1921 Cleveland Avenue, in one of a row of two- and three-story dwellings where freshly washed clothes flopped from wires strung on rooftops. The father's lack of business sense kept the Weissmullers in financial hot water. He failed as a saloonkeeper and often drowned his failures in drink. Johnny recalled his father berating the children and beating his mother. "I ran away once and slept under an elevated railroad but then came back to the beating I knew he would give me."

Heartbreak came in varied packages for Johnny. He saved money for a secondhand sled, a possession of which the youngster had always dreamed. Johnny skimmed along the snow-covered streets and thought his luck had changed. Wanting more speed, he hooked his sled by rope onto a passing truck. But, after a short and delightful sprint, Johnny decided to break loose. To his horror, the rope wouldn't drop off the truck and the angry driver sped away with Johnny's precious sled dangling behind.

"I remember sitting in the snow, crying my heart out," he said. "It was so cold that tears froze on my cheeks."

Then Weissmuller's father died and Johnny tried to help his mother by working, first as an errand boy for a church supply business and later as a bellhop and elevator operator at the Chicago Plaza Hotel. "I had to quit school. You know, your guts get so mad when you try to fight poverty and its constant and inevitable companion—ignorance. I made up my mind to fight myself out anyway I could."

Swimming was his passport.

Just when Johnny, then 16, was beginning to believe there was no way out, he bumped into childhood pal Hooks Miller, who had gone

Weissmuller churns through Japanese waters in 1928 meet.

on to earn a place on the famed Illinois Athletic Club swim team. Miller told Johnny about his coach, a 350-pound dude named "Big Bill" Bachrach. The next day, Weissmuller's lithe body was torpedoing through the waters at the Illinois A.C. as Big Bill watched.

"You come back tomorrow," Bachrach told Johnny. "I'll start you on a real training course. I want you to change your stroke and do everything I say . . . to the letter. No questions, no excuses. First, you've got to forget all you've learned about swimming. It's all wrong. So what if you can stay afloat. That's no miracle, all fish can swim. You have no system in breathing . . . you've got to relax. Relax, boy, relax." The training hours were to drag on endlessly, Johnny wondering whether he wouldn't be better off selling newspapers back in his old neighborhood.

Finally, one day Big Bill up and asked, "How'd you like to be a world champion?" Johnny, his eyes igniting, said, "When?" Bachrach broke into an uncustomary grin and said, "Soon as I say you're ready."

Weissmuller was soon allowed to enter his first real race, the 100-yard men's junior event. In his excitement, Johnny made three false starts. He finally got started but finished second in the nonsanctioned race. The reason for his failure had nothing to do with swimming. It seems that Johnny decided to wear a swimming cap to control his hair, which was already at Tarzan length, and, during the race, the cap slipped and covered his eyes. Even half-blinded, he almost won.

Johnny got a haircut.

After Weissmuller won a 100-yard freestyle title in the 1921 Central AAU championships, defeating Abe Seigel, his coach decided to withdraw his prize pupil. Bachrach didn't want his superswimmer to become famous just yet. At least not before he could entice well-heeled businessmen to come down to the Illinois A.C. and bet that the unknown kid couldn't break a world record. Big Bill would say, "Pick any distance, fifty yards to a half-mile, bring your own stopwatches and I'll provide the listed records." Johnny seldom failed his coach and was usually rewarded with a free lunch.

Weissmuller's true debut into big-league events came at the National AAU later that year, and he clocked a 23.2 in the 50-yard freestyle, a scant fifth of a second off the world mark. Before 1921 ended, Johnny established his first legal world record at 150 yards, turning in a 1:27.4 at Brighton Beach, New York. Big Bill wasn't holding his boy back any longer.

Weissmuller, later to have five wives, had has first romance at the age of 17 when he encountered a seaside blonde named Lorelei, but Big Bill Bachrach's heart wasn't touched. "Here I am, trying to train you for the Olympics, to make you a national hero, and all you do is moon about the first girl who crosses your path." The urge for companionship subsided for the moment. Just to make sure, Bachrach transported his young ace to Hawaii where Johnny was to swim in an exhibition against two-time Olympic Games champ Duke Kahanamoku for the entertainment of delegates to a Shriners convention.

It was a rough sea journey from San Francisco to Honolulu, the violent Pacific tossing the ship so that all the fresh water was washed out of the swimming pool. Johnny paddled around in salt water for the first time and found it more buoyant. He needed much less leg kick to keep his body in a high, hydroplaning position. He learned that by varying leg beat, he could better challenge distances of over 100 yards.

Duke Kahanamoku, who later became the official silver-haired welcomer for the Hawaiian Islands, was a proud competitor but also a smart athlete. As Weissmuller worked out in preparation for the Shriner swim, the Duke put a stopwatch on him. Johnny blazed 100 yards, four laps of the Punahou pool. Duke looked at his watch. "Must be broken," he said, gaping at Bachrach. "It stopped at fifty-two and two-fifths seconds." Big Bill smiled pompously and said, "Sorry to disappoint you, Duke, but look at my watch." Kahanamoku suddenly remembered he had another engagement that required him to leave Hawaii "within the next hour." Weissmuller and his teammate put on a show for the Shriners, anyway, and set 13 world records on the trip.

Johnny had a brief scare in 1923 when his heart functioned improperly. It was blamed on staying underwater too long. Weissmuller was back in prime shape for the Olympic trials prior to the 1924 Games at Paris. For luck, he always tapped on a wooden ring before each competition. Rapping on wood was one of Johnny's idiosyncrasies, and since trees are hard to find around swimming pools, he had a wooden ring made to serve the purpose. He qualified easily, beating even the famed Duke of Hawaii's time, and sailed from New York on a bright June morning for France along with 100 track performers, 66 swimmers, 20 fencers, 15 oarsmen, 25 boxers, 11 gymnasts and 16 wrestlers, as well as 12 coaches, 10 managers, 10 trainers and 6 massagers.

Weissmuller dashed to easy victory in first trials for the 100 meters and then stroked to an even easier triumph in the semifinals. But, as the finals—the shot at his first gold medal —approached, the 20-year-old became nervous. "Relax, you're the world's champion," said Bachrach. "Remember to keep relaxed. Relax, boy." Fellow finalists represented the cream of world swimming . . . the Duke and his younger brother, Sam Kahanamoku, Arne Borg of Sweden and Katsuo Takaishi of Japan. "Don't get your head too high," Big Bill cautioned, "it's like flooding a carburetor with too much gasoline and not enough air. You'll flood yourself and stall."

Johnny was in a middle lane, a Kahanamoku brother on either side. He wondered, "Which one will set the pace, tiring me to let the other win?" About then, Duke stepped up, his bridal-white teeth flashing, and said, "Good luck, John. Remember, the most important thing is to get the American flag up there three times. Let's go do it." For the first time that day Johnny relaxed. The swimmers took their marks, curling toes over the edge and crouching into the ready position. The gun sounded and the five human bullets crashed into the pool. The race was on.

Weissmuller waited for no one. He quickly stretched away from the brothers Kahanamoku with Arne Borg and the finalist from Japan laboring to keep up with the dazzling Americans. Johnny won the gold medal in Olympic record time of 59 seconds flat, the Duke was second, Sam third, Borg fourth and Takaishi last in the spangled field.

It was the beginning of Weissmuller's reign as the world's greatest swimmer. He captured golds in the 400-meter freestyle at 5:04.2 and was also first in the 800-meters relay at a time of 9:53.4. All three victories were in record Olympic time. It was much the same story four years later in Amsterdam. After carrying the U.S. flag in opening ceremonies, Weissmuller smashed his own records with a 58.6 clocking in the 100 meters and a 9:36.2 effort with three teammates in the 800-meter relay. From the time of that first Olympic race through the next 10 years of international competition, John Weissmuller never lost a race.

A tour through Europe after the 1924 Olympics delayed Johnny's return to Chicago, but when he finally got home, the new international hero called the number of his old girl friend, Lorelei. Weissmuller had been chased and, at times, caught by his dozens of shapely admirers on the long stay in Europe. But he yearned for Lorelei, and it was a blue day when he called and her mother answered, "She doesn't live here anymore. She's home with her husband."

Weissmuller traveled after that, thinking he had nothing waiting for his return to Chicago. On one jaunt, he stopped by Hollywood and met Douglas Fairbanks, Sr., who prided himself on knowing the top athletes of his day. He welcomed the Olympic hero warmly and invited him to the back lot at Goldwyn Studios where Fairbanks was filming *The Black Pirate*. Johnny's eyes brightened as he ventured into the backstage world. He saw a redskin leaning against a totem pole but was later told it was a Swede in makeup who couldn't handle a word of English. He spotted a Russian cossack, a grand dame and a honey-dipped sweetie from down South. Johnny had found a new world.

Fairbanks took the impressed young man to lunch where they joined a producer who was introduced as Sol Lesser. Lesser leaned to Fairbanks and asked, "Have you given some thought to playing Tarzan?"

Douglas thought a moment and answered, "That's not my cup of tea. You need a new face to play your hero. Now," he continued, nodding to Johnny, "there's a lad who'd be sensational in the part. He looks like Tarzan and he's a marvelous swimmer besides." Lesser, obviously disappointed at not getting Fairbanks for the role, said, "The kid's okay, but we need a star."

Weissmuller began spending much of his time in Florida after Hollywood had temporarily decided against him as an actor. It was there that he met his first wife, Bobbe Arnst, a blonde singer with the Ted Lewis band. Two weeks after they met, Johnny asked Bobbe to marry him. They were united in Fort Lauderdale by a justice of the peace with no relatives or friends to bear witness.

Big Bill Bachrach was still around, and on one summer day in 1930, he approached

Johnny as the swimmer pulled himself from a pool. "Sign here," he ordered and Weissmuller scrawled his name without a second thought. "What did I sign?" he finally asked. "My boy," said Bachrach, "you've just become a pro. I can't handle you anymore. You're a married man and need some income. So you're getting five hundred dollars a week from BVD swimsuits to promote them."

Johnny appeared shell-shocked at his new position. Suddenly, he had an extra buck. It was to change his life. For the next decade, he would struggle to control and retain the money that sifted through his poorly managed account.

Johnny's work with BVD led him to Hollywood where he set up promotional shop at the local athletic club on Sunset Boulevard. Bobbe had begun to enjoy swimming and especially liked what it did for her legs. Cyril Hume, one of the movies' highest-paid writers, visited the club regularly and was impressed by Weissmuller's body as well as his heroics in the water. Hume had been assigned to do the first screenplay about Burroughs's hero of the jungle, the script for *Tarzan of the Apes*. He asked Johnny, "How'd you like to do a test for Metro?" Weissmuller was stunned and didn't speak as Hume continued with his idea of playing Tarzan, the jungle man who swims like a fish yet who is strong and muscular.

"Me? Tarzan?" said Weissmuller and thus one of the screen-world's most famous lines was born.

Johnny was told that over 100 flat-bellied young men would be tested for the part. "That's fine with me," he said, "will Jean Harlow be around?" She was, and so were Joan Crawford, Norma Shearer, Clark Gable, Wallace Beery, Marie Dressler, Jackie Cooper and even the great Garbo.

The screen test was given and Johnny passed. He had already left town and was promoting his BVDs in Oregon when word came. His wife, Bobbe, didn't want her man going to show business and had even asked an MGM official to make sure he failed the screen test. He had laughed and sent her away. But, when Weissmuller was picked as the movies' first talking Tarzan, the studio—once a contract for seven years with pay scaled from $500 up to $2,000 a week was in the vault—gave him the cold-blooded order to get rid of his wife. Johnny said no, saying he loved Bobbe. But, the couple got into violent arguments over the situation, and she finally packed and went home to her mother. Bobbe later confessed that Metro had bribed her with $10,000 to leave her husband.

John's hair grew long, over the ears, and MGM's contract specified that it never be cut, only trimmed. Johnny enjoyed the animals in his movies, especially the chimpanzee Cheetah. And, there was a golden lion named Jackie. Johnny and Jackie hit it off immediately when the beast licked Tarzan's liquid makeup from an arm. Before long, Weissmuller had to discourage the lion since Tarzan's skin was getting red from repeated lickings by Jackie's sandpaper tongue.

Maureen O'Sullivan, a gorgeous Irish colleen, fit perfectly into Johnny's muscular arms and was immediately accepted as the heroine of Burroughs's jungle stories. They were big box office from the time Tarzan rescued his Irish Jane from her first hazard of the wilds. People wondered whether Tarzan and Jane would become real-life mates, but Maureen had fallen deeply in love with director John Villiers Farrow, whom she married and bore seven children, including actress Mia Farrow.

Lupe Velez, a Hollywood tamale from Mexico, became Johnny's second wife. She was a human tiger who earned such nicknames as "Whoopee Lupe" and "the Mexican Wildcat." Long after they were divorced, Lupe committed suicide with an overdose of drugs.

So went life for Johnny Weissmuller, the oft-turbulent love affairs and the big money. The series of Tarzan movies ended at 19 in 1947 with *Tarzan and the Mermaids*. Johnny's son, 6-foot 6-inch John, Jr., tried to replace his father as the jungle king, but it didn't work and the boy became a stevedore in Sausalito, California.

Weissmuller's career was extended another 10 years with Jungle Jim movies, which depicted him as somewhat of an overage, overweight Tarzan who traipsed the jungle wearing khakis and a big hat rather than the loincloth scanties of the previous 17 years.

"I had more talking as Jungle Jim," Johnny said years later. "After all, I didn't have much acting to do as Tarzan. It had mostly been stunts and my big line was 'Tarzan no like guns.'" As late as 1955, his income-tax return showed $94,000 in salary, but it dropped to $39,000 in 1956 when the Jungle Jim string ran out. By 1957, Weissmuller was being sued for

back alimony by one of his wives and the old Tarzan's fiscal world never seemed to get completely straight after that.

"Sure, I've had my problems," he said. "Some bad investments. Four marriages that didn't last. Some battles with booze. But, I'm a pretty tough guy to sink. I lived an exciting life and I've been an awfully lucky fellow. I just don't think I'd have been happy without the Hollywood part. I can't picture myself as a retired swimsuit-company executive with a little place in the country and eighteen grandchildren running around."

Maria, his fifth bride, gave him three children. Johnny became involved in idea after idea to make a return to the big money days but most failed. One of the highlights of his life after age 60 was being a director and featured member of the International Swimming Hall of Fame in Fort Lauderdale, which became his home. "I paddle around the pool with kids. You'd think they wouldn't know Tarzan the way their parents and grandparents did. But, thanks to television showing my old movies, I'm still Tarzan to them. Like I said, it's been a wonderful life."

HUBERT MIZELL

Top: Weissmuller's strong pull kept him undefeated in international competition. Right: Fond of kids, John gives a swimming lesson in London.

Bronko Nagurski
The Big Ukrainian

They like to tell about the time the Chicago Bears, en route to the first official championship of the National Football League, were playing at home in Wrigley Field against the Portsmouth Spartans. The Bears were trailing late in the game when they handed the ball to the Bronk. He smashed through—not over or around—left end, sending two defensive linemen flying in opposite directions, barreled through the secondary, stampeded over several would-be tacklers and dragged along a few others, then completed a 45-yard run for the winning touchdown by crashing into a goal post, caroming off and plowing headlong into a brick wall beyond the end zone.

"That last guy hit me awful hard," the Bronk said.

That, in essence, was what Bronko Nagurski was all about. He wasn't huge—although at 6 feet 2 inches and 230 pounds, he wasn't exactly underweight—but he was as solid as they came. In Nagurski's case, it wasn't always easy to separate fact from fancy. Perhaps it wasn't true that he used to enter a room holding his wife, Eileen, out at arm's length in the palm of his hand, although he swore that he did and still could, "only Eileen won't let me." Maybe he didn't actually once knock over a horse and the mounted policeman sitting on it as he was falling out of bounds. Perhaps it's not true that after missing a particularly fierce tackle at the Bears' training camp in Wisconsin, he sheared off the side of an automobile parked along the sidelines. Maybe he didn't—but he could have.

Nagurski, after retiring from the gridiron and the professional wrestling ring where he spent many years following his football career, remained a massive man, although he admitted that the additional 40 pounds was not all muscle. He admitted it quietly, almost shyly. For despite the ferocity with which Bronko Nagurski tore up the opposition on the football field, he was always a gentle man.

He was born on November 3, 1908, in Rainy River, Ontario, Canada, where his parents, Michael and Eamelia, had recently settled after emigrating from their homeland, the Polish Ukraine. His name wasn't Bronko; it was Bronislau. The nickname came later.

"My father," Bronko said, "was very diversified. He was a laborer mostly. He helped build the Trans-Canada Railroad, then he worked in farming for a while in North Dakota. He also spent time in sawmills. And when I was little, we moved to International Falls, Minnesota. He started into the grocery business then, and he also had some farmland and a portable sawmill. He built and rented houses, too. Like I said, diversified.

"He was a big man too, although he never got to the size that I did. And even though I was big, I never really thought about going into football when I was young. I'd spent most of my years on farms and in the woods and liked it, so I figured I'd do something in agriculture or forestry. Football was one of the things I just sort of grew up with. Don't forget, International Falls was a backwoods community in those days."

It was at Falls High School that Bronislau became Bronko—and became a football player. "My mother took me down to register. She couldn't speak English very well. She kept trying to explain my name and the teacher just couldn't understand her. So finally the teacher said, 'Do you mean Bronko?' and my mother decided she'd had enough so she just nodded in agreement.

"When I got to Minnesota, all I knew was that I wanted to go to school. My mind wasn't really set, although I was still thinking about agriculture. But after my first year, when I found out I had to have things like a major and a minor and I'd already gotten involved in sports, it was a sort of spur-of-the-moment thing. I thought I'd go toward physical education and follow school by going into education—coaching or something like that."

He made his reputation as a fullback at Minnesota, although he also played end, tackle and guard. "Back then, the linemen were often called tackle backs. We'd play on the line for a while, then go back and carry the ball for a while."

Bronko played the line for most of his first

Nagurski of the Chicago Bears poses for a running picture. Red Grange said, "If you hit him above the ankles, you were likely to get killed." Nagurski's top salary: $5000.

year, 1927, because the Gophers already had an all-American fullback in Herb Joesting. In 1928, though, still bouncing from position to position, he spent most of his time at fullback. It was then that he established himself as a steamroller. Against Wisconsin, for example, he scored the winning touchdown by dragging six tacklers with him over the goal line.

That was just a prelude to his senior year. His coach, Dr. Clarence W. ("Doc") Spears, was still moving him from the backfield to the line and back again. Nagurski, Doc said, could have been an all-American at any position. And he proved to be quite correct. In 1929, Bronko was named to every all-America team. The catch was that some selectors placed him at fullback while others listed him as a tackle. His versatility was so frustrating that one newspaper solved the problem by naming a 10-man team— with Nagurski at both tackle and fullback.

Recently he was accorded still another honor, his selection to the all-time modern college team, missing unanimity by a single vote. The National Football League, which inducted him into the professional football Hall of Fame in 1963, put him at fullback on its all-time, all-league team. In his three seasons at Minnesota, the Gophers lost just four games. Said Ernie Nevers, a Minnesota teammate, "Tackling Bronko was like trying to tackle a freight train going downhill."

It was no different when he joined the Bears in 1930. "When you hit Bronk," Chicago teammate Red Grange recalled, "it was like getting an electric shock. If you hit him above the ankles, you were likely to get killed." With his talents, there was no way to guess what kind of salary Nagurski might have commanded were he offered up on the affluent player market of the 1970s. Even in the Depression years of the 1930s, George Halas got him at bargain rates.

"I never made over five thousand dollars a season with the Bears," Bronko said. "I wrestled for fifteen years, and I probably made more out of that than I did from pro football. Halas's first offer was thirty-five hundred. But my backfield coach at Minnesota, Dutch Bergman, told me to ask for sixty-five hundred. So five thousand was what we settled for. But I got cut the next year. You know, it took me seven years to get back up to five thousand."

But Bronko didn't feel cheated nor did he resent the sometimes astronomical salaries

being paid to latter-day superstars. "Football doesn't owe me a living," he said. "For the times, I made good money. If I had it to do all over again, I'd try harder—get a little more money. More power to these boys who get big bonuses. A football player deserves whatever he can get these days. It works the other way, too. Whatever an owner or a coach can get out of you, he'll do it. They don't throw much sympathy your way after you're all through and crippled up. I still feel a lot of my injuries, especially on rainy days. . . . I don't reminisce much any more. Of course, I still watch the game. If they're playing interesting ball, I follow them. If they're playing stupid ball, who wants to watch?"

When, in 1930, Nagurski donned uniform number 3 for the Bears, he helped raise the team to third from a ninth-place finish the preceding year. They were third again in 1931, the season that Bronko, in a game with the Bears' cross-town rivals, the Chicago Cardinals, showed he had not only power but speed as well by dashing 65 yards for a touchdown. Then came the glory years, when the Bears earned their reputation as the "Monsters of the Midway." In 1932, the first of the three straight years he was named an all-pro, they met the Portsmouth Spartans for the title. It was Na-

Left: Nagurski cuts through wide hole in Redskins' line during game in 1937. Above: Bronko gets instructions from Gino Capelletti in varsity–alumni game in Minnesota.

gurski who passed to Red Grange for the winning touchdown.

The next season, the league adopted divisional play, with the winners meeting for the championship. En route to the Western crown, the Bears collided with Green Bay. Nagurski relived that game with Cal Hubbard, a Packer tackle.

"The Packers always seemed to beat us," Bronko said. "We were playing you in Green Bay and the pattern was the same. You had us seven to nothing with about two minutes to go. Then Luke Johnsos and Bill Hewitt cook up a pass play on the field. Hewitt crosses over on an end-around and throws a touchdown to Johnsos, the other end. The score is tied and we get ready to kick off. 'Please, God,' said Hewitt just before we lined up, 'make them fumble.' By way of helping the miracle come to pass, Hewitt tackles the receiver so hard he fumbles. We recover and go on to score. We beat the Packers fourteen to seven. We shower and dress. We leave by way of the field and notice that only

one man is left in the place. It's the coach, Curly Lambeau, still sitting on the Packer bench and still holding his head in his hands."

Then came the championship against the best of the East, the New York Giants, who had beaten the Bears during the regular season. Bronko who had piled up 553 yards during the year—"most of us thought we had had a good year when we gained three hundred, maybe four hundred yards a season"—kept the Bears in the game with his ball carrying and occasional passing. On one play, he faked a run into the line, then completed a jump-pass to Bill Karr for a touchdown. On another, the most spectacular play of the game and the one that gave Chicago the 23–21 victory, he jump-passed to Bill Hewitt who, in turn, lateraled to Karr, who scampered 25 yards for a touchdown.

In 1934, the two teams met again for the title, with the Bears taking an 18-game winning streak into the contest, one that was destined to become known as the "sneaker" game. It was played on a field of ice. That circumstance appeared to give Chicago a slight edge, and the Bears used it to take a 10–3 half-time lead on a touchdown run by Nagurski. But New York coach Steve Owen had an ace up his sleeve. When the Giants came out for the second half, they did it wearing tennis shoes borrowed from nearby Manhattan College.

Suddenly able to maneuver on the frozen turf, they caught the Bears flatfooted and ran away to a 41–21 victory. "The sneakers didn't bother us early," Bronko said. "We knew they had them. Had we been able to change our cleats at half-time, I didn't think they could have beaten us. But we never carried around any extra sets."

Despite the loss, it had been another superb year for Nagurski, and not just as a runner. When Beattie Feathers set his rushing record of 1,004 yards, it was Bronko who led the blocking. "Beattie always ran with a hand in the middle of my back," he said, "so that he could sense which way I was going to block and I could sense which way he wanted me to turn the play."

In 1935, arthritis hampered Nagurski, keeping him off the all-league team for the only time in his career and dropping the Bears out of title contention. The next season he rebounded to churn up 529 yards, but again Chicago fell short of a title. They got another shot at it in 1937 but lost again, this time to the Washington Redskins. By now, Bronko was back up to his first-year salary of $5,000. He wanted a raise and asked Halas for $6,000. When Halas said no, Nagurski announced his retirement and headed into professional wrestling. It had been a short career by some standards and one that Nagurski could have made even shorter had he taken advice—and a check—from Detroit Lions' Dick Richards, who offered Bronko $10,000 just to quit the game. It happened in a New York restaurant. He was making $3,000 when Richards made his offer, wailing, "You're ruining my team. Just quit and get the hell out of the league."

Nagurski blinked. "We were sitting with Cliff Battles and Halas and I looked over at Cliff and asked him what to do. 'Well,' he said, 'that's more money than you'd make in three years with the Bears. If it were me, I'd take it.' I said I would. Halas was sitting across the table. Richards wrote out the check and shoved it across at me. Halas reached out and raked it away 'I'll give it to you later,' he told me. I never saw it."

It had been a career that had prompted Giants' coach Steve Owen to proclaim; "There's only one defense that could stop Nagurski— shoot him before he leaves the dressing room." And the career had one more chapter to go.

In 1943, with pro football's ranks depleted by World War II, Halas talked Bronko out of retirement. "They used me at tackle at first because they had four or five fullbacks. But as the season progressed, they pressed me into fullback because all ours were being drafted." The Bears again won the divisional title, and in the final game of the season, Nagurski played all the way at fullback, grinding out 84 yards and a touchdown in 15 carries. Then they walloped Washington for the championship, and the Bronk bowed out for good. In his nine pro seasons, he had carried the ball 872 times for 4,031 yards—unofficially since the league did not keep statistics in 1930 and 1931.

He returned to the wrestling circuit until 1950, picking up the world championship belt three times along the way. "Wrestling wasn't fixed on the scale it is now," he said, "but I wish I hadn't done it. I wasted a lot of time." He spent 10 more years as a wrestling referee. "Then I decided it was too much traveling. My wife and I had raised our first two children, and I hardly got to know them, I was away so much."

So Bronko retired to Rainy Lake, Minnesota, first as a fishing guide, then as owner of a service station, which he ran until going into full retirement in 1970. "I had to give it up," he said, "because it took too many hours. My legs started bothering me. Too much time on the pavement. And I didn't want to pull customers in there just on account of the name."

The name lived on in another way, however. The Nagurskis had seven children and the oldest of their five sons, Bronko, Jr.—that's his real name—starred for the Hamilton Tiger-Cats of the Canadian Football League. Bronko, Sr., said that as in the case of other latter-day players who found football a lucrative profession, his son lost a great opportunity. "This country was started by pioneers," the Bronk said, "and so was football. I think those people who missed out on the pioneer days missed out on a lot. I was a pioneer."

BRUCE LOWITT

Nagurski takes posed hand-off from Sid Luckman.

Babe Didrikson Zaharias
Wonder Woman

She was a big, raw-boned girl from Texas. Her legs were long and lean with muscles that rippled. She had a strong, expressive face, not pretty, not unattractive, a face with strength and character, a face painted by the rays of a boiling sun and the bite of piercing winds. No one would ever accuse her of being feminine— or dare to—although in later years, as a housewife, she projected a kind of fragile delicacy. But the façade never fit. She was always the Babe.

Her name was Mildred Babe Didrikson Zaharias. It was only natural that to a sports-minded world, she should immediately become known only as the Babe. In the preceding decade, the name had been synonymous with another hero of the time—the great Babe Ruth of the New York Yankees—but as sports moved from the Golden Twenties into the Depression Thirties, the mantle slid easily onto the broad shoulders of the girl who could do everything.

"This truly is the athletic phenomenon of our time, man or woman," wrote the great Grantland Rice. There was hardly a sport in which she could not—and did not—excel. She played baseball with all the free-swinging, base-sliding verve of a Pepper Martin. She donned pants and head gear and bumped against male counterparts on the football field. She swam, she ran, she jumped. She was a whiz at basketball, handball, lacrosse. She played tennis, boxed, bowled, fenced, skated and excelled in shooting, cycling, billiards and handball. Yet she made her greatest fame as an Olympic champion and as a woman golfer who captured titles on both sides of the Atlantic.

Asked once what was her favorite sport, the Babe replied, "I'm sorry, I don't have one." Then she added, "The best way to take athletics is to like them all. Athletics are all I care for. I sleep them, eat them, talk them and try my level best to do them as they should be done. You must feel that way."

She credited her broad interest in sports to her father, a Norwegian ship's carpenter who sailed 19 times around the Horn before settling in Texas. Mildred was born June 26, 1913, in Port Arthur, the sixth of seven children. The father had a mania about physical condition. He required each of the children to exercise, and he got each of them interested in some sport.

As a small girl, the Babe recalled later, she never had a doll or played house with toy dishes and furniture. When she grew up, she disdained makeup, and perfume was obnoxious to her. Instead, she exercised on a weight-lifting machine that she improvised from broomsticks and her mother's flatirons and set up in her backyard.

It was common for her in those days to walk up to a boy who lived on the same block and say, "I'm going to lick you." She normally did. She also challenged the boys to footraces, jumping contests and other jousts involving skill and muscle. The boys learned to dodge her as if she were a plague. She always won.

The Texas tomboy resented being called a "natural athlete." She felt such a label did not recognize her grit and perseverance. She reasoned that if she could not beat other women at sex appeal, she would beat them at everything else. Not only was she a remarkable athlete, but she was talented in many other fields. She could type between 80 and 100 words a minute. She boasted, "There's not a crossword puzzle I can't finish in a half hour." She was a graceful ballroom dancer. She was an accomplished harmonica player. She was an expert cook, and she was so good at gin rummy that no one wanted to play against her.

Still, she bristled when she was charged with having a lack of femininity. In 1931, she tried to shake the tag, but it didn't work. That year, she was scheduled to have a boxing exhibition against the brother of Young Stribling, a ranking heavyweight contender. But shortly before the bout, the Babe said: "I've decided to give up boxing. I'm going to be a lady now. I'm eighteen, you know."

She could beat almost any man in any sport, this phenomenon.

Even though she gave up her boxing career then, she continued to excel in sports—many of which were usually reserved for men—and beat several male counterparts.

It wasn't until she married 300-pound George Zaharias, a former wrestler known as "the Crying Greek from Cripple Creek," in 1938 and later devoted herself strictly to the women's professional golf tour, that her femininity began to assert itself. Taking pride in her womanhood, she wore lace. She started using makeup and going to beauty parlors. And she cooked, sewed and kept house.

But she didn't lose her sense of humor. In 1947, after becoming the first American in 47 years to win the British Women's Amateur golf championship at Gullane, Scotland, she was asked about her success. Cracked the Babe: "I just loosen my girdle and let the ball have it."

Neither was she one for observing amenities. Once in a golf tournament at Philadelphia, she called several girls around her—in a football-style huddle—and removed her slip while thousands of spectators watched in stunned amazement.

The slender, 5-foot 6-inch, well-muscled, agile, blue-eyed, short-haired Babe first attracted national attention in 1929. As the star player on the Beaumont High School basketball team, she was offered a position to play with a Dallas insurance company that sponsored a strong amateur squad. The team, known as the Dallas Cyclones, won the national Amateur Athletic Union (AAU) title three straight years, and twice the Babe was named an all-American forward.

In 1930, she represented the Dallas team in the national women's baseball-throwing championship at Jersey City, New Jersey, and hurled the ball an amazing 296 feet. Many major league managers would have been glad to have outfielders who could throw that distance.

Later, she became a pitcher for the House of David baseball team. She pitched an inning for the Brooklyn Dodgers against the Philadelphia Phillies, and she once struck out Joe DiMaggio, the great slugger of the New York Yankees. DiMaggio fouled off the first two pitches by the Babe and then tried to back off, swinging his bat in self-defense, as the third pitch came whizzing past his ear. It was called a strike.

That same day, before 72,000 fans in Yankee Stadium, the Babe decided to do some fielding at third base. Wearing a tight-fitting skirt, she bent over to field a grounder, and the skirt split all the way to the waist.

"I dove for the dugout," she said later with a wide grin. "I wasn't going to give any striptease for a three-dollar top."

In 1937, the Babe pitched in an exhibition game for the St. Louis Cardinals against the Philadelphia Athletics and faced A's slugger, Jimmy Foxx. "I gave him my high, hard one," she recalled, "and he knocked it into the adjoining county. But Paul Dean, then playing the outfield [he normally was a pitcher], came out of a clump of peach trees with the ball. He said he caught it."

She took on another great hitter, Boston's Ted Williams, but not on the diamond. She engaged Williams and former heavyweight boxing champion Jack Sharkey in a fly-casting contest. After winning with unerring marksmanship, the Babe said "All that Williams can do is bat."

One of the Babe's greatest accomplishments came on July 16, 1932. Only 19 years old, she entered the National AAU women's track and field meet and Olympic tryouts at Evanston, Illinois, as a one-woman team representing the insurance company she worked for in Dallas. She competed in 8 of 10 events, winning 5—the 80-meter hurdles, baseball throw, shot put, broad jump and javelin—finished second in the high jump and fourth in the discus. She set three world records and won the team title with 30 points.

From there, she went to the 1932 Olympic Games at Los Angeles, where she won the javelin with a toss of 143 feet 4 inches and the 80-meter hurdles in 11.7 seconds—both Olympic records at the time. She also tied for first in the high jump with a record leap of 5 feet 5 inches but was disqualified for diving over the bar head first. The technique was ruled illegal, although it never had been questioned before. Later, it was legalized. The Babe also wanted to enter the sprints and the broad jump but was prevented by a three-sport limit imposed by Olympic officials.

Her Olympic feats in 1932 helped the Babe win the first of her five Woman Athlete of the Year awards from the Associated Press. She later was chosen for the award in 1945, 1946, 1947 and 1950. And in 1950, she was named the woman athlete of the first half of the twentieth century by the AP.

"If I can impress sportswriters and the sports public fifteen or twenty years more, I'll enjoy it," she said. "In fact, I'm working on the second half of the twentieth century. And, like port wine, the older I get, the better I get."

As the Babe got older, it was golf that occupied most of her time in sports. Her entry into golf was purely accidental. One day in 1931, she was walking down the main street in Dallas looking for a party dress. Instead, her eyes caught a green-trimmed golf bag with shiny, steel clubs glistening in a sporting goods store. The dress had to wait. The Babe was unable to resist the temptation of buying the golfing equipment. "That was it," she said later. "The bug got me."

The Babe took her golfing implements to the Stevens links, a public course in Dallas, and swung a club for the first time. She said it was a strange feeling at first, but it didn't take her long to get accustomed to the weight. After all, the clubs were lighter than baseball bats, and with a bat, she once had hit three home runs in a game.

Playing every hole in her first round, she came in with a remarkable score of 95. A short time later, her employers at the Dallas insurance company made arrangements for her to play at the Dallas Country Club, where she fell under the tutelage of club pro Pat Green. After only three lessons, the Babe played a round of golf in the amazing total of 83. She could drive a golf ball more than 250 yards, often outdistancing her opponents by 100 to 150 yards.

Golf, however, was temporarily put aside while the Babe concentrated on her track-and-field performances in preparation for the 1932 Olympics. Following her sensational Olympic accomplishments, the Babe became one of the most revered athletes in American sports. People and groups throughout the country requested to see her. So it was not surprising that an enterprising promoter seized the opportunity to put her on tour. Shortly after the Olympics, she signed a contract for $3,500 a week to sing and play the harmonica. She lasted one week and quit, exclaiming, "I want to see the sky again."

Grantland Rice convinced the Babe she could become the best woman golfer in the world and encouraged her to take up the game seriously. Her first golfing appearance after the Olympics—and her first in more than a year—was at the Brentwood Country Club in Santa Monica, California. The Babe, using borrowed shoes and clubs, easily broke 100, playing the back nine in 43.

Then came a mixup in which the Amateur Athletic Union ruled that she was a pro because an automobile company had used her name in an advertisement. She asserted her name had been used without her permission. But not until 1937 did she regain her amateur standing. In 1935, the United States Golf Association ruled her ineligible because of her professionalism in other sports. In June of that year, she announced she was turning pro. Nine years later, she regained her amateur status in golf.

The Babe had entered her first golf tournament in 1934 at Fort Worth, Texas, winning low medalist honors with a 77. Once she started golfing in earnest, she hit as many as 1,000 golf balls in an afternoon, playing until her hands were so sore they had to be taped.

Once a man offered her the honor of teeing off first in a match. "You better hit first," she said, "because it's the last time you'll get the honor. And you better bust a good one if you don't want to be outdriven twenty yards by a gal."

The Babe was no egomaniac. She played sports with a refreshing abandon. She was completely aware of her athletic capabilities and usually backed up her boasts with accomplishments. She once scored 106 points in a basketball game. She worked out with the Southern Methodist University football team and impressed everyone with her left-footed kicking. She was good enough at billiards to make a cross-country exhibition tour. And, at one time, she decided she wanted to be the world's champion skier. So she started workouts, first on small hills, then on larger ones. But before she could achieve her goal, she was caught by the golf "bug."

In 1935, she went on a nationwide tour with golfer Gene Sarazen. She blasted long drives down the fairways. She clowned between shots, and she learned trick shots that she exhibited to the galleries. She was a colorful, crowd-pleasing player.

"The Babe is the player they pay to see," a sponsor reported. "As long as the galleries

Babe Zaharias liked to put on football gear and play in actual games. As a basketball player, she led the team that won the national AAU championship for three years in a row.

trail her around the fairways, the Babe will get the money."

The Babe's short game needed polishing before she could become a strong contender in major tournaments. Determined to be the best woman golfer in the world, she spent two years in California trying to make her game complete. After that, she hit the tournament trail and was the top gate attraction. But her game still lacked.

Again, she went back to the practice tees, this time under the tutelage of Tommy Armour, one of the best teachers of the day. She practiced for hours. She soaked her hands in brine, bandaged them and kept playing. Her game improved steadily.

As a pro, however, the Babe could not establish herself. In 1935, there were only two tournaments that women pros could participate in—the Western Open and the Texas Open. There were only a few more by the early 1940s. The major tournaments then were open only to amateurs—the U.S. Women's Amateur and the British Ladies Championship. With that in mind, the Babe applied for reinstatement as an amateur in 1944—and the U.S. Golf Association approved.

Reinstated as an amateur, the Babe won the Western Open title for the third time in 1945 and won 15 consecutive matches in 1946 before heading for the 1947 British Ladies tourney in Scotland. One victory in her long string was the 1946 U.S. Women's Amateur at Tulsa, Oklahoma, where she crushed Clara Callender Sherman of Pasadena, California, 11 and 9, in the scheduled 36-hole final. It was a record margin for the championship.

The British Ladies title had never gone to an American, and the Babe was confident she would bring the championship home. She had little trouble reaching the final round, in which she was paired against Jacqueline Gordon of England. The Babe, who had worn faded blue slacks throughout the tournament, tried to be a lady in the final round and switched to a sweater and culottes. But she got off to a poor start, and by the eleventh hole, she trailed for the first time, falling 2 down. By the eighteenth, she evened the match, and for the afternoon round, she changed back into her corduroy trousers—her "lucky pants."

They seemed to inspire her. The fabulous Babe won five of the first six holes of the afternoon round, including one with an eagle, and went on to beat Miss Gordon, 5 and 4. When she clinched the victory at the thirty-second hole, she went into a Highland fling on the wind-swept Firth of Forth course, and a Scotsman said, "It was a shame to send our girls out against a game like that."

Later, a London sportswriter said, "We have not seen a fairway phantom like her—not in forty-seven years. What a 'Babe!'"

The Babe returned to the United States and won another tourney, stretching her streak to 17 victories—a record that still stands. In August, 1947, she turned pro again—this time for keeps—to accept a $300,000 motion picture offer "which I could not very well reject." She said she turned pro for three reasons: "My common sense told me the prospect of earning over $500,000 in three years outweighs any advantages the thrill of amateur competition could have given me. I had reached the pinnacle of amateur golf while pro golf was still a challenge. And I hoped that by turning pro I would better women's golf by forcing more open tournaments."

Spearheaded by the Babe, the women's pro golf tour began to take shape, both literally and figuratively. Interest increased in the tour as the women became more proficient golfers and their scores begain to dip—while their style of clothes became more fashionable and their skirts rose above the knees.

The Babe had set her goal on becoming the best woman pro that ever played golf. "Then," she said, "maybe I'll be content to retire."

She set out quickly to achieve her goal. She won the Women's World Championship at Tam O'Shanter in Illinois for three straight years, 1949–51. She set a 72-hole record—at the time —of 228 in winning the Tampa Open in 1951. She was the leading money winner on the women's tour for four consecutive years, 1948–51. She won the Women's Open in 1948 and 1950.

Babe Zaharias would soon retire, not out of her own desire. In the spring of 1953, she contracted terminal cancer. She was operated on in Beaumont, Texas, and returned to the tournament trail. In 1954, drawn and haggard yet still able to hit strongly, she somehow managed to win the Open one last time.

She died September 27, 1956, at the age of 43—the greatest woman athlete in history.

BERT ROSENTHAL

Jesse Owens
The Master of Race

The prowess of Jesse Owens, who reached his peak in the mid-1930s, became a mark of almost superhuman versatility and achievement in track and field.

On a balmy spring day in 1935, the silk-smooth, sleek-striding Owens came gliding out of Ohio State University to astound the sports world by shattering five world records and matching a sixth.

And then, the lithe, 160-pound sprinter–hurdler–jumper one year later captured everything but a handshake from Adolf Hitler at the 1936 Olympics in Nazi Germany.

Owens's world marks were broken later and his collection of four gold medals was matched by other Olympians. But no athlete left a more wondrous imprint on a single sport than did the slender black product of the Depression era playgrounds of Cleveland, Ohio.

In the 1936 Olympics at Berlin, when war clouds hung heavily over the great German metropolis, Owens withered the Nazi pride of Hitler by winning the 100- and 200-meter sprints and the broad jump and whisking off with his fourth gold medal in the arduous grind of intense international competition by leading off the triumphant United States 400-meter-relay team.

Hitler, from his festooned stadium box, congratulated German medal winners as superspecimens of his pure Aryan forces but missed medal presentations involving Owens.

"It was all right with me," Owens recalled many years later. "I didn't go to Berlin to shake hands with *Der Führer* anyway. That's too long, long ago to bear any resentment, even toward a man like Hitler. And the German people since have made me a welcome guest."

In any other prime sport, Owens could have become a wealthy professional. But from the amateur sublime, young Owens, who was married at 18, was forced by economic necessity to the almost absurd by having to exploit his fame professionally.

For quick money he ran against a racehorse in Cuba and then led a dance band. In 1939, he lost $25,000 as a Negro baseball promoter. "It was easier to start from scratch on the track than at a bank, I soon found out," ruefully recalled Owens.

But, as Owens met frequent discouragements in the hard world of cash-and-carry, he never lost the poise that typified his glorious, if brief, success on the cinder paths.

"I buckled down and proved to myself that I had the talent to think as well as to run," he reminisced.

A measure of his success, which included giving about 200 speeches a year as a most talented and articulate orator, was the sprawling ranch house in Paradise Valley, Arizona, to which he moved from Chicago in 1972.

That was a much more auspicious move than when Owens's family came to Cleveland from Damville, Alabama, when he was nine. Jesse shined shoes to help out at home until his speed distinguished him from the rest of the kids at Cleveland's Fairmount Junior High. At Fairmount coach Charley Riley spotted and groomed the skinny kid, who at 14 ran his first timed 220 in 25.2 seconds.

"Riley always tried to make me run like I was carrying a glass of water on my head," said Owens, whose style always remained a picture of poetry in motion.

Trackdom's Fabulous Sixties spewed world records that backed Owens's great performances at Ann Arbor and Berlin into an obsolete category—but not when the differences in track surfacing and techniques are considered.

The 100-yard-dash world mark in the early 1970s was 9.1, shared by a half-dozen. The 220 dash and 220 low hurdles, seldom run on a straightaway as Owens did in his classic Ann Arbor clockings of 20.3 and 22.6, were eclipsed by Tommie Smith at 19.5 in 1966 and Don Styron at 21.9 in 1960.

"Records, as they always say, are made to be broken," commented Owens. "But things were a little different. In the 1930s, we didn't have composition, all-weather tracks and rubberized jumping runways, and we didn't have starting blocks for the sprints. In my era, the cinder or clay tracks all were different, no two ever were the same.

"I take my hat off to the great modern

Jesse Owens takes baton from Frank Wykoff during 400-meter AAU relay. Owens led off the United States relay team that captured the gold medal in the 1936 Olympics in Berlin.

track stars. They have been superb and are getting better. But I would say the competition of my day was just as great as today's, maybe not as much in numbers. From all parts of the world, we have more international class performers emerging every year."

Owens considered his one biggest thrill the winning of the 100-meter dash in the 1936 Olympics. "It was a million thrills packed into one," he recalled. "Ralph Metcalfe of Marquette University still was ahead of me at seventy meters, and one hundred twenty thousand people were roaring.

"Between seventy and ninety meters, Ralph and I were streaking neck-and-neck. Then I was in front at the finish. My eyes blurred as I heard the 'Star Spangled Banner' played, first faintly and then loudly, and then I saw the American flag slowly raised for my victory.

"That 1935 Big Ten meet was fine, but the Olympics are the Olympics."

Thirty-seven years after he starred at Ann Arbor, the Big Ten record book still listed as conference meet marks Owens's memorable one-day achievements in the 100- and 220-yard dashes, the 220-yard low hurdles and the long jump.

That day to remember, May 25, 1935, was launched when, at 3:15 P.M., the slender black athlete, clad in the scarlet and gray of Ohio State, got off to a perfect start in the 100-yard dash finals and streaked to a 9.4 clocking, matching Frank Wykoff's world record.

At 3:25 P.M., Owens took his first and only long jump, arching 26 feet 8¼ inches to surpass by nearly a half-foot the world mark of 26 feet 2⅛ inches held by Japan's Nambu.

At 3:34 P.M., Owens floated across an easy winner in the 220-yard dash with a 20.3 clocking, slashing three-tenths of a second from Roland Locke's world record.

And at 4:00 P.M., Owens gracefully scissored over the 220-yard low hurdles in 22.6, shaving four-tenths of a second from Charles R. Brookins's 11-year-old world mark.

"What I remember best about that sunny, perfect afternoon was leaning against a flagpole watching the people, some ten thousand I guess, file into the wooden stands of Michigan's old Ferry Field," recounted Owens.

"I was wondering whether my bad back would permit me to run at all. When the pre-meet warm-up came, I couldn't even jog because of a stiff back from a stair-fall at a fra-

Above: Owens wins the long jump for Ohio State at meet in Los Angeles. Right: He jumps 26 feet 5⅜ inches in 1936 Olympics, breaking former Olympic record by 13 inches.

ternity house only two weeks before the meet.

"At the call for the hundred-yard dash, Larry Snyder, our Ohio State coach, suggested I scratch because of the sudden strain in the jolting start of that bang-bang sprint.

"But I told Larry, 'Let me try it, maybe I'll snap out of it,' even though my buddy, Charlie Beetham [ace half-miler], had to help me remove my sweatsuit. Charlie slapped me on the hand and said, 'You'll be okay, kid.'

"My back hurt when I went into the starting crouch. But when the starter said 'Get set,' I felt no pain at all. I jumped in front with the gun and stayed there. I could hear Bobby Grieve of Illinois pounding behind me, but I took him by five yards."

By that time, the long jump was under way. After a 10-minute rest, Jesse sauntered to the jumping pit with Snyder's instruction to take only one leap and rest up for the 220 dash and 220 low hurdles.

"I skipped a practice jump but put a handkerchief beside the pit at the world-mark distance of the Japanese Nambu," Owens remembered. "I tried a couple of runs for stride and then barreled down the runway for keeps.

"I took off perfectly and I thought I'd never come down. When I leveled off in the pit, I saw that handkerchief behind me and knew I had a world record."

The crowd, which had watched silently, burst into a rousing cheer. So did other athletes who had completed their competition and lined the runway. The officials huddled over the steel tape and then field announcer Ted Canty, holding Owens's hand, led him to the edge of the track and said through his megaphone to the hushed crowd, "I wish to introduce a world champion."

Later, when the field lined up for the 220 dash, the crowd was quiet as the participants toed their marks. The gun barked and Owens

jumped into the lead out of the chute on the long straightaway.

"I didn't start pushing until the hundred-yard mark," Owens recalled. "But I could feel being all by myself. I didn't dare look back, but I felt I was flowing. About fifty yards from the finish, I began bringing up my knees, which you do when you are tiring. I guess I broke the tape about ten yards ahead of Andy Dooley of Iowa."

Again the crowd waited quietly and then broke into a roaring cheer when Canty announced, "The winner, Jesse Owens of Ohio State, and a new world record, twenty and three-tenths seconds."

"Oh boy," said Owens in retrospect, "the pain really was gone from my back then. I had about fifteen minutes before my last event, the two-twenty lows. During that time, I took off my shoes to let the blood flow into my feet—my spiked shoes were very tight—then put them on and jogged a few minutes."

At the crack of the starter's gun for the 220 hurdles, Owens again was off perfectly.

"I always figured in the hurdles, not my favorite race, that if I got to the first hurdle first, I'd win," recounted Jesse. "I got to it first this time. Then I started the cadence count Coach Snyder had us do—one, two, three, hup—getting seven strides in the twenty yards between hurdles. That cadence was music to my ears, a beat that just kept me runnin' and bobbin'. I finished five yards ahead of Northwestern's Phil Doherty."

That was it. Another world record. The crowd went wild. Many rushed onto the field to congratulate Owens, including then Big Ten commissioner K. L. ("Tug") Wilson.

"He was a floating wonder, just like he had wings," said Wilson, who later became president of the U.S. Olympic Committee.

That evening, Owens recalled, "I had the damnedest cramps in my legs I ever had, before or since."

Until Owens's superb performance in the 1936 Olympics, only Finland's Paavo Nurmi, first of the classic world distance runners, had captured as many as three individual gold medals in one Olympics. The Flying Finn scored a grueling sweep of the 1,500-, 5,000- and 10,000-meter runs in the 1924 Paris Games.

Jesse's more-noteworthy records in the 1936 Olympics were in his gold medal 200-meter-sprint and broad-jump performances. His 20.7 clocking in the 200 marked the first time in the nine Olympics since 1900 that the 21-second barrier was broken. And it stood for 20 years, until the United States' Bobby Morrow sped to a record 20.6 in the 1956 Games at Melbourne.

Owens's long-jump triumph at Berlin was on a leap of 26 feet 5⅜ inches, more than a foot better than the best previous in Olympic history—25 feet 4¾ inches by the United States' Edward Hamm in the 1928 Amsterdam Games. And it was to stand 24 years, until the 1960 Rome Olympics when Ralph Boston barely shaded it with 26 feet 7¾ inches.

"In long jumping," Owens once said, "a guy has to have speed and get height. If he has the speed and gets the height, the momentum will carry him to a great leap. The trouble with the long jumpers today is that they get no height."

That commentary was made by Jesse just about a decade before a long-legged Bob Beamon, a rangy black from Texas-El Paso University, really did get up in the air over the long-jump pit in the 1968 Mexico City Games.

Beamon sailed an incredible distance of 29 feet 2½ inches to smash in one prodigious leap not only the long-assailed 28-foot barrier but also the unbelievable 29-foot barrier.

Owens, who attended the Mexico City Games as a United States Olympic Committee consultant, as he also did in the 1972 Munich Games, commented: "I thought the man had gone into orbit. Not only was it a superhuman jump, but the same perfect conditions may never again be available to any broad jumper. The thin air of the most altitudinous Olympic site ever picked for the Games, plus the Tartan runway, plus a flawless takeoff and execution, combined to make Beamon an almost certain track immortal."

Owens never did forget that jump nor did he forget his own background.

"Regardless of his color, a man who becomes a recognized athlete has to learn to walk ten feet tall," said Owens. "But he must have his dignity off the athletic field. You can't tell an athletic star that his conduct must be impeccable because thousands of kids idolize him and will emulate everything he does and then forget about his problem of living in his community."

JERRY LISKA

Owens dons the victor's oak-leaf crown during presentation of gold medal at Berlin following his triumphant long jump, one of four firsts.

The Transition Years

The elixir of the Golden Twenties was heady stuff. It had to leave a hangover. That rollicking, reckless, unrestrained period was followed in the early 1930s by a depression, which itself was followed by World War II. Sport found it was never to be just a game again.

Athletes were no longer men in short pants engaged in athletics for the love or glory of it. They were cold operatives, doing their work for a price. Vitamins and scientific eating habits produced a superior type of athlete—bigger, faster, stronger. Records continued to fall. But it was a different ball game. From the seventh-floor headquarters of the Associated Press in New York, a directive went out to all bureaus and all writers: "Never use the word *hero* in describing an athlete. Be discreet in the use of such terms as *courage* and *bravery* in reporting sports contests." It was ruled that such phrases were empty and ludicrous when held up for comparison with the sacrifices and valor exhibited by the armed forces on Iwo Jima and the Anzio beachhead.

The athletes themselves returned from the wars with a soberer and more mature frame of mind. Exhortations in the locker room to "go out and die for dear old alma mater" fell on deaf ears and drew icy stares. "It's not the same," one coach remarked after one of his impassioned locker-room speeches had fallen flat on the hardwood floor. "These guys have been through a lot and they have a different attitude. You have to reason with them. They don't buy that old malarkey anymore."

Just as athletes adjusted to the changing times, so did the bankrollers of the various professional teams. Club owners who were wedded to the sport—such as the Horace Stonehams of the baseball Giants, the Phil Wrigleys of the baseball Cubs and the Tim Maras of the football Giants—became more rare. The big businesses and conglomerates moved in. Even the New York Yankees became a subsidiary of the Columbia Broadcasting System. Then followed a mad chess game with franchises. The baseball structure took on a new look. The St. Louis Browns moved to Baltimore, the Philadelphia Athletics to Kansas City, the Boston Braves to Milwaukee, the Dodgers and the Giants to the West Coast. Major league baseball, in an expansion from 16 to 24 teams, tapped the rich metropolises of the Deep South and Texas. Pro football kept pace with expansion; so did basketball and hockey.

Excellence of the individual athlete, however, didn't suffer. Instead it escalated. Ted Williams, the Splendid Splinter of the Boston Red Sox, became the first baseball player in 11 years to bat more than .400. Joe DiMaggio thrilled fans at Yankee Stadium almost as much as Babe Ruth ever did. Joe Louis, Rocky Marciano and Sugar Ray Robinson brought new glamour to boxing. An icy-nerved, cold-eyed Texan named Ben Hogan dominated golf. A black thunderbolt named Jimmy Brown shredded professional football lines for Cleveland. Sammy Baugh and Johnny Unitas gave a new dimension to the art of quarterbacking. An Englishman, Dr. Roger Bannister, shattered the 4-minute mile in foot racing. In basketball, it no longer was a matter of being either fast or tall. Bill Russell proved that one had to be both. In the 1940s, 1950s and 1960s, sports matured. They donned long pants.

Sammy Baugh
The Air Game

He was skinny and tall, with a Texas drawl, and his one big ambition was to play major league baseball. But he wound up as the pro football quarterback who almost single-handedly revolutionized the offensive concept of the game. By anybody's yardstick, he was one of the greatest quarterbacks ever to throw a football. Many said, and still do, that he was the greatest—better than Johnny Unitas, better than Joe Namath, better than any of the great modern quarterbacks.

He didn't even get his nickname from pro football. It came from baseball, the sport he really wanted to master but in which he spent only one summer as a professional—in the minors at Sacramento, Columbus and Rochester. They called him "Slingin' Sammy Baugh."

Slingin' Sammy was a string bean from Sweetwater, Texas, whose bulletlike passes gained 21,886 yards and accounted for 186 touchdowns in 16 years—from 1937 through 1952—with the Redskins of Washington. He started out at a time when coaches looked upon the forward pass with dismay—something to be used only with caution and never, never inside one's own 30-yard line. Baugh made the forward pass a potent offensive weapon, setting the stage for the barrages of passes by pro football quarterbacks in later years.

In 1937, Baugh's rookie season, he led the Redskins to the National Football League championship game against the Chicago Bears. There was snow and ice on Wrigley Field. The footing was treacherous. Baugh had never before played under such conditions. The Redskins were behind and backed up to the shadow of their own goal line. It was clearly, in the offensive theories of the day, the time for a punt.

As the Redskins huddled in their own end zone, they heard Baugh drawl, "We're a goin' into punt formation but we're really gonna pass." Baugh, also the team's punter, stood in the end zone and took the snap from center. The Bears rushed in, trying to block the kick. Baugh straightened up and hurled the ball straight as an arrow downfield to Cliff Battles, his halfback, for a 42-yard gain. The Redskins

went on to score, winding up with a 28–21 victory and the championship.

In that title game, Baugh gained 335 yards on 18 completions and had touchdown strikes of 35, 55 and 78 yards. While those figures wouldn't be considered high for the pass-conscious NFL of the sixties and early seventies, they were extraordinary for 1937. And when the rest of pro football saw how Sammy could sling the pigskin and the results he produced, the owners started looking for quarterbacks who could throw. Then and there the game of pro football opened up.

Even though Baugh was hailed as a cowboy when he arrived in the nation's capital in 1937 to play for George Preston Marshall's Redskins, he really wasn't. Sweetwater, Texas, was a railroad switching stop and Sammy's father worked for the Atchison, Topeka and Santa Fe. As a boy, Sammy threw a football through a rubber tire suspended from a tree in his backyard. Gradually he increased his distance from the tire. As part of a practice session, he'd start the tire swinging like a pendulum, run back and throw at the moving target.

His high school football coach wasn't aware of this, however, and when the tall, skinny kid went out for football at Sweetwater High School, he was arbitrarily assigned to play end. At an early practice session, Sam picked up a poorly thrown ball 40 yards downfield and fired it back, like a bullet. The amazed coach shook his head and said, "From now on, you're the passer." Actually, he was the tailback in the single-wing formation and didn't become a quarterback until Washington switched to the T formation in 1944.

Still, Baugh's first love was baseball, and he could throw one as unerringly as he could a football. He became the best third baseman in his section of Texas, attracting the eye of Dutch Meyer, then the baseball coach, as well as freshman football coach, at Texas Christian University. Meyer told TCU's head coach at the time, Francis Schmidt, "I found me a real baseball player. Incidentally, I think he plays a little football, too." Schmidt, however, wasn't impressed after his first look at the 6-foot 3-

Despite his renown as a quarterback, Baugh was a superb kicker, often punting for more than a 50-yards-per-game average. Here he boots one in a game against the Chicago Bears.

inch, 175-pound Baugh, who, incidentally carried approximately the same weight throughout his playing career. "Too fragile," growled the Horned Frogs' head coach. "He won't last."

A year later, Meyer had become TCU's head football coach and Baugh was his boy. The colleges in those days didn't share the professionals' aversion to the forward pass. Meyer installed a passing attack off his single wing, and even though the Southwest Conference at the time was air crazy, TCU outdid the other teams. Baugh's passing led TCU to the Sugar Bowl in his junior year, and in a heralded game, he guided the Horned Frogs to a 3–2 conquest of Louisiana State on a wet, sodden field. Actually, his punting prowess (14 for an average of 50 yards) helped the Frogs as much as his passing did.

In three years at Texas Christian, Baugh completed 274 passes in 599 attempts for 3,439 yards and 39 touchdowns. Compare this with his totals for his first three years in the NFL (197 of 395 for 2,498 yards) and the reluctance that pro football exhibited at the time to use the forward pass is clearly illustrated. In 1947, after Sammy had made believers of the no-pass fraternity, he threw the ball 354 times, completing 13 more passes and gaining nearly 500 yards more than he did for his first three seasons combined.

Although Baugh earned all-American laurels in his final two years at TCU, he still wasn't convinced that football was his forte. He signed a contract after graduation with the baseball Cardinals of St. Louis. During the summer of 1937, he played for three teams in the Cardinal farm system. He whipped the ball so hard from third base that he was switched to shortstop for the longer throw and the preservation of the first baseman. It was from this brief baseball stint that he was first called Slingin' Sammy. Two things went wrong in baseball—he couldn't hit a curve ball and the Cardinals were bringing along another shortstop that year, a young player named Marty Marion, who eventually became a Cardinal star.

George Preston Marshall, meantime, had just moved his Redskins to Washington, D.C., from Boston, where the fans preferred Harvard football. He was looking for someone to attract customers. He went after Baugh, finally signing him to a contract at the unheard-of price of $8,000, including a bonus. Marshall talked Baugh into playing for one fall, telling him to

go back to baseball the next spring if he wished.

When Baugh arrived in Washington, he came to stay. The Redskin coach, Ray Flaherty, doubtful whether Sammy could throw the ball the way his Texas admirers said he could, took one look at his new player in a practice session and told Marshall, "You did it, Chief. You got him. That's the greatest passer the world has ever seen. We'll take the big one this year."

Flaherty's promise to Marshall was just as good as the one center Ki Aldrich had made to the Texas Longhorns. Baugh started in the Redskins' first game of the season, against the defense-minded New York Giants. He passed 16 times, completing 11. The 'Skins went on to win 13–3. Later in the season when the Redskins played the same Giants for the Eastern Conference title, Baugh connected on 11 of 15 passes in a 49–14 rout. Then came that championship game with George Halas's Bears on icy Wrigley Field in Chicago.

For the next decade the Redskins prospered, posting a winning record each season and capturing five division titles and one more championship. It wasn't all a bed of roses, however, for Baugh. In 1940, playing the Bears once again for the league crown, the Redskins and Baugh took a licking that stands out in the annals of NFL championship play, losing 73–0. Baugh, who had developed a reputation for witticism, was asked whether the game would have been different had his end not dropped a touchdown pass in the first quarter. "Yeah," he drawled, "it would have been seventy-three to seven."

Later he would say this about the rout: "It was one of the those games where you get behind early and you have to play catch-up. You'll find games like that where you have to start gambling. That was the best Redskin football club I've ever played on. The score was no indication of the two teams. We'd beaten them three weeks before, and two years after that, with the same group of boys, we beat them in the championship game."

The Bears started using the T formation in 1940, and Chicago's rout of the Redskins enhanced its popularity. By 1944, the Redskins had switched to the T. Although reluctant at first, Baugh successfully made the switch, saying, "Why that's the easiest position in football, quarterback in the T formation. All you do is hand the ball off and pass." Later he said that had the T been used when he first began play-

ing, he could have lasted until he was 40, which would have been only two seasons more than he did play.

In 1945, his second campaign with the new formation, Baugh completed 70.3 percent of his passes. In a game that year with the Pittsburgh Steelers, he connected on 18 of 21. Two years later, fans watched him gain nearly 3,000 yards through the air and hurl 25 touchdown passes. It was that same year, 1947, that Baugh had what he considered his finest day as a passer. It so happened that it was "Sammy Baugh Day" in Washington, and the fans had chipped in to give him a new station wagon. Baugh was facing the Chicago Cardinals, a team that included such players as Charley Trippi and Paul Christman and that went on to win the Western Conference title that year. On a muddy field, Baugh completed 25 passes for 355 yards and six touchdowns. "It was my day and I did pretty good," he later drawled.

In his last game, except for a token appearance later to hold the ball for a placement kick and his official retirement ceremonies, Baugh, then 38, completed 11 straight passes against a blitzing St. Louis Cardinal defense. As he threw his eleventh completion, big Don Joyce, the Cardinal defensive tackle who had been going after Baugh each time, slammed him to the turf. Baugh's throwing arm was hurt, and

he and Joyce fought furiously for a few seconds. Both Joyce and Baugh were kicked out of the game—the end of Baugh's career as a passer.

It wasn't until many years later that Baugh's career records would be equaled. During his 16 campaigns, he led the league in passing six times, completing a total of 1,693 passes for an equivalent of slightly less than 14 miles. His career completion percentage was a healthy 56.5. But Baugh wasn't only a passer. He averaged 44.9 yards with his punting and, in 1940, averaged a nifty 57.4 yards on 35 punts. Much of his career coincided with the era of the 60-minute player, and he was a capable safety on defense. He once intercepted four passes in one game, setting a league record that stood for many years.

After retiring from pro football as a player, Baugh became head coach at Hardin-Simmons University in Texas and later was head coach of the New York Titans, forerunners to the Jets, as well as of the Houston Oilers. After George Preston Marshall had turned him into a rootin', tootin' cowboy, Baugh bought a ranch in his native Texas and spent the time between seasons there. In early 1972, with his five sons grown up, he was actively engaged in operating a 35,000-acre spread near Rotan, slingin' a lot of bull, perhaps, but still slingin'.

BEN THOMAS

Baugh lines up a pass in Bears' game in 1942. His career statistics include 1,693 passes, totaling almost 14 miles, as well as a completion average of 56.5. He even played defense.

Joe DiMaggio
Maker of Managers

On December 11, 1951, Joe DiMaggio turned his back on the highest salary ever paid a man in his profession and announced his retirement from the game of baseball. "I feel that I have reached the stage where I can no longer produce for my ball club, my manager, my teammates and my fans the sort of baseball their loyalty to me deserves," he said at that press conference. And if he could not provide the quality of baseball that the world had come to expect of the Yankee Clipper over the past 15 years, then the time had come to bow out. The gracefulness that had been DiMaggio's trademark on the field was there even at his retirement.

In 1969, when major league baseball celebrated the game's centennial, DiMaggio was acclaimed by a poll of sportswriters and broadcasters as the greatest living player and best center fielder in the history of the game. Joining him in that all-time outfield were two of baseball's earlier nonpareils, Ty Cobb and Babe Ruth. Each member of that dream outfield had his own distinctive style; the graceful ease of DiMaggio would have been a perfect complement to the fiery explosiveness of Cobb and the brash power of Ruth. If the good baseball player is one who makes the difficult plays look easy, DiMag took it one step further—he made even the "impossible" plays look routine.

The many facets of DiMaggio's baseball ability earned him universal respect among baseball men.

"I've never seen anybody who could surpass this guy," raved Joe Dugan, a Yankee third baseman who played with immortals Babe Ruth and Lou Gehrig.

Lefty O'Doul, the former major league star who managed the young DiMaggio with the San Francisco Seals of the Pacific Coast League, called him "a maker of managers" because he could do so many things so well.

Upon being named one of baseball's greatest living players in 1969 as a right fielder, Willie Mays had this reaction: "Isn't this something here? I've played right field maybe two or three days in my life. Center field must be reserved for my idol—Joe D."

The two top center fielders of the 1950s and 1960s, Mays and Mickey Mantle, took time to attend DiMaggio's fiftieth birthday party in 1964. "This guy was my hero," Mays declared. "I tried to do things like him, but you know only he could do them." Mantle, DiMaggio's successor in center field for the New York Yankees, added, "He was my idol, too. I think he was the greatest player ever."

Hall of Fame pitcher Lefty Gomez, DiMaggio's longtime roommate on the Yankees, was lavish in his praise for Joe. "He helped put me in the Hall of Fame," Gomez grinned, "chasing down all my mistakes out there in center field. In fact, if he hadn't been my roommate, I might never have gotten to know what his face looks like. All I ever saw out on the field was that number 5 on his back as he was going out to chase those long ones."

DiMaggio's appeal was not limited to baseball players, or even baseball fans. U.S. Open golf champion Ken Venturi once said, "In my athletic career, the greatest honor I ever had was meeting Joe DiMaggio." And Lyndon B. Johnson, president of the United States, wired this greeting to Joe on his fiftieth birthday celebration: "Happy birthday to an American sports hero."

In 1954, Joe DiMaggio married actress Marilyn Monroe in what was planned to be a secret ceremony in San Francisco. Nobody knows how word got out, but before the ceremony could be performed, a crowd estimated at over 500 people had jammed the corridors of city hall. But that was very little compared to the throng of 30,000 San Franciscans who turned out for DiMaggio's first wedding, to actress Dorothy Arnold.

How good a baseball player was DiMaggio? For 13 major league seasons he compiled a career batting average of .325 and slugged 361 home runs, despite playing his home games in Yankee Stadium, a ball park which takes away many homers from right-handed hitters because of its spacious power alley in left center. He drove in 1,535 runs, an average of better than 118 per season. He was the American League's Most Valuable Player three times, was picked

Charlie Silvera (29), Phil Rizzuto (10) and Tommy Henrich (15) greet Joe DiMaggio after the first of his two home runs in a 9–7 triumph over the Boston Red Sox in 1949.

for the All-Star Game in every single one of his major league seasons and led the league in batting, home runs and runs batted in twice each. In his 13 seasons, the Yankees won the American League pennant 10 times and the World Series 9 times. His most remarkable statistic was achieved in 1941, when he collected at least one hit in each of 56 consecutive games, stretching over a period of more than two months.

But DiMaggio's greatness goes beyond numbers. In 1951, DiMaggio's last year, he batted only .263, hitting just 12 homers in 116 games. But the Yankees won the American League pennant. Manager Casey Stengel told why.

"He was our silent leader," Stengel said, pointing to the Yankee Clipper. "Without him we couldn't have won the pennant last season. He always gave everything he had, no matter how badly he felt. He served as an inspiration to the rest of the club. He was more than just a player—he was an institution."

One of the players on that 1951 Yankee team put it more bluntly.

"The boys feel that if they are going to win a third straight American League pennant," he said, "Joe will have to play center field, even if he doesn't hit a lick. He means so much to us just to be in the lineup."

If ever there was a candidate for the perfect baseball player, it was DiMaggio, who stood a shade under 6 feet 2 inches and weighed between 190 and 200 pounds. He excelled in each of the five categories by which ballplayers are traditionally rated—hitting for average, hitting for power, fielding, running and throwing. His only weakness was that throughout his career he was plagued by injuries, which really serves only to enhance his accomplishments. Seven times he was unable to open a season because of injuries. In 1949, he missed the first 65 games because of an inflamed heel. Three full seasons came out of the middle of his career because of World War II. Nevertheless, he came closer to perfection than any other player of his —or perhaps any—day.

Famed sportswriter Grantland Rice, writing in the foreword to DiMaggio's autobiography, *Lucky to be a Yankee*, described the special appeal DiMaggio had for the public.

"No matter how many years you look at sporting events . . . you never grow blasé or apathetic to the thrill of perfection. Even the sport itself dwindles beside the coordinated rhythm of perfection. I've seen it in golfers, in tennis champions, in boxers, runners, in ball players, yes, and even in racehorses. Joe DiMaggio possesses that magic gift of perfection in his swing at the plate. If ever an athlete was meant for a sport, DiMaggio was meant for baseball. I know of no athlete who gives you quite the same sense of effortless ease that DiMaggio does in the performance of his baseball tasks."

And when DiMaggio felt he could no longer approach that level of perfection, he retired, even though the Yankees offered him $100,000 just to play 75 games in 1952. "If I couldn't play ball all out," he explained, "I didn't want to play."

Joseph Paul DiMaggio was born November 25, 1914, in Martinez, California, one of nine children of Italian immigrant parents. His father, Giuseppe, operated a fishing boat out of San Francisco, and it was expected that the five sons would also become crab fishermen. But Joe, for one, never liked cleaning a crab boat, so he took to playing sandlot baseball on the North Beach playgrounds. When his older brother Vince moved from sandlot ball to the San Francisco Seals of the Pacific Coast League, Joe began wondering whether that might be a way for him to make money, too.

Joe joined a boys' club that entered an industrial league. "We beat the Maytags in the playoff for the championship, and I belted a couple of homers," he recalled. "For winning the title, each of us got a gold baseball and a merchandise order worth exactly eight dollars. We were rich. The following season I was with the Sunset Produce Club in a Class A league. I played short. They offered a pair of spiked shoes to the batting champion of the league, and I won with .632 for eighteen games."

It was not until the next year, 1932, that Joe's professional career really got off the ground. It was his brother Vince who got him the chance to join the San Francisco Seals. Vince had been signed by the Seals and then farmed out to Tucson in a lower minor league, where he batted .347 in 1932 and was recalled late in the season by San Francisco. Joe, then 17, went to watch his brother play one day, and Spike Hennessey, a scout for the Seals who knew Joe's sandlot reputation, offered him a tryout with the club. It was late in the season, the Seals were in sixth place and going no-

The Yankee Clipper beats throw home in 1948 game against Senators.

where, and the team's shortstop, Augie Galan, asked if he could leave the club a little early to go to Hawaii with one of the team's outfielders, Henry Oana. The club agreed, but then found itself without a shortstop. Vince DiMaggio had the answer. "My kid brother can play short," he volunteered. And so, Joe DiMaggio got his professional start in baseball at age 17 —as a shortstop.

In his first trip to the plate, he belted a long triple off a veteran pitcher named Ted Pillette. He got one more hit in the three games left in the season to finish the year with a batting average of .222.

In the field, it was another matter. As he says in his autobiography, DiMaggio did not exactly make the San Francisco fans forget Frank Crosetti. "On the first fielding chance I had," DiMag recalled, "I just lobbed the ball

over to first, because I was afraid if I cut loose it would go over the first baseman's head or into the dirt. Julie Wera, a former Yankee who was playing third, yelled, 'Throw the ball, you dumb busher!' I cut loose the next time and the ball went well up into the grandstand."

Despite his scatter-arm, Joe's hitting earned him a place with the Seals during spring training tryouts prior to the 1933 season. But because of his erratic fielding, shortstop DiMaggio opened the season on the bench. One afternoon manager Ike Cavaney decided to use Joe as a pinch hitter for the Seals' right fielder, Ed Stewart. DiMaggio drew a walk, then returned to the bench expecting one of the other players to be sent in to play right field. Instead, Cavaney said, "Go out to right field, Joe." DiMag thought he was kidding, picked up his glove and started for the clubhouse, but his brother Vince stepped

miss 87 games that season. Even though he batted .341, nearly all the major league scouts lost interest because they were afraid to spend money for what looked like damaged merchandise.

William Earl Essick, a West Coast scout for the New York Yankees, was different. He persuaded Ed Barrow that the injury was only temporary, that this kid was worth taking a gamble on. The Yankees made a deal with the Seals, sending San Francisco five minor players and $25,000 cash in exchange for DiMaggio, who would be delivered following the 1935 season. It was a bargain, to say the least. Joe showed that Essick knew what he was talking about by burning up the Pacific Coast League in 1935, batting a torrid .398 with 34 homers and 154 RBIs.

His major league career, however, was delayed by another injury. During spring training prior to the 1936 season, DiMaggio was having an injured foot treated under a diathermy lamp. He left the lamp on too long and burned his ankle. He finally broke into the Yankee lineup on May 3, 1936, when he played left field and collected three hits. He went on to play in 138 games that year, batting .323, with 29 homers and 125 RBIs. He also led the Yankees to their first of four consecutive world championships—no other player had ever played on World Series winners in each of his first four seasons.

His sophomore campaign was even better. Although he again missed the season opener, this time with a sore arm, he played in 151 games, batted .346, led the league in homers with a career-high 46 and knocked in 167 runs, another career peak. The Yankees breezed to the pennant, beating Detroit by 13 games. Many experts have called that 1937 Yankee team the greatest of all time, or have placed them neck-and-neck with the 1927 Yankees of the Babe Ruth era. Their lineup in 1937 was awesome. The catcher was Bill Dickey, who hit .332 with 29 home runs and 133 runs batted in. At first base was Lou Gehrig, whose consecutive game streak was nearing 2,000. He batted .351 with 37 homers and 159 RBIs. The double play combination of Tony Lazzeri and Frank Crosetti was second to none, and Red Rolfe was an all-star at third base. The outfield had DiMaggio in center, with four men sharing left and right —George Selkirk, .328; Tommy Henrich, .320; Myril Hoag, .301, and Jake Powell, .263. The pitching staff had only two consistent winners,

in. "He meant it, Joe. Go out to right field," Vince said.

Playing regularly in the outfield, DiMaggio batted .340 for the season, with 28 home runs and 169 runs batted in over a 187-game schedule. He hit successfully in 61 consecutive games, a portent of things to come. That streak drew attention to Joe and made a baseball fan out of his father. Boccie had previously been Giuseppe's game, but with the attention Joe received for his hitting streak, Giuseppe began to see the possibilities of that American game. "Boccie ball?" he asked. "No money in boccie ball. Baseball, that's the game." And he was proud of his sons' talents for the game, as three of them—Vince, Joe and younger brother Dom—reached the major leagues.

Scouts flocked around Joe in 1934, until in June he sustained the first of a series of injuries which were to mar his career. While riding in a bus to a Sunday dinner at a sister's house, he sat with his left leg cramped in an unnatural position. When he got off the bus, his knee crumpled under him—a tendon sprained. He later reinjured the knee and was forced to

Joltin' Joe connects for his seventeenth homer of the 1941 season.

but with such batting support it didn't matter. And those two aces—Lefty Gomez and Red Ruffing—were among the best moundsmen in the game.

DiMaggio missed the 1938 season opener, but this time not because of injury. He was a holdout, having balked at the Yankees' offer of $25,000. Looking back on that year, Joe calls it his toughest season because of the booing he heard from fans all around the American League—and even at Yankee Stadium—for having held out so long. He was not ready to play until April 30. Nevertheless, his batting figures were nothing to be ashamed of—.324, 32 homers, 140 RBIs—and the Yankees went on to their third straight American League crown. They beat the Chicago Cubs in four straight games in the World Series.

Joe made it for opening day in 1939, but after eight games he was sidelined by an ankle injury. He played in only 120 games that year, but batted a career-high .381, leading the American League. He topped the league again in 1940 with a .352 mark, but the Yankees did not win the pennant, losing to the Tigers by two games.

By now DiMaggio was an established major league superstar. In five years in the majors he had never batted lower than .323 and he had averaged 32 homers and 138 RBIs over that period. He had led his team to four American League pennants, and had narrowly missed a fifth. But the year that made DiMaggio a household name was 1941, the year of the streak.

The season did not start off particularly well. In one stretch of 10 games early in the season, he managed only six hits for a .177 average. "Off the figures, I look terrible," Joltin' Joe conceded at the time. "But I have belted a good many hard balls, only to have them caught. Mind, I am offering no excuses." How can a ball player shake himself out of one of those slumps? "There is no remedy," he conceded. "Time and confidence in yourself are about all you can look to."

Apparently Joe was looking in the right direction. On May 15 he got a hit off Edgar Smith of the Chicago White Sox and his streak was under way. For 56 games—more than a third of the major league season—Joe was to get at least one hit in each game. He was not to be blanked until July 17, more than two months later. "It's the greatest record in baseball," declared Lefty Gomez, "and one that's not likely to be broken by anybody —ever."

The streak didn't attract much attention in the early going. But soon he passed Rogers Hornsby's National League record of 33 and took dead aim on the modern American League record of 41 set by George Sisler in 1922 and the all-time record of 44 notched by Wee Willie Keeler in 1897. With the Yankees' manager, Joe McCarthy, cooperating by giving Joe the "hit" sign on every pitch, DiMaggio continued to crack out the base hits. As he approached 40 games, Joe recalls the one time in his life he publicly questioned an umpire's decision.

"It was a called strike that caused me to turn around and look back," he remembered, "but before I could say anything, the umpire blurted out, 'Honest to Gawd, Joe, it was right down the middle.' The idea of an umpire being apologetic for his decision appealed to me and helped ease the strain."

DiMag broke Sisler's record in a doubleheader in Washington June 29, tying the mark with a double off Dutch Leonard in the sixth inning of the opener and breaking it with a single off Arnie Anderson in the nightcap. In another doubleheader, against the Red Sox July 1, he collected two hits off Mike Ryba in the opener to pull within one game of tying Keeler, then equaled the record with a single off Black Jack Wilson in the first inning of the second game. He received a break when the game was called on account of rain, but not until five innings had been completed—just long enough for it to be an official game.

DiMaggio broke Keeler's record the next day against Heber Newsome, a pitcher who won 19 games for the Red Sox that year. He describes that game vividly in his autobiography:

"In the first inning, I really lit into a pitch. I thought it was going right out of the Yankee Stadium, but Stan Spence went back and made a great catch. The next time up, it was my own brother Dom who got on his bike and took out after a long drive to make the catch. I felt a little down at that moment, because I had hit Newsome hard twice and that's about as often as I figured to hit him under the law of averages. And when Dom came up with the ball, I thought that while it might have been a great tribute to the integrity of baseball, it was kind of rubbing it in to be robbed of a record by your own brother, especially when he was coming over to my house for dinner that same night!"

But DiMaggio was not to be stopped. In the

fifth inning, he made sure nobody was going to rob him by tagging Newsome for a home run, and the record was his.

The streak went over 50 and finally came to a halt after 56 games, when the Yankees played a night game at Cleveland July 17. A throng of 67,468 turned out in cavernous Municipal Stadium for that contest, to see Cleveland's starting pitcher, lefty Al Smith, try to bring a stop to the hitting streak.

Joe came to the plate four times that night. He drew one walk and hit the ball solidly three times—but got no hits. "I hit two balls down the third base line, right on the line," he said. "Ken Keltner of Cleveland grabbed both and the momentum carried him outside the foul line for the throw to first. Both times the ball and my foot arrived, bang-bang. That's how close they were—but the ball was first." In the eighth inning, DiMag came to the plate against relief pitcher Jim Bagby. Again he hit the ball cleanly, but this time shortstop Lou Boudreau came up with the grounder—even though it took a bad hop—and turned it into a double play. The streak was over.

For the record, his statistics for those 56 games were 223 times at bat, 91 hits, an average of .408, 56 runs scored, 55 runs batted in, 15 homers, 21 walks and just seven strike-outs. What's more, the Yankees just about wrapped up the American League pennant during DiMag's streak. And immediately after he was stopped, he went out on another tear, this one lasting 16 games. Had Keltner not made one of those stops, Joe's streak might have gone an incredible 73 games.

Needless to say, Joe called that streak his greatest thrill in baseball. "I was lucky and I'm not trying to be modest," he said. "A fellow must have every break in the book to enjoy such a run of good fortune. Manager Joe McCarthy and my teammates gave me plenty of help that year. I remember one road game, I went into the final inning without a hit and three Yankees had to bat ahead of me. If they all went out, the streak was over.

"Red Rolfe opened with a single and the next batter flied out. McCarthy gave Tommy Henrich the bunt sign. The only reason for a one-out bunt was to keep the inning alive so that I'd get up again. If the batter had hit away, there was the possibility of a game-ending double play.

"Henrich nodded joyously at the command and dropped his bunt. He was thrown out, but I got my chance. I managed to hit a double. You would have thought we had just won the pennant. Rolfe, on crossing the plate, threw his cap high into the air. The players on the bench danced, whistled and hollered. When I finally came in, Henrich hugged and kissed me. You couldn't help but admire men like McCarthy, Rolfe and Henrich for their desire to help a teammate. It was one big happy family playing for the Yankees."

In 1942 DiMag managed to play in 154 games—highest total of his career—and batted .305. The next three years were spent in the army, and in 1946 he rejoined the Yankees and batted .290, certainly not a figure to be ashamed of, but his first below the magic .300 level nonetheless. But in 1947 he led the Yankees to another pennant with a .315 average, then had a great year in 1948, batting .320 and leading the league in homers, 39, and runs batted in, 155.

In 1949, Joe DiMaggio became the first major league baseball player ever to be paid a flat salary of $100,000 a year. The top figure Babe Ruth had earned was $80,000, although the difference in taxes actually made Ruth's take-home salary larger. Nevertheless, it was another milestone for the Yankee Clipper. But 1949 was also the year of DiMaggio's heel troubles, which caused him to miss the first 65 games of the season. It also, however, provided the setting for what Joe called his "second greatest thrill" in baseball. When he finally was ready to play, New York was headed for a three-game series against Boston, the Yankees' chief rival for the pennant that year.

"I hadn't played a game and the season was ten weeks old," he recalled. "There was considerable doubt that I'd ever play again. Many believed the bone spurs in my heel spelled the finish." They were wrong. In his first game, he singled and homered—and the Yankees won. In the second game, he cracked a pair of homers—and the Yankees won again. In the finale of the three-game set, he hit yet another homer—and again the Yankees won. DiMag was back, and the Yankees were on their way to another pennant.

"It was a fantastic series," he said, "simply unbelievable. At the time I had said, 'It takes more than ability and luck for anybody in my physical shape to get off to a start like that, hitting four home runs and a single to drive in nine runs in three games.' Something

114

else must have been helping me, I guess."

Another of his career thrills came in 1950, in the World Series. DiMag had led the Yankees to the American League pennant with a .301 average, 32 homers and 122 RBIs, and they were to face the Whiz Kids, the Philadelphia Phillies, in the Series.

With DiMaggio's marriage to actress Dorothy Arnold having ended in divorce (as would his later marriage to actress Marilyn Monroe), his son, Joe, Jr., held a special spot in DiMaggio's heart.

In the sixth of the second game, Joe caught a 400-foot drive off the bat of Del Ennis. When he made the catch, he had one foot on the ground and the other up against the wall. In the bottom of the ninth, he made a running stop of a ball hit by Granny Hamner which appeared to be heading up the alley. That stop cut off a Phillies' rally and sent the game into extra innings, tied 1–1. In the top of the tenth, DiMaggio came to bat against Robin Roberts, a fire-balling young right-hander.

"I had hoped to hit one all day," Joe recalled. "I knew little Joe, my son, then eight, and some of his schoolmates in California were listening to the game on the radio. I was thinking of this situation with Joe, Junior and said to myself, 'I must hit this one.'" The ball rocketed out into the upper left-field stands, and Joe (and Joe, Jr.) had the home run which gave the Yankees a 2 to 1 victory.

The 1951 season, which was to be DiMaggio's last with the Yankees, provided yet another thrill. It happened in the World Series against the Giants.

"It's nice to wind up with a World Series home run," he said. "That's why I think the Polo Grounds home run against Sal Maglie gave me a big kick."

In the fifth of the fourth game, Joe hit his eighth and final Series homer. "I got a boot out of hitting that homer because when the ball disappeared the fans started to applaud. I think the fans knew this might be my last big World Series hit. It was one of the nicest receptions I ever received. Yogi Berra was waiting for me at home plate. He jumped all over me and I practically carried him to the bench. It was a great feeling."

After his retirement in 1951, DiMaggio worked as a broadcaster for the Yankees, doing the pregame and postgame shows. He devoted some time to the restaurant on San Francisco's Fisherman's Wharf, which was run by his brother Tom, and held numerous other positions. But baseball, the game he loved, never lost its appeal. For a number of years Joe went to spring training, putting on his old number 5 —a number since retired by the Yankees—to help tutor the young hitters and outfielders. Although he repeatedly said he did not want to become either a coach or a manager, claiming he was not suited for the jobs, he did return to baseball for a brief time in 1968 as a vice-president and coach with the Athletics, the team which had been in Philadelphia during Joe's playing days but which had since moved through Kansas City to Oakland, just across the bay from DiMaggio's San Francisco home.

In 1955, to nobody's surprise, Joe was inducted into baseball's Hall of Fame in Cooperstown, New York. Then, in 1969, he was named the game's greatest living player and all-time top center fielder. At the dinner honoring the players named to the all-time teams, DiMaggio was his usual gracious self.

"To play this wonderful game that I enjoyed so much would have been enough," he declared. "I never thought I'd be honored this way. Getting into the Hall of Fame was the ultimate for me—I didn't realize something like this would come along as well."

In 1949, his fans jammed Yankee Stadium for Joe DiMaggio Day. There were presents, too numerous to mention, and cash gifts, too, which were donated to the Cancer Fund and the Heart Fund. DiMaggio, clearly more than a little embarrassed by all the attention he was receiving, summed up his feelings when he stepped to the microphone.

"When I was in San Francisco, Lefty O'Doul told me: 'Joe, don't let the big city scare you. New York is the friendliest town in the world.'

"This day proves it. I want to thank my fans, my friends, my manager Casey Stengel and my teammates—the gamest, fightingest bunch that ever lived.

"And I want to thank the good Lord, for making me a Yankee."

ALEX SACHERE

Bob Cousy
Houdini of the Hardwood

"I hope you can make this team. If you can, I'll be glad to have you. If you can't, don't blame me. A little guy always has two strikes on him in this business. It's a big man's game."

Those were the words of Red Auerbach, hard-boiled coach of the Boston Celtics professional basketball team, in 1950, to an all-American fresh out of Holy Cross College—Bob Cousy. It was midway in his second season before the 6-foot 1½-inch Cousy, a dazzling play maker, came into his own in the National Basketball Association. He was named Rookie of the Year for the 1950–51 season, finishing ninth in the league in scoring, but his overall play wasn't that impressive. Often he was too fast for his teammates with his razzle-dazzle ball handling, fooling them almost as much as the opposition.

But with Auerbach setting up a fast-break offense and pointing out mistakes, Cousy blossomed halfway through his sophomore season and took charge in the backcourt. It didn't take long for word to spread of Cousy's magical doings with a basketball. He became a drawing card throughout the NBA cities. Schoolboys everywhere were trying to emulate the Cooz. "Who do you think you are—Cousy?" became the common expression when someone tried a fancy move on the court.

Cousy's moves prompted Auerbach to quip: "The only knock I have with Cousy is that he makes practice sessions hard on a coach. All the other players just want to stand around and watch him." Cousy had a full repertoire, including the twice-around pass, in which he put the ball behind his back once and then fed a teammate after he brought it around the second time. There also was his behind-the-back switch, in which he transferred the ball from his right hand to his left and put in a left-handed lay-up. Both maneuvers were accomplished while in the air.

"I can grip a basketball like a baseball," said Cousy, who had hamlike hands, exceptionally long fingers and arms that were two inches longer than those of the average 6-footer. He had powerful thighs and calves, which enabled him to change direction quickly. He also possessed unusual peripheral vision. "I can see

more than most people out of the corners of my eyes," he said. "I don't have to turn my head to find out what's going on at either side. Sometimes it appeared that I was passing off without looking. But I was looking out of the corners of my eyes."

It's likely that few would have heard of Bob Cousy if his parents hadn't worked hard to escape their East Side tenement in Manhattan. Bob's main involvement in sports were stickball, stoopball and boxball, sidewalk variations of baseball. His father, who drove a taxicab seven days a week, finally moved the family to a house on a quiet, tree-lined street in St. Albans, Queens, a New York suburb, when Bob was 12.

Bob had been born August 9, 1928, only a short time after his parents arrived in the United States from France. For the first five years of his life, he spoke only French. Bob had never played basketball and knew nothing about the sport until he moved to St. Albans. There he worked hard with his friends at the playgrounds so that he could make the basketball team at Andrew Jackson High School. A playground director named Morty Akin was the first adult to give the 12-year-old tips about playing the sport. He pushed Cousy, a natural right-hander, into using his left hand.

"I dribbled by the hour with my left," Cousy recalled. "I didn't have full control, but that year I got so I could move the ball back and forth from one hand to the other without breaking the cadence of my dribble. I wasn't dribbling behind my back or setting up any trick stuff, but I was laying the groundwork for it." One of 250 turnouts, Bob failed to survive the cut for the junior varsity squad. Disappointed but not discouraged, he played in various outside leagues, including the Catholic Youth Organization and a Jewish league. As a sophomore in high school, Bob got lost in the shuffle and was cut again. But the Andrew Jackson coach, Lew Grummond, spotted Cousy playing each night at the Jackson community center and put him on the junior varsity.

He was ready for the varsity by his junior year but wasn't allowed to play because he flunked citizenship. "Really," Bob said, "it wasn't

Cousy in college play-off between Holy Cross and North Carolina State.

a course. Just conduct or deportment. It was crowded and I had to double up in a seat with a wise guy who was always making me grin and fool around." It was another setback for Bob, and he wasn't permitted to play until February. He didn't let up, however, playing outside ball and getting an *A* in citizenship the next semester. He became a standout addition to the team, and as a senior he led the city in scoring and was named to the all-city team. The college offers came pouring in, but Bob narrowed it to two schools—Holy Cross and Boston College. He had promised his grandmother that he would go to a Catholic college.

Ken Haggerty, a former Jackson player who was a junior at Holy Cross, helped Bob make up his mind to go to the college in Worcester, Massachusetts. When he entered Holy Cross in 1946, freshmen were allowed to play varsity ball. The Crusaders went on to win the NCAA championship under Doggie Julian, but Cousy was upset because he didn't see enough action. He wanted to return home. He wrote a letter to Joe Lapchick, coach of St. John's in Brooklyn, in an effort to transfer. But Lapchick advised him to stick it out at Holy Cross. He saw more action in his sophomore season but still wasn't satisfied with his playing time.

In his junior and senior years, he got his chance to play and took advantage of it. Unveiling his sleight of hand with a basketball, Cousy led the Crusaders to two great seasons, including a 26-game winning streak in his senior year. In fact, the whole Holy Cross starting five could handle a ball so well that they were nicknamed "the Fancy Pants A.C." Cousy was dubbed "the Houdini of the Hardwood."

Cousy's reputation was nationwide. His goal now was to play with the Boston Celtics. NBA teams in those days were allowed to exercise territorial draft picks, and Cousy was confident he'd be number one with the Celtics. Auerbach, in his first year on the job, bypassed the Cooz and chose 6-foot 11-inch Chuck Share of Bowling Green. Much to Bob's disappointment, he was chosen by the Tri-Cities Black Hawks. "Where is Tri-Cities?" Cousy wanted to know. He discovered that the team operated out of three cities—Moline and Rock Island, Illinois, and Davenport, Iowa.

Boston sportswriters, incensed that New England's favorite player had been spurned by the Celtics, pressed Auerbach for an explanation. "We need a big man," Red said. "Little

Bob, a natural right-hander, learned when he was 12 to dribble with
his left hand from a New York suburban playground instructor.
At Holy Cross, Bob led his team to a 26-game winning streak.

Cousy, the pro (above), deftly passes off to Celtic teammate.

men are a dime a dozen. I'm supposed to win, not go after local yokels." After some months of wrangling with Tri-Cities owner Ben Kerner, Cousy signed a contract for $9,000. Kerner then traded Bob to the Chicago Stags, who folded before the start of the season. The Stags were dispersed throughout the league, except for Max Zaslofsky, the NBA's top scorer, Andy Phillip, a leading play maker, and the rookie named Cousy.

There remained three teams with choices —the Boston Celtics, New York Knicks and Philadelphia Warriors. All three clubs wanted Zaslofsky, with Phillip their second choice. To settle the situation, NBA president Maurice Podoloff had the names picked out of a hat. Boston went first—the name on the slip of paper was Cousy, much to Auerbach's chagrin at the time. The Knicks got Zaslofsky, leaving Phillip for the Warriors. Auerbach's first words to the press were "Cousy will have to make the club."

Years later Red was to say, "We got stuck with the greatest player in the league when we drew his name out of a hat."

Before the end of Cousy's first season, Auerbach had accepted Cousy as a coming star. But Red was always dropping remarks to the press downgrading Cousy's game. If someone said his passing was great, the coach would reply, "Yeah, but his shooting was off." It was Auerbach's method of keeping Cousy angry.

The Celtics had finished last in 1949–50, the season before Auerbach and Cousy arrived on the scene. Cooz averaged 15.6 points a game to help the Celtics jump to second place in the East. After a year, Red dealt Chuck Share to Fort Wayne for deadly Bill Sharman, who was to team with Cousy to form one of the game's best all-time backcourt tandems. It was a coup for Auerbach. The Celtics continued to improve as Auerbach built his powerhouse around Cousy, the NBA's number-three scorer the following two seasons. The Celts finished second and third in the East. Easy Ed Macauley and Cliff Hagan were acquired.

With Auerbach calling the shots and Cousy doing his thing, the Celtics were solid contenders for Cousy's first four seasons, pulling owner Walter Brown into the black. A great asset of Bob's was his ability to finish strong. In a 1953 Eastern Division semifinal play-off game against the Syracuse Nats, Cousy hit 17 of the Celtics' last 21 points in a 111–105, four-overtime victory. He finished with 50 points. He hit for 10 field goals and 30 free throws in 32 attempts, a play-off record.

Despite their resurgence, the Celtics couldn't win an NBA championship until the big man Auerbach was looking for—6-foot 10-inch Bill Russell—came along halfway through the 1956–57 campaign. Tommy Heinsohn, Frank Ramsey and Jim Loscutoff were other additions. Russell, who played on the 1956 Olympic squad after being an all-American at San Francisco, revolutionized the game with his shot-blocking and defensive work as much as Cousy did with his play-making.

The Celtics emerged as the dominant force in pro basketball, much as the Yankees were in baseball. They won the championship in 1957, lost out in the final to St. Louis in 1958 with Russell playing with an injury, then came back to win from 1959 through 1963 with Cousy and Russell leading the way. After 1963, Cousy, with capable backcourtmen such as Sam Jones and K. C. Jones to take up the slack, decided to retire at age 34. Sparked by Russell in later years, the Celtics ran up an amazing record of 11 NBA titles, including 8 in a row.

Crowds turned out to bid him farewell in each NBA city where Cousy was making his final appearance. It was only fitting that the Cooz went out a winner at Boston in the 1963 championship game, dribbling away the last few seconds before the clock ran out.

After 12 seasons of traveling around the NBA circuit, Bob took over as coach at Boston College, a position that gave him more opportunity to spend time with his wife and two daughters. But because the recruiting end of the college game was something he disliked, he moved back into the pro ranks as coach of Cincinnati, later Kansas City-Omaha, in 1969. He was less than successful and quite daring in trading away the likes of Oscar Robertson and Jerry Lucas in order to build his type of club. Once, in desperation, he suited up for a few brief appearances with the Royals to give them some needed backcourt help.

However, the dark-haired, stoic court magician was always remembered for his feats in Boston. "The image of the Celtics is the image of Bob Cousy," said Bill Russell.

DICK JOYCE

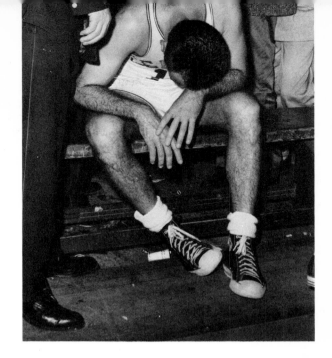

Top: Cousy exhausted after Boston beat the Hawks to win third NBA crown. Above: Cousy wipes away a tear as fans honor him on his retirement from Boston.

Joe Louis
America's Brown Bomber

Heavyweight champion Joe Louis camouflaged a burning desire for revenge under his usual deadpan expression when he climbed through the ropes the night of June 22, 1938.

Facing him was the only man to have previously defeated him—former heavyweight champion Max Schmeling. Only two years before, Schmeling had astounded the boxing world by hammering Louis senseless, knocking him out in 12 rounds. Even after he won the heavyweight crown by stopping Jim Braddock, Louis often remarked, "I won't be champion until I get that Schmelin'."

Schmeling had studied films of Louis's bouts prior to their initial encounter and had detected a flaw in his defense. Louis tended to drop his left hand whenever he threw a hard right, making him vulnerable to Schmeling's vaunted right cross. The German belted Louis repeatedly with rights before putting him down for the count.

Louis had taken the former champion lightly and had absorbed a humiliating defeat. Determined, eager to prove that that knockout loss was a fluke, Louis spent several minutes warming up in his dressing room. When he entered the ring, beads of perspiration rolled down his muscular body. When the bell clanged, two years of waiting to make up for a heartbreaking defeat turned Louis into a sleek brown cobra that struck with power-laden fists.

As Louis told it:

"He tried a right to my head but it went around me. I left-jabbed him mean and brought his guard low. I drove a right to the jaw with all I had. I put my body into it. It threw him on the ropes and his knees buckled. I caught him coming off the ropes and ripped one into his belly. He screamed like a stuck pig."

Louis floored Schmeling three times before referee Arthur Donavan halted the one-sided affair at 2:04 of the first round.

Two years before, racial violence had erupted in parts of the nation. But after Louis destroyed Schmeling, celebrations took the place of angry protest. There were parades. Louis, standing in the ring as Schmeling was half-carried to his dressing room, said, "I waited two years for my revenge, and now I got it." He would later remember that evening as his biggest hour. "Bigger almost than getting to be the champ."

Although Louis had wanted to defeat Schmeling simply for revenge, the bout was shrouded in an aura of international politics because of Germany's aggression in Europe and the mounting feeling in America that it, too, would eventually be swept up in the winds of war. The press had a field day when Schmeling was invited to visit Hitler after he won the crown from Jack Sharkey on a foul.

After the war, it was learned that Schmeling had not joined the Nazi party and was credited with using his influence to combat prejudice against black GIs in Germany following the war. But Louis was not one to be embroiled in politics. Schmeling had beaten him, and he merely wanted to avenge that setback.

Louis reigned as heavyweight champion for 11 years 8 months—much longer than any other man in the history of modern prize fighting—and defended his crown a record 25 times. He earned over $4 million and finally retired in 1951, after he had returned to the ring as a balding, flabby old man attempting to earn enough to wipe out a huge income-tax debt.

A somber, reserved man, Louis plied his brutal trade with the dedication of a skilled craftsman. A potent puncher whose sparring partners often felt the full impact of his fistic bombs, he could knock a man out with a single punch. He asked no quarter and gave none.

Once asked how he felt about knocking men out, he replied, "Those guys I fight are wanting to beat me up as bad as they can, so I can't feel sorry when I beat them up."

While he packed a hard wallop in the ring, he gained a reputation as a soft touch outside the squared arena. He earned approximately $2 million before entering the army in 1942. Half of that went to his managers, Julian Black and John Roxborough. High living and poor investments exhausted most of the remainder. He invested large sums in shaky business ventures and loaned vast amounts to people he hardly knew. Louis took up golf, and although

Challenger Billy Conn on his way down from Brown Bomber blows.

he could hit soaring drives, he never mastered the precise art of putting. Golf-course hustlers knew him as an easy mark.

"I took to having a good time with my winnings, and I had plenty of people to help me," he said.

Born into a poverty-stricken Alabama sharecropper's family in 1914, he moved to Detroit's Black Bottom with his mother and stepfather in 1926. The Motor City ghetto was an improvement for the family, which had not known the benefits of indoor plumbing and electricity before.

For the first time in his life, Louis attended school. It was a frustrating experience for both Joe and his teachers. Barely literate, he was placed in a class for slow learners. Finally he was sent to a trade school to learn furniture making.

One day he wandered into a community center and began paying for boxing instructions with money his mother was giving him for violin lessons. His mother soon learned what Joe was doing with the money when his violin playing failed to improve and he began to come home with a bruised eye or swollen lip.

His first amateur bout was a catastrophe—he was spilled seven times and given a thorough lacing by a more-seasoned opponent. The sound thrashing he received in his ring debut probably would have discouraged most youths, but Louis was adamant about developing into a polished fighter. He slowly learned how to put his weight behind a punch and how to punch in flurries. He ran up a string of victories and won the National Golden Gloves light heavyweight title. He attracted the attention of Roxborough, a successful black attorney, who, together with Black, agreed to manage him. His managers gave him pocket money, established

him in an apartment and hired the great Jack Blackburn to train him.

Blackburn, a leading lightweight around the turn of the century, took a no-nonsense approach to training fighters. He was the boss. He started Louis over with the fundamentals of jabbing, hooking, blocking and slipping.

Louis turned pro in 1934 and earned $52 for flattening Jack Kracken in one round. He sailed along, racking up 26 consecutive victories before he knocked out former heavyweight champion Primo Carnera in 1935. Despite his 60-pound weight advantage, the ambling Carnera was no match for the lethal-fisted Louis. After he won the title, Louis dominated the sport as no heavyweight titleholder had done since Jack Dempsey. He wore the crown with a quiet dignity and preferred to let his fists talk for him in the ring.

Louis was a contrast to the only previous black heavyweight king, Jack Johnson. A cocky, boisterous man who laughed at society's institutions and delighted in taunting an opponent in the ring, Johnson criticized Louis as a "clumsy greenhorn." Louis, quiet as usual, said nothing. But Blackburn seethed at Johnson's remark and claimed, "He wouldn't have no piece of cake fighting Chappie," using the nickname Blackburn and Louis called each other.

Although the loss to Schmeling was the only blot on his record, critics claimed that the Brown Bomber was a mechanical fighter, able to devastate sluggers with blurring combinations of punches but having trouble with fighters who kept away and boxed him.

He had trouble the first time he fought Billy Conn. While lacking a knockout punch, Conn was a superb ring artisan who could feint an opponent dizzy and befuddle him with nimble footwork.

Although Louis outweighed Conn 199½ pounds to 174, he was unable to corner him and was peppered with quick left jabs. Near the end of the twelfth round, Conn jolted Louis with a whistling left hook. Louis's handlers had a worried look when the champion returned to his corner.

"Chappie, you gotta knock him out," Blackburn said.

Ahead on points, Conn was not content to box Louis to a decision. He was also looking for a knockout. He attempted to swap punches with Louis in the following round and was soon in trouble from a succession of rights to the jaw.

124

His senses numbed and his flashy footwork deadened, Conn absorbed a solid barrage of punches before being counted out with only two seconds remaining in the round.

Louis entered the army in 1942 and spent his hitch traveling the globe, fighting exhibitions for troops. But time was beginning to take its toll of the Brown Bomber's talents.

Louis and Conn fought again on June 19, 1946. Conn, displaying his usual Irish confidence, boasted that he would confuse Louis with his speed. The Brown Bomber, on hearing the challenger's prediction, retorted, "He can run but he can't hide."

Both Louis and Conn had engaged in scores of exhibition bouts during the war, but a fighter needs the competition of actual ring combat to maintain his sharpness. The 45,266 fans who paid $1,925,564—the second largest gate in boxing history—to attend the bout at Yankee Stadium were bitterly disappointed with the ring-rusty boxers. A chorus of boos filled the air as Conn, more intent on survival than mixing it with Louis, ran and clinched while the champion shuffled in pursuit. Louis found an opening in the eighth round, buckled Conn's knees with a jarring right to the jaw and then knocked him out with a left hook and a right cross.

Just how far Louis had skidded was evident when he met Jersey Joe Walcott in New York in 1947. A crafty, 37-year-old veteran, Walcott electrified the crowd by dumping Louis for a count of two in the opening round, eluding the champion's heavy artillery by keeping out of range. He dropped Louis for a count of seven in the fourth and had turned the Brown Bomber's face into a swollen, bruised mask by the end of the 15-round bout. Louis was so disgusted with his showing that he left the ring before the decision was announced and had to be called back by his cornermen. He retained his crown via a split decision—the two judges voted for the champion, but the referee cast his ballot for Walcott.

Louis admitted that his reflexes weren't working that night. Instead of shooting his punches on instinct when he spied an opening, he had to think before he punched. The two fought again six months later. This time Louis caught up with Jersey Joe in the eleventh round and knocked him cold. It was Louis's final title defense. He announced his retirement on March 1, 1949.

Left: Joe takes time out from training for typical phony publicity pose. Above: At Camp Upton, after his induction into the U.S. Army as a private.

Saddled with a burdensome tax debt, Louis toured the nation fighting exhibitions. Finally, unable to extricate himself from debt, Louis returned to the ring on September 27, 1950, and met Ezzard Charles for the title. Charles had gained recognition as champion by defeating Walcott for the vacant crown. Determined to prove his claim to the title, Charles methodically outboxed the 36-year-old Louis. The Brown Bomber was a mere shell of his former self that night. His balding head shone under the ring lights and a layer of fat jiggled around his middle.

"I'll never fight again," Louis said through puffed, bleeding lips. Fans hoped he would keep his word. But he didn't.

Embarking on a new comeback, Louis reeled off eight straight triumphs before he was matched with a brawling, crude puncher from Brockton, Massachusetts, named Rocky Marciano.

It was a familiar tale of boxing, the up-and-coming youngster being thrown in against the aging warhorse. It was an important bout for both. For Marciano, it was a test against one of the biggest names in boxing. For Louis, a defeat would surely end his career.

Louis held off Marciano for the first couple of rounds, but even those sitting far back in the cheap seats could tell that sooner or later Marciano would corner the aging warrior and finish him off. Marciano floored Joe with a left hook in the eighth round. Slowly, painfully, Louis arose at eight on unsteady legs. Rocky backed him against the ropes, measured him and then knocked him onto the ring apron with a crippling right, flush on the jaw. Louis lay there, sprawled across the bottom strand of rope, feebly attempting to rise. The referee didn't even bother to count.

Marciano was apologetic about his victory. "I feel bad about beating Joe. He was my idol," he said. "I am sure I was very lucky that I didn't get to fight Joe ten years earlier."

Finally, Louis retired for good after compiling a record of 68 victories, 3 losses and 54 knockouts.

The Internal Revenue Service still held a tax bill, however, so Louis turned to a variety of ventures. He loaned his name for promotional purposes to a milk business and even turned to wrestling, a move that saddened many.

Louis, who commanded respect even in de-

feat, defended his decision to turn to the side-show atmosphere of professional wrestling by saying, "It's an honest living and it's better than stealing."

The government forgave Louis's tax debt, but in later years Joe was plagued by failing health and, in 1970, was briefly confined in a veterans' hospital for what was termed a mental breakdown.

After his release, some of the important names of sports and show business organized an appreciation night for his benefit. His fight films were shown. The guests watched the Brown Bomber on the screen, shuffling forward, battering opponents with machine-gun rapidity. That was Joe Louis.

EARL GERHEIM

Left: With Lena Horne. Above: Marciano belting an older Louis.   127

Maurice Richard
The Rocket

"and the Rocket's red glare . . ."

There were some ice hockey enthusiasts who said they thought about Rocket Richard when this portion of the American national anthem was sung before a game in a National Hockey League arena.

For those who saw him play, it is not difficult to remember Maurice("Rocket")Richard, even though he retired in September, 1960. During his time, he was hockey's hottest scorer and the player with the hottest temper. His actions once provoked a riot in his hometown of Montreal, and his performances on the ice prompted his early election to the sport's Hall of Fame. He undoubtedly would have been voted by opposing goalies as the player most determined to score. "When he hit that blue line," said Glenn Hall, a goaltender for Detroit, Chicago and St. Louis, "and he saw an opening, his eyes would light up like a pinball machine. It was scary."

For 18 seasons, Richard, a black-haired French-Canadian with intense deep-set eyes, tormented NHL goalies, and when he was through, he had scored 544 regular-season goals—more than any player before him. He set a standard for single-season excellence when he totaled 50 goals in 1944–45, becoming the first player in history to reach that plateau. His accomplishments become even more impressive when they are considered in the light of some of the obstacles he had to overcome. He was a left-handed shot playing right wing—much the same problem a naturally left-handed batter faces who has to swing from the right side of the plate. He was a native of Montreal, playing before the most demanding fans in all of hockey —fans who are uncompromisingly critical of anything less than perfect hockey from the Canadiens. But perhaps his toughest obstacle was an early series of injuries that threatened to end Richard's career before it ever got started.

Richard grew up in the north end of Montreal, a predominantly French section of the bilingual city in which English is rarely spoken. As a youngster, he had an abiding love for the Canadiens and their hero of those dark, Depression days, Howie Morenz. Young Maurice, like most boys in Canada, skated early and played hockey in Montreal's playground leagues. There wasn't a day in the winter weeks in the 1930s that Richard wasn't on skates, involved in hockey.

"Being a spectator wasn't important to me," said Richard. "I wanted to play. I never went to see the Canadiens. I was too busy playing my own games. I played six days a week in organized games, and on the seventh day, I would practice."

Richard's thirst for hockey was unquenchable. But he never considered a professional career because he didn't think he was good enough. He studied to be a machinist, figuring he would earn a living that way and play his hockey for fun. But soon he found his trade being squeezed out of his life by the sport.

"I was playing two games a night, and on weekends I played Saturday afternoon and night and Sunday afternoon and night," recalled Richard. Inevitably, the Canadiens learned about young Maurice's talent, and he was invited to play for their Montreal-based farm club.

In his first game with the team, Richard was tripped in front of the net. He went crashing into the boards and his ankle snapped. He was through for the season and, naturally, depressed by the accident. His run of tough luck wasn't through yet.

The next season, Richard was back in training camp with the Canadiens' Seniors, the farm club that was considered a short hop away from the NHL. He made the team and got off to a good start. Again injury struck. Richard was making a play near the net when an opponent cracked a stick across his leg. Maurice lost his balance and began to fall. Instinctively, he threw out his hand to break his tumble. "My body went forward but my wrist rapped against the steel upright at the side of the net," said Richard. "I could hear that terrible sound of the bone breaking. Once again, I was badly injured, and once again, I began asking myself whether this was worth all the pain and frustration."

The broken wrist cost Richard another season and left him deeply depressed. "I don't think I could be blamed for my pessimism," he said.

Hottest hockey scorer, hottest temper, early Hall of Famer.

"After all, I had suffered the fractures in two seasons with the Senior Canadiens and had very few goals to show for it."

That's the reason Richard was surprised when the NHL Canadiens invited him to their training camp for the 1942–43 season. Other than an annoying inclination for injuries, Richard had shown very little with the Seniors. Nevertheless, he was getting a chance to make the big team. Many NHL players had been tapped for military service and that had created opportunities for youngsters such as the Rocket, who might otherwise not have gotten a chance.

Richard made the team and got off to a fast start with five goals and six assists in his first 15 games. Then disaster struck again. The Canadiens were playing Boston and Maurice was carrying the puck into the Bruins' zone when Johnny Crawford, a defenseman, crunched him to the ice with a heavy body check. As Richard landed, Crawford came down on top of him. Maurice's leg had twisted under him as he fell, and once again he heard that terrible sound of bone breaking. Again it was his ankle, and for the third straight season Richard was forced to sit on the sidelines. It left the Canadiens' management wondering whether he'd ever be able to make it in the NHL.

"It looks as if we have a brittle-boned player on our hands," said Tommy Gorman, manager of the team. Still, Gorman, coach Dick Irvin and the rest of the Canadiens' management refused to give up on Richard. They invited him back to camp for the 1943–44 season. Again he made the team and, incredibly, again the early-season injury struck. This time it was his shoulder that snapped after a hard check. As he staggered off the ice, Richard was convinced he was jinxed for life.

This time, Maurice was lucky. The injury was not a major one, and he missed only a few games. When he returned to action, coach Irvin decided to put him on a line with two Canadiens' regulars—center Elmer Lach and left wing Toe Blake. It was a big thrill for Richard, who had idolized Blake when Toe was a Montreal star and Maurice was still learning his hockey in the city's playgrounds. It was also a big break. The trio clicked in a hurry, and Richard started scoring regularly—perfect medicine for restoring the confidence of the moody young man.

Soon, Blake, Lach and Richard developed into one of the NHL's most potent scoring lines.

The success of a line can be measured by whether they're together long enough and play well enough to earn themselves a nickname. Blake, Lach and Richard measured up on both counts, and soon they were tagged "the Punch Line" because of the way they juiced up Montreal's attack. And on the Punch Line, Richard was the most prolific scorer.

The unit scored 82 goals in its first season together, and 32 of them belonged to the young right winger. In practice, they would fly up and down the rink, sometimes embarrassing their teammates. Once, as Richard came streaking down the right side during a scrimmage, one of the defenders shouted, "Look out, here comes the rocket." The nickname stuck, and after that it was Rocket Richard.

Led by the Punch Line, the Canadiens lost only five games in the 1943–44 season and finished in first place by 25 points. But the regular season statistics go out the window when the play-offs begin. Stanley Cup play is hockey's second season, and third-place Toronto, matched against Montreal in the first round of the play-offs, was determined to knock off the Canadiens. The Maple Leafs took the series opener, 3–1, and two nights later faced Montreal in game two of the series at the Forum. The date was March 23, 1944.

Richard's scoring pyrotechnics had earned him his own defensive shadow, a big, close-checking Leaf forward named Bob Davidson. Wherever the Rocket went, Davidson was sure to follow. The tactic had worked in the opening game of the play-offs and through the scoreless first period of game two. But it didn't last much longer.

At 1:48 of the second period, Richard took passes from Blake and defenseman Mike McMahon to score. Seventeen seconds later, the Rocket connected again, this time on feeds from Blake and Lach. Richard's two goals forced the Leafs to open the game up. They discarded their tight checking pattern, trying to get their own offense moving. But on this night, the offense was all Richard.

After Reg Hamilton had cut Montreal's lead in half, the Rocket struck again, scoring at 16:46. That gave him a Stanley Cup hat trick—three goals, and not only in a single game, but in a single period. Richard was not through. The capacity Forum crowd of 12,500 fans gave him a standing ovation as the Canadiens left the ice after the second period, and

Richard versus Gump Worsley and a goal for the Montrealer.

they had plenty more to cheer about later on.

One minute into the third period, the Punch Line struck again, with Lach and Blake feeding Richard for his fourth goal of the night. And at 8:34, incredibly, the Rocket exploded his fifth goal of the night into the Toronto net. The final score of the game was Richard 5, Maple Leafs 1.

Traditionally, at the end of hockey games, the three stars are chosen and skate out for a bow. Sometimes the announcer builds the suspense, revealing the stars in reverse order, starting with number three and building up to number one. The public-address man began his pronouncement routinely. "Tonight's number-three star," he said, "Canadiens' number nine, Maurice Richard."

There was a murmur of incredulity from the crowd. How could it be? The Rocket had scored all five Montreal goals and he was being named third star. Who was better? How could this be? *Sacre bleu!*

"Tonight's number-two star," the announcer continued, "Canadiens' number nine, Maurice Richard." Now the murmurs turned to laughs and then cheers as the fans realized what was happening. Soon, the announcer confirmed it. "And tonight's number-one star, Canadiens' number nine, Maurice Richard."

"I only had six or seven shots on goal all game," said Richard, recalling his explosive record game, "and every goal was scored in a different way. The funny thing is that when we beat the Leafs eleven to nothing three games later, I only scored two goals."

When the 1944–45 season began, Richard picked up where he had left off in the previous season's play-offs. The Rocket was becoming

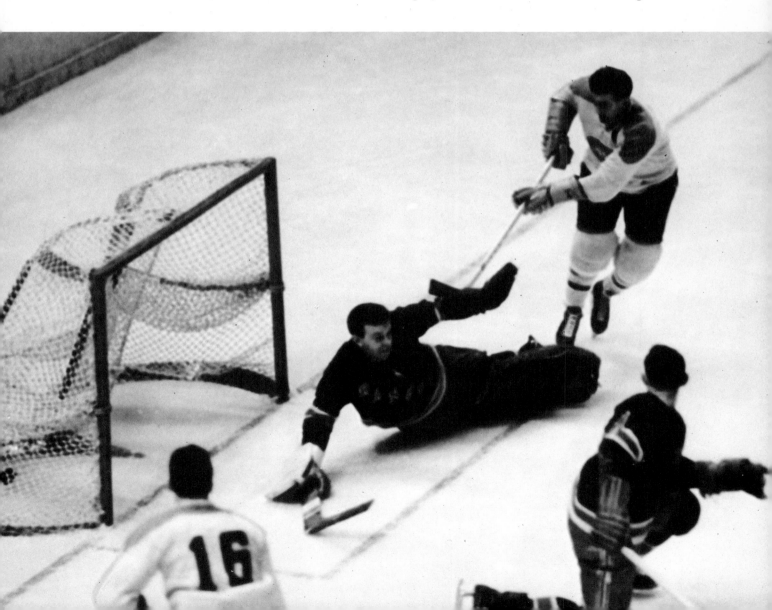

unstoppable, and he scored goals at a furious pace. Richard scored in bunches. If he scored once, there was a good chance he'd score again. And if he scored a second goal, the hat trick was almost expected. Ten times during the 50-game schedule, he scored more than one goal in a game. One night he matched his play-off game explosion with a five-goal show. He scored 15 goals over a 13-game stretch early in the season and 14 over 9 games later on.

Richard broke Joe Malone's single-season record of 44 goals and zoomed on to 50, reaching that total in the final game of the season. No other player scored more goals in a single season until 21 years later, when Bobby Hull zoomed past the plateau. But Hull and other shooters who subsequently topped Richard's figure all played longer seasons than the Rocket did. Richard was the only man to have scored 50 goals in a 50-game schedule.

His scoring naturally attracted attention, and other NHL teams plotted defenses designed to "defuse" the Rocket. They rarely worked and, in fact, often spurred Richard on to greater accomplishments. "Actually," said Richard, "I wanted somebody on the other team to make me work."

Richard was by no means a placid player. When he was hit, he hit back. He had a hair-trigger temper and often lost it. The Rocket found himself in frequent scraps with other players and sometimes even with game officials. More than once he was called on the carpet by NHL president Clarence Campbell and fined or suspended for misconduct on the ice. The most infamous of these confrontations took place in March, 1955, and resulted in what was later called the St. Patrick's Day riot—a black day in the otherwise proud hockey history of Montreal.

Richard, who had never won a scoring title, was leading the race. The Canadiens were in a neck-and-neck battle with Detroit for first place as the 1955 season moved into its final week. The Canadiens were in Boston for a game against the Bruins when Richard got into a fight with defenseman Hal Laycoe. In the scrap, Laycoe cut Richard, and the sight of his own blood sent the seething Montreal star into a frenzy. He took off after Laycoe, bound for vengeance, and when linesman Cliff Thompson jumped Richard from behind, trying to break up the fight, the Rocket swung at the official. Campbell punished Richard by suspending

him not only for the last three games of the regular season but for the entire Stanley Cup play-offs as well. The news hit Richard like a knockout punch. "I've never been so shocked in my life," he said. "I felt numb from head to toe."

Campbell's decision, which eventually cost Richard the scoring title he coveted so much and also cost the Canadiens first place, left Montreal fans in an ugly mood. Reprisals were pledged against Campbell if he dared to show up in the Forum for the next game, which was to be on March 17, 1955, against Detroit. The NHL's chief executive refused to be intimidated, and midway through the first period, he showed up to take his usual seat. As soon as he arrived, some spectators started pelting him and his party with debris. One hoodlum sneaked past the cordon of police around Campbell's box and slugged the president. With the Red Wings skating to a 4–1 first-period lead, the mood of the fans grew uglier. During the intermission, a tear-gas bomb was thrown, and the building turned into total turmoil. Campbell, removed to the safety of the Forum's medical office, ruled the game forfeited to Detroit as the crowd spilled into St. Catherine Street, the hoodlums spreading destruction along Montreal's main thoroughfare.

When it was over, police had made some 40 arrests and damage was estimated at $100,-000. Richard made an appeal on local radio stations to restore calm, and only then did the city return to normal.

Ironically, that was Richard's best scoring season. He finished with 74 points, one less than teammate Bernie Geoffrion, who overtook the Rocket on that tumultuous final weekend. Richard never came closer to the scoring title—the only major honor he missed in his career. He was named to the first or second all-star team 14 times in 18 seasons and was honored as the league's Most Valuable Player in 1947.

Perhaps the ultimate honor came when Richard could no longer continue to play. An Achilles' tendon injury limited him to 28 games in 1957–58, and two years later, at the age of 39, the Rocket retired. Normally, a player must wait five years after retirement to be considered for the Hall of Fame. Richard was voted into the shrine in June, 1961. He had been retired nine months.

HAL BOCK

The Rocket's temper flares; a linesman tries to pacify him.

Jimmy Brown
Brain and Body

Years after the highly publicized Jimmy Brown–Sam Huff duels had ended, people were still interested in hearing about their confrontations during the days when Brown ran for Cleveland and Huff defended for the New York Giants. Whenever he was asked, the Giants' middle linebacker would invariably cite the same instance to illustrate the intensity of their rivalry.

"I remember one game in particular," Huff recalled. "The first time Jimmy carried the ball, he rammed into the middle of our line. I came up fast, hit him hard and stopped him for no gain. As the pile untangled, I sneered at him and said: 'Brown, you stink.' Jimmy didn't say anything. He just got up slowly, as he always did, and walked back to the huddle.

"The second time Jimmy carried, the same thing happened. He rammed into the middle, I dived into the hole and stopped him. As the pile untangled this time, I sneered harder and said even louder: 'Brown, you stink.' Again Jimmy didn't say anything—just got up slowly and walked back to the huddle.

"The third time Jimmy carried, he drove into the middle. But nobody stopped him. He got a couple of key blocks, exploded past me and the secondary and raced sixty-five yards for a touchdown. Trotting back to the Browns' bench, he turned toward me and I could see he had a big grin on his face. Then he shouted: 'Hey, Huff, how do I smell from here?' "

Huff, of course, could consider himself fortunate, having managed to stop Brown two out of three times. Many defenders got only a whiff of Brown as the 6-foot 2-inch, 228-pounder sped by during a nine-year career in which he built a record of achievement that probably never will be bettered—even in an era when records are made to be broken. Brown disdained records. "Records are nice," he said, "but they don't tell the full story." Nevertheless, the full Jimmy Brown story can't be put in its proper perspective without citing his records.

When he retired following the 1965 season to take up a career in the movies and to deepen his commitment to the racial struggle, Brown had set the existing standard for every career category in rushing:

Most seasons leading the league—8 (1957–61, 1963–65)
Most attempts, lifetime—2,359
Most yards gained, lifetime—12,312
High average gain, lifetime—5.22 yards per carry
Most touchdowns rushing, lifetime—126

In addition to the above, he set records for most consecutive seasons leading the league (5), most yards gained in a season (1,863), most 1,000-yard-or-more seasons (7) and most 100-yard-or-more games (58, or almost half the games he played). In all the history of pro football, only Brown gained more than 1,500 yards in one season, and he did it three times—1,527 in 1958, 1,863 in 1963 and 1,544 in 1965.

Huff often complained that the only way to stop Brown was "to grab hold, hang on and wait for help." Alex Karras, the tough Detroit defensive tackle, said that that didn't work: "You had to give each guy in the line an ax." But, of all the compliments paid Brown, the one that probably gave the truest picture of the splendid athlete was offered by Henry Carr, an Olympic sprinter who, during the 1965 season, caught on with the Giants as a defensive back. As he watched Brown career downfield, he noted: "He runs like he has a halo over his head saying you can't touch."

There was no halo, but Brown had vast skills, a bronze V-shaped body carefully honed and two other dimensions—instinct and intelligence. The instinct was for survival, and it enabled him to establish an unofficial record for durability by a running back—he was forced out of only one game during a career that encompassed 118 regular season games, one divisional play-off and three championship games. The intelligence was put to use to maximize the physical equipment, enabling him to establish all the other official records.

Despite the splendid physique he displayed to millions in his movie roles, Brown always pointed to another part of his anatomy when he analyzed his success on the football field—at Syracuse University, where he gained 2,091 yards rushing and scored 25 touchdowns in

Jim Brown cracks a Philadelphia tackle. Brown led the league in rushing eight years, gained 12,312 yards, scored 126 touchdowns and averaged 5.22 yards per carry.

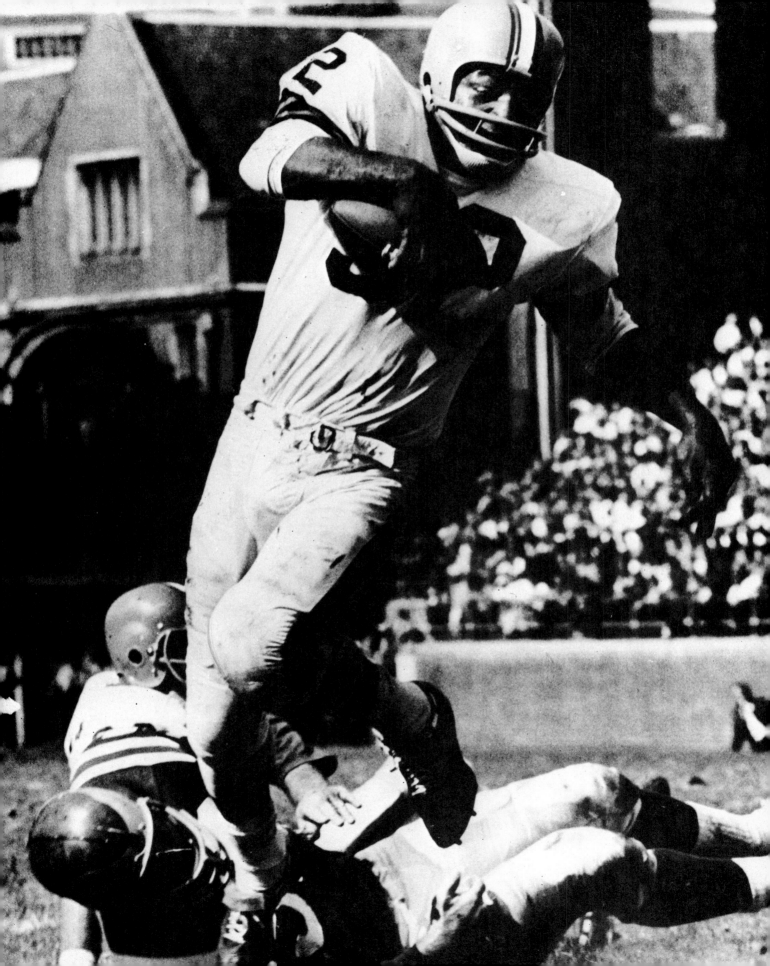

1954–55–56, and at Cleveland, where he began piling up yardage in 1957 and continued to do so until his retirement. He quit just prior to the 1966 season in order to continue his work in *The Dirty Dozen*, the movie that made him a star in that medium.

"I always made it a practice to use my head before my body," Brown explained. "I looked upon playing football like a businessman might. The game was my business; my body and my mind were my assets and injuries were my liabilities. The first basic was to be in absolutely top-notch physical condition. I always tried to train harder than anyone else. I even developed my own set of calisthenics, things I could do in a hotel room if I had to. And over the years, I made a study of what things usually cause injuries, and, as much as I could, I avoided doing those things.

"By the time I was in pro ball, I figured that if I was going to make it against guys who outweighed me sixty or seventy pounds, I was going to have to develop something extra, something more than sheer muscle and flashy footwork. I was going to have to outthink the opposition. I would say that I credit eighty percent of the success I had to the fact that I played a mental game. It's just common sense. Physically, many guys in pro football were more than my equals—big, strong, fast. But some simply didn't get as much out of themselves as others. Their mental game didn't match their physical capacity. My game pivoted on having planned ahead of time every move I intended to make on the field.

"The nine years I was in pro ball, I never quit trying to make my mind an encyclopedia of every possible detail—about my teammates, about players on other teams, about the plays we used and about both our and other teams' collective and individual tendencies. Every play I ran, I had already run a thousand in my mind. You get a jump on the game when you visualize beforehand not only the regular plays you run but also the hundred and one other things that might happen unexpectedly. So, when you're in the actual game, whatever happens, you've already seen it in your mind and plotted your countermoves—instantly and instinctively."

Brown scores off-tackle in game against St. Louis Cardinals.

That's what Brown brought to football. What it gave him was an outlet that, in his own words, kept him from being a gangster; one that brought him the financial rewards of stardom and the satisfaction of winning a National Football League championship, that gave him the platform that enabled him to move on to other fields he felt were more challenging, particularly his black activist role as the founder of the National Negro Industrial and Economic Union. It took him a long way from his traumatic childhood at St. Simons Island, off the Georgia coast, where he spent his early childhood with his great-grandmother, playing on the beaches after his father, a gambler called "Sweet Sue," had gone off to do his thing and his mother had gone north looking for work.

At seven, Brown was sent to rejoin his mother, who was doing housework for a family in Manhasset, Long Island. What his mother couldn't provide, football did—the way up. "I loved playing football," Brown said after he had retired. "It changed my life. Otherwise, I could have been some kind of gangster. I led a gang when I was a kid." The gang was called the Gaylords. But sports were a greater lure, and by the time he reached his senior year in high school, Manhasset High School was drawing standing-room-only crowds to see Brown in action—in football, basketball, baseball, track and lacrosse.

He was steered to Syracuse by Ken Molloy, a local citizen who had taken an interest in Brown. A Syracuse graduate, a lacrosse enthusiast and an attorney, Molloy played a large role in guiding Brown. He was singled out by the great running back the day he was enshrined in pro football's Hall of Fame. Brown started at Syracuse as a fifth-string back but soon was recognized for his ability and was playing first-string before the end of his sophomore year. During the next two years, he built the national following that made him a first-round selection in the NFL draft, although two other running backs—Paul Hornung and Jon Arnett—were picked ahead of him. When he joined the Browns, no one was particularly impressed, not even Ed Modzelewski, the incumbent fullback.

"He didn't know the plays very well and wasn't sure of himself," Modzelewski recalled after Brown had taken his job. "I figured, 'He's just another challenger.' There'd been others. So my first reaction to Jim was that he probably was just another guy who would wind up selling

encyclopedias. Then there was another thing against him—the law of the jungle. I had a lot of friends on the team. They'd try to hit Jim just a little harder than they normally did in practice. But he'd bust out of their arms, and gradually you could see him gaining respect. The writing was on the wall for me, so I became his number-one rooter. When we all saw what he had, I felt just like the guy who played behind Babe Ruth."

The Browns had finished with a five and seven record in 1956, but with Brown's coming, they accomplished an amazing flip-flop in 1957 and ran off with the Eastern Conference title after compiling a nine, two and one record. Brown, who gained 237 yards during one game, won his first rushing title with 942 yards. A year later, he surpassed 1,000 yards for the first time and was the Most Valuable Player in the NFL. He was to achieve both several more times. But, by the early 1960s, he was beginning to chafe under the rigid rule of coach Paul Brown and starting to emerge as the straightforward talker and black activist that made him a controversial figure.

"Although I was billed as Paul's star performer, I had no relationship with him," Brown said. "His aloofness put him beyond approach. It seemed to me that he thought of me as nothing more than a weapon. I felt he had no interest in me as an individual." He also said he felt that the coach's attitude had led to having a team that "lacked spirit and had become stereotyped." The initial result was twofold: In 1962, for the first time since his rookie year, Brown did not gain 1,000 yards, and in a Brown versus Brown confrontation, owner Art Modell went with the player, dumping Paul Brown.

The ultimate result was, in 1963, the finest year in Jimmy Brown's career—1,863 yards—and in 1964, a National Football League championship. The key to that was Brown, who led the team to a ten, three and one record and into the championship game against the highly favored Baltimore Colts. The two teams battled to a scoreless first half, and then Brown provided the impetus that enabled Cleveland to break it open. Lou Groza gave the Browns a shaky 3–0 lead with a field goal as the second half started, then Brown turned the left corner and galloped 46 yards to the Baltimore 18-yard line. On the next play, Frank Ryan passed to Gary Collins for a touchdown, and the Browns were in. In all, Brown carried 27 times for 114 yards and caught three passes for 37 more, but the satisfaction was not statistical. "I have had better days as an individual," he said, "but this is the most satisfying day of all."

The 1965 season, surprisingly, turned out to be Brown's last, but he left no one short-changed as he put together a 1,544-yard year and the Browns again won the Eastern title, although they lost to Green Bay in the NFL championship game. Brown already had appeared in his first movie, *Rio Conchos*, and when he was offered *The Dirty Dozen*, he decided it was time for him to change careers. He decided that despite the fact he was just 30 and it was obvious that he still could play at top proficiency for several more years. But other vistas had opened, and Brown's head was turning in different directions.

"It wasn't a question of whether I could play three more years or five more years," Brown explained. "Taking a realistic look at my life and my ambitions, at the things I wanted to achieve, it was time for a change. I had some concerns about giving up football's certainties for the movies' uncertainties. But the hard fact is I feel I quit just in time. I got out still in my prime and without any injuries. I got out before I ever had to be like I've seen so many guys—sitting hunched over on the bench, all scarred and banged up, watching some hot young kid out there in their place.

"I found movies more rewarding financially, and something I could keep at far longer than I could have in football. Besides that, my other activities benefited, especially working to increase Negro participation in the country's economic life. That's very important to me. I believe a man grows up. He discovers there are other worlds, other interests. His horizon widens. He has aggravations in his athletic life. He has to rid himself of them if he is to flower as a complete individual."

Freed of his ties to the establishment, Brown answered some of the questions he had put off before, becoming something of a critic of the sport and some of its leading figures. He was also totally outspoken about relationships between white and black players, citing the problems that arise in relationships off the field, particularly when it comes to a black man dating a white woman. During the same period, he became the center of a widely publicized court case in which he was sued by a young lady who first accused Brown of molesting her and then tried again with a paternity suit. Brown was acquitted, but his outspoken frankness, the court case and the publicity that emanated from some of the sites of his movies—such as a reported escapade with Raquel Welch—added to the picture of a controversial figure.

Brown remained aloof, at least verbally, from offering any self-defense, and when he became eligible for election to pro football's Hall of Fame, there was some strong sentiment for barring him, despite his unmatched achievements, because of all the adverse publicity attached to his off-the-field activities. But, the first time he was eligible for election, 1971, he was elected. The odd thing is that he neither needed nor campaigned for a spot in the Hall of Fame, but he did, indeed, covet it. Still, on the eve of the festivities preceding the ceremonies, there was some concern that he would embarrass the establishment by not showing up.

Jim Brown was there, however, on a bright sunny day in Canton, Ohio, on the glistening steps of the polished shrine to the game's greats, resplendent himself in a white knit jumpsuit that underscored the bronze body that had run for so many yards and so many touchdowns. When he was called forth to be honored, he received a standing ovation, responded with a peace sign and then said he wanted to talk about three things that had made him particularly happy on the occasion of his enshrinement.

"During this morning's parade, I had a fantastic time," Brown said. "That was because the people responded and made me feel wanted. It was all natural and spontaneous. And my mother is here today—she had a tough struggle when I was a little boy. She worked very hard. I want to thank her—because I never tell her. Finally, I want to thank the people of Manhasset, Long Island, New York, where I grew up, who were instrumental in my life and came to me when my life could have taken any turn." Then he paused and added:

"You've heard some bad things about Jimmy Brown. But the arrogant, bad Jimmy Brown can be humble when he is given true love."

There were 8,000 people there that day, July 30, 1971, but at that moment their applause rang out as loudly as if Brown had just completed a long touchdown run before 80,000 fans in Cleveland's Municipal Stadium.

MIKE RATHET

Ben Hogan
The Greatest Comeback

In a fabulous career interrupted by service as an army officer in World War II, Ben Hogan won four U.S. Open golf championships, captured two Masters titles and the only British Open in which he competed. In 1953, he swept the Masters, the U.S. Open and the British Open in a feat that golf authorities rate as being at least equal to Bob Jones's Grand Slam of 1930. He was the fairway king of his day, a dour, machinelike craftsman hailed by most observers as the greatest shot maker who ever lived. Yet Hogan will always be remembered most for the courage and unshakable will that marked his comeback from a near-fatal automobile accident—an experience later dramatized in story and movies.

On February 2, 1949, Hogan and his pretty, dark-haired wife, Valerie, were driving along a lonely Texas highway en route from Phoenix, Arizona, to their home in Fort Worth, Texas. Suddenly, out of the haze and with no advance warning, a transcontinental bus skidded and lunged across the path of the Hogan car. Instinctively, Hogan flung himself across the seat to protect his wife. The act probably saved both their lives.

The impact of bus and car collision drove the steering wheel through the driver's seat, as a javelin might be thrust. Valerie escaped with minor injuries, but Hogan was less fortunate. He suffered a double fracture of the pelvis, a broken collarbone, a fractured left ankle and a smashed right rib.

He was rushed to an El Paso hospital where doctors began putting the broken body back together. The sports world waited anxiously but pessimistically. Surgeons performed operation after operation on Ben's scarred, battered legs. It seemed impossible that even the most modern medical science could restore to the gritty Texan the endowments that had made him the best professional golfer in the world.

Just after it appeared that Hogan had weathered the crisis, he developed thrombosis. In order to halt the clotting of blood, doctors performed a two-hour abdominal operation and tied off the principal veins in his legs. It saved the golfer's life, but it seemed to assure that Hogan's golf career had ended. There was doubt that he would ever walk again.

The pessimism was not only premature, it was ill-founded. It failed to reckon with the fierce determination and unflagging fighting qualities of the blacksmith's son, whose life from boyhood had been spent overcoming obstacles and defying critics.

As soon as he was able to stand up, Hogan asked for his putter. He practiced putts on the rug and on the hospital lawn. After leaving the hospital, he trudged to the practice tee on unsure, aching legs and hit practice shots by the hour.

It was less than a year after the horrible accident and golf fans had turned their attention to new personalities when the shock announcement came: "Hogan to Try Comeback in the Los Angeles Open." It was at the Riviera Club in Los Angeles—the course that became known as "Hogan's Alley"—that Hogan had won his first U.S. Open title in 1948, scoring a record 276 that was to last 19 years.

Now in January, 1950, sports fans watched with wonder and admiration as the little battler trudged over the fairways on legs that appeared to be held together by wire and adhesive tape. He walked slowly, in laborious stiff-legged fashion. But there was no mistake about his swing. His shots still carried a machinelike crispness. His jaw was a vise of determination. Sam Snead took an early lead but admitted he was uncomfortable. "I keep looking over my shoulder," Snead said. "The little man is coming." Come he did. In his first tournament outing in 12 months, Hogan tied Snead for the title. The play-off was delayed by bad weather. It was immaterial that in the postponed play-off, weeks later, Snead was the victor. Hogan had returned.

If there was a feeling that the Los Angeles venture had been a freak, this doubt was erased five months later in the Golden Anniversary Open at the Merion Golf Club outside Philadelphia. Still so bothered with circulation problems in his legs that he had to return to his hotel room at night after play and put his legs in traction, Hogan tied Lloyd Mangrum and

Hogan returned to the tour after the war, winning the PGA championship in 1946. He finished the year the leading money-winner, with earnings totaling $42,500.

George Fazio at 287 and then won the 18-hole play-off by four strokes.

The historic triumph, however, failed to convince some cynics. A nationally syndicated sports columnist, in the men's washroom at Merion after the presentation ceremonies, was loud in expounding his private theories to a small coterie of friends. "Well, the Little Man has done it," the writer said. "He might as well enjoy it. Now he's proved himself. He's been given a big financial settlement by the bus company because of the accident. He's rich and contented. He'll never win another big tournament—mark my words."

Hogan, unnoticed, happened to be within earshot. Flushed and angry, he confronted his critic. "You wouldn't want to make a bet on that, would you?" The writer was shaken. But he recovered sufficiently and said, "Sure, let's make it a half-dozen ten-dollar ties."

Less than ten months later, Hogan had won the bet. He captured the 1951 Masters. He also repeated in the U.S. Open, and in 1953, he pulled off his amazing sweep of the Masters and the U.S. and British Opens.

If Ben Hogan was a great golfer before the 1949 accident, he became an even greater one later. Most of his friends acknowledged that the ordeal had left him a mellower man but, if anything, it had toughened an already competitive spirit. He had new inspiration and a stronger psychological approach to the game.

Hogan had always been something of a loner. He was a cold, detached artisan on the course, likened by some observers to an undertaker weaving a shroud of defeat for all his adversaries. If there was any softening of his nature, it was relative. The iron rod of self-discipline, forged by early years of adversity and supported by suspicion of outside influences, did

The Battler continued his tournament success through 1947 and 1948, but in 1949 a car accident left him with a fractured pelvis and seemingly without a career.

not bend easily. Much of the hard crust remained.

To many of the new and younger golfers who followed on the tour, he was always "Mr. Hogan." They looked to him with awe and respect. His best friends—chief of whom were Jimmy Demaret and Claude Harmon—never really got close to him. Demaret, a wisecracking, flamboyant extrovert whose personality was a direct antithesis of that of his favorite golfing partner, had his own term of endearment for Hogan. He called him "Blue Blades." "I don't understand why people say Ben is so untalkative," Demaret once quipped. "When I play with him he speaks to me on every green. He says, 'You're away.'"

"Those steel gray eyes of his," a friend once remarked. "He looks at you like a landlord asking for next month's rent."

Rivals on the tour dubbed him "the Hawk." Adoring Scots at Carnoustie, where Hogan won the British Open in 1953, christened him "the Wee Ice Mon." To the thousands of fans who pressed at the restraining ropes and stampeded down the fairways behind him in the big tournaments, he was a robot with a frozen face who turned out golf shots with such perfection that there was suspicion he may have been made of nuts and bolts.

Hogan went to major tournaments as much as two weeks in advance and subjected the course to microscopic study. He memorized the best placement positions for drives on every fairway. He stepped off yardage and made a note of markers, information that he filed in some invisible cabinet in his brain—never making a penciled note. Contemporaries said that his shot-making was so precisioned that he played from one round to the next out of his own divots.

"From tee to green, there never was anyone to compare with Hogan," said Gene Sarazen, the old, beknickered squire whose tournament career spanned half a century. "He was a veritable machine. If he had been able to putt as well as Bob Jones or Jack Nicklaus, no one could have come close to him. Yet he was such a superb shot maker that his putting was never put to too severe a test. He was always rifling his approach shots at the pin."

Hogan liked to refer to himself as a shot manager rather than a shot maker. "Management—that is, placing the ball in the right position for the next shot, knowing exactly where to be on the green—is eighty percent of winning golf."

Intensity of purpose was drilled into Hogan at an early age through necessity. He was born August 13, 1912, in the little town of Dublin, Texas. He was 10 years old when his father, the village blacksmith, died and his mother gathered up her family and moved to Fort Worth. Ben sold papers on street corners to help provide food for the family, and at the age of 12, he became a caddie at the Glen Garden Country Club, earning 65 cents a round.

Another caddie at the same club was Byron Nelson, who in later years was to become one of Hogan's strongest rivals. Ben was 15 when he won his first tournament—the Christmas Day caddie championship at the Glen Garden Club. At 19, he turned pro and, with $100 in savings in his pocket, headed for Los Angeles to take his first shot at the winter tour. He lasted a month. He came back to Fort Worth, saved for another grubstake and in 1933—at the age of 20—set out for the West Coast again. For the second time he failed to make the grade. The root of his problems was an atrocious hook. "Look, son," well-wishing pros advised him, "why don't you go home and get a good job in some store. With a hook like that, you'll starve to death on the golf tour."

Ben took only part of the advice. He returned home, broke, disillusioned, but far from beaten. "I know I can make it," he told friends. He spent the next three years slaving to get all the kinks out of his game. He was encouraged when he qualified for the U.S. Open championship at Baltusrol in Springfield, New Jersey, in 1936. However, he failed to survive the 36-hole cut.

In 1937, the determined Hogan set out on tour again but with increased responsibilities. He took with him his bride, the former Valerie Fox. He managed to survive with a third-place finish at Lake Placid and tenth place in the Canadian Open, but by this time discouragement and frustration were beginning to eat away at his once-flaming hopes. With $1,400 in savings, he and Valerie decided between them to make one more try on the winter tour of 1938 and agreed that if this attempt were not more successful, Ben would give up golf and go into another business.

A change in careers appeared imminent as Hogan moved from Pasadena to Los Angeles to Sacramento, spending more money for subsist-

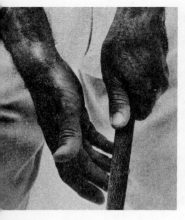

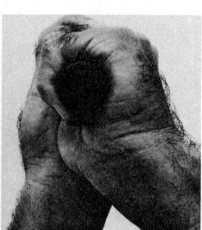

ished in a tie for the sixty-second place.

In the spring of 1940, he won his first tournament, the North and South Open at Pinehurst, North Carolina, and before the campaign had ended, he had added three more. By this time people were beginning to notice the Texan with the mechanical swing. Sportswriters dubbed him "Bantam Ben," although at 5 feet 9 inches and 160 pounds he qualified as a middleweight. He was leading money-winner in 1941 with $18,358 and again in 1942 with $13,143. He finished in a tie for third in the 1941 U.S. Open at Fort Worth, and in 1942, he tied Byron Nelson for the Masters crown, losing in a play-off.

But at this stage, golf was of little consequence. Hitler's Nazi legions were slicing through Europe, and the Japanese had bombed Pearl Harbor. Hogan entered the Army Air Corps as a lieutenant midway in the 1942 season. In special services, he was permitted to play in some tournaments but competition was limited. His old rival, Nelson, unable to enter the service because of medical reasons, immediately took charge of the tour, setting a record at one stage of 11 straight tournament victories.

Returning to the tour after the war, Hogan won the match-play PGA championship, beating Ed ("Porky") Oliver, 6 and 4, in the final at Portland, Oregon, on August 25, 1946. He finished the year as the number-one man on the money list with $42,556. Two years later he won the first of his four U.S. Opens, shooting rounds of 67–72–68–69—276 for a new record. Eight months later he was lying in an El Paso hospital, in traction, his career seemingly shattered.

The comeback in the 1950 Los Angeles and U.S. Opens proved to be only a catapult to greater victories. He won the first of his two Masters in 1951, closing with a methodical 68, and went on to Oakland Hills in Detroit to capture another Open. The massive Oakland Hills course had been converted into a golfer's nightmare for the occasion. New fairway traps had been planted in the normal hitting areas. The fairways were so narrow that golfers complained they had to walk them single file. The rough was like knotted barbed wire.

Through the first three rounds no one was able to break par and none of the competitors was more frustrated than Hogan. In the final round, his face a chiseled picture of determination, Ben carved out a 3-under-par 67. At the formal presentation ceremonies, he said quietly,

ence than he could pick up in prize money. By the time he and Valerie reached Oakland, they had exactly $85. Then they suffered another setback when a thief jacked up their secondhand car and made off with the two rear wheels.

Hogan acknowledged that he was at rope's end. "I knew unless I won enough to give us a new start, I would have to sell the car and head back to Texas," Ben recalled later. "The night before the first round, I didn't sleep at all. I knew how desperate our circumstances were. I don't think I have ever gone into a tournament with more determination. Instead of tightening up and pressing, I forced myself to play every shot with the utmost concentration."

Hogan shot a 66 in the opening round for the tournament lead. He cooled off a bit after that, finished third and collected $385. It was the turning point in his golf career. He managed to survive—little more—by earning $4,150 in 1938 and $5,600 in 1939. He qualified for the United States Open again in 1939 and fin-

Above: The Hogan grip.

"I'm happy I brought the beast to her knees."

Hogan, beaten out in the 1952 Open at Dallas by Hungarian-born Julius Boros, had his greatest year in 1953. In the Masters he shot successive rounds of 70, 69, 66 and 69 for a record 274. In the Open at Oakmont, Pennsylvania, he won by six strokes over runner-up Sam Snead. Then came the British Open.

The Texas Hawk had won every major championship and golfing honor in the United States, but no golfer could call his career complete without once tackling the capricious winds and native treacheries of the Scottish and British seaside links where the game was born. Hogan felt he needed a British Open victory to cement his recognized position as the number-one player in all golf.

The golf-loving British were delighted, but they conceded him little chance of victory. The conditions were different from anything Hogan had experienced in America. The course was hard, craggy, pockmarked. The greens, by Hogan's own description, were "like putty." The British ball was smaller than the American ball. The weather was windy, rainy and cold.

On top of this, Hogan, shortly after his arrival, developed a severe cold. Weak and feverish and draped in layers of sweaters, the Wee Ice Mon finished the tournament with a brilliant 68, winning by 4 strokes. The Scots gave him the greatest ovation any American had received since Bob Jones. His name became a household word. He came home to a ticker-tape parade up New York's Broadway and saw his iron personality crack on the steps of city hall. "You just want to cry," he said. "I owe it to God and my wife, Valerie."

Completion of this Little Slam—the Masters, U.S. Open and British Open in a single season—left Hogan with one remaining goal. He wanted to win a fifth U.S. Open title and move into an exclusive sphere ahead of Bob Jones and Willie Anderson, who shared his record of four.

He appeared to have it in 1955 at San Francisco's Olympic Club, finishing with a 287. But a little-known pro named Jack Fleck from Davenport, Iowa, came out of nowhere with a streak of birdies on the closing holes to tie. The next day, a drained, discouraged Hogan lost the play-off.

In the 1956 Open at Rochester, New York, Ben needed only to par the last two holes to tie Cary Middlecoff for the championship. On the seventy-first hole, he froze over a 30-inch putt, backed off from it and then jabbed at the ball futilely, missing. It seemed to sound the knell of a fabulous career.

"My nerves are shot," Hogan acknowledged later. "I've been feeling my putting going for a long time. It's not the legs that go first—it's the nerves.'"

In the few following years that he competed on a reduced scale, Hogan found himself standing over putts for minutes before bringing the blade through. His confidence shattered, he experimented with putters and techniques, open to any suggestion. "I just don't seem able to bring the club back," he said. "I feel the people's impatience and I can hear them say, 'Go ahead and hit it,' but I just can't."

Hogan made two other strong charges at the Open. In 1959 at Winged Foot in Mamaroneck, New York, he was in the running most of the way but finished five shots back of Bill Casper, the winner. In 1960, at Denver, he was pressing Arnold Palmer until he came to the seventy-first hole. A gambling shot missed by inches and fell into the water. Perhaps an inch more and he would have been on the flag for a birdie and within reach of the coveted fifth Open.

After that, Ben Hogan faded from the scene. With new rules by the U.S. Golf Association exempting only the last five champions, Hogan declined to demean himself by trying to qualify for the Open. He sold his golf club business to American Machine and Foundry Company for a figure reported in the millions but remained on to run the Fort Worth factory. He built a $200,000 home in Forth Worth and settled down to the life of a businessman weekend golfer.

He made only periodic forays into the big time. He played in tournaments at Fort Worth and Houston, where the young Turks of the modern tour would rush out on the course to watch the master strike the ball. In 1967, at the age of 54, Hogan shot a 66 in the third round of the Masters and thousands hugged the eighteenth fairway, standing 40-deep around the eighteenth green to give him a roaring ovation.

Ben tipped the bill of his white cap and smiled one of his rare smiles.

Said a man, walking to an adjoining tee, "He's still the greatest."

WILL GRIMSLEY

Satchel Paige
"If He'd Only Been White"

"If you were only white. . . ."

It was a phrase LeRoy Robert Paige heard for the first time in 1924, the first time he'd mowed down batters who happened to be a different color. It was a phrase still uttered in 1971 when Satchel Paige entered baseball's Hall of Fame through the back door.

For more than two decades he toiled in the Negro Leagues, barred from the majors by skin that happened to be black. Yet despite baseball's color line—or perhaps because of it since the records of the black leagues are sketchy at best—Satchel Paige became a legend.

He never professed bitterness publicly about being kept out of the majors until he was at an age when most players had long since put away their gloves and spikes for good. "I always felt," he said, "like I was a keynote for the colored."

Uncovering his exact records in the Negro leagues from 1926 to 1948 is just as unlikely as uncovering his exact age. And those mysteries, far from being solved by Satch, were rather gleefully encouraged by him.

Even on February 9, 1971, the date of his selection to the Hall of Fame, he sidestepped questions about the year of his birth. Was he 60? Or perhaps 65? Or older? "I really can't hold it in one place," he replied laconically. "Besides, that's pretty close—just like it's always been."

It is also close to the truth that Satchel Paige was the best man ever to pick up a baseball and throw it at—and past—an opposing batter. It is estimated that in his lifetime, Paige pitched in more than 2,500 ball games. He claims to have won 2,000 of them. And of those 2,000 victories, the best estimates credit him with possibly 250 shutouts, including perhaps 100 no-hitters.

More accurate, of course, are the records of his major league performances from his 1948 debut with the Cleveland Indians to a day in 1965 when he threw his last hesitation pitch for the Kansas City A's. By major league standards, his record—28 victories, 31 defeats and an earned run average of 3.29—hardly calls for his enshrinement in the Hall of Fame.

But it was not his major league records that got him there. It was the years in the Negro leagues that did, the years before he followed Jackie Robinson, Larry Doby and Roy Campanella across the color line.

According to the *Baseball Register*, Paige was born July 7, 1906, when a birth certificate in Mobile, Alabama, was made out in the name of LeRoy Page.

"My folks started out by spelling their name *Page* and later stuck in the *i* to make themselves sound more high-tone," disclosed Satch, the seventh of eleven children of his father, John, a gardener, and his mother, Lula, a washerwoman. "But my mom didn't put much stock in that certificate. She told a reporter in 1959 that I was 55 instead of 53—said she had it down in her Bible. Seems like Mom's Bible would know, but she ain't ever shown me the Bible."

Several years later when the subject came up once again, he dismissed it with a shrug and the comment that "the midwife and all the books burned up."

It wasn't until he was about seven that LeRoy became "Satch." It was a day when, in order to bring a little more money into the household, he found himself among the neighborhood youngsters working at the Mobile railroad depot, carrying bags. He got a dime for each one.

"We weren't going to be eating much better if I made only a dime at a time so I got me a pole and some ropes," he said. "That let me sling two, three or four satchels together and carry them at one time. . . . My invention wasn't a smart-looking thing, but it upped my income.

"The other kids all laughed. 'You look like a walking satchel tree,' one of them yelled. They all started yelling it. Soon everybody was calling me that, you know how it is with kids and nicknames. That's when LeRoy Paige became no more and Satchel Paige took over. Nobody called me LeRoy, nobody except my mom and the government."

As the years passed, Satch, just as about any other kid does, became interested in baseball, partly from hanging around or working as

a cleanup boy at the semipro park where the Mobile Tigers played. But he couldn't afford a baseball. So he threw rocks. "That's when I first found out I had control. It was a natural gift, one that let me put a baseball just about where I wanted it about anytime I wanted to. I could hit about anything with one of those rocks."

He was 10 when he switched from rocks to baseballs, making the team at W. H. Council High School—as an outfielder. But one day, after two of the team's pitchers had been hit hard, he got his chance. "I was all arms and legs. When I let go of the ball, I almost fell off that mound. But that ball whipped past three straight batters for strike-outs. I kept pumping for eight more innings. When I was done I had struck out sixteen and hadn't given up a hit."

Suddenly he was the team's number-one pitcher. And just as suddenly, two years later, he was in reform school, the Industrial School for Negro children at Mount Meigs, Alabama, for playing hooky, for fighting and rock-throwing and for getting caught while trying to swipe some toys from a store.

Along with the usual reform school duties, Satch refined his pitching. About five years after entering Mount Meigs, he left and began making a name for himself in sandlot and semipro ball. In 1926, Alex Herman, owner and manager of the Chattanooga Black Lookouts of the Negro Southern League, got a look at Satch.

He liked what he saw and headed straight for the Paige house. Mrs. Paige refused to let Satch go until Herman promised to look after him like a father and send his $50-a-month salary home. And so at 17, Satch, a gangling 6 feet 3 inches, 140 pounds, packed his bags and became a pro.

For the next five years, with teams such as Chattanooga, the Birmingham Black Barons, the Nashville Elite Giants and others, Satch built his reputation. He got his best chance at the end of the 1930 season when he joined the Baltimore Black Sox, a club that barnstormed the country against the Babe Ruth All-Stars.

"Babe wasn't the only big gun on that club," Paige recalled "They had Hack Wilson. He hit over fifty homers and knocked in about a hundred ninety runs in the 1930 season with the Chicago Cubs. And there was Babe Herman. He batted almost four hundred with Brooklyn. I was real curious to see those boys. They were just as curious to see me. I'd done pretty well and they'd heard about it. Fact was, a couple

of my boys told me those major leaguers were laying for me. I was laying for them, too. I beat them Stars easy and struck out Hack Wilson and Babe Herman to boot. Hack came up to me after the game. 'That was some pitching,' he said. 'It looked like you were winding up with a baseball and throwing a pea.' "

The tour wound up in Los Angeles, where he climaxed his performances by striking out 22 batters. "I never counted those twenty-two strike-outs as my one-game record," Satch said years later. "I always said it was eighteen even though I got twenty-two in other games, lots of times. I don't count exhibition games. I know some of the boys ain't in shape when I whiff them in those games."

In 1931, he reached one of his goals. He signed with one of the era's best teams, black or white—Gus Greenlee's Pittsburgh Crawfords. One of his teammates was Josh Gibson.

"There's never been power like Josh's," Paige once said. "He wasn't just a slugger, either. He was a high-average man, too. If I had to rate top hitters, I'd put him ahead of Ted Williams of Boston, Joe DiMaggio of New York and Stan Musial of St. Louis, and right in that order."

With Gibson, Cool Papa Bell, George Perkins, Oscar Charleston and other stars, Paige continued to improve in his years with the Crawfords. In 1933, he appeared in 41 games, compiling a 31–4 record with 16 shutouts. The next season, he made the East Squad in the Negro Leagues' second All-Star Game—and won it with four scoreless innings of relief.

By this time, with more money coming in and other offers waiting to be considered, Satch had become a year-round pitcher, jumping from team to team, sometimes playing for each on a one-day basis—some 250 teams between 1926 and 1948—sometimes working every day for a full week, sometimes hopping down to Mexico, Venezuela, Puerto Rico or the Dominican Republic or barnstorming the country in the off-season.

As he had considered Pittsburgh his home base in the early 1930s with the Crawfords, Kansas City became his home base in the 1940s with another of the Negro leagues' top teams, the Monarchs.

By this time, too, he was advertising himself as "Satchel Paige, world's greatest pitcher, guaranteed to strike out the first nine men." Wearing a shirt with either "Satchel" or "Paige"

Dave Barnhill, New York Cubans, and Paige of the Monarchs.

emblazoned across the front, he would pitch for any team that could meet the $500 to $2,000 he commanded for three innings of work. More often than not, those first nine men would stride up to the plate and trudge back to the dugout, strike-out victims all.

More and more, he was displaying his talents to teams loaded with major league stars —Jimmy Foxx, Hank Greenberg, Ralph Kiner and Joe DiMaggio. His talents were a baffling assortment of pitches—fastballs and curves delivered over the head, submarine style and everywhere in between with any number of speeds. And there was his famous hesitation pitch, in which he planted his foot, halted in midthrow, then fired the ball plateward.

In one memorable game during a barnstorming trip, he and Dizzy Dean hooked up in a scoreless duel through nine innings. As Paige went out for the tenth inning, he met Dizzy coming off the mound. "I don't know what you're going to do, Mr. Dean," Satch drawled, "but I'm not going to give up any runs if we have to stay here all night." And he didn't allow even one run. He won the game when his team scored a run off Dizzy in the thirteenth inning.

"Satchel and me," Dean said afterward, "would be worth a quarter of a million to any major league club. We'd clinch the pennant mathematically by the Fourth of July and go fishin' until the World Series. Between us, we'd win sixty games."

Satch went him one better. "Heck, maybe I'd win all sixty by myself." He just might have. In one exhibition, he faced Rogers Hornsby, one of the game's great right-handed batters, and struck him out five times. In another in 1935, he faced Joe DiMaggio, only one season away from joining the Yankees. In his first three at-bats, DiMaggio struck out twice and fouled out once. Finally, in the tenth inning, he bounced a single through the infield to win the game. One former Yankee scout remembers sending the Yankees a telegram: "DiMaggio all we hoped he'd be; hit Satch one for four." And DiMaggio would say sometime later: "He was the best I ever faced. After I got that hit off him, I knew I was ready for the big leagues."

Paige, of course, had been ready for the big leagues for years. But it wasn't until Robin-

son and Branch Rickey of the Brooklyn Dodgers broke down the racial barrier that the big leagues were ready for Satch.

Bill Veeck's Cleveland Indians were in the middle of an American League pennant fight. And so Veeck, baseball's maverick owner, signed Satchel Paige on July 7, 1948. "That was the day I celebrated my forty-second birthday," Satch would say. "Some liked to say I was forty-two going on forty-nine."

Some called it a publicity stunt—but Veeck said otherwise. "We are convinced he is the best available player who has a chance to help us win the pennant."

Two days later he made his big league debut, coming in to relieve Bob Lemon in the top of the fifth inning. The visiting St. Louis Browns were leading 4–1.

"It seemed like a mighty long walk from the bullpen to the pitcher's mound," Paige recalled. "I didn't go fast. No reason wearing myself out just walking. I just shuffled along, and every time I shuffled, the stands busted loose like they never was so happy to see anyone in their life.

"When I got to the infield, out came all these photographers. There must have been ten of them, popping flashbulbs in my face. They tried crawling over one another to get pictures of me. It was such a mess I just dropped my mouth open and stood there for a minute. I guess maybe history was being made. I was only about ten feet away from being the first Negro ever to plant a spike on an American League pitching mound."

When the bedlam finally died down and Cleveland Manager Lou Boudreau had given him the ball, Paige made it official. He fired, and Chuck Stevens singled. Then Gerry Priddy sacrificed him to second. Up came Whitey Platt. "I gave him my overhand pitch and my side-armer and my underhander and my hesitation. He struck out." Then Al Zarilla hit a flyball for the third out. After one more scoreless inning, Paige was removed for a pinch hitter. "I hadn't set no records, but I'd done what the Indians was paying me for. I'd gotten the side out without giving up any runs in the fifth and sixth innings."

Soon after that, American League president Will Harridge banned Satch's most famous pitch, the hesitation. "He said he'd never seen a pitch like that," Paige said. "He said I was tricking the batters and umpires—having the batters swinging at balls when all the time I had the ball in my hand, having the umpires calling strikes when the catcher thumped his glove, making them lie."

After a two-inning stint against Brooklyn in an exhibition game, Paige got his first victory with a three-hit, three-and-one-third inning relief appearance against the Philadelphia Athletics on July 15. "I was one and nothing in the majors, one and nothing against guys who were in knee pants or weren't even born when I'd started pitching."

On August 3 he became a starter, going against the Washington Senators. By then his record was 1–1, he'd been used eight times in relief and allowed four earned runs in 18 innings. He started off poorly against Washington, giving up a two-run triple to Ed Stewart in the first inning. But he settled down and when he left for a pinch hitter in the bottom of the seventh inning, the Indians were ahead. They stayed there, and Paige had his second victory. And the Indians had a share of the league lead.

He got another victory in relief against the Yankees. Then, on August 13 in Chicago, he shut out the White Sox 5–0 with a five-hitter. A week later before an incredible 78,382 fans in Cleveland, he did it again, this time stopping the White Sox 1–0 on three hits.

Satch finished the 1948 season with a 6–1 record and a more-than-commendable 2.48 earned run average, striking out 45 batters and walking 25 in his 21 games covering 72⅔ innings of work. Veeck had called him "the best available player who has a chance to help us win the pennant." The Indians did, indeed, win it, beating the Boston Red Sox in a play-off game, then winning the World Series in six games against the Boston Braves with Paige getting in for two-thirds of an inning.

However, he was never again to reach such heights. After resuming his usual life of barnstorming following the World Series, he played again for Cleveland in 1949, finishing with a 4–7 record, barnstormed again in 1950 and returned to the majors for three undistinguished years with the St. Louis Browns. He then faded into the minor leagues and beyond before making his farewell appearance on a major league mound with three scoreless innings with the Kansas City A's in 1965 at the incredible age of 59.

But he still wasn't officially finished with the majors. In August, 1968, he donned uniform number 65 for the Atlanta Braves and wore it for the 158 days he needed to qualify for a baseball pension.

"Right now, he is a pitcher," said Atlanta manager Luman Harris who, at 53, was nine years the junior of his pitcher. "He's one of our twenty-five active players. Now I've got to find out if he can pitch." Braves chairman William C. Bartholomay said, "We expect him to get into shape and be ready to pitch when called."

But the call never came. And with the passing of the 1968 season, the career of Satchel Paige finally ended. The man who had spent 22 years as a rookie and had made as much as $44,000 a year waiting to break into the big leagues, retired for good, to live with his wife, Lahoma, and their children in Kansas City.

And on the day he returned to the spotlight, his selection to the separate-but-equal wing of the Hall of Fame, he again pronounced the rule that had kept him going: "Don't look back. Something might be gaining on you."

He had once explained it this way: "When you look back, you know how long you've been going and that just might stop you from going any farther. And with me, there was an awful lot to look back on. So I didn't. That let me keep on going, and keeping going more than anything else made ol' Satch the reputation he had. That and a good fastball."

BRUCE LOWITT

Left: Satch gives a few pointers to Mickey Mantle, Allie Reynolds and Dom DiMaggio at 1952 All-Star game.

George Mikan
Basketball Revolutionist

George Mikan, big number 99 of the Minneapolis Lakers, was the dominant player of his time in professional basketball. With an elastic holding his thick eyeglasses in place, Big George lumbered downcourt and planted himself in the pivot. Grabbing the ball with his huge hands, the 6-foot 10½-inch, 245-pound Mikan then used his elbows and bulk to good advantage as he moved toward the basket before spinning and scoring with his hook shot. Once too awkward to obtain a basketball scholarship at Notre Dame, Mikan developed into a skillful, coordinated athlete at De Paul University in Chicago, where he won all-American honors in 1944, 1945 and 1946 and led the school to the national championship in 1945. From 1947 through 1954, when Mikan was the central attraction in the National Basketball Association, the Lakers were the best team in the game. And only three years after George joined the Minneapolis team, an Associated Press poll of sportswriters and broadcasters named him the best basketball player in the first half of this century.

He became the NBA's first big gate attraction and gave the sport impetus that carried it to popularity in the two decades following his retirement. When he left the NBA after the 1953–54 season, Mikan had scored 11,376 points —about 5,000 more than any other player had compiled at that time. While pacing the Lakers to five league titles in six seasons, he won three scoring championships, finished second twice and third once.

The son of Joe and Minnie Mikan, owners of a restaurant–bar in Joliet, Illinois, George gave little evidence before he was 15 that he would turn out to be something special. Mikan once recalled that winning a marbles championship gave him one of the few pleasures of his early life. Yet he could not enjoy this victory to the fullest. Self-conscious because of his gawkish appearance, Mikan remembered, "In my neighborhood, winning the marble championship was a high honor. Yet all the joy was taken out of it by barbed remarks about 'the big kid taking advantage of all the little kids.' " George also recounted that his primary ambi-

tion had been not to play basketball in Madison Square Garden but to perform as a pianist in Carnegie Hall. "I loved music and I felt I had enough talent to become a concert pianist," he said. "But I was foolish enough to let myself be laughed out of it." George was referring to the derisive jeers from neighborhood youngsters he would encounter on the way to the Joliet Conservatory of Music where he studied. Eventually he left the school rather than be kidded by the others.

He was tall well before he put his name in the record books. George was 5 feet 9 inches when he was 8 years old and reached 6 feet at age 11. "I remember how I used to stoop all the time to make myself look shorter than I really was. I became round-shouldered, ungainly and so filled with bitterness that my height nearly wrecked my life." As a junior in high school George began playing basketball. His younger brother Ed, who was a member of the varsity team, encouraged George to try out.

However, during the summer George broke a leg in a school-yard game. Because the injury did not heal properly, he was bedridden for 18 months. During this period his height reached 6 feet 7 inches. Fed up with being taunted because of his size, George left Joliet Catholic High School after he recovered. He enrolled at Quigly Prep, a seminary in Chicago, 50 miles from his hometown. He said to his mother, "You always wanted one of your sons to become a priest, so it's going to be me." However, a kindly priest at the seminary, suspecting that George wasn't happy in his new surroundings, advised, "When you finish here, George, better just go to a regular college. The priesthood is no place for anybody who's trying to run away from something."

During his last year at the seminary he played basketball for a Catholic Youth Organization team. In 1942, the coach of the CYO team arranged to get him a tryout at Notre Dame. George Keogan, head coach of the Irish, told Mikan, "Your height is a fine asset and you've got the spirit, but you're hopelessly clumsy." However, Ray Meyer, Notre Dame's assistant coach, suggested that George try another college.

Mikan is fouled but manages to put in the basket against the Knicks in 1949. Big George made the Lakers the best team in pro basketball and was named best player of the first half-century.

He decided on De Paul and was accepted. When he arrived at the school, he received a pleasant surprise. Meyer had left Notre Dame and had become the head coach at the Chicago college. Meyer, acknowledging Mikan's potential, put the big guy through a rigorous training schedule. He had him skip rope, shadow box and run. He practiced for long periods with George, feeding him the ball from behind the free-throw circle, and, in alternating 15-minute periods, the tall center worked on left- and right-handed hook shots and tap-ins.

George had a tendency to pivot away from the basket instead of toward it. So that George could learn to pivot correctly, the coach placed folding chairs on both sides of him as he moved toward the basket. Mikan wound up with numerous bruises after a week of knee-banging, but Meyer was satisfied that his mission had been accomplished.

In a short time, George developed an effective hook shot. His coordination improved. He grew more confident. He grew taller. He also found he was no longer easily rankled by spectator taunts such as "Frankenstein" and "monster." In 1945, he led all college basketball players in scoring with a 23.9-point-per-game average. He topped the nation again in 1946 with 23.1. In a magnificent performance in Madison Square Garden in 1945, he poured in 53 points against Rhode Island State.

By the time Mikan had graduated from De Paul in 1946, professional basketball had emerged from the dance halls and church gymnasiums but it had yet to be nationally accepted as a major sport. There were two pro leagues, the National Basketball League and the new Basketball Association of America. The latter circuit sought to sign Mikan, hoping to cash in on his college reputation, but Mikan joined the Chicago Gears of the NBL, signing a five-year contract at $12,000 a year. He came to the Gears in midseason and averaged 16.5 points for 25 games.

When the Gears folded after that season, Mikan became a member of the Minneapolis Lakers. They were among the few clubs in a position to pay off the remainder of his $12,000-a-year contract. In his first full season as a pro, 1947–48, Mikan led the Lakers to the NBL championship, winning the scoring crown with a 21.3 average and gaining unanimous recognition as the league's Most Valuable Player. The following season the NBL and ABA, which had been struggling as separate entities, merged and became the National Basketball Association. Joe Fulks of the Philadelphia Warriors and Max Zaslofsky of the Chicago Stags had been the best-known players in the BAA, but Mikan overshadowed them that first NBA year, pacing the loop in scoring. Interest in professional basketball was increasing. Fans wanted to see this massive giant who was breaking all records. When the Lakers played in Madison Square Garden that year, the marquee outside the storied arena read: Geo. Mikan vs. Knicks.

In that first NBA season Mikan established a single-game scoring record of 48 points. Fulks later eclipsed that mark by scoring 63. Mikan never broke Fulks's mark, but during one period early in 1949, he went on an amazing spree. He hit for 48 points against the Knicks; four days later he tallied 53 against Baltimore; two weeks later he got 51 against New York and, the next week, he poured in 46 against Rochester. Although the Lakers placed only second in the West Division at the regular season's end, they captured the NBA title in the play-offs, as Mikan, despite a broken wrist, averaged more than 30 points in each of the 10 play-off games.

With solid support from big, rugged forwards Jim Pollard and Vern Mikkelsen and speedy guards Slater Martin and Whitey Skoog, coach John Kundla's Lakers built the league's first dynasty. In six years the Lakers had finished first in their division four times and won five play-off titles. Maurice Podoloff, then NBA president, later called the Minneapolis club the greatest contributing factor of the success of the NBA. He also called the Lakers the greatest team in the history of basketball.

Despite Mikan's success, he was occasionally criticized for throwing his weight and elbows around, but he also absorbed considerable punishment. Yet he missed only two games in six NBA seasons, as a result of a respiratory infection.

In 1951–52, attempting to make the league race more competitive, the NBA rules committee widened the foul lanes from 6 to 12 feet and made it illegal for a player to stay in the lanes for more than three seconds. The move was made to thwart the sport's big men, particularly Mikan. However, the altered regulation didn't stop Big George. His average dropped 4 points—to 23.8—but Minneapolis came away with the league title again. Mikan had a number of big nights, scoring 61 points against Rochester and netting 44 or more points nine times that season.

"My big job was to score and rebound," Mikan explained, "but when they ganged up on me, that meant some of my teammates were free. That's when I concentrated on handing off or passing to players breaking around me." Joe Lapchick, who coached the Knicks in many crucial games against the Lakers during Mikan's career, called George "the best feeder out of the pivot the game ever had."

Mikan averaged 18 points a game in 1953–54 and then announced his retirement to begin the practice of law. When asked why he quit basketball at 30, an age at which he obviously could have continued, Mikan said, "I want to quit at a peak of my career, while George Mikan is still George Mikan."

After Mikan retired, the Lakers dropped in the standings and home attendance dipped accordingly. Urged to do so by club management, Mikan made a brief comeback in 1955–56. In the first game of his comeback, he scored only 2 points but 12,000 fans turned out to see him play in Boston Garden. The next night against New York, he scored 20 points. He totaled 370 points in 37 games, increasing his career point total to 11,764. At that time he held the record for career points, single season points—1,932— and career scoring average—22.6. Mikan returned to the game two more times, each in a nonplaying capacity. He took over as coach of the Lakers in 1957–58 but resigned when the club lost 30 of its first 39 games. In 1960, the team moved to Los Angeles. Seven years later, Mikan became the first commissioner of the American Basketball Association. However, when the league office was moved from Minneapolis to New York in 1969, he elected to remain in the Midwest to practice law.

Still, Mikan had left his mark on pro basketball. As he matured, he also found an inner tranquillity. "Once I got rid of my obsession that my height was a frightful bugaboo, I came to realize that for every shortcoming of an oversized body, there is a plus quality to compensate. For instance, I was able to score off bullies without lifting a finger. Once when I was driving on a Minnesota highway, a car in front of me stopped short and I rammed into its rear bumper. The driver rushed at me, fists clenched and shouted, 'Get out of that car!' I stepped out slowly and drew up to my full

Mikan brings ball downcourt in 1950. When he left the NBA in 1954, he had scored 11,376 points and had led his team to five championships.

height. The driver's face paled and he backed away. 'All my fault,' he mumbled. 'Guess I shouldn't have stopped so short.' "

Critics of the lumbering center's playing ability maintain that Mikan would not have been a star had he played during the 1960s and 1970s because the game had become faster and the centers needed to be more mobile. The introduction of the 24-second clock placed a premium on speed and agility. However, Red Auerbach, who saw all the top players while serving as coach and general manager of the Boston Celtics, said about Mikan: "Sure, he had an advantage that there was no 24-second rule. But he would have adjusted to it. That man would have been a stickout anytime, anywhere and under any conditions."

DICK JOYCE

155

Pancho Gonzales
Latin Fire and Fury

A 51-cent tennis racket, a Christmas gift from his Mexican-born mother in 1940, started it. A decade later he was the hottest thing in tennis, equipped with not only a torrid game but also a fiery temper, the kind of temper typically associated with a fiery Latin. A giant-killer when a youth, he maintained that billing into the 1970s. In between, he retired countless times, but he always returned to competition.

Other tennis stars rose and descended during the period from 1948 to 1971. Richard Alonzo ("Pancho") Gonzales was always there. Most of the time his temper stood out as blatantly as the scar on his face that always seemed a barometer of his anger.

So obscure were his beginnings that even his name was invariably misspelled. Pancho himself couldn't decide whether it should be Gonzalez or Gonzales, at times demanding the *z* and later using the *s*.

Regardless of the spelling, Pancho Gonzales captured the favor of the American public in much the same way that another Chicano, Lee Trevino, has done in golf today. Pancho could easily have used Trevino's self-acclaimed title of Super Mex many, many years before the golfer began using it.

Unlike the loquacious, wisecracking Trevino, however, Gonzales was a dour, mechanical workman on the court. He was a killer who put his opponents in a vise with an aggressive attack, who never relaxed the pressure. In his prime, he possessed a magnificent, style-book game with few flaws. He moved around the court like a jungle cat, effortlessly but with lightning quickness. His serve, like a rocket, once was clocked at 110 miles per hour. The racket, which he held with the Eastern, or shake hands, grip, appeared an extension of his right arm. He had remarkable concentration and—according to his fellow players—possessed perhaps the best tactical mind in the sport.

Pancho—called Gorgo by his contemporaries—was a handsome figure, 6 feet 3 inches tall, 185 pounds. Even as he reached his forties, there never was the trace of paunch. Raven-black hair, which developed snowflakes as the years went by, curled around his dark, coppery features. The scar on his left cheek—the result of a childhood car crash—seemed to ignite into a sliver of flame when he became aroused—which was often.

Once locked in battle, Pancho lost all compassion. He carried on constant feuds with his adversaries, linesmen and even spectators. Once, in Boston, he clambered into the stands and grabbed a heckler by the throat. He had to be wrenched from his tormentor, a man who quickly left the arena, pale and shaken.

At the age of 20, he blazed out of nowhere to win the U.S. championship at historic Forest Hills, the U.S. Clay Courts championship and the U.S. Indoor championship, becoming the first player to hold all the titles simultaneously.

His first triumph at Forest Hills had a hollow ring, however, because Ted Schroeder, rated in 1948 as the best amateur player in the United States, hadn't competed. A year later Pancho would prove himself in what has been described as one of tennis's most historic games.

On a hazy September afternoon in 1949, Gonzales squared off against Schroeder in the men's singles final at Forest Hills. Each had resolutely advanced through the pairings in a fashion that later prompted Gonzales to say: "This whole thing resembles the plot of a corny Grade B movie." Gonzales had seethed throughout the entire tourney because he, the defending champion, was seeded number two, behind Schroeder, who hadn't even played the previous year. As the two warmed up for the title match, Schroeder was confident, clowning, laughing and wisecracking. Gonzales, in contrast, was grim and quiet.

Gonzales would later recall how Schroeder would "psyche" him before a big match as they changed clothes in the same dressing room. The outgoing Schroeder would walk over to Pancho and say, "Hello, Pancho."

"Hi, Ted," Gonzales responded.

"Good day for tennis."

'Yeah."

"You know I'm going to beat you again, Pancho. . . ."

The championship match began dramatically. The laughing Schroeder suddenly became

Gonzales at center court, Wimbledon, after one of many retirements.

deadly serious, smacking the ball with vengeance off both sides and lunging to the net behind his high-bounding service. The sellout crowd of 13,000 saw the two giants battle relentlessly. At last, with the score 17–16 in Schroeder's favor in the first set, Pancho fell behind 0–40 on service and finally, after 73 minutes, it was Schroeder's set.

The second set lasted only 24 minutes with Schroeder winning 6–2, giving him an imposing two-set lead. Gonzales decided that his only chance was to go for broke, and he began hitting all out. The strategy worked. Schroeder, who was experiencing a natural letdown, seemed stunned by the savagery of Gonzales's attack. Pancho won four games in a row and took the set 6–1.

During intermission, Gonzales was consoled in the dressing room by Frank Shields, a friend and later a captain of the Davis Cup team. "That was a tough first set to lose," Shields told the young Gonzales.

"I'll get him," vowed Pancho.

And he did, getting an early break in the fourth set and going into a 3–1 lead. Schroeder never came close to cracking Pancho's murderous serve and Gonzales won 6–2, evening the match. As the fifth and decisive set began, Gonzales's confidence was booming, although he realized that his scrappy opponent was considered the best fifth-set player in the world.

Through the first eight games, the set went with the service. In the ninth game, Gonzales got his first break with two magnificent backhand returns and took the lead 5–4. In the next game, Gonzales, serving, fell behind 15–30 with a nervous double fault but forced Schroeder into a volleying error and brought the score to 30–30. Once again, as tension mounted, Gonzales fell behind 30–40, then deuced the score a second time and moved to match point with a perfect placement. The duo engaged in a long rally on the next point until Schroeder hit a blazer down the line. The linesman yelled "out" and the drama was over. It was Pancho's match and his championship.

Born May 9, 1928, the oldest of seven children, Richard Alonzo Gonzales was the son of a Mexican immigrant to Los Angeles. "We had few luxuries in our house," he would later recount. "Food wasn't abundant, but it was simple and filling, and we never went hungry."

He was a good boy, but presented a problem to his hard-working father, who sought to

give all his children the education that he didn't have. Pancho, however, hated school and its regimen, playing hooky whenever possible. He picked up an interest in tennis while hanging around the neighborhood playgrounds. This upset Manuel Antonio Gonzales, who felt that tennis might prevent his son from becoming a success. The mother, nevertheless, bought young Richard that 51-cent tennis racket, and every day he would take it, race to a nearby tennis court and play for hours. His truancy, meanwhile, became more frequent. The boy became very close to Frank Poulain, pro at the Exposition Park Shop, and it was Poulain who told the elder Gonzales that his son should devote even more time to tennis.

"My son doesn't need tennis. He needs an education," insisted Manuel Gonzales.

"The boy will have made more money from tennis by the time he is thirty than you will make in your lifetime," countered Poulain.

El Gorgo at Forest Hills in 1957 (left) and with championship cup in 1949. Gonzales, seeded second, beat defending champion Ted Schroeder, 16–18, 2–6, 6–1, 6–2, 6–4.

The parents gave reluctant approval and young Richard, soon picking up the natural nickname—Pancho—for a Chicano, began playing in junior tournaments, winning his share of matches. Through Poulain he was introduced to Perry Jones, the sport's czar in Southern California who designated the players who went East to the prestigious matches. Pancho discovered quickly that Jones was a stern disciplinarian. When Jones learned that young Gonzales was skipping school, he suspended the youngster, preventing Pancho from playing in big tournaments. Finally Pancho quit, after trying five high schools, and thus no longer had to answer to truant officers. He served a brief stint in the navy.

Eventually, he was reinstated. His first big break came in the Southern California championships when he was 19. He defeated Herbie Flam, who two years earlier had won the national junior crown.

Gonzales made his first appearance at Forest Hills in 1947, winning in the first round but losing a five-setter to Gardnar Mulloy. A year later, Gonzales was the number-eight seed among the U.S. entrants at Forest Hills. He swept past Ladislav Hecht, Gus Ganzenmuller and Art Larsen. Then he won over the top seed, Frankie Parker, a two-time U.S. champion, in four sets; beat Jaroslav Drobny in the semis and downed South Africa's Eric Sturgess for the championship. Gonzales, however, felt that his triumph was by default because Ted Schroeder hadn't competed.

After defeating Schroeder the following year in the historic match at Forest Hills, it was inevitable that Gonzales would go into the professional ranks. He signed for 30 percent of the proceeds in a tour involving himself and the great Jack Kramer. Kramer defeated him in 96 of their 123 matches, and although Gonzales accumulated $75,000 in professional earnings, he got no offers the following year, being told, "People pay only to see winners."

The disillusioned Gonzales returned to Los Angeles, buying the tennis shop at Exposition

Park. He passed his time stringing rackets and selling balls, playing social matches and an occasional exhibition.

By 1954, Kramer had taken over as the promoter of the pro tour, remaining its star as well. He was looking for a new name and turned to Gonzales, who rejoined the tour and began a stormy relationship with Kramer that would go from the tennis courts to the law courts.

Returning from oblivion, Gonzales became the ace drawing card and for the next eight years reigned as the undisputed pro champion. He was never satisfied by his financial arrangements with Kramer and sued to raise his take from 20 percent to 25 percent of the gross. Gonzales claimed that he, and he alone, was responsible for increased crowds in such places as New York, Chicago, Cleveland, Washington and Boston. The courts upheld Kramer.

This didn't stop the feuding, however, and Gonzales continued to press for more money. Kramer finally quit promoting the professional tennis tour, leaving the business to an association of players. Tony Trabert became the association's director and inherited Kramer's controversy with Pancho, who went into temporary retirement again as crowds clamored for his appearance. Without Gonzales, attendance declined.

Pancho wrote several books and bought a tennis ranch in California. In 1964, he was back, winning tournaments in New York and Cleveland. He frequently threatened to retire again, but didn't, more than holding his own on the pro tour and periodically defeating the new champion, Rod Laver.

By 1969, Gonzales was announcing his retirement after almost every tournament he played. In the fall of that year, Pancho crushed Arthur Ashe, Jr., 6–0, 6–2, 6–4, in the finals of the $50,000 Tournament of Champions at Las Vegas, Nevada. "This is the end," he proclaimed. "I now will retire to my tennis ranch."

When the 1970 pro tour opened in Madison Square Garden, Gonzales ended his retirement once again. To the delight of a crowd of 18,000 at the Garden, he whipped Laver, the heavy favorite in a winner-take-all $10,000 match.

Explaining his triumph, the ageless veteran said, "I can't attack and keep attacking. I have to outthink the men I beat now."

Before he turned pro, Gonzales represented

the United States on the 1949 Davis Cup squad. He led the United States to a 4–1 victory over Australia with straight set victories over Frank Sedgman and William Sidwell. The following year, without Gonzales, the U.S. team lost 4–1 to practically the same Australian squad. Later, he served the U.S. Davis Cup team as a coach. A stern disciplinarian who demanded hard work and near perfection, he won the respect of his pupils. But they also feared him. In Australia one year, Gonzales became infuriated over the lackadaisical play of Dennis Ralston, whom he had taught and guided as he would have his own son. Gonzales stormed off the court in a huff, taking the next flight back to the United States.

A national magazine once described Gonzales as "easygoing." A friend's description was much better and more accurate: "Pancho's the most even-tempered man I ever knew," said the friend. "Always mad."

BEN THOMAS

Pancho's fierce temper led him to quit high school as well as the tour several times. In 1971 (above), he was still arguing with officials. Left: With son, Richard.

Rocky Marciano
The Brockton Bull

In 1946, a would-be major league catcher left a Chicago Cubs tryout camp—rejected because of a poor throwing arm. Five years later the power in that same arm brought Rocky Marciano one of the most prestigious prizes in sports, the heavyweight championship of the world. The fierce dedication and pride mixed with that power made him the first heavyweight champion to retire without having lost a professional fight.

"What could be better than walking down any street in any city and knowing that you are the champion?" he asked. Before defending his title against Archie Moore he said, "It would hurt—it would hurt a lot—to find a guy who could lick me. So far, I haven't. It's everything. You lose the title and you lose people's respect and admiration and, of course, you lose money."

But there came a time when the title wasn't everything. "I think it would be taking advantage of my family if I tried to fight any more," Rocky said seven months after the Moore fight September 21, 1955. So he quit, switching his dedication from the ring to his family and business until he died in the crash of a light airplane on a misty Iowa night August 31, 1969, the eve of his forty-sixth birthday.

"You're thinking only of ending it as quickly as possible," said Rocky in explaining his pressure-applying, take-one to-get-one style of fighting. "You find yourself wishing he'd go down, save himself more pain. People say, 'Do you enjoy hurting the other fellow?' Of course not. But it's another man against me. I got to get cruel at fight time. When he's on the verge, I got to get meaner. After a couple of rounds, you feel the guy is your enemy. You got to feel that way. Otherwise you couldn't hurt him. And you got to hurt him."

Marciano hurt Carmine Vingo badly and almost quit fighting because of it. On the night of December 30, 1949, Rocky and Vingo were engaged in a toe-to-toe battle at New York's Madison Square Garden when Vingo was knocked out in the sixth round by a smashing right-hand punch and rushed unconscious to a hospital. Rocky vowed to himself that he would quit fighting if Vingo died. Vingo survived, although he was paralyzed from the waist down. Rocky, noted as a tough man with a dollar, paid $2,000 toward hospital expenses. The day he got married, Rocky said, "I was never so happy in all my life as when I saw Carmine Vingo at the wedding."

It was this compassion that helped make Marciano a popular champion, both to the public and to other fighters. "When he defeated me, I think it hurt him more than it did me," former champion Joe Louis said after Rocky sent him into permanent retirement with an eighth-round knockout October 26, 1951. "He was always talking about it. After the fight, he sent a message to my dressing room saying how sorry he was the fight turned out the way it did." The night he won the title from Jersey Joe Walcott, Rocky said, "I started to holler and I wanted to whoop it up because I was so thrilled at winning. But when I looked at him, all I could think of was how awful he must have felt."

On the night of September 23, 1952, in Philadelphia's Municipal Stadium, Rocky became champion at the age of 29 by knocking out the 38-year-old Walcott in the thirteenth round of one of the great heavyweight title fights. Walcott, expected to circle and box, went after Rocky from the opening bell and dropped him for the first time in his career—his only other knockdown was by Moore in his final fight. "I wasn't hurt," said Rocky, who jumped up quickly. "I took a count of four because I was in good condition and didn't need more rest."

From the time Rocky got up until the time that Walcott didn't, the fight was one of Walcott's experience and aging strength against Rocky's power, stamina and determination. Walcott bled from a gash above his left eye while Rocky was cut above the right eye and on top of the head from contact with Walcott's chin. Rocky had trouble seeing in the seventh and eighth rounds because a foreign substance, possibly the dripping solution from the cut over Walcott's eye, got into both of his eyes. At the end of 12 rounds, Rocky was behind on the cards of the referee and two judges. Then, he

162

Rocky pounds a left to the face of Ezzard Charles.

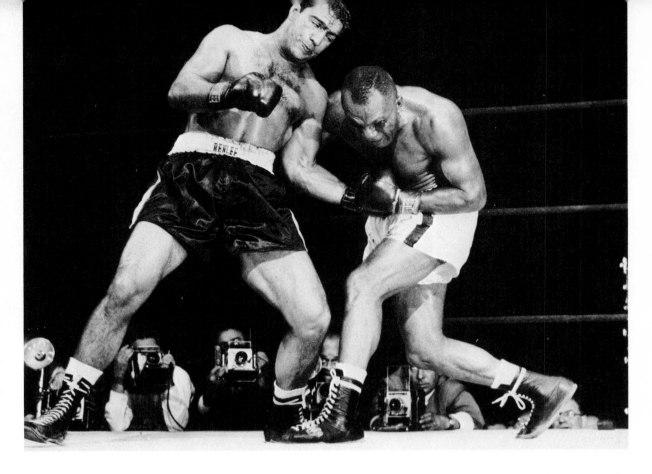

caught Walcott with a clubbing right to the jaw and knocked him out at 43 seconds of the thirteenth round. "I felt that punch down to my heels," said Rocky of the blow that traveled about 12 inches. "I never hit a guy harder in my life."

Rocky defended the title six times. He knocked out Walcott in one round; knocked out Roland LaStarza in 11; outpointed former champion Ezzard Charles, a classy boxer, in 15; shook off the effects of a split nose and knocked out Charles in 8; knocked out Don Cockell in 9 and then knocked out Moore in 9. On April 27, 1956, the man who was called "the Brockton Blockbuster" announced his retirement as the undefeated heavyweight champion of the world. Rocky compiled a pro record of 49 victories, with 43 knockouts, and he did it as one of the smallest men ever to hold boxing's premier title. He stood 5 feet 11 inches and fought at about 185 pounds—Bob Fitzsimmons was the only champion who was lighter —and his 68-inch reach was the shortest of any heavyweight king's.

The eldest of six children, Rocky Marciano was born Rocco Francis Marchegiano in Brockton, Massachusetts, to an Italian immigrant couple, and he came into the world as a heavyweight, weighing 13½ pounds. One of the congratulatory cards that Pietro Marchegiano received upon the birth of his son carried the drawing of a pair of boxing gloves and the words "Hail to the Champ." "I always knew Rocky was going to be champion of something," Pietro once said. "I didn't know whether it was going to be boxing, baseball or football. But I knew he was going to be champion." Rocky liked football and baseball, but he had to quit school at 14 to help support the family. His father was a shoemaker, and Rocky held a variety of jobs, such as ditch digging, candy mixing and truck driving.

Marciano's boxing career unofficially began at an army camp in Wales during World War II when some of his G.I. buddies asked him to take on the camp bully who was making things increasingly unpleasant. "No, I wasn't boxing then," said Rocky. "But I had a reputation of being a tough guy because I was pretty rough in football and baseball games. I had also had some sessions with three wrestlers who tried to pin me and couldn't. Finally, I agreed to fight this guy. It was on a Saturday afternoon, I think. The boys formed a circle and

Heavy going for Jersey Joe Walcott. Above: Marciano digs left into ribs. Left: Rocky measures his opponent backed into the corner. In thirteenth, with a KO, he became the world's champ.

we put on the gloves. I stopped him in two rounds. He quit while he was on the ground. He stopped bothering the fellows."

Rocky began to fight seriously as an amateur after being sent to Fort Lewis, Washington, and he continued to fight as an amateur after his discharge. He lost a championship fight as an amateur, dropping a decision in the Eastern Golden Gloves finals to Coley Wallace, whose main professional claim to fame was a starring role in the movie *The Joe Louis Story*. Then, with his hoped-for baseball career out of reach, Rocky decided to become a pro fighter. Soon after this decision came a move that played a major role in his climb to the title. He got Al Weill as a manager and Charley Goldman as a trainer. Weill was one of the shrewdest managers in boxing history, and Goldman was equally adept at his job.

"Listen, I trained many clean-living fighters—guys like Lou Ambers and Marty Servo—but they didn't live as strict as this guy," Goldman once said in admiration of Marciano's dedication to his craft. "He's always thinking about his condition." But the little trainer's first impression of the future champion was a mixture of doubt and awe. After watching Rocky spar for the first time, Goldman reacted by saying, "He's hopeless. But he can hit like the kick of a mule."

Goldman got an indication of Rocky's power in that first sparring session, against a heavyweight named Wade Chancey, when after two rounds of looking futile, Rocky landed a right hand high on the head that staggered Chancey. Rocky, who had engaged in one pro fight before joining Weill—he knocked out Lee Epperson in three rounds March 17, 1947—

Philadelphia, September 23, 1952, and Jersey Joe is down.

made his first start for Weill and Goldman July 19, 1948, when he knocked out Harry Balzerian in the third round at Providence, Rhode Island. He then closed out the year with 10 more knockouts, 9 of them in Providence where he fought 28 of his 49 fights. He won all 13 fights in 1949, including the one with Vingo, but in two of them he was unable to knock out his opponent. However, it wasn't until the next year that Rocky the brawler proved he could win by decision over a clever boxer by outpointing LaStarza, a later knockout victim in a title fight, in 10 rounds March 24, 1950.

In 1951, Rocky moved closer to the title by knocking out another brawler, Rex Layne, in six rounds and by knocking out Louis. However, it was another fight that year that revealed just how devastating Marciano was in the ring. For six rounds Rocky smashed away at 35-year-old Lee Savold, a 19-year veteran of professional fighting, but when the fight was stopped, Savold was still on his feet and Rocky was criticized in some quarters for his failure to knock down Savold. But the next day Savold went into a hospital with the inside of his mouth ripped, both lips split, gashed above both eyes and in a state of shock. Rocky said he was sorry he had not been able to knock out Savold. Savold was sorry, too.

The fight that earned Marciano his shot with Walcott came July 28, 1952, in Madison Square Garden against highly regarded Harry ("Kid") Matthews, managed by veteran Jack Hurley. Matthews never had a chance, going down and out after a series of left hooks in the second round. Although it was his right-hand punch that was publicized all through Rocky's career, his left hook could render an opponent unconscious with almost equal ease. In the Louis fight, the former great champion kept a careful watch for Rocky's right. Then in the eighth round three left hooks sent Louis crashing to the canvas, where, lying on a strand of the lower ropes, the top half of his body on the ring apron, he was counted out.

After Matthews came Walcott, and the big right hand that brought him the championship of the world. Then came a parade in Brockton, a license plate bearing the word *kayo* and a European tour. Sharing Rocky's triumphs was his wife, Barbara, who also shared with Rocky the price for that glory. Asked once about the grind of training, Rocky replied, "Look, a guy with a bankroll has got something, right? A good-looking guy's got something, right? Well, a guy with a good body, he's got something, too. I always wanted to have strength more than the average guy. It makes you feel proud. As a kid I always admired guys with muscles." But this Spartan drive for the strength and stamina that served him in the ring also kept him away from his family for long periods of time. He complained that every time he returned home from a fight, he had to be reintroduced to his little daughter.

It was these absences that finally drove the man who had earned $1.7 million in purses away from the ring when he was 33 and still at the peak of his earning power as a fighter. "Barbara has been after me to quit for some time," Rocky said in announcing his retirement. "I think it would be taking advantage of my family if I tried to fight any more. At first, I was single. It didn't make any difference then. But the baby makes a lot of difference."

On retiring, Rocky said he would never attempt a comeback, "barring a complete and dire emergency." No such emergency arose, although Rocky did make some investments that proved to be bad. And there was always present the unexplainable urge that has pulled other proud champions out of retirement, most to their regret. In fact, in 1959, Rocky was tempted to make a comeback to the point of working out in secret for a month, but he resisted the temptation to return and concentrated on his post-fighting career, which included investments in a bowling alley, a construction firm, a boat-building company, real estate and fighters. He also tried television performing and nightclub work, and he became active in civic affairs in Fort Lauderdale, Florida, where he eventually settled.

Then in the summer of 1969, Rocky did something he really enjoyed. He went into training and shed 50 pounds so that he and Muhammad Ali could film a series of fight sequences that would be made into a film based on information received and digested by a computer. A month later Rocky was killed in an airplane crash while his wife, 16-year-old daughter and 17-month-old son waited to give him a birthday party. He died not knowing that the computer would declare him the winner over Ali by a knockout in the thirteenth round, the greatest heavyweight who ever lived.

ED SCHUYLER, JR.

Wilbur Shaw
Flirtation with Death

Though his life had been a constant flirtation with death, now for the first time, Wilbur Shaw was not in control of himself or his surroundings. Only minutes before, he had been leading the Indianapolis 500 by more than a full lap with enough fuel to go the distance. If his Maserati held together, Shaw would become the first driver ever to win the biggest auto race in the world three years straight and the only driver to win it four times. There was big money ahead, more than any amount he had ever seen before, enough to make him and his wife, Boots, secure for life.

It was there, just ahead, 48 more laps around the famed Indianapolis Motor Speedway—a fabulous 2.5-mile oval that Shaw knew like the palm of his hand. He had practically lived at the Speedway for 13 years; he loved it as no man before or since. It had been good to him, it had made him famous the world over; it had opened doors that would have been available in no other way. He was about to conquer the old Brickyard again. All he needed was for the Italian-made car to take that extra deep breath and carry him the final miles to victory.

The Maserati was an old friend. He had driven it to victory in 1937 and in 1939. He had driven it in races around the country and it had never failed him. True, it was now showing its age, a bag of nuts and bolts, but it was still a good car, the best around—that is, when Shaw was driving it. He had helped unload it from the boat a few years before, he had given it its first shakedown runs on American soil, and he and the car had become good friends, buddies in a common cause. He had nursed the sleek, red machine as a mother nurses her first-born, as a father takes pride in his son.

But as Shaw swung the heavy machine into the Speedway's first turn, the Maserati faltered. It seemed to sway a bit, as if a gust of wind had lifted her tail and swung her around. Whatever it was—later, it was found that some of the spokes in the right rear wheel had come loose—the red monster tore itself from Shaw's grasp and headed for the concrete retaining wall. Nothing the slight but muscular Shaw could do would prevent a collision. The Maserati

crumpled, and Shaw had finally lost control.

Wilbur Shaw had had narrow escapes before during a full racing career that had carried him around the world twice, to the hell-for-leather dust-bowl racing tracks in every nook and cranny of this country and Canada. Once, he had been seriously hurt in a crash at a track in California, but he had survived, largely without the help of doctors. Now he lay flat on his back in a hospital, surrounded by doctors. Faced with serious consequences for the first time in his racing life, he pondered the future while the doctors worked.

"My mind was in a turmoil," he said later in his official biography. "Although I was comparatively free of pain, I couldn't move my legs. What if my bowels and kidneys were paralyzed? What if I could never race again? What if I was destined to be a wheelchair invalid for the remainder of my life? All these thoughts flashed through my mind, over and over."

He also pondered, as perhaps only a Wilbur Shaw would do at a time like that, the loss to his bank account. "I couldn't help thinking about all that cash which had been knocked out of my hands by the crash. My share of the prize money, for winning, would have been peanuts compared to what I would have been able to get for endorsements of certain products as the Speedway's only four-time winner and three in a row to my credit. At a conservative estimate, I would have been in a position to collect between $150,000 and $200,000 simply by signing my name to some contracts."

Wilbur Shaw, one of America's greatest racing drivers, did survive the accident. Not only that, he himself tore the cast off his body a few days later and let his crushed vertebra heal by itself. Indeed, he was back behind the wheel of a passenger car within a matter of days—off to California. There were always parties, big parties, just around the corner and Shaw wasn't the kind of person who would miss them, serious injuries or not.

Wilbur Shaw, adventurer, sportsman, a tiger on the tracks, flier, husband and father, was born in Edwardsville, Indiana, not far from Indianapolis, in October, 1902. His father, a

A grimy Shaw signals a third victory in Indianapolis 500.

policeman on the Edwardsville force and later an insurance executive, was an outdoorsman, an inveterate tobacco-chewer and "the best parent a son could ever have." His mother was a cultured, God-fearing woman, a practical, industrious person who valued security and loved music and the arts. They divorced while Wilbur was young, and his mother later remarried.

After completing the fifth grade, Shaw moved to Indianapolis with his mother and a stepfather to whom he became attached later in life. He became the star diver on the YMCA swim team, joined the Boy Scouts and delivered the *Saturday Evening Post*. Later, at Muscle Shoals, Alabama, he worked part-time as an office sweeper, where his stepfather, Clay Morgan, was working. He then moved up to a $50-a-week job as a "spy" for the project superintendent, reporting on the other workers. But he returned to Indianapolis in time to finish high school, in time to deliver the class speech.

The Speedway was not too far from the Morgan home, but Shaw took no more interest in it than most normal boys; that is, until May, 1916, when Stutz became a factor. Though a foreign car and driver won that year, Shaw became a Stutz fan and moved up to Cloud Nine when he went to work at the Stutz factory installing batteries in the new cars. He also learned to chew tobacco.

Another big disappointment of his life came when, at the start of World War I, he tried to enlist in the Marine Corps and was turned down for being too small. The fact that he had donned his first pair of long pants only the day before he went to the recruiting office didn't help. He broke down and wept in the office when they rejected him. He went back to work in the battery factory.

Shaw was 19 when a friend introduced him to Bill Hunt, who built and drove race cars from his shop, the Speedway Engineering Company. He got a job there washing parts, and he also took the first step toward a career that was to lead him to the Indianapolis Motor Speedway, where during a period of seven consecutive years he was first three times, second twice and seventh once—a record no one matched for years. Salvaging parts from Hunt's shop, he built his first race car in the upstairs portion of a building he took over in a remote section of Indianapolis. He and a friend were forced to bump a hole in the rear of the second floor to get the racer to the street.

He saw his first race when he drove a truck bearing Hunt's racer to Hamilton, Ohio. Hunt overturned the car and was injured, and he gave some words of advice to the pint-sized Shaw—"This isn't a very safe business. Anyone who doesn't want to die young ought to stay out of it."

The spark had been struck, however. Shaw described his first visit to a race track like this: "Almost overnight, my already intense desire to become a race driver developed into what might be termed a mania. I didn't even want to take time out to sleep." He hardly did. Working night and day, he got his "Imperial Special" ready for the debut of both driver and car at the Hoosier Motor Speedway, a half-mile course on the outskirts of Indianapolis. He had completed two laps of practice, hardly at speed, when he was flagged off the track and told to go home. Two weeks later, he showed up at another half-mile track at Lafayette. Hunt was also there in that spring of 1921 and again cautioned Shaw that "racing is a risky business and these dirt tracks can be treacherous," adding with some force, "You haven't got a chance." Shaw's reply: "I have got to start somewhere, and it might as well be here." Hunt finally prevailed on Shaw to let him qualify the car, and he put it on the front row. Wilbur Shaw, destined to become one of America's sports celebrities, though success was still a long way off, got his long-awaited chance to prove his mettle.

After some hasty instructions from Hunt, mainly "Don't worry, you'll feel it in the seat of your pants after a few laps," the field was flagged off and Shaw was on his way. The cars hadn't completed a lap before, as Shaw put it, things started happening all at once. His car got sideways, then slid into a rut, then leveled off as the wheels came down. But another rut grabbed the right wheels, pulling the car into a complete roll and taking a big section of the fence with it. Shaw climbed out of the wreckage with nothing more than a few bruises and dejection on his face.

Though his first race had been a disastrous one, Shaw had made an impression. His spirit, his obvious determination to be a race driver, his courage and his natural talent had caught the eyes of other car owners. He got rides on several Midwestern tracks and he won, first a heat race that paid the magnificent sum of $18, then later feature events. By 1924, he had won the National Light Car champion-

ship, and promoters were seeking his services with "deal" (appearance) money. He became a driver to be reckoned with, and the people who operated the big speedway at Indianapolis took notice.

Shaw arrived at the Brickyard for the first time in 1927, having first met, hurriedly courted and married Beatrice Patrick, whom he described as a "blonde Irish Madonna." He was assigned a car owned by Fred ("Fritz") Holliday. The car had a history. It was the one in which Jimmy Murphy had been killed at Syracuse in 1924. It had been rebuilt by a little-known California mechanic named Louie Meyer, who later became a three-time Indianapolis winner. It was named the "Jinx Special," a fact that alone should have scared the daylights out of a 23-year-old rookie. The car was known around Gasoline Alley as "Murphy's death car," and no one else would touch it— particularly against the likes of Lou Schneider, Tommy Milton, Frank Lockhart, Pete DePaolo,

Dutch Bauman, Al Cotey and Benny Shoaff, all of whom were old hands at the Speedway. Milton was Shaw's personal idol and the two later became fast friends.

The prerace tension almost got to the slightly built rookie even before his first race. He described it: "My temples were throbbing, my lips seemed dry and parched, my heart was in my throat and the muscles in my chest seemed to have such a stranglehold on my lungs that I had to make a conscious effort to breathe."

Shaw had been brought up as a "Sunday School kid" by his doting mother. Racing men as a rule aren't demonstrably religious, but Shaw always maintained that men who live dangerously, such·as race drivers, are a little closer to their Maker than is the average person. Thus it was that Shaw spoke his private prayer, "Thy will be done," as the cars moved off. He drove well and had the car in seventh place when Meyer relieved him for a spell mid-

Shaw pushes his Maserati to 1939 Indy triumph.

way in the race. Attrition among the cars ahead allowed him to finish fourth for a payoff of $3,500. It was a highly creditable showing for a rookie with a car that admittedly was 10 to 12 miles per hour slower than the regulars.

Shaw was one of the original "spit and polish" men of auto racing. The first one was Ralph dePalma, the 1915 winner, who always dressed at the peak of fashion, who made his mechanics do the same when they were out of the garage area, who ate at the best places, who ran with the best people and who carried himself as a gentleman always. Shaw was a chip off the same cultural block. Always nattily dressed, he was articulate, polished and a storyteller of note even before he became the Speedway's personal ambassador in later years. He lived "high off the hog," drank often but wisely and liked parties where he and his friends could regale each others with stories of racing. As

he became more famous, his circle of friends widened to include the Ford family of Dearborn and top officials of Chevrolet, Firestone and other big auto and accessory concerns. He was himself a top mechanic, an exacting supervisor of his crew and a strategist of the first order when it came to planning the execution of a race.

He became a regular on the big-car championship circuit that stretched from one side of the country to the other, including dirt tracks, board tracks, road courses and later the paved ovals. He was at Milwaukee for a race when informed that his wife, Beatrice, had died in Detroit during childbirth. It was months before he recovered from the shock, but recover he did and a few months later came into what he called the luckiest day of his life. He walked into a showroom in Detroit, bought a new Auburn Speedster and met Cathleen Stearns. Be-

Above: Wilbur Shaw poses with friends before Indy race in 1940, a year before his big accident. Afterward, Shaw would become the track's president and general manager.

cause she reminded him of the shapely girl who played the title role in the comic strip *Boots and Her Buddies*, Shaw promptly named her "Boots." And he married her after another whirlwind courtship. She was his constant companion and his tower of strength throughout the most successful part of his career.

Shaw made several speed record runs, both at Bonneville Salt Flats, Utah, and at Daytona Beach, Florida. He also drove in a high-speed boat race in Cuba and won it. During the height of his career, he went to Europe to race, and it was there that he became familiar with, and an admirer of, the Italian Maserati that carried him to victory at Indianapolis in 1939 and 1940. He had won in 1937 with a Miller that he co-owned.

Shaw had implicit confidence in his ability as a race driver. His friends said he never hesitated to admit he was the best. Thus, when he once traveled to the West Coast with Mauri Rose, who became the next three-time Indianapolis winner behind Shaw, he became somewhat irritated with Rose's opinion of himself. "Mauri spent almost all of the time telling me what a wonderful driver he was," Shaw told friends later. "According to him, no one else knew half as much about racing as he did and this was particularly irritating to me because I was equally certain I was the best in the business. Frankly, I have never known any top-ranking driver who didn't have such an opinion of himself, but Mauri had not yet learned to voice his opinion with a proper amount of restraint." Shaw and Rose later became friends, and Shaw in the years to come was to gain increasing respect for the latter's ability as a driver.

It was in California that Shaw suffered his first serious injuries in a race car. At the famous old Ascot track near Los Angeles, he slammed into the wall and wound up with several broken ribs. Another time, he blew a tire at Ascot and wound up upside down on the retaining fence, giving West Coast photographers one of the best action pictures ever taken in racing. He also got "skinned a bit" when he and his riding mechanic sailed over the wall at Indianapolis in 1931.

But Shaw was always in control until that near-fatal day at Indy in 1941 when the Maserati failed him. He had been "too little and too young" to get into World War I, and he was "a bit too old" to make it into World War II.

But his contribution to the war effort was important, nonetheless, for he became director of the Firestone Tire and Rubber Company's aviation products division. His fertile mind first developed a puncture-proof fuel cell for fighter planes and later for tires that would keep the heavy aircraft from sinking into the mud and mire of European landing fields.

His ride in the Maserati in 1941 was his last at the old Brickyard he loved so well. But he was not finished there. He arranged for the sale of the Speedway property to Anton ("Tony") Hulman, Jr., acting as the principal agent between Hulman and the former owner, Eddie Rickenbacker. Not only that, Shaw became the track's president and general manager under Hulman and began the task of restoring the vast plant to a high plane of respectability. He pushed himself to make the Speedway a success, and it was under his direction and that of Hulman that the old Brickyard began its unbroken string of crowd sellouts in the mid- and late-1940s.

He pushed himself so hard that he suffered a major coronary while flagging a Soap Box Derby event at Akron in 1949, and for the second time in his life, he lost control. He recovered, as only Wilbur Shaw could, and for several years lived the life of a country gentleman with his wife and son, Warren Wilbur Shaw, Jr., born to the couple after almost 16 years of marriage, on a small ranch he bought outside Indianapolis.

Wilbur Shaw, crack race driver, man-about-town, slight, powerful, handsome with a small thin mustache that was a trademark for 30 years, had learned to fly during one of his many winters in California. Ironically, it was his second love, an airplane, that placed him for the third time in a position over which he had no control. He and two companions were returning to Indianapolis in a light plane from a trip to Michigan on October 30, 1954. The sky was overcast; the temperature on the ground two degrees. Snow was falling and two other planes in the area reported "icing" conditions.

At 4:19 P.M. that day, Shaw's plane crashed to earth in a cornfield near Decatur, Indiana, carrying its three riders to their deaths. The flirtation was over.

BLOYS BRITT

Ted Williams
Last of the .400 Hitters

The final day of the 1941 season for the Boston Red Sox dawned cold and dreary in Philadelphia. It was one of those late September days when a blanket of dull gray clouds blocks out the warming rays of the sun, a miserable day for baseball. So, why the turnout of 10,000 bundled-up fans at old Shibe Park on that particular afternoon? The New York Yankees long since had eliminated the runner-up Red Sox from the pennant race, and Connie Mack's Athletics were in eighth place—the cellar—for the fifth time in seven seasons. The Philadelphia faithful, along with a contingent of visitors from Boston, had shown up for a single purpose: to see whether Boston's tall, gangling young left fielder, Theodore Samuel Williams, would make baseball history.

Not since Bill Terry of the New York Giants had turned the trick 11 seasons earlier had a major league player batted .400. Not since Terry's big year had any player gone into the final day with a real chance to do so. The Kid had a shot at it, a good shot. This slugging Red Sox outfielder, a month short of his twenty-third birthday and already a national celebrity, was hitting .39955.

Williams wasn't particularly happy about that day. He always said he was a warm-weather player and, in fact, might not have been carrying that lofty batting average had it not been for a preseason accident. He chipped a bone in his ankle while on a fishing trip and sat on the bench until warm weather arrived. When he finally got into the lineup, he hit like a man with a mission and at one point in June possessed an unbelievable .436 average. And this was during that brief period when the sacrifice fly counted as both a time at bat and an out.

Every opposing pitcher had been aware of that .436 average. Each one had saved his best stuff for the Kid, and the average dipped to .402 until a spurt sent it back to .413. Then the cool weather returned and Williams lost nearly a point a day the last two weeks before the closing-day doubleheader. His .39955 would have gone into the record books as an even .400 had he not played on September 28 at Philadel-

phia. They round it off for the books. But that wasn't for Williams. "Hell, Joe, I want to play," he told Joe Cronin when the Boston manager suggested he could skip the games. "If I'm going to be a four hundred hitter, I want to earn it all the way."

Williams recounted the story years later, how he and Johnny Orlando, Boston equipment manager, walked the streets of Philadelphia for hours the night before that doubleheader, talking about this and that but mostly about baseball and mostly about Dick Fowler and other Philadelphia pitchers and about Ted's chances of getting some hits. It was Orlando who, when Williams showed up at the Red Sox spring training camp at Sarasota, Florida, in March of 1938, sized him up and asked, "Who are you?"

"Ted Williams."

Orlando, alluding to the fact that the heralded 19-year-old prospect was two weeks late in reporting, commented wryly, "So, the Kid has finally arrived. You dress over there with the other rookies, Kid."

The nickname stuck. Williams was known as the Kid to all of baseball when he went to the plate in that season finale against Fowler, a right-hander who later would pitch a no-hitter. Williams recalled that catcher Frank Hayes wished him luck and added, "Mr. Mack told us if we let up on you, he'll run us out of baseball. So, we're not giving you a damn thing."

The Kid took the first pitch—he usually took the first pitch the first time up in a game—then lashed a liner between first and second base for a single. The next time up he unloaded, sending the ball over the right-field wall for a home run. Now, most of the 10,000 were on their feet, roaring in approval as Williams rounded the bases. Two for two, and the batting average was up to .402. If they expected the Kid to acknowledge the applause, they would be disappointed. But, of course, no one in the crowd expected him to.

Let other players respond to the cheers, not Williams. This had become his trademark. Not once since his rookie season of 1939—when he

The Kid shows his batting stance in 1940, a year in which he hit .344 and led the league with 134 runs scored. A year later he would become the last man to hit .400.

did it regularly—not once had he tipped his cap in appreciation, not even when he hit a home run in what he and the fans knew was his final time at bat in a big league career spanning more than two decades. That was at Boston's Fenway Park in 1960 on another cold, cloudy September afternoon. They presented him with a plaque and silver bowl in a ceremony at home plate and formally retired his uniform number, number 9. He was almost 42 years old and had been mellowing. He recalled years later that he almost tipped his cap that day, but he didn't. "I vowed I'd never do it again when I realized that a lot of those guys cheering on a home run or a good catch were the same ones who led the boos at other times," Williams explained. "Maybe an inning before, they were knocking my brains out for making an error. I hate front runners, people who are with you when you're up and against you when you're down."

There were no boos in Philadelphia for the Kid. The Athletics brought on Porter Vaughan, a lefty he'd never seen pitch, and Williams rapped him for two singles. In the second game, he singled again and hit a towering double to right. That was it, six hits in eight trips and a season average of .406, best in the majors since Rogers Hornsby's .424 for St. Louis in 1924. Not a single player hit .400 in any of the next 30 seasons, and only one even made a real run at it, an old fellow named Ted Williams. It was 1957 and he said that summer, "I'm getting the breaks, but I don't have the legs. I never was real fast, but if I had the speed I once had, I'd have a chance. You have to have the legs to beat out a few hits." The Kid—they still called him that—finished with a .388. He needed only five additional hits to finish above .400. Most of baseball agreed as the seasons passed that in all likelihood Williams would be the last of the .400 hitters.

All of baseball agreed that Williams was the greatest hitter of his time, if not the greatest of all time. And, certainly no one could argue that the Kid was for two decades the most controversial sports figure in America. He was called more things than just "the Kid" or "the Splendid Splinter" during his stormy, colorful career as a player. He was called a draft dodger, a spoiled brat, a malcontent, an individualist without team spirit, unpatriotic, a slacker. Fans in the bleachers said worse things. Writers dubbed him "the Splendid Spitter" or "Tempes-

tuous Ted" when angry at him, "Mr. Clutch" and "Our Teddy" when reveling in his success.

Our Teddy was born in San Diego in 1918. His father ran a small photographic studio, specializing in passport pictures and portraits; his mother was a full-time Salvation Army worker. Ted and his younger brother, Danny, didn't see much of their parents. The small frame home was less than two blocks from a city playground, where you would find Ted whenever he could get a friend to accompany him. He liked most sports, but mostly he liked baseball. The playground was lighted until 9 P.M., and Ted usually was the last to leave. On the playground or in the schoolyard, you'd usually find him at bat or yelling to someone that he was next up. Hit, hit, hit—that apparently was all he wanted to do. In his book on batting, written some 40 years later, Williams claimed that he practiced batting more than any other person in the world. He maintained that hitting a baseball is the most difficult feat in all of sports. When he retired, he estimated that he had been at bat 200,000 times, only 7,706 of which were in regular major league games.

"I'd rather swing a bat than do anything else in the world," he confided to a reporter midway through his career. He didn't know any reporters when he secretly decided he wanted to be the greatest hitter of all time. As a youth, he made this wish whenever he spotted a shooting star. It was during the formative years that Ted also got interested in fishing. Ted, a perfectionist at everything he attempted, would spend hours fly casting from his front porch. He claimed that if he weren't the greatest hitter of all time, he had to be one of the best fishermen who ever lived.

Williams was taller than most kids his age, but extremely thin. He was sensitive and worried about it and constantly tried to gain weight. He developed an affinity for milk shakes at an early age but seldom had the money for them. When he reached Boston, he averaged four or five a day, earning from his teammates the tag "Malted Milk Kid." Williams was 6 feet 3 inches but weighed only 148 pounds when, at the age of 17, he was signed by the San Diego Padres of the Pacific Coast League. One scout advised Ted's mother not to let him play baseball, saying he was so frail that one season would kill him. Perhaps not Splendid at that point, but certainly a Splinter.

Ted was a good hitter, both for distance

and average, even as a tenth-grader. On his first day of practice at Herbert Hoover High, he hit a couple out of sight. His coach's one reservation was the youngster's apparent lack of speed. The coach was always after him to run faster. Ted wished throughout his career he had been endowed with the speed of a young Mickey Mantle or Willie Mays, saying it would have meant at least 30 additional hits a year for him.

His first time at bat in organized baseball was anything but auspicious. Williams recalled that he was petrified when he made his debut as a pinch hitter. He went out on three strikes down the middle without a swing of the bat. A few weeks later, after the Red Sox picked up his option, he volunteered as a relief pitcher in a game hopelessly lost. He got two doubles but wasn't doing too well on the mound. Manager Frank Shellenback put in another pitcher but sent Williams to left field, where he played the remainder of the season.

He hit .271 that season and, in 1937, collected 132 hits, 23 of them home runs, and drove in 98 runs while hitting .291. Then the Red Sox signed him, and he reported to the Boston club for 1938 spring training. He had to float a loan to get to Sarasota and was farmed almost immediately to Minneapolis of the American Association. His parting shot, after borrowing bus fare for the trip to the Minneapolis camp from his new friend Johnny Orlando, the Boston equipment manager, was: "Tell 'em I'll be back. And tell those outfielders I'm going to wind up making more money than all three of them put together." Williams by his own admission was a cocky youngster. He called everyone "Sport." Perhaps addressing manager Cronin in this manner helped speed his departure to the farm club.

Minneapolis was a picnic. Williams scored 130 runs, hit 43 home runs, batted in 142 and averaged .366, best in the league in all four

Williams avoids Birdie Tebbetts's tag as he leads the 1946 Red Sox to their first pennant in 28 years. He batted .342 that year and was voted Most Valuable Player.

departments. He was extremely popular with the fans, who weren't concerned about his mental lapses in the field and some occasionally inept base-running. He could hit. Williams was back in Sarasota the next spring, just as he had promised, and he remained with the Red Sox for the next 22 seasons, with time out for two tours of duty in the Marine Corps. He became the highest-paid player in baseball, and when his salary reached $100,000, it far exceeded the combined pay of the team's three regular outfielders of 1938.

Ted now was a much better hitter than when sent to the farm club the previous spring, thanks to a gradual physical maturing and to the many hours he spent with Rogers Hornsby. The Minneapolis coach talked hitting with Williams day after day and ordered extra batting practice for the budding star on every possible occasion. Even after his playing days ended and Williams was manager of the Washington Senators and then the Texas Rangers, discussing the science and theory of hitting was a favorite pastime of his. He was never too busy to talk batting, and he wouldn't be in camp a week before he would know pretty much what to expect of most of the pitchers in the league.

The Kid was now 6 feet 4 inches tall and had fleshed out to 175 pounds. He played a good exhibition season and was the regular left fielder when the Red Sox broke camp. The Boston writers already were predicting stardom for the Kid, and 10 months later they voted him Rookie of the Year. He batted .327 and his 145 RBIs led the league. Overall, 1939 was a happy season for the youngster. With only a few exceptions, he kept his temper and tongue in check and he got along well with the reporters and fans. That was the year he tipped his cap.

Then came 1940. He began to hear some boos and began to read stories written about him that he considered unfair. The writers noted that he didn't hit to left field, that he occasionally didn't seem to run to first base as fast as they thought he should, that he wasn't the best at covering ground or handling the ball in the outfield, that he wasn't particularly chummy with his teammates. Some of the wolves in the bleachers took their cue from what the columnists wrote, and they wrote plenty when Williams commented one day that he would rather be a fireman than a baseball player. From that day on, Williams firmly believed that a large

segment of the Boston press was the enemy. And, he marked down those bleacher fans as allies of the press. He said years later, "I felt a lot of people didn't like me. I did things I was ashamed of and sorry for and yet know I would do again under the same circumstances because that was me."

After a particularly trying day in August, when he had heard the boos—in a crowd of cheers, he could always pick out the few boos—the Kid criticized the Boston community, its newspapers and reporters and its fans. And, he told the writers, he wanted to be traded to Detroit. They printed it. The next day there were more boos. Williams hit at his tormentors again, this time complaining about his $12,500 salary, calling it "peanuts." When that got into print, teammate Jimmy Foxx called Williams "a spoiled boy." The columnists wrote that Williams was creating dissension on the team. The Kid seethed, but he also thrived on the controversy that engulfed him. He hit .344 that season and led the league in runs scored with 134.

It was perhaps strange that this great player, so outspoken so often, never argued with umpires. He occasionally questioned a decision but never argued about it. He was never thrown out of a game. He also was rarely at odds with either his teammates or players from other teams. The few player feuds involving Williams that the columnists reported were mostly figments of their own imaginations. Williams said that he had never had a dispute with Tom Yawkey, owner of the Red Sox, not even over contracts. He never was a holdout.

How could this man live in apparent harmony with one segment of baseball and be so much at odds with the writers and fans? Even Williams had difficulty trying to explain it. He wrote in his biography nine years after retiring as a player: "I was and am too complex a personality, too much confusion of boyish enthusiasm and bitter experience to be completely understood by everybody. . . . I think, however, that The Kid who made the sports page jump was never the same person to himself as he was to the reader, and maybe not the same even to the people who knew him. I think it is natural that I regret that deception."

Indeed he did make the sports page jump.

He won the 1941 All-Star Game with a dramatic three-run homer in the bottom of the ninth inning when the American League was trailing 5–4 with two outs. He called it the most

thrilling hit of his life, even more exciting than batting .406 that season. It must have been quite a disappointment not to have been named Most Valuable Player. That award went to Joe DiMaggio of the Yankees, who hit safely in 56 consecutive games.

America was now at war, and before the next season rolled around, Williams received a military deferment as the sole' supporter of his mother. He was booed everywhere he played. He was termed a draft dodger. He won his third batting championship, averaging .356. Two months after the season ended, he began the first of two tours of duty with the Marine Corps that took more than four-and-a-half seasons of baseball from him. On the second tour, called up at the age of 34, he flew jet planes in 38 combat missions over Korea and returned a hero.

He led the 1946 Boston team to its first pennant in 28 long years, batting .342 and also being named Most Valuable Player. But that year brought one of 'the great disappointments of his career. The Kid got only five hits, all singles, and drove in only one run in the World Series against St. Louis. His batting average for the Series was .200. DiMaggio nosed him out by one point in MVP balloting the next year, but Williams received the award for a second time in 1949. In 1950, the Red Sox star became the highest-paid player in baseball, signing a contract reported at $88,000. He was to receive as much as $135,000 before his retirement.

If he wasn't making headlines one way, the Kid was doing it another way. He made an obscene gesture and spat toward the crowd during a game at Fenway Park in 1950; he criticized his team's spirit in a radio broadcast in 1951; he called draft boards, politicians and writers "gutless" during an interview in 1956; he spat toward the stands when booed for dropping a flyball and was fined $5,000; he threw a bat that struck a woman spectator after being called out on strikes in 1958; he spat at the fans again.

All the while, Williams was steadily compiling a lifetime batting average of .344. He won the last of his six batting championships in 1958 at the age of 40, the oldest player in the majors to win a title. He was a member of the American League all-star team for 16 years and, at the conclusion of his career, held a host of major league records, among them runs scored and bases on balls the most consecutive playing years. He led the American League in runs batted in three times and tied for the lead once. He led in doubles two years, in home runs four years and in runs scored six years.

Three years after his retirement, Williams told a group of newsmen he had no regrets. "I don't think I'd do a single thing differently if I were starting out again—except maybe concentrate a bit more on fielding. And I certainly wouldn't feel any different about most of you writers! You haven't changed a bit. Just the other day you misquoted me again."

Perhaps some of the writers changed a little, and maybe the Kid changed some, too. In 1969, Williams was lured back into baseball as manager of the Washington Senators by a five-year contract at $65,000 annually and an option to buy 10 percent of the club. The columnists speculated on whether this loner, this man with the terrible temper, could handle a group of players. He handled the players so well that he was named American League Manager of the Year. He also handled the press all right, so well in fact that stories described him as cooperative and patient during interviews. He was relaxed and smiled a lot. Several columnists from Boston even went so far as to describe him as downright friendly.

It could be that the writers had softened him up a little bit back in 1966 when they paid him the ultimate tribute. That was when the chips were down, when it came time to rate him on ability alone. The writers voted him into baseball's Hall of Fame on a landslide vote the first time he was eligible.

JACK SIMMS

Williams came out of retirement to manage the Washington Senators. In his first year he was named Manager of the Year.

Gordie Howe
Silken Scoring Touch

Bryan Watson, a small but aggressive defenseman in the National Hockey League, remembers his first game in the big leagues. It was against the Red Wings. "I was with the Canadiens then, and they threw me out to kill a penalty. I went into the corner with Howe, knocked him down from behind and skated away with the puck. I hadn't gone very far before I heard heavy strides coming up behind me, and then I felt a stick slipping under my arm. Then there's the blade—not an inch from my nose. It's Howe and he says, 'Check out, junior.' I got so scared I fell down."

Gordie Howe spent 25 years of his adult life on ice. His performances excited spectators and left opponents hot under the collar. "Howe is everything you'd expect an ideal hockey player to be," a rival once said. "He's soft-spoken and thoughtful. He's also the most vicious, cruel and mean man I've ever met in a hockey game."

"Gordie took a lot of unnecessary abuse his first year or two in the league," recalls Lefty Wilson, the Red Wings' trainer. "We were on an overnight trip from Montreal and I told him that. I got him riled up a bit, and the next game in Boston he tagged the first guy that bothered him. Then it went around the league, 'Don't fool with Howe.' "

The goalies in hockey's big league had an even tougher time against Howe. While there was some small doubt about whether he was the game's best fistfighter of his era, there was no doubt that he was the game's most prolific goal scorer of his or any other era. When he retired at 43 on September 9, 1971, he had accumulated 786 goals in regular season play, 232 more than the runner-up, Bobby Hull of Chicago. He held the records, too, for most games played, 1,687; most assists, 1,023; most points, 1,809; most games, including play-offs, 1,841; most goals, including play-offs, 853; most assists, including play-offs, 1,114, and sundry other records compiled in Stanley Cup and all-star game competition. In career regular season penalty minutes, he trailed only Ted Lindsay, a former Detroit teammate, 1,643 to 1,808. He had been named the league's Most

Valuable Player six times and was its top scorer six times. He was on the all-star first or second team a total of 21 times.

"If I had my choice of any one player—at the age of twenty-one—I'd have to take Howe," said Frank ("King") Clancy, whose own career in the NHL spanned 50 years as a player, coach, general manager and referee. "He is the complete hockey player—the greatest ever in the NHL."

Howe kept his motor running at an accelerated pace during most of his 25 years with the team that represented Motor City. He loved to score. But he also derived considerable satisfaction from setting up a teammate for a goal. In the last game of the 1959–60 season, for example, Red Wing rookie Murray Oliver needed one goal to collect a cash bonus for netting 20 goals. Midway through the game Howe told Oliver, "The next time we're on ice, get in front of the net." Oliver followed instructions. Howe carried the puck to the blue line, shot and Oliver tipped the puck into the net for the score. Then, in an uncharacteristic burst of bravado, Howe skated to the Detroit bench and called out, "Anyone else need any bonus money?"

Gordie himself was earning $100,000 annually for playing hockey during the two years preceding his retirement, but his Hall of Fame career began most modestly in Floral, Saskatchewan, Canada. Gordie's family—he was the sixth of nine children—was suffering through the Depression. They were on relief, and Gordie got his first pair of ice skates when he was five years old in a grab-bag parcel his mother bought for a dollar. By wearing several pairs of socks, Gordie was able to get them to fit, and he started out as a goalie on the frigid 50-below-zero outdoor rinks of his hometown. "When I played goalie," he once recounted, "I used to skate a mile from my house to the rink, holding the pads up in front of me to cut the wind. At one rink they had a heated shack. A guy would ring a cowbell and the forward lines and the defense for both teams would go off and sit in the shack by the potbellied stove to warm up while the alternates played."

Howe is taken out of the play by Rangers' Walt Tkaczuk, although word around the NHL was "don't fool with Howe." Gordie's reputation was as the league's most dangerous man.

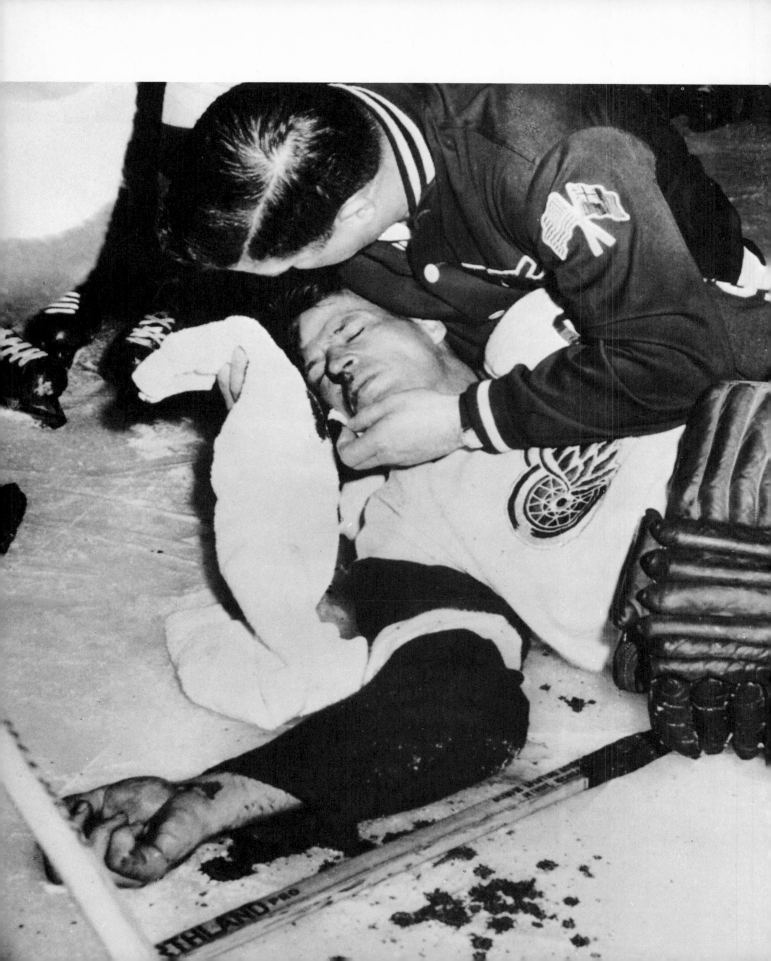

The kid got cold feet about playing goal after two years, moving out of the cage in order to become a forward. He was shy and had few friends. While other boys spent their time pranking together, Gordie remained alone, usually practicing his hockey. Such dedication sharpened his skills. Added strength came from his job on a construction gang, where he worked pouring concrete. He had quit high school after one year.

Organized hockey beckoned when Howe was 14. A New York Ranger scout named Russ McCorry sent him off to Winnipeg, 500 miles from home, where a tryout camp was being held. Some people in hockey have claimed that the Rangers overlooked the quiet prairie youngster, but Howe explains that he was homesick and fled back to Saskatoon, where his family had moved. Two years later, the Red Wings managed to hogtie the young prospect. Fred Pickney, a Detroit scout, saw Gordie in a church league and sent him to the club's tryout camp in Windsor, Ontario. There Jack Adams, then the autocratic general manager and coach of the team, saw him for the first time.

"Gordie was a big, rangy youngster who skated so easily and always seemed so perfectly balanced," Adams was to recall later, "it tickled me to watch him. So I called him over to the boards and said, 'What's your name, son?' A lot of kids that age choke up when they start talking to you. But he just looked me in the eye and said real easy, 'My name's Howe.' I then remember saying, 'If you practice hard enough and try hard enough, maybe you'll make good someday.' "

Shortly after signing with Detroit, Howe was standing in the hallway outside Adams's office. He looked heartsick. "What's the matter?" Adams asked. "Well," Gordie replied, "you promised me a Red Wing jacket, but I don't have it yet." The youngster got his jacket.

Howe scored 7 goals as a rookie, 16 as a sophomore and 12 his third year in the major league when injuries held him to only 40 games. But from then on, he was a superman. He played the full 70-game schedule for five straight years and produced goal-scoring totals of 35, 43, 47, 49 and 33. Even at 40 years of age—in the 1968–69 campaign—he wound up with 44 goals, and in his final season he recorded 23. Although few players would tangle with him in a corner of the rink or anywhere else, Gordie showed about 300 stitches in his face, had had ribs broken three times, had suffered a shoulder dislocation, had undergone operations on both knees, had had several toes broken, a wrist fractured and two serious head injuries. He played 15 games one year with a broken right wrist in a cast and still won a scoring title.

One head injury occurred in 1961 when he ran into Eddie Shack in Toronto. The other, more serious, happened during the 1950 Cup play-offs, just three days before Gordie's twenty-second birthday. It came as a result of a collision with Ted Kennedy of the Maple Leafs, and at 3 A.M. Howe underwent brain surgery to save his life. In that one accident, he fractured his skull, cheekbone and nose and received deep cuts on his right eyeball. In moments of stress, he still suffers from a compulsive blinking of his eyes because of that accident.

"I once went out on the ice and tried to imitate Gordie," said the low-scoring Bryan Watson. "I hit a few guys, took a few shots and blinked all over the place. But it didn't do me much good. There's only one Gordie Howe."

Gordie considered a good season one in which he scored from 30 to 35 goals. He scored 30 or more goals 14 times during his career. He also considered it a good year when stitches in his face were kept at a minimum. In hockey it is not unusual for a player to be gashed by a stick or skate blade, taken to the rink clinic, sewn up and hustled back to the ice. Stitches are merit badges.

"They add up fast when you get the big ones," Howe said. "I remember that Continental Life used to insure us. They'd give you five dollars a stitch. But they cut that out in a hurry. They changed it and gave you five or ten dollars per cut requiring a stitch and that turned out to be a losing proposition for them, too. Once, I had a real good year. I had less than five stitches."

His first serious injury was not incurred in a hockey game. "I got hurt while playing with friends in Saskatoon," he said. "I conked my head on the ground. It was frozen during winter. I was jumping and horsing around and whatever I was jumping at, I didn't make it. I couldn't have been more than seven or eight years old. I was knocked out for something like twenty-four or twenty-six hours. The other kids ran and told my mother I was dead."

He suffered his most serious injury in that Stanley Cup game on March 28, 1950. Early

Howe's life on the ice was always perilous. In 1950, he suffered a collision that led to brain surgery. In another (left), he fractured his skull, cheekbone and nose.

in the second period, Ted Kennedy was carrying the puck and Howe skated close to the sideboards, looking to throw a check. Suddenly Kennedy stopped short and the Detroit star tumbled face-first into the thick wooden sideboards. The Toronto player had lifted his stick just before Gordie fell and some accused him of deliberately hitting Howe with it.

"The only thing I remember," Howe explained later, "is that Kennedy was coming down the left side and I was trying to squeeze him off. His stick blade came up. Then I went into the boards and that's all I remember."

Gordie remembered next that he was being prepared for brain surgery. Adams, the general manager, had telephoned Saskatoon for permission from Howe's mother to drill into his skull. "It looked pretty bad," Adams recounted a few years after the incident. "When they got him into bed, he started to bleed from the nose and mouth. I stayed there and held his hand until the doctor sent me out."

"I did awake and realized something was going on," the young right wing related after recovering. "Then they started shaving my head and I thought, 'Hell, no.' They kept scraping the bottom of my foot with something. Then I remember the drilling to relieve the pressure."

A 90-minute operation by Dr. Frederic Schreiber, a brain specialist, saved Gordie's life. Twenty-six days after surgery, Gordie was released from the hospital and permitted to attend the Red Wings' seventh game of the final Cup series against the New York Rangers in Detroit. The Wings won the game 4–3 on Pete Babando's goal in the second sudden-death overtime period. When the ancient silver mug was pushed out to center ice, the crowd spontaneously shouted, "We want Howe! We want Howe!" Gordie walked onto the ice, a soft fedora covering his scarred head. Ted Lindsay, a teammate, grabbed the hat and sent it flying into the stands, then fondly tapped Gordie's head and joked, "You big lucky stiff. You sit in the seats and watch us go out and make a couple of thousand dollars for you." When the Cup presentation ceremony at midice had ended, Howe was given the Cup and he carried it through the milling, cheering crowd to the Detroit dressing room.

From 1950–51 through 1954–55, the Red Wings placed first in the six-team circuit, extending their string of pennants to seven. They won the Cup in 1952, 1954 and 1955. Howe's greatest play-off game as a scorer came in the 1955 finals against Montreal. The series was deadlocked at two games apiece when he beat goalie Jacques Plante for three goals as the Wings recorded a 5–1 triumph in Detroit's Olympia Stadium. The Canadiens evened the series once more by winning in Montreal, but Detroit won the Cup on its own ice with a 3–1 victory. Howe got the opening goal, his ninth of the play-offs, and a linemate, Alex Delvecchio, scored the other two. Howe led all scorers in goals and total points with 20.

Howe, the goal scorer, could flick his huge wrists with silken strength and mongoose quickness. His wrist shot once was timed at 114.2 miles per hour. It was the game's most accurate shot, and Gordie, the only truly ambidextrous player in the NHL, could score with equal facility from either side of his body. He used a 21-ounce stick made of Canadian ash that had only a slight bend of the blade and an extremely stiff handle. "Give Gordie a stick with an ordinary handle," said Lefty Wilson, the trainer, "and he'll break it like a toothpick. He is so strong that when he shoots, that handle bends like a banana."

"The only way to stop Howe is to crowd him, stop him before he gets started," explained Kent Douglas, a defenseman. "But nobody wants to crowd him. Nobody even wants to get near him."

Howe's surgical touch with the stick would not have made him the menace he was without the physique behind it. The 6-foot, 205-pounder had the long, thick neck and sloping shoulders that distinguished a number of other powerful athletes, among them Joe Louis and Paul Hornung. His neck measured 17 inches and his arms were so long that the shoulders of some of his jackets had to be padded to give definition to his upper body. Strength, shot, savvy— all these combined in Howe with a deep, smoldering drive never to be beaten.

In the 1956 play-offs against Toronto, someone threatened to "come after" Gordie Howe and kill him. The Wings had won the first two games of the series in Detroit and were hoping for number three on the night of March 24. "In the second game I gave Tod Sloan of the Leafs a hard body check. He was hurt bad enough to sit out the rest of the game, and it looked as though he would have to be sidelined for the next few days, at least," Howe said. "The following day, a Toronto newspaper

received a letter from an unidentified person that said that if Ted Lindsay and I played for the Wings in Maple Leaf Gardens the next night we both would be shot."

Although the threat was regarded as the work of a crackpot, Toronto's chief of detectives, Alex McCathie, ordered 12 special plain-clothes policemen to guard Howe and Lindsay around the clock and accompany them to the rink.

"We were sure it was a crackpot," Gordie said. "We joked about it in the dressing room. We even had a plan to really drive the guy nuts. Marcel Bonin was playing for our club, and we decided to put number nine on the front of Bonin's uniform and Lindsay's number seven on the back. But our coach wouldn't let us do it."

Both Howe and Lindsay scored in the third period, enabling Detroit to overcome a Toronto lead and sending the game into overtime. In the extra period, Gordie and defenseman Bob Goldham set up Lindsay for the winning goal. "As soon as he scored, Ted turned his stick around, aimed it at the crowd and made like he was shooting a machine gun," Howe recalled afterward. "But I think that Ted and I hustled off the ice into the dressing room just a little faster than usual that night."

Canadiens' followers, most of them French Canadian, revered the memory of the retired Maurice Richard's colorful and dramatic performances for the Flying Frenchmen. They had been reluctant to concede that Howe was as good or better than their Rocket, who

Teammate Alex Delvecchio helps Howe off ice.

had scored 544 goals, the league record until it was shattered by the Detroit right wing. Applause for Gordie in the Montreal Forum usually was polite, but unenthusiastic. How could it have been otherwise for Howe in the Rocket's domain? It was different, though, on October 20, 1965.

A capacity crowd of 13,531 looked on as the All-Stars, of which Howe was a member, and the Canadiens stood on the sidelines while awaiting introductions by the public address announcer. The All-Stars were introduced first, and as each player's name was called, he skated out to take a position on the blue line designated for his team. Cheers greeted each All-Star. However, when the PA system blared, "And wearing number nine, Detroit's Gordie Howe," the stadium vibrated. Feet pounded the floor and cheers thundered through the vast building for several minutes. And then Howe characteristically showed why he deserved the unusual ovation. He scored two goals and assisted on two others as the Stars won 5–2.

Between 1957 and 1964, Howe averaged between 40 and 45 minutes for each 60-minute game—almost twice as much as most forwards. This once prompted Toronto's Dave Keon to remark: "There are four strong teams in this league—Toronto, Chicago, Montreal and Gordie Howe." On November 10, 1963, Gordie scored career goal number 545—eclipsing Richard's record—beating goalie Charlie Hodge of Montreal at 15:06 of the second period. He reached 600 goals on November 27, 1965, once more at the expense of the Canadiens, although Gump Worsley was in the nets. Goal number 700 came on December 4, 1968, with Les Binkley of Pittsburgh the victim. That night he recalled that he had scored his first NHL goal 23 years earlier by putting the puck past Toronto's Turk Broda. "I also lost two teeth in that game," he said.

He rarely lost anything in subsequent games, winning many newspaper decisions in the fights in which he participated. The most celebrated battle took place in Madison Square Garden during the 1958–59 season when Lou Fontinato was playing defense for the Rangers.

The initial spark had been ignited between Howe and Eddie Shack, a wild skating wing who was assigned to cover the Detroit star. Shack came out of a tangle with Howe sporting a cut that took three stitches to close. As Shack quarreled behind the net with Gordie, Fontinato zeroed in on Howe and smashed him into the boards. Both dropped their gloves and Fontinato went in low at Howe, firing the first punches. Gordie used his left hand to grab Fontinato's sweater, then drove his right fist into Lou's nose. Fontinato crumpled to the ice, his nose broken. A Red Wing teammate related in awed tones: "Howe's punches went whop-whop-whop —just like someone chopping wood." A few months after being pounded by Howe, Fontinato and Gordie met at a dinner in Canada. A mutual friend was in the middle and said to Lou: "I guess you know Gordie Howe." Fontinato replied, "I guess so, but I'm not sure I should lower my hands to shake with him." Then Lou smiled and the two shook hands.

There was considerable handshaking in the team's front office on the afternoon of September 9, 1971, when Howe officially announced his retirement after 25 years as a Red Wing playing star and accepted an executive position with the club. Four months later during a nationally televised ceremony at the Olympia, the club management retired Howe's number 9 jersey. Among those present was Vice-President Spiro Agnew.

A year before Howe retired, his wife, Colleen, had remarked, "You know, everybody has always expected so much from Gordie and he's never let them down. I just hope it's remembered when his legs go."

She needn't have worried.

BEN OLAN

In 1969, Howe was still battling for the puck (left), but his career was coming to a close. In 1971, at a luncheon with his wife, he finally quit.

Dr. Roger Bannister
A Barrier to Break

On a chilly, blustery May evening in 1954, a few hundred people at the Iffley Sports Ground on the outskirts of Oxford, England, watched the most historic track-and-field meet of all time. Roger Bannister, a tall and slimly built English medical student of 25, became the first man in the world to run the mile in less than 4 minutes. His time was 3:59.4.

The medical student was an essential part of the record breaker. Bannister, with his knowledge of the human body, had spent years calculating by trial and error how much stress the heart and lungs would stand. He had learned how to push himself onward—onward until he could go no more—and how to time that moment of collapse to the very second when he crossed the finish line.

Breaking the 4-minute barrier had been the dream of milers for years. At one time it really was just a dream, for many coaches and medical experts held it was physically impossible. No human being was capable of such effort, they argued.

That was in the days of Thomas Conneff, the Irish-American who set a world record of 4:15.6 for the mile in 1895 and held it for almost 16 years. During the twenties, the era of the great Paavo Nurmi, the record stood at 4:10.4.

In 1933, Jack Lovelock, the black-vested New Zealander, pushed it down to 4:07.6 and the barrier seemed less a dream. Immediately after World War II, in July, 1945, Gundar Haegg of Sweden set a record of 4:01.04 and suddenly the barrier actually appeared vulnerable. Sydney Wooderson, setting a new British mark of 4:04.2 in the same year, gave British runners new incentive.

Bannister's interest in the mile started at age 18 when he began medical studies at Oxford University. Rowing had been his sport at school, and his first thoughts at Oxford were to row for the university against Cambridge in the historic Varsity Boat Race on the Thames River. But one of Bannister's strong points throughout his athletic career was his remarkable capacity for self-analysis and self-criticism. He soon decided that he was too light to be a top-rank oarsman and concentrated on cross-country running instead.

They were short of milers at Oxford that year. Bannister was persuaded to run against Cambridge in the intervarsity track-and-field meet and, in the first time he had run the mile in a competitive race, stunned everybody by winning.

From then on the mile became Bannister's obsession. The experts agreed he had a look of greatness. With his elegant, flowing action he covered 7 feet 6 inches at one stride, compared with the average miler's stride of about 5 feet.

In 1948, he won the intervarsity mile again and was invited to join the British team preparing for the Olympics, which were to be held at the White City, London.

Bannister rejected the offer. Even at 19, with the Olympic dream of every young athlete in front of him, he knew how to pace himself. "I'm too young," he told the British selectors.

While he remained at Oxford, victory in the intervarsity mile each year was a foregone conclusion. He won it four years running. The third time was in 1949, when he set an intervarsity record of 4:16.2.

That was the year Bannister began to think seriously of attacking the 4-minute barrier. He toured the United States with a combined Oxford and Cambridge team and clocked 4:11.9 against Harvard and Yale and 4:11.1 against Cornell and Princeton. In the race at Princeton he was watched admiringly by Lovelock, who had set his world record on that same track in 1933.

All this time the tall, gangling Englishman was studying his lap speeds, varying them by a second here and a half-second there, experimenting with his finishing burst and trying to squeeze the last fraction of a second out of the final quarter.

In 1952, Bannister's friends found their faith slipping. He ran in only one competitive mile and clocked 4:10.6. And in the Olympics at Helsinki, he managed only fourth place in the 1,500 meters. Josef Barthel of Luxembourg scored an upset victory. Bannister finished the race with his face contorted in pain after a

Roger Bannister is held up after winning mile in 3:58.8 at British Empire Games in 1954. A doctor, Bannister made it a point to know how much the heart and lungs could take.

lung-tearing burst down the home straight and complained he had had to run three strenuous races in four days.

Then came 1953. In that year Bannister found a friend and pacemaker in Chris Chataway, who became an important part of track history. Chataway was among Britain's best milers in his day, but he knew he wasn't as good as Bannister, so he unselfishly dedicated his efforts to helping Bannister to attack the 4-minute barrier.

In May, 1953, the pair teamed up for the British Amateur Athletic Association (AAA) team against Oxford University at Motspur Park. Chataway set the pace for three laps and then pulled out and let his friend get on with it. Bannister ran a last lap of 58.6 and finished in 4:03.6, cracking Wooderson's British record, which had stood for nine years.

One month later Bannister and Chataway ran unexpectedly in an invitation mile in a children's event at Motspur Park and did even better. This time, after Chataway had done his pacing act, Bannister clocked 4:02.0, the third-

fastest time ever recorded. It was calculated that on the stroke of 4 minutes, Bannister was about 14 yards short of the finish line.

But this time there was trouble. Bannister had entered the race quietly and without advance publicity because he wanted to see whether he could run better if he were freed from the pressure of public interest. Hardly a soul knew that he and Chataway were going to be there. And the British Amateur Athletic Board didn't like it. It refused to recognize Bannister's time as a British record.

For one thing, the board said, this was not a bona fide competitive event. And for another, "the Board does not regard individual record attempts as in the best interests of athletics as a whole."

Bannister was not the first ambitious athlete to be rebuked and hindered by administrators bound by the letter of the rules. He didn't let it bother him. It wasn't the British record he was after. He was edging closer and closer to that 4-minute barrier.

"I have just reached Camp Six on the way

England, May 6, 1954. Bannister (41) let Chris Brasher (44) set the pace, then allowed Chris Chataway (left) to take over. At the end, Bannister had broken the 4-minute mile.

up the runner's Mount Everest," he said.

It was a well-timed analogy. Edmund Hillary and Sherpa Tenzing had just become the first mountaineers to reach the very peak of the great mountain. All Britain was Everest-conscious. And as Bannister prepared for his final assault on the citadel, Britons became 4-minute-mile-conscious too.

In August that year Bannister claimed his first world record—or at least a share in it. Teaming with Chataway, Bill Nankeville and Don Seaman, he ran as anchor man in 4:07.6 and helped to set a world mark of 16:41.0 for the 4-mile relay.

Then came the evening at Iffley—May 6, 1954. It was a fantastic night in many ways. Bannister and his friends had again avoided publicity as much as possible, believing that a quiet atmosphere would be of psychological help in shattering the barrier. Only a handful of newsmen and photographers, scenting that something big might happen, turned up to watch.

The attempt on the 4-minute barrier almost never took place. An hour before the race, a 25-mile-an-hour wind was blowing and the flag on the tower of historic Iffley Church, overlooking the field, stood straight out. Bannister's friends told him it was no night to attempt a fast speed.

He agreed—until five minutes before the start. The wind had begun to drop. Bannister looked at the church. The flag was still out but fluttering quite gently.

"I'm going ahead," he said, rather like Eisenhower leading the invasion of Normandy across the rough English Channel in 1944. "I feel this is a chance to do it."

Bannister not only wanted to crack the 4-minute barrier, but he wanted to be the first man. And he knew that John Landy of Australia and Barthel of Luxembourg were training hard in America, bent on the same idea. It could be now or never.

This time British track officials were prepared for anything. They sent three official timekeepers and made sure that the match, between the AAA and Oxford University, was properly constituted.

Chris Brasher and Chris Chataway acted as pacemakers. Bannister made a special request that progress times be announced over the loudspeakers at every 220 yards instead of the usual 440 yards. Every yard of that mile was mapped out in his mind.

Brasher set the pace for the first two laps. He finished the first circuit in 57.4, with Bannister one-tenth of a second behind him. At the half-mile Brasher was timed in 1:58.0 and Bannister was two-tenths of a second later. On the third lap Chataway, acting to a finely judged plan, sprang forward and took over the lead. Brasher, his job done, dropped back. At the bell Chataway was timed in 3:00.4 and Bannister in 3:00.5.

The crowd, small but knowledgeable, knew exactly what was happening. Bannister ran at Chataway's heels and a wave of excited cheering followed him around the track.

He glanced at the church. The flag was hanging limply now at the side of the staff. Chataway slowed 250 yards from home and Bannister surged to the front. Every spectator was dancing up and down in the mounting excitement.

Bannister said afterward that as he ran down the home straight, everything started to go black and the tape at the finish line contracted to a dim shape in front of him. As he crossed it, he collapsed into the arms of waiting friends. Spectators swarmed across the track and the other runners were lost in the throng.

A minute later the official result was announced over the loudspeakers with typical stiff-lipped British formality. "The event of Event Number Nine, the One Mile," the announcer said as if he were reading the lesson in church. "R. G. Bannister, three minutes. . . ."

Nobody heard any more. The announcer's voice was drowned by the cheers. Bannister stood panting with his arms around the shoulders of two friends for support. His mother was there to give him a hug.

Later Bannister explained that he had listened to the 220-yard progress times as he ran and that everything had gone exactly as he had planned. The times:
220 yards–28.7
440 yards–57.5
660 yards–1:27.5
880 yards–1:58.2
1,100 yards–2:29.6
1,320 yards–3:00.5
1,540 yards–3:30.4
1,760 yards–3:59.4
Bannister was exactly two seconds inside Haegg's world record, which had stood for nine years. The Swede had run the first and third laps faster, but it was the final lap that made

the difference between the two performances. Below the two great runners are compared, lap by lap:

Haegg, 1945	Bannister, 1954
56.6	57.5
61.9	60.7
61.2	62.3
61.7	58.9

Bannister's world record stood for only a short time. Seven weeks later Landy set a new mark of 3:58.0 at Turku, Finland. But Bannister had been the first man to break the barrier and his glory was undimmed. In the next year or two, as one runner after another got inside 4 minutes, his image remained larger than any of them.

When the news of Landy's Turku run reached London, a telephone call was made to Bannister, who was delighted at hearing of the Australian's success. The reaction was genuine and spontaneous.

"I'm so pleased," he said warmly. "The boy has tried so hard. Records are made to be broken." Then he wanted to know Landy's lap times.

Bannister never held the world record again, but he mastered Landy in a memorable face-to-face encounter at the Commonwealth Games at Vancouver that same summer. The race was heralded as the greatest mile of all time. The two rivals went away on their own and nobody else was ever in the race. Landy, taking short steps against Bannister's long, flowing stride, led all the way until the final bend, but the Englishman's finishing burst was decisive. He crossed the line in 3:58.8, with Landy at his heels in 3:59.6.

Afterward it was learned that Landy had cut his foot the day before the race, but he insisted that it hadn't affected his running. "I can never beat Bannister," he said. "He is the greatest of us all."

Analyzing himself, Bannister once said that he was too long in the legs to be a sprinter and lacked sustained stamina for distance running. "In a sprint you have to run as fast as possible," he said. "In a distance race you can almost forget everything until the last two laps. But in a mile you are thinking all the time of what the other runners are doing, and planning, and of when not to be provoked into making your effort, of when you should make it, and many other things."

Later, in the games at Vancouver, Jim

Above: The day after breaking the "barrier," Dr. Bannister is hoisted high by fellow medical students. Right: With his wife, Moyra, and four children.

Peters, British marathon runner, collapsed near the finish line, and doctors were seriously worried about his condition. Bannister took him into his personal care and looked after him until the team reached home. It was a reminder for the British public that their 4-minute-mile hero was now a qualified doctor as well as the world's greatest middle-distance runner and that the days of his athletic career were numbered.

Bannister went straight on to the European Games at Berne and won the 1,500 meters gold medal in 3:43.8 after producing a tremendous finishing burst over the last 300 meters. The next Olympics at Melbourne were two years away, and British fans felt that at last they had a gold medal coming their way in the 1,500 meters after having spent more than 30 long years in the wilderness. But the doctor had run his last big race.

At the end of 1954, Bannister took a post at a London hospital and announced his retirement from athletics. "I will not have the same time for training now," he said. "I could get little satisfaction from a second-rate performance and, anyway, it would not be right to give a second-rate performance when representing my country."

He never ran again, but he continued giving his spare time to sports and helping young athletes. He became one of the most respected men in Britain. He served on various national committees that helped sports and planned new playing fields, and in 1971, he became the chairman of the Sports Council, a national advisory body set up with government backing.

Bannister the athlete was a man of deeds, not words. He seldom had much to say to interviewers, just a polite word or two explaining his tactics. But in later years he spoke out fearlessly whenever he considered it his duty. He constantly warned young athletes against drinking, smoking and taking drugs.

He protested loudly against the choice of Mexico, with its high altitude, for the Olympics of 1968 and said that athletes were being used as guinea pigs. He campaigned against government taxes on sports events and equipment. He pleaded repeatedly for more playing fields for British youth and launched public appeal funds to pay for them. He called for a British national academy of sport.

His own boyhood was spent in Harrow, on the northwest corner of London, at the foot of the hill on which the famous school stands. Harrow School playing fields have helped to produce many world class runners but, as Bannister said, the ordinary boys and girls of the Harrow district were less fortunate.

"When I was a schoolboy, I had to climb fences to find fields big enough to run about in," he said. "One night I ran into some concrete blocks and I ended up in the hospital. I want to see playing fields available to every youngster in Britain so that nobody need have an experience like that."

Bannister became a physician at a hospital for nervous diseases. He and his Swedish wife, Moyra, had two boys and two girls.

"The human spirit is indomitable," he declared. "There will never be a time when the human spirit will not be able to better existing world marks. Man is capable of running a mile in three-and-a-half minutes."

Every year, on the anniversary of the first sub-4-minute mile, Bannister, Chataway and Brasher meet with their wives for a celebration. Bannister always insisted that the other two had as much to do with his achievement as he did.

Bannister's time of 3:59.4 was overshadowed by a wave of sub-4-minute miles, but, viewed in retrospect, it was the most important time of all. He was the athlete who proved, more than any other, that nothing is impossible. His words became the clarion call of every athlete who set out to achieve a great goal.

"The mental approach is one of the most important things in running," he said. "The man who can drive himself further, once the effort gets painful, is the man who will win. Most people train by racing. I tried to make each race an event in my life."

GEOFFREY MILLER

194

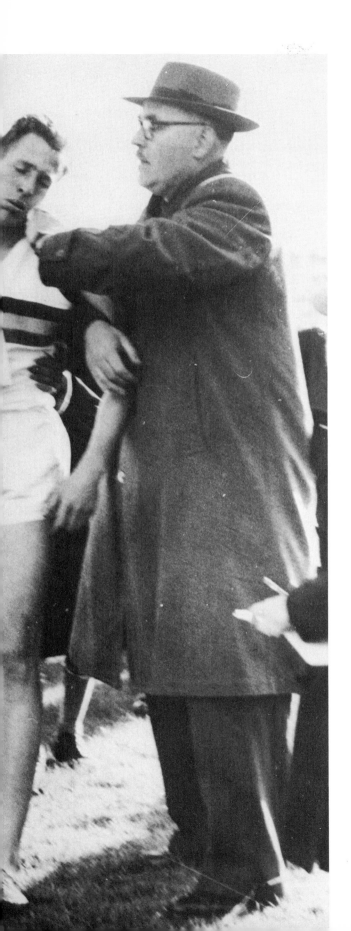

The doctor gets help after running historic mile.

Johnny Unitas
The Six-Dollar-a-Game Quarterback

There is much truth to the legend of how Johnny Unitas became a Baltimore Colt but, as is the case with most legends, mixed in are sizable portions of myth. It is true that Unitas was rejected by the Pittsburgh Steelers and that he did indeed play one fall of semipro football for the Bloomington Rams on fields in Pittsburgh strewn with rock and pieces of shattered glass. It is also true that Unitas appeared at the Colts' tryout camp in the spring of 1956 along with the usual number of "rinky-dinks," males of various shapes, sizes and ages who turn up at such camps hoping to win a place on the roster of a pro football team.

His appearance at that camp and his subsequent climb to greatness made him the ultimate hero of those who make those often-pathetic pilgrimages. However, the truth is that Unitas was never really one of them. He arrived at the Colts' camp by invitation, with an offer of a $7,000 contract, and bringing with him some strong recommendations. He was by no means typical of the tryout brigade.

Nor did he prove to be an ordinary player. In commemoration of the National Football League's fiftieth anniversary, he was voted the greatest quarterback of all time. The sportswriters and sportscasters of the nation voted him the player of the decade for the 1960s. Three times Unitas was voted the league's Most Valuable Player; he was named all-pro quarterback six times and in 10 of his 16 years he was selected to play in the Pro Bowl. Sid Luckman, himself ranked among pro football's all-time great quarterbacks, said, "Johnny Unitas is the greatest quarterback ever to play the game, better than I was, better than Sammy Baugh, better than anyone."

Unitas completed more passes for more touchdowns and more yardage than anyone else in football history. In 16 seasons, he completed 2,708 of 4,953 passes for 38,657 yards and 283 touchdowns. During that time, the Colts won one Super Bowl, three NFL championships and one American Conference title—also managing one other visit to each of those championship games. Unitas got them there with more than just superb passing. He called his own plays,

and did so under all three coaches he played for—Weeb Ewbank, Don Shula and Don McCafferty. His success as a play-caller was traced to his ability to read quickly and correctly the opposition's defense and, if necessary, to change at the line the play he had called in the huddle.

Even after the ball had been snapped and the defense was reacting, Unitas had the knack for quickly erasing what had been planned, taking advantage of the new situation. It was a talent that went back to his college football days at Louisville. His coach there, Frank Camp, said, "Unitas had the quickest reactions I've ever seen, aided by the fact that he had peripheral vision. He could see the whole field in front of him and could anticipate the positions of the receivers and the defenders when the ball would reach them."

Though Unitas often sought suggestions from his receivers and running backs, he was a stern commander in the huddle. Any breach of discipline was dealt with through a tight-lipped reprimand, and he made it clear at all times that he alone would call the plays. John Mackey, the Colts' big tight end, once marveled, "It's like being in a huddle with God." Aside from some moments at preseason training camp when he would purposely befuddle rookies by using double-talk in the huddles, Unitas was all business on the field, always calm, always seeming to be in control of the situation.

"I don't know what he uses for blood," Sid Gillman once said of him, "but I'll guarantee you it isn't warm. It's ice cold."

He was amiable enough off the field; some even described him as shy. There was nothing in his dress or manner to make people turn to stare at him, nor was there anything especially noteworthy about his physical appearance—certainly not the superman image his gridiron feats would suggest. An inch over 6 feet tall and weighing just under 200 pounds, his torso widened gradually into a deep chest and broad shoulders, but he was not especially muscular. There was a noticeable curve to his right arm, evidence of the thousands and thousands of passes it had thrown. Other symbols of his oc-

As late as 1971, Unitas stood as the game's most respected quarterback.

cupation were various scars, some of them surgical, souvenirs of his encounters with legions of opposing defensemen. The most serious injury of all, suffered in April, 1971, one month before his thirty-eighth birthday, was sustained, ironically, while playing paddleball with teammate Tom Matte in the Towson, Maryland, YMCA. The Achilles' tendon in his right leg was torn.

That injury, the way he reacted to it and the way he overcame it, offered a great deal of insight into the man. Matte recalled that Unitas, as they were playing, suddenly felt a sharp pain above his right heel. He asked Matte whether he had kicked him, and when Matte said he hadn't, Unitas declared matter-of-factly, "I've snapped my Achilles' tendon." Just as matter-of-factly, he showered, shaved, dressed and drove home to pick up some toilet articles. While home, he called the Colts' team physician, told the doctor what had happened and to meet him at the hospital and then drove there to undergo surgery. Matte was so unnerved that his ulcers acted up, and he, too, had to be hospitalized.

Recovery from a ruptured Achilles' tendon normally takes six months, possibly longer for someone of Unitas's age, but there was the nagging possibility that the tendon might never heal sufficiently to allow Unitas to play again. Unitas did not need six months. He embarked on an intensive program of therapy and exercise, insisting by the beginning of September that he was ready to play in preseason games—he wasn't permitted to do so. After being reactivated on the eve of the 1971 season, Unitas said, "There was never any doubt in my mind that I would be back, only in the minds of the coaches and other people."

His medical history reads like an emergency-room report on a Saturday night—broken ribs, punctured lung, shoulder contusions, knee injuries that required surgery and a variety of arm problems, one of which, in 1968, threatened his career. In that instance, a tendon in Unitas's right arm was tearing away from a bone, causing him intense pain. The trouble had plagued him, on and off, for several years, but in 1968 it grew so severe that he spent most of the season on the sidelines, barely able to lift his right arm. Again, therapy, exercise and a grim determination to overcome obstacles carried him through. The explanation was offered that Unitas's determination to overcome injuries was part of the competitive drive seen in most top athletes. This trait played an important role in guiding Unitas around the many obstacles on the road that led him to the Colts.

Unitas, born of Slavic background in Pittsburgh, was one of four children. He was four years old when his father died and the task of supporting the family fell to his mother. Unitas played high school football at St. Justin in Pittsburgh, and it was there that the story of Unitas the football star really began.

Having played halfback his first two years, Unitas was converted to end as a junior. He wasn't on the receiving end of passes for long, however. St. Justin's quarterback suffered a broken ankle in the second game of the season, and coach Jim Carey turned to Unitas as the replacement. Carey had seen in the youngster the most powerful arm on the team—so strong, in fact, that receivers at first had difficulty holding onto his passes. The team enjoyed no great success, but Unitas was elected to Pittsburgh's all-Catholic high school team that and the following years.

Still, there was no great rush by college coaches to recruit him. Lack of interest undoubtedly was due to Unitas's unimpressive size—he weighed only 145 pounds at graduation from high school. He had tryouts at Notre Dame and Indiana, both ending in rejection because coaches felt he was too light. Coach Carey fumed, "Nonsense, he's only a kid. He's going to fill out nicely." Carey, Unitas's earliest believer and one of his most ardent, again proved to be an excellent judge of potential. In one year Johnny put 20 pounds on his frame.

Following the rejections at Notre Dame and Indiana, Unitas knocked on a hometown door, that of the University of Pittsburgh. Len Casanova was then the head coach at Pitt, and he was impressed. All that remained was for Unitas to pass the entrance exam, considered only a formality since he had shown adequate scholastic aptitude in high school. But in one of those ironic twists that cropped up often in Unitas's life, he flunked the exam. Unitas's determined effort to find a place in college football next took him to Louisville. There, he made the team and was enrolled.

One inducement that had lured Johnny to Louisville was that the school permitted freshmen to play varsity football. There was no agreement that he would be a starter, however, and for the first four games he rode the bench.

Johnny U throws against Green Bay. In 16 seasons, Unitas completed 2,708 of 4,953 passes for 38,657 yards and 283 touchdowns. The Colts won many championships under Unitas.

Louisville's fifth game was against St. Bonaventure; it was in that game that Unitas made his college football debut. His first moments were embarrassingly inept—he obviously was very nervous—and coach Camp yanked him from the game. When the second half began, however, Unitas was back at quarterback. By then, St. Bonaventure had built a 19–0 lead. Unitas promptly began to lead Louisville to a comeback, at one point completing 11 consecutive passes. He threw three touchdown passes in the second half—not enough to prevent a 22–21 victory by St. Bonaventure but enough to impress Camp and virtually everyone else who saw the game.

Unitas led Louisville to four successive victories that season. Louisville had a mediocre campaign the following year, and then its fortunes dipped even further because 15 scholarship players had been lost through academic deficiencies. Yet, Unitas's talent continued to be apparent. In Unitas's senior year, one rival coach, Bowden Wyatt of Tennessee, called him the best quarterback he had seen all season.

In the NFL player draft that year, Pitts-

burgh made Unitas its ninth choice. The Steelers' training camp was in Olean, New York. Unitas felt that the location of the camp was a good omen since it was there that he had made his college debut. Again, however, as had happened at Notre Dame, Indiana and Pitt, Johnny's hopes were not fulfilled. Head coach Walt Kiesling and his staff gave him scant attention. Somehow, some way, he was lost among the scores of other players, and the Steelers released him.

Dejectedly, not even waiting for the morning bus out of Olean, Unitas hitchhiked back to Pittsburgh. Of all the mistakes ever made at football training camps, the Steelers had made one of the biggest. To compound the sin, as far as Unitas was concerned, the Steelers had waited until late in the summer before cutting him. When he called the Cleveland Browns' coach, Paul Brown, who knew Unitas by reputation, Johnny was told that not sufficient time remained for a tryout that year. Brown, however, invited Unitas to contact him again the following summer.

So, Unitas spent the fall of 1955 playing semipro ball with the Bloomington Rams of Pittsburgh for six dollars a game. Meanwhile, he worked as a pile driver with a construction company. Late that fall, Ewbank, then Baltimore's coach, received a letter from a fan extolling Unitas's play for the Rams and urging the Colts to get him. Although it was never learned who wrote that letter—later Ewbank laughingly accused Unitas of being its author—it planted the quarterback's name in Ewbank's mind.

Weeks later, when Camp, Unitas's college coach, mentioned Johnny to Ewbank as a talented prospect, the computer in Ewbank's brain brought Unitas's name out of the recesses and the coach did some investigating. He found a favorable scouting report on Unitas in the Colts' files, with a notation indicating that Baltimore would have drafted him had he still been available in the later rounds. A scout confirmed that the Steelers had not paid much attention to Unitas at training camp. Ewbank went to the front office and asked Don Kellett to invite Unitas to spring tryout camp.

For the first three games of the 1956 season, Unitas fulfilled the role of backup, sitting on the bench. Although the fourth game, against the Chicago Bears, began with Unitas still there, an important chapter of pro football history was to have its start before that game ended. Shaw suffered a broken leg, and Unitas was thrust into his professional debut. Within moments he was living a nightmare. The first pass he threw was intercepted by Chicago's J. C. Caroline, who ran it back for a touchdown. On the ensuing kickoff, Unitas promptly collided with his teammate Alan Ameche and bobbled the hand-off. The Bears recovered and went in for another touchdown. Unitas later botched another hand-off; Chicago recovered, setting up another score. The Bears won that game, 58–27.

Ewbank's explanation for that atrocious performance was that Unitas was not really prepared for the game since he had not worked out with the Colts' starting backfield. That problem was solved as Baltimore prepared for its game with the Green Bay Packers the following Sunday. Unitas led the Colts to victory over the Packers and to three more victories before the season ended. He finished that campaign with the highest completion average ever recorded by a rookie, 55.6 percent. He had become Baltimore's starting quarterback.

Two years later, Unitas led the Colts to the Western Conference title and a victory in the championship game over the New York Giants. That championship contest has been called the greatest football game ever played. The Colts won it in sudden-death overtime, by a score of 23–17.

The Giants were leading 17–14 with time running out in the final quarter when Baltimore, deep in its own territory, gained possession. Unitas told his teammates, "We've got eighty yards to go and two minutes to do it in. We are going to find out what stuff we're made of." With his passing, he then drove the Colts into position for Steve Myhra to boot the field goal that tied the score and sent the game into overtime. In those excruciating moments of sudden death, Unitas, mixing runs by L. G. Dupre with passes to Raymond Berry, Ameche and Jim Mutscheller, brought the Colts 80 yards in 12 plays to the 1-yard line. From there Ameche slammed through the Giants' defensive line for the winning touchdown. Unitas's role in that drive was one of the most significant performances in pro football history.

Johnny Unitas had many other memorable moments as he was establishing himself as one of the great all-time athletes. Of course, anyone who achieves such heights finds himself the target of those who delight in seeking imperfections. The worst that has been said of Unitas is that as his fame grew, he became conceited. To that criticism, Unitas replied, "There is a difference between conceit and confidence. A quarterback has to have confidence. Conceit is bragging about yourself. Confidence means you believe you can get the job done. I have always believed I could."

MARVIN SCHNEIDER

Left: Johnny holds ice pack against bruised ribs during game in Super Bowl against Dallas. Above: Rushed hard, Unitas still manages to get off pass.

Eddie Arcaro
King of the Stakes Riders

Eddie Arcaro, "the Big A" of the jockey ranks for 30 years, sat a horse with such graceful arrogance that he seemed to be doing the animal a favor by riding him. Eddie had the cold, haughty confidence of a dancing master. He had the kind of face that goes with a star tango performer. A compact 5 feet 2 , 114 pounds, like all great jockeys he was strong in the wrists and shoulders. His olive skin reflected his Mediterranean ancestry.

The railbirds, especially at the New York tracks where he rode most of his races, called him "Banana Nose." His nose, however, more closely resembled a wedge of pie—thin at the start and fat at the end. Arcaro had a tough, tensile strength. He had the sensitive hands of a maestro and the icy nerves of a high-wire man who disdains a net.

Eddie was, in the judgment of most racing people, the greatest rider in the history of American turf. His fabulous career raced through three historic decades, from 1931 to 1961. The other jockeys called him "the Master," and not in jest. Arcaro was the king of the Triple Crown events—the Kentucky Derby, the Preakness and the Belmont. He rode 17 winners in those races, a record nobody else has threatened.

Arcaro was the only man to double in the Triple Crown. He won it with Calumet Farm's Whirlaway in 1941 and won it again with that same stable's Citation in 1948. In all, Heady Eddie rode five Derby winners, a record he shared with Bill Hartack; six Belmont victors, a mark shared with Jimmy McLaughlin, a nineteenth-century rider, and six Preakness champions, a record unequaled by any other jockey.

When Eddie retired in 1961, his 554 stakes winners constituted a record. It later was broken by his good friend and golfing buddy Willie Shoemaker. Arcaro was a magnificent money-rider. Although he never led the national jockey list in number of winners for any one season, he topped it six times in money earned by his mounts.

Eddie's career spanned 31 seasons, but he actually rode for only 30 years. He spent one full year, September, 1942, to September, 1943,

on the sidelines because of a suspension resulting from an incident at the old Aqueduct track in New York. The hot-blooded Arcaro, angry at another jockey, Vincent Nodarse, tried to crowd Nodarse through the rail and into the infield during the running of a race. The stewards asked Eddie a simple question: "Why?" They got an equally simple reply: "I wanted to kill him."

Eddie rode 24,092 mounts, winning with 4,779. He was second with 3,807, third with 3,302 and out of the money with slightly more than half his horses, 12,204, mathematical evidence of what a difficult sport racing is. His mounts earned the immense sum of $30,039,-543, a total surpassed only by Shoemaker. Eddie's first race was at Bainbridge Park, near Cleveland, on May 18, 1931. He was 15. His finale was at old Pimlico in Baltimore on November 16, 1961. He was 45.

Race riding is a dangerous profession, and Eddie knew how it felt to dance with disaster. He fell dozens of times but badly only twice. In 1933, at a Chicago track, he was spilled from a horse named Gun Fire. A fractured skull and punctured lung sidelined him for four months. In June, 1959, riding the star-crossed Black Hills in the Belmont, Eddie was thrown violently into the mud on the stretch turn. He lay there in a mud puddle, limp as a rag doll, as the field tore past him, some of the horses jumping over his body. That time, with a concussion and other injuries, Arcaro missed a month.

Arcaro's great rides numbered in the hundreds. Many times his ability to stage a raging finish seemed to be the difference between winning and losing. The question of how much a jockey contributes to a horse's victory is always a subject for strong debate around the race tracks. Arcaro himself doubted the value of the jockey. But there was something special about a great ride by Arcaro. It was a work of art.

An example was his Kentucky Derby victory on wild, wacky Whirlaway in 1941. No other jockey had been able to keep the erratic colt on a straight course. Eddie gave it the master's touch, keeping the long-tailed stretch

202

Typical Eddie Arcaro charge, leading in race at Aqueduct.

in front every step of the way to win by six-and-a-half lengths.

Even Arcaro sometimes made mistakes. There was the Devil Diver–Shut Out incident in the 1942 Kentucky Derby. Both horses were racing in the pink-and-black silks of the Greentree Stable. Eddie had his choice of the two colts as a Derby mount. He picked Devil Diver. Shut Out drove to the wire, a handy winner, with Devil Diver a laboring sixth. Had Arcaro chosen Shut Out, it would have given him a lifetime total of six Derby winners and he would have stood alone at the top of the list instead of being tied with Hartack.

Arcaro himself insisted that he tossed off the 1947 Derby on C. V. Whitney's Phalanx. In that race, Eddie started his drive for the lead at the half-mile pole. After placing second to Jet Pilot in a photo finish, Arcaro concluded that he had made his move too soon. His horse was exhausted in the final yards.

The topper, however, in the small list of Arcaro blunders came on November 12, 1949, at Pimlico. Eddie was riding Brookmeade Stable's Blue Hills in the Pimlico Cup, a grinding gallop of two-and-a-half miles, more than twice the distance of the average race. The start was on the backstretch and the horses were scheduled to pass the finish line three times. The second time around, Arcaro had Blue Hills two lengths in front and flowing smoothly, but as he went under the wire, he pulled up the horse, thinking the race was over. Several horses drummed by him. Jockey Jimmy Lynch, riding Bayeux, came past Arcaro and called out, "Eddie, old buddy, we have to go around again." The startled Arcaro got his horse moving again but could do no better than second, eight lengths behind Pilaster.

"I feel worse about the mistake than anyone else," said the chagrined Arcaro after the race. "I guess I'll have to go back to school and learn how to count to three. Maybe I should have carried three peas in my hand and thrown one away each time we went by the stands."

Although trainers were falling all over each other to get Arcaro to ride for them, especially in a stakes race, Eddie went on record as believing that the importance of the rider is overrated. He stated that the principal function of the jockey is to make the horse run to its full potential and that in a given race any one of two dozen jockeys at a track would get home in front with the best horse in a race.

runner on the rail for the first six furlongs, making his bid along the fence on the last turn and blazing away from the field in the straightaway to win by eight lengths.

Eddie himself always mentioned the 1948 Santa Anita Handicap in which he steered a South American horse named Talon through the pack, weaving through and around the field to win in a driving finish. In 1947, he literally rammed a charging chestnut colt named Assault between the leaders in the deep stretch at the old Jamaica oval to win the Butler Handicap.

The Nashua–Swaps match race held in 1955 at Washington Park, Chicago, was another Arcaro classic. Eddie rode Nashua. Shoemaker was on Swaps, the speed horse of the pair, and was expected to take the lead at the break. Arcaro got Nashua out of the gate like a hunting cheetah. Riding and yelling like a Plains Indian on a raiding party, Eddie had Nashua

Eddie in 1939, just beginning to be recognized as "the Big A." Already the railbirds were affectionately calling him "Banana Nose." Right: After winning Derby in 1952.

"A jockey does a good job if he makes the horse perform to his potential," Eddie said. "You have to remember that about seventy percent of the horses running don't want to win. Horses are like people. Everybody doesn't have the aggressiveness or ambition to knock himself out to become a success. Most horses will dog it and goof off if you let them get away with it."

Curiously enough, after the Shut Out boner in the Derby of 1942, Arcaro teamed with that son of Equipoise to form a winning combination. Eddie rode Shut Out to victory in the Belmont Stakes, the Travers at Saratoga and the Arlington Classic. It was after the Arlington that he called Shut Out "the best ugly horse I ever rode," a curious compliment if that's what it was intended to be. Years later Eddie was asked about the remark.

"I'll tell you about that dude," he said. "He was a mean horse, and every time I worked him out in the morning, he used to try to throw me. He really didn't like me. One morning I took him out on the track and he reared high in the air. I think he wanted to go over on his back and squash me. I had had enough. I turned my whip around and I hit him across the nose with the butt end just as hard as I could. That dude never gave me any trouble after that."

Shut Out, of course, was omitted when Arcaro mentioned his all-time favorite horses. He named Citation and Kelso as the best distance runners. Bold Ruler was tabbed as the top sprinter and Round Table as the number-one grass horse. He also said that Calumet Farm's Two Lea was his favorite mare, despite the finish of the 1950 Santa Anita Handicap.

Early in 1950, Arcaro went to Caliente, where future book is made on the Santa Anita Handicap. He made a sizable bet on Two Lea to place in the big race and got excellent odds. In a future book bet one wagers on a horse, not on an entry. It so happened that Calumet sent three horses to the post for the Santa Anita 'Cap that year. Arcaro was on the great Citation. Steve Brooks rode Ponder, the 1949 Kentucky Derby winner. Johnny Gilbert was in the irons on Two Lea.

"Trainer Jimmy Jones had ordered Two Lea to make the pace," Arcaro recalled. "I was making my move along the rail with Citation in the stretch, and I thought I had the race locked up. But Noor came flying on the outside. At that moment I got blocked by my own stablemate, Two Lea. I had to check my horse. Noor

Top: Eddie is greeted on return after his one-year suspension in 1942. Above: At Belmont in 1955 when "Sunny" Jim Fitzsimmons was honored for his fabulous years as a trainer of thoroughbreds. Opposite: The Arcaro family comfort him after spill—daughter Carolyn, wife Ruth, son Bobby.

got the lead. I got Citation rolling again, and I was so excited I went right by Two Lea and beat her out of the place. I couldn't catch Noor, but by finishing second with Citation, I beat myself out of eight thousand dollars."

It's a strict rule of racing that jockeys may bet only on their own horses or stablemates in a race in which they are riding. Arcaro once said that he could still feel the pain from a bet he made at Tropical Park. He was the contract rider for the Greentree Stable, and he was listed to ride a fast three-year-old who seemed ready to move into the handicap ranks and who was in against inferior company.

"I knew the colt was a stickout," Eddie sighed, "so I bet ten thousand dollars to win on him. He opened up a big lead, and as we turned into the stretch, I began to think, 'If I win by too much, the handicappers will load him up with weight.' I began to ease him up. He starts to drift toward the outer rail. I'm not worried. He's leading by eight lengths. All of a sudden he jumps the rail, tosses me flat on my back and runs off to the stable area. I wasn't hurt but, oh, that ten thousand."

Although he was always called Eddie, he was christened George Edward Arcaro. He was born on February 19, 1916, in Cincinnati, Ohio, the son of an Italian immigrant taxicab driver. Eddie, always sports-minded but too small for baseball and football, ended his formal education at the age of 13 to seek his fortune at the race track. It was hard going. Trainers, by repeatedly telling him he would never make a jockey, often reduced the slim youngster to tears.

Working as an exercise boy, Arcaro galloped horses for $20 a month when he could get it, but often for no pay other than experience. He was working at Latonia, a track near Cincinnati, when a trainer named Clarence Davison took the young Arcaro under his wing. A long time later Eddie would say, "Davison taught me everything I know."

Eddie was the top apprentice in New Orleans in 1933. He then moved along to Chicago. His first big contract was with Warren Wright of the Calumet Farm. He rode that stable's Nellie Flag in the 1935 Kentucky Derby, Eddie's first appearance in the "Run for the Roses." He could do no better than fourth that day. But in his next try, on Lawrin in 1938, Eddie made it to the winner's circle. He returned for four more visits.

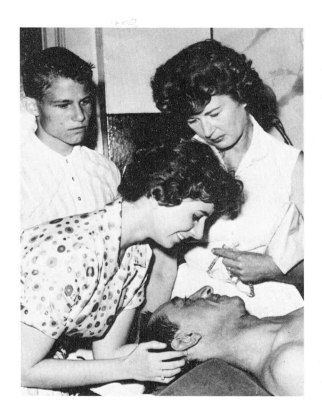

Arcaro's widely quoted credo about race riding was "Don't get beat by no noses." He did, of course, hundreds of times. But any racing man will tell you that Eddie won more photo finishes than he lost. He was 114 pounds of concentrated fury in a close finish, pumping and pushing his mount frantically to ensure victory. It is a turf oddity that not one of Arcaro's 17 Triple Crown triumphs came in a photo finish.

His five Kentucky Derby winners were Lawrin, winner by one length in 1938; Whirlaway, by eight in 1941; Hoop Jr., by six in 1945; Citation, by three-and-a-half in 1948 and Hill Gail, by two in 1952.

Eddie's Preakness victories were on Whirlaway, who breezed by five-and-a-half in 1941; Citation, also by five-and-a-half in 1948; Hill Prince, by five in 1950; Bold, by seven in 1951; Nashua, by a length in 1955, and Bold Ruler, by two in 1957.

In the Belmont, it was Whirlaway, winner by two-and-a-half in 1941; Shut Out, by two in 1942; Pavot, by five in 1945; Citation, by eight in 1948; One Count, by two-and-a-half in 1952; Nashua, by nine in 1955.

Shortly after retiring, Arcaro modestly said that he thought he belonged among the top five jockeys of the American turf. Sam Renick, a former jockey who rode against Arcaro before becoming a television sportscaster, went a step or two beyond that. "I believe that he became aware of his greatness after winning his first Derby in 1938," Renick said. "He was good before that, but after it he became great. He had confidence like no one else I've ever seen on a race track."

An international turf authority, Baron Fred d'Osten, added his appraisal of Arcaro at the same time: "Since 1920, I have seen all the top jockeys of the world. I have watched races in many countries and I have seen men such as Steve Donoghue, Sir Gordon Richards, Charley Elliott, Earl Sande, Roger Poincelet, Rae John-

stone and many, many others. Eddie Arcaro is far superior to any of them."

Arcaro knew fear, of course. Any race rider does. There are close calls every day. Horses swerve and bump each other. Riders get into close quarters where one false move means an ugly spill. Looking back at his days as a rider, Arcaro recalled how he felt.

"I figured that when I signed my name to be a jockey, death might be a part of it. There were plenty of times when I was afraid. Every day something would come up that would give me a scare. Every jockey has to live with it. Jockeys know what hard competition is, and in racing, if you want to make it real big, you can't be afraid of dying. That day at Belmont when I fell from Black Hills didn't bother me. Afterward you couldn't have put a gun to my back and made me stop riding and being a jockey."

Eddie enjoyed his fame as the country's top jockey. When he reached the age of 40, he was asked whether he planned to retire in the near future. His answer was quick. "Let's face it. I'm a celebrity. It's fun and I like it. You know what will happen after I retire? I'll be just another little man."

Arcaro had successful open-heart surgery in November, 1970. After a period of convalescence, he seemed as jaunty as ever. During his riding days he was regarded as being as strong as any jockey on the turf. When talking about what makes a successful rider, Eddie mentioned the physical part of it.

"Race riding is as much physical exertion as the jockey can put into it," he said. "Every top rider has strong back and shoulder muscles. Even a really little guy like Shoemaker is built like a lightweight fighter from the waist up. You develop those muscles by pushing with the horse on every stride, by showing him you're boss and making him keep his mind on his job."

Eddie studied the horses he rode. "When a horse is doing his best, his ears are always laid back close to his head," he said. "If he flicks his ears, he's admiring the scenery or thinking about something else besides running. But the best tip-off is his breathing. It's deep and regular when he's relaxed, but he grabs for air when under tension. Breath control is the secret of handling horses. It's no accident that stables like the Phipps outfit, Greentree and Rokeby consistently come up with good horses. They're taught breath control as colts."

The use and misuse of the whip is a frequent subject for discussion around the race track. The whip is designed to sting a sluggish horse into action. In the stretch, however, if a horse is tiring, all great jockeys prefer—and are masters at—the hand ride, which, in effect, holds a horse together in the vital closing yards.

"There is no sense in whipping a tired horse, because he'll quit on you," Arcaro said. "Some jocks put on a big show by whacking their horses in the stretch, but I think more horses are whipped out of the money than into it. A horse resents it when he's leveling for you."

On one occasion, however, in the 1950s, Arcaro did resort to the whip. He was riding an odds-on favorite in the feature race of the day at Belmont Park, and the horse simply would not respond. The angry Arcaro popped the whip a dozen times, but to no avail. He finished sec-

ond, and as he weighed out, those in the stands who had backed the losing favorite began to vent their feelings. The boo-birds were still chirping as the field for the following race paraded into the walking ring in the Belmont Park paddock, which at that time was a beautiful tree-lined area behind the clubhouse. As Eddie, astride his mount in the race, came abreast of one particularly loud heckler, the pest screamed, "Banana Nose, you're a bum. You never tried with that horse, you phony."

It was too much for the irate Eddie to take. He leaned over, ostensibly to fix his boot on the left side, and as he passed the heckler, he said softly, "My friend, I wish you had the stripes on your rear end I left on that horse."

CHARLES MOREY

Left: At a party in a New York restaurant in 1969, Eddie acknowledges the bald pate of Johnny Longden. Above: Wife and son congratulate Arcaro on Preakness win.

Bill Russell
The Worth of a Dollar

The year 1968 was one of transcendent individual performances in the world's athletic arenas. It was an Olympic year. Graceful, green-eyed Peggy Fleming dazzled everyone with her figure-skating triumph at Grenoble, France, and a handsome, rugged Frenchman named Jean-Claude Killy scored a triple sweep in Alpine skiing. Al Oerter, an American marvel as a discus thrower, became the first Olympian in history to win four gold medals in the same event. A rail-thin U.S. black, Arthur Ashe, Jr., an amateur, outclassed the pros in winning the first U.S. Open tennis championship at Forest Hills. The sports pages rang with the exploits of such stars as Debbie Meyer, O. J. Simpson, Kipchoge Keino and Gordie Howe. When time came for *Sports Illustrated* to award the Grecian urn to its Sportsman of the Year, the prize went to none of these. It went to Bill Russell, the remarkable player–coach of the Boston Celtics professional basketball team.

It was the year that Russell drove a team of veterans to their tenth world championship since he had joined Boston as a raw, uncoordinated rookie 12 years before. He added still another National Basketball Association title—his eleventh—before retiring in the summer of 1969 to pursue a career as an actor in the movies and on television and as a popular sports commentator for the American Broadcasting Company.

Russell's career reached its zenith in 1968. Although second in their division, the Celtics eliminated Detroit in the first round of the play-offs and then went into the Eastern finals against the Philadelphia 76ers, quickly dropping behind three games to one—a step away from elimination. It was at this point that Russell, by personal performance and inspiration, rallied his reeling forces and won three games in a row.

The victory sent the aging Celtics into the NBA championship series against the flashy and favored Los Angeles Lakers, which featured superstars Elgin Baylor and Jerry West. The Celtics won in six. The next season—1968–69—Russell brought his team to a peak again after finishing a disappointing fourth in the East. The Celtics knocked off Philadelphia again and went against the Lakers, who had been strengthened by the addition of Wilt Chamberlain in the finals.

It was a dramatic series, touch and go all the way with the two rival giants dominating the battle, a fierce struggle in which blocking and rebounding set up the fast break. In the end it was Russell's hand that was raised.

"I think Wilt is the better all-around basketball player," said Jerry West, a teammate of Chamberlain's with the Lakers. "But for one game, I'd rather have Russell."

Six feet nine inches tall, a black, goateed figure of a man who seemed to run on stilts, with arms and legs like the tentacles of an octopus, Russell brought a new dimension to this rough, tough, fire-engine-fast, sharpshooting game of towering titans. Although he had a good eye and a fantastic touch, he never concentrated on scoring. His forte was ball control and play-making. In these categories, the game never produced an equal. Russell operated on the theory that a team cannot shoot if it doesn't have the ball. He dedicated himself to the job of seeing that the other team didn't get the ball.

"No one ever blocked shots in this league until Russell arrived," said Arnold ("Red") Auerbach, the Boston coach for whom Russell played for 10 years before inheriting the team's reins himself in 1966. "He could upset them all. They knew they couldn't outmaneuver him, so they tried to beat him with physical punishment. They hoped he couldn't take it."

He could. Russell finished his career with an astounding total of 21,721 rebounds. In a single game as a rookie he accounted for 49, a record.

Rebounding always was one of the slightly appreciated and frequently overlooked facets of basketball. Only after the explosion of the professional game and the introduction of sophisticated statistics was any note made of rebounding at all. The fans became obsessed with the obvious—the tossing of the big round ball through the meshed hoop. No one paid much attention to how a team got the ball and engineered it down the floor.

210

Bill Russell at San Francisco in 1958. Bill led the Dons to a 55-game winning streak and two NCAA titles. With teammate K. C. Jones he led the Olympic squad to victory in 1956.

mother died at the age of 32. "After that, Charlie and I took turns signing each other's report cards," Bill recalled later. "Our father was always busy working."

As a youngster, Bill was gangly and unco-ordinated. He appeared to be all arms and legs. He wasn't a sensation in sports, although no one could fault him for trying. He failed to make the football team at McClymonds High School and became very discouraged. Meanwhile, Charlie, two years older, was a basketball star at Oakland Tech.

Failing in football, Bill decided to take a stab at basketball at McClymonds. He struggled but it seemed his feet were always getting in the way. He failed to make the squad as a sophomore. "One day I heard the coach say in front of the whole team, 'Why is it that if there are two brothers in school, we always get the bum?'" Russell recalled. "It left me shaken, almost broken."

If it hadn't been for an understanding junior varsity coach named George Powles, Bill might have given up basketball completely and basketball might have been deprived of his ulti-mate talents. Powles invited Russell to come out for the jayvee squad. There were only 15 uniforms, but Powles let the lanky youngster, sixteenth in rank, share a uniform with another boy. It was a profitable move. By the time he had reached his senior year, Russell had stretched to 6 feet 5 inches and was moving well enough to clinch the varsity center spot. Yet college scouts were not especially impressed.

In the final game of his high school career, Russell went against Oakland Tech and an all-city star named Truman Bruce. In the crowd was a scout from the University of San Fran-cisco, on hand to watch Bruce. The scout, Hal De Julio, hardly noticed the Oakland Tech star. Russell scored 14 points, his best ever in high school, but what impressed De Julio most was the youngster's defensive and ball-blocking abil-ity. Before the evening was over, Russell was committed to an athletic scholarship at San Francisco.

"They didn't even have a gym," Russell said later. "But it was a college and some place I thought I'd never get to." Bill attained his full height of 6 feet 9 inches as a sophomore and became one of the team's standout players. His roommate was K. C. Jones.

"I never had any money," Russell remi-nisced years afterward. "But I used to go every-

To accept the role of basketball thief and play maker while the headlines and plaudits were going to the big men pushing the ball through the hoop certainly required a certain measure of unselfishness. Bill Russell's early life geared him for that.

William Felton Russell was born in the Jim Crow South—in the little town of Monroe, Louisiana, on Lincoln's Birthday—February 12, 1934. He was nine when his mother and father packed up their meager belongings, Bill and an older brother named Charlie and headed west. They settled in Oakland, California. There life for the Russells took on a slightly brighter hue. Both parents worked, on different shifts, and one of them usually was at home. However, the Russell boys fended largely for themselves. Bill's

Above: Russell drives for a lay-up in 1963 game against the Lakers.

where K. C. would go. He would buy me shoes if I needed them. But he never said much."

Russell fitted in well with the plans of Phil Woolpert, the defense-minded coach of the San Francisco Dons. In Russell's junior year, the Dons began a winning streak that became the longest in the nation, 55, and which included two National Intercollegiate Athletic Association (NCAA) titles. It was only natural that both Russell and Jones should be named members of the 1956 Olympic team and that they should both play key roles in another of America's gold medal victories at Melbourne.

The tall, black boy who was so awkward that he couldn't make his high school football team found his bearings in college. Associates contended he could have excelled in any sport he chose, but Bill's affinity was for basketball and track. At San Francisco he went out for the track team because, he said, the track team had a monogrammed sweater that buttoned down the front. The other sweaters were pullovers. "The first meet, I went out and jumped six feet seven inches for the sweater," Bill boasted.

Russell liked track because he felt it to be a sport in which it was easy to psyche the opponents. Psyching the foe was a maneuver that Bill carried into his basketball with success. "Track is really psychic," he said. "There wasn't a guy I jumped against I couldn't beat if I had a chance to talk to him beforehand. I talked to Charlie Dumas and we tied. After that he went on to those world records. I recall one meet with thirty-four jumpers. They wanted to start the bar at five-eight. I said, 'Let's start it at six-four—let's get rid of the garbage.' I wore a silk scarf, basketball shoes and black glasses. I had no trouble. . . ."

John Havlicek, a teammate of Russell's with the Celtics, said, "He's a fantastic athlete. He could have been the decathlon champion. He could broad jump twenty-four feet. He did the hurdles in thirteen-four."

While at San Francisco, Russell caught the eye of Boston scouts, who persuaded coach Red Auerbach that the big center would be a welcome adjunct to the Celtics. However, prospects of landing him were thin. The Celtics had finished second in the NBA race in 1955-56, pushing them next to last in the draft. Besides, the Harlem Globetrotters were allegedly waving big money in front of Russell's nose and there was a chance that Russell might choose basketball show business over big-time competition.

The Rochester Royals had first choice but bypassed Russell when Russell purposely dropped word that he would demand a $25,000 salary, big for that period. "Can you imagine spending a winter in Rochester?" Russell said years later. So Auerbach, determined to land the San Francisco star, went to work on the St. Louis Hawks, who had the next pick. Ben Kerner, the Hawks' owner, had moved the team from Milwaukee the previous season and hoped to turn a last-place club into a winner in a hurry. Kerner was amenable when Auerbach suggested trading Easy Ed Macauley, an aging veteran who had been all-American at St. Louis University, and Cliff Hagan, a one-time all-American at Kentucky, for the untried Russell. The deal was made.

Auerbach got his first look at the new Celtic jewel when the 1956 U.S. Olympic team played an all-star squad at College Park, Maryland. "He was horrible," Auerbach said. "He was awful. I thought, 'God, I've traded Ed Macauley and Cliff Hagan for this guy!' I sat there with my head in my hands."

The Boston coach recalled that Russell came over to him after the game and apologized for his poor performance. He promised he'd do better next time. "I hope so," Auerbach said. "If this game is an indication, I'm a dead pigeon." Russell wasn't much better in his first game as a pro.

"Harry Gallatin of the Knicks ate him up," Auerbach said. "Russell—well, he didn't seem to want to hit anyone. Timid. He'd just been married, and that doesn't do a guy any good. So the next time we played the Knicks, I thought I'd play Russell at corner and let Arnie Risen play center against Gallatin. Russell came to me and said he wanted to try again against Gallatin. What a job he did—Gallatin got one shot, maybe two. Russell destroyed him."

Russell signed with the Celtics for $19,500 a year, the highest ever paid an NBA rookie, but after the first six games, he was on the verge of giving it back and quitting the game. "I was the worst shooter in the National Basketball Association," Russell confessed in a personal magazine article written several years afterward. "The opposition walked all over me. I got pushed, pulled, pinched, punched, bumped and stepped on because I was too clumsy to get out of the way. My all-American reputation meant nothing—there were all-Americans by the dozen in the pro league. My height, while hardly a handicap, was no longer exceptional. A number of men matched my six feet nine inches and some topped it."

By this time, however, Auerbach was convinced he had made no mistake. He saw in Russell a quick, agile, ball-hawking wizard who could dominate the game and cow the opposition without scoring. "Forget about the points," the Boston coach told his expensive rookie. "Just get me the ball." Then he enunciated his own personal philosophy of winning basketball: "Nobody can win in this league without a big, rugged man who can grab rebounds and keep the other team from scoring."

Auerbach referred to Russell as his "destroyer." "That's the word you use for him," the coach added. "He destroys players. Take Neil Johnston—a good set shot and a great sweeping hook shot, a big, long-armed guy who played

for Philadelphia and who was the leading scorer in the NBA the year before. Russell destroyed him. He destroyed him psychologically. He practically ran him out of organized basketball. He blocked so many shots that Johnston began throwing his hook farther and farther from the basket."

Russell's great rebounding ability resulted in a 19.6 average—948 for 48 games—his first year. Only Maurice Stokes of Rochester grabbed more during Russell's first year, but Stokes played in 24 more games. Havlicek said of his teammate: "I've seen him in plays on a basketball court when he not only blocks a shot but controls the ball and feeds it to his forwards, and then he's up at the other end of the court trailing the fast break, and if there's a rebound, there he is, ready for it. He might be the fastest man on the Celtics." Havlicek recalled that Archie Clark of the Lakers stole the ball three

times in a game against the Celtics and each time had a five-step lead on Russell and a free lane to the basket. Each time Russell overtook him and blocked the shot.

It was only natural that Russell should become involved in a personal duel with the great Wilt Chamberlain, who joined the NBA in 1959–60. Not only was Chamberlain four inches taller than Russell but he had the strength of a blacksmith. "Russell will never block Wilt's shots," many pro basketball buffs contended. "He's never met a man like Chamberlain."

Chamberlain, out of the University of Kansas, broke in with the Philadelphia Warriors and immediately went on a scoring binge. All he had to do was stand on tiptoes to stuff the ball into the basket. He averaged 37.6 points a game his first year, scored a record 100 points in a single game and went on to amass point-making records that were staggering.

The first major confrontation of these two titans of the court came in 1960. Boston won the Eastern Division title of the NBA and Philadelphia finished second. They met in the play-offs. Wilt continued to stuff the ball into the basket. Russell blocked, intercepted, stole and ran. In the end, Russell was the victor, the Celtics beating the Warriors, four games to two. This was merely the first of a long series of head-to-head battles between the pair, most of them won by Russell.

"I had rather be what I am for a first-place team than a big scorer for a third-place team," Russell said, applying the needle to his rival and giving it a twist. "If I scored thirty or more points a game, the rest of my game would suffer." Teammates recalled that Russell became so intense before a game that he inevitably would go into the bathroom and throw up. "It was a welcome sound," Havlicek said. "It meant he was keyed up. In later years he didn't do it as much except in the big challenge games where he was meeting someone like Chamberlain."

The Celtics won the NBA title in Russell's rookie year, but the next season, 1957–58, with Russell suffering an ankle injury in the third game of the play-offs, they lost to the St. Louis Hawks, bolstered by the addition of Macauley and Hagan. The Boston dynasty began the following year, 1958–59, the Celtics winning eight consecutive championships under the sharp tutelage of Red Auerbach and the aggressive leadership of Russell and Bob Cousy, who retired after the 1963 season.

With the departure of Cousy, Russell stepped in as the Celtics' captain and quickly destroyed the myth that the Celtics could not operate without their great play maker. The Chamberlain–Russell rivalry continued with intensity. "If he is better than I am, he's got to go out and show me every game," said Russell. "I'm never convinced." When it was announced that Chamberlain signed for $100,000 in 1965–66, Russell balked. "If Chamberlain is worth a hundred thousand, I figure I am worth one dollar more," he said. He got $100,001.

The Philadelphia 76ers, with Chamberlain as the spearhead, won the Eastern Division title in 1965–66, beating out Boston. But the Celtics, traditionally coming up for the big moment, struggled by Cincinnati, routed Philadelphia four games to one and then beat the Los Angeles Lakers in the play-off final. It was after this victory that Auerbach decided to step out as coach. He named Russell as his successor. "The best player I've got is me," Russell said immodestly. "I'm the one I have to bear down on the most."

In Russell's first year as coach, the Celtics finished second in the Eastern Division and lost in the play-offs to Philadelphia. The next year, the Celtics again finished second, but in the play-offs they eliminated Detroit, were behind three games to one and rallied to beat the 76ers and then whipped Los Angeles in six games for the title. Russell was back on top again. In 1968–69, Russell again landed the Celtics in the play-offs despite a disappointing fourth-place finish in the Eastern Division, then proceeded to knock off Philadelphia, New York and finally the Lakers. Russell gave one of his greatest performances in the seventh and final game, then decided he had had enough basketball.

Proud of his African heritage, he bought rubber plantations in Liberia and made frequent visits there. He embarked on a college lecture tour, acted in the movies and on television and did some commentary for the American Broadcasting Company. He sprouted a beard and affected Nehru jackets, love beads and caftans. He became one of the most militant spokesmen against racial injustice. "I can honestly say I have never worked to be liked," he said. "I have worked only to be respected."

DICK JOYCE

Auerbach's "Destroyer" scores against St. Louis Hawks' Charlie Share. Hawks drafted Russell but traded him to Boston for veterans Ed Macauley and Cliff Hagan.

Sugar Ray Robinson
"I Never Liked Fighting"

Sugar Ray Robinson's face was tight with worry as the bell sounded for the tenth round in his middleweight championship bout with Randy Turpin of England at the Polo Grounds in New York on September 12, 1951. The fight was too close. Ray had a slim lead on points but not enough to feel secure. The British fighter had taken the title from Ray in a momentous upset in London two months before. There was only one way for Robinson to get it back—with his fists. But Turpin was a sturdy foe, just unorthodox enough to be dangerous.

Robinson flicked a jab and Turpin ducked under it. Then it happened. Some scuffling inside, elbows thudding against sweaty ribs, arms pinning gloves, heads bent and bobbing. An accidental butt by Turpin. An old cut over Robinson's left eye spewed blood. In a second the battlewise Robinson recognized the danger. They stop fights for bad cuts. If Turpin took the title back to England a second time, it would be gone for good.

Ray's eyes narrowed. They were a killer cat's eyes now, burning brightly. Ray stalked his man. There were no feints. No jabs. Ray ripped a right. It crashed against Turpin's jaw and Randy hit the deck. Referee Ruby Goldstein tolled the count. It reached nine and Turpin gamely got to his feet.

It was a mistake. A red ribbon of blood was running down the left side of Robinson's face, but he followed Turpin. Ray threw combinations that blurred the eye. Turpin lurched back into the ropes. Robinson leaped after him. Randy rolled and squirmed along the ropes. There was no escape. Randy tried to hide behind his upraised gloves. Ray went to the body busily. Turpin dropped his gloves to protect his stomach. Ray planted his feet and delivered a right to Turpin's jaw.

Referee Goldstein jumped in, threw his arms around the helpless Turpin and stopped the bout. The time: 2:52 seconds of the tenth round. Only eight seconds left—not time enough to count a man out—but Goldstein could not chance it. Sugar Ray had regained his middleweight championship and had almost made a prophetess of doom of his sister. In London, after the first Turpin fight, she had said: "I don't want to see the rematch. I know Ray. He'll kill Turpin the second time."

This second meeting with Turpin was one of the most dramatic in the incredible ring career of Sugar Ray, who fought as a pro for a quarter of a century, from 1940 to 1965. He held the welterweight championship early in his career and then for a decade juggled the middleweight crown like a magician making things disappear and reappear. He won it five times. He lost it three times to other fighters, vacated it once himself because of retirement and had it taken away by a boxing commission another time. Nobody else in the history of the ring juggled a title that often.

There was no telling how much money Ray earned. The Sugar Man liked high living. It was estimated that his share of purses in 25 years of fighting was about $4 million. At one time he owned all or most of several blocks of Harlem in New York. He had apartment houses, a beauty parlor, a cafe, a barber shop and a few other side enterprises. He toured New York in a fuchsia Cadillac. He frequently had an entourage that dwarfed a maharajah's on a state visit.

Ray somehow managed to dispose of all that money. When he became 50 years old in the 1970s, he was working as an actor. He took bit parts, walk-ons, small speaking roles, in television and the movies. He did some stage work, and he had a nightclub act. The entourage consisted of his second wife, Millie.

Most ring authorities rated Ray the greatest fighter, pound for pound, in the history of boxing. Anything any other fighter could do, Ray could do as well if not better. He could do everything. His left jab was a straight stab. He was a master of the feint. His right cross came as though shot from a cannon. His left hook was a jaw-breaker. His combinations were classic in their speed and accuracy. His ring brain was a veritable computer. And he had a searing will to win.

A veteran fight manager, sitting at ringside and watching Robinson when Ray was at his peak, commented, "When Sugar Ray fights,

Sugar Ray Robinson, bloodied but strong, absorbs a punch from Randy Turpin in 1951 match that Ray won on a technical knockout in the tenth. Only two months before, Turpin had scored an upset.

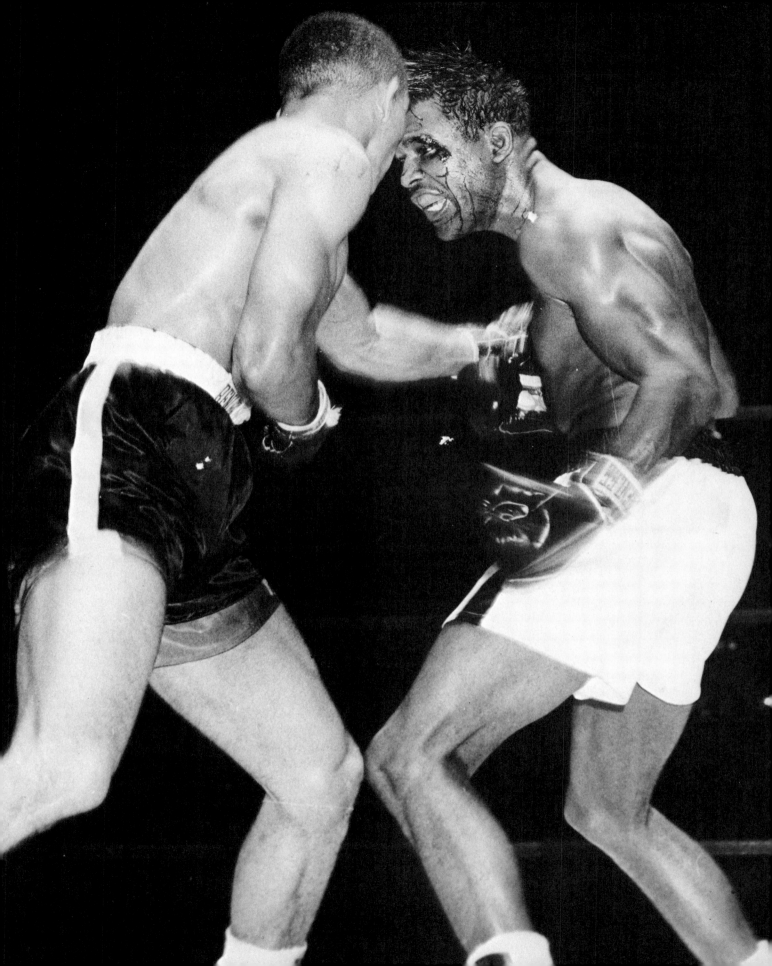

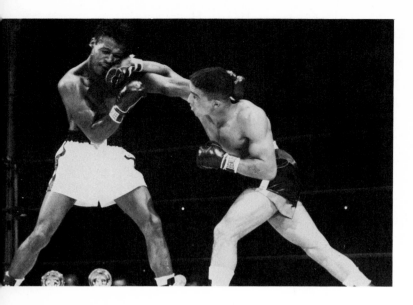

watching the older boys work out. One of the older boys was an earnest young heavyweight named Joe Louis, who worked with Ray's father in an auto plant. When Ray was about 12, his parents separated and he moved to New York with his mother and two sisters. For a time he scratched out walking-around money by tap-dancing in the streets. He was inspired by Bill (Bojangles) Robinson, the legendary tapper, who gave the Harlem kids lessons in dancing around the celebrated "Wishing Tree."

One fine afternoon, when the fates were in a whimsical mood, Ray got into a dice game on a Harlem street, right in front of the Salem Methodist Church. Ray was rolling and had the dice in his hands when, without warning, the other kids bolted, leaving him with the cubes and the money in the pot. At the same time he became conscious of a large shadow falling over him. It belonged to the Reverend Cullen of the Salem Church.

The good reverend took the lively youngster into the church for a little discussion. It dragged on for some time. Reverend Cullen found out a few things about Ray's ambitions, and the discussion ended with his sending the youth to his friend, George Gainford, who held forth at the Salem Crescent Gym. Gainford took the young hopeful in hand. He soon discovered the boy was right-hand crazy. So he tied his right hand to his chest, put him in the ring with another boy and told him to learn how to use his left. There didn't seem to be much choice.

When it came time to get an amateur fighter's card, Walker Smith discovered he was too young. He borrowed a former boxer's Amateur Athletic Union card made out in the name of Ray Robinson. He later legally adopted the name. As an amateur, Ray was sensational. He won 89 bouts, 69 by knockouts, 44 of which were in the first round. It was on an amateur card in Watertown, New York, that he earned the nickname that was to stay with him throughout his life.

The year was 1939. Ray was 18 and weighed 133 pounds. Before his turn to go on, he entertained the handlers and hangers-on in his dressing room by tap-dancing to the music of a portable phonograph. A few minutes later he was in the ring disposing of an opponent with a lightning flurry of punches. A sportswriter at ringside leaned over to Gainford and said, "That's a sweet boy you have there." George re-

every boxer in the country should pay his way in to see how it's done." Oddly enough, early in his pro career, Robinson had atrocious dietary habits when not in training. He was fond of pie and ice cream and other foods that would make any trainer turn pale. But he watched his diet when training for a fight.

Ray was a tough bargainer and did his own negotiating despite the presence of his manager of record, George Gainford, who was overbearing enough to win the title of "Emperor Jones." Robinson was known to run out on fights when things didn't suit him. He always seemed to want just a little more. "Why take a half-dollar when you can get the whole buck" was the code he lived by.

A handsome man, Ray also was vain. In his younger days when the "living was easy," he regaled the press before a fight by announcing, "See this face? Ain't no man ever going to bust up this face. I won't stay in this business too long." But, of course, he did. Years later there was scar tissue around the eyes and the skin of the handsome face was rough and grainy from too many punches from too many fighters.

He was born Walker Smith in Detroit, Michigan, on May 3, 1921, although *Ring Record Book* listed the year as 1920. The disparity, Ray insisted, was because he posed as a year older than he actually was when he started fighting. His early days in Detroit found him hanging around the Brewster Center Gym

Clockwise from above: Ray misses with a left and is hit
with a counter-right from Turpin; the Sugar Man dances in Paris;
Robinson jars Kid Gavilan with a left in 1948 fight.

plied: "Sweet as sugar." From then on he was
Sugar Ray.

Robinson made his professional debut at
Madison Square Garden on October 4, 1940.
He knocked out Joe Echeverria in two rounds
and earned $100. After taking a shower, he
returned to the arena and watched his idol,
Henry Armstrong, take a beating in a welterweight title bout from Fritzie Zivic. Ray later
recalled that he had tears in his eyes watching
Armstrong destroyed by the artful Zivic. He
later fought and beat Zivic twice and conceded
that he learned a lot from the clever Fritzie.

The victory over Echeverria launched Ray
on a victory string of 40 fights, which was
broken on February 5, 1943, by a brawling
bulldog of a middleweight named Jake La
Motta in Detroit. Ray was a welterweight then,
but he seemed unable to get a shot at the 147-
pound title. On August 27, 1943, he went
through a 10-round waltz with the aging Armstrong, holding Henry up when necessary. Ray
took the fight only because Armstrong needed
a purse.

There was time out for a hitch in the army,
and late in 1944, Ray began his pursuit of the
welterweight crown. He finally got his chance
in December, 1946, against Tommy Bell, a
tough and underrated fighter. Bell put Ray on
the floor during the hard-fought match in Madison Square Garden, but Sugar got up and belted
out a decision. In the next four years, he defended the 147-pound title five times. But each
year he found the weight harder to make.

Ray's first welterweight championship defense was a tragic one. He met an outclassed
opponent named Jimmy Doyle in Cleveland on
June 24, 1947, and knocked him out in eight
rounds. Doyle suffered brain damage and died.
After that Ray stopped Chuck Taylor, outpointed
Bernie Docusen and defeated Kid Gavilan, a
really fine fighter. That was in 1949. In 1950,
Ray toyed with Charlie Fusari in a title bout
in Jersey City. That was his last 147-pound title
match.

Sugar won the middleweight championship
for the first time on February 14, 1951, in Chicago, a lucky city for him throughout his career.
He stopped the stocky La Motta, who had an-
nexed the crown, in 13 rounds. The winning of
the middleweight title vacated his welterweight
crown. Five months later, he lost the 160-pound
championship to Turpin in London after making
a grand tour of Europe. Ray fought in Paris,

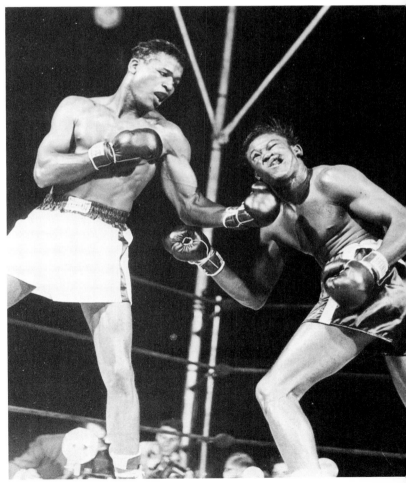

Antwerp, Liege, Berlin and Turin before meeting Turpin. He also took time off to taste the heady night life of Paris, accompanied, of course, by his entourage.

After winning the title back from Turpin, Ray made two defenses early in 1952. On March 13, he went 15 rounds against Bobo Olson in San Francisco. Ray got the decision. Five weeks later, in Chicago, he hammered Rocky Graziano out in three rounds. There seemed no real competition for Ray in the middleweight division, so once again he looked upward—right at light-heavyweight champion Joey Maxim.

Maxim was a fairly clever journeyman. He was ringwise. His footwork was good. His hands were experienced. But he was no puncher and at no time a menacing rallier when in trouble. Ray felt sure he could spot Maxim the difference in weight between the 160-pound division and the 175-pound class. They met in Yankee Stadium on June 25, 1952. It was a hot night. The temperature at ringside was 104 degrees when Robinson and Maxim entered the ring. The referee was Ruby Goldstein. The standby referee at ringside was Ray Miller.

From the start it was obvious that the streamlined Sugar was too fast for the plodding Maxim. His jabs were popping Joey's head back. Ray's combinations shook Maxim and made him hold. From time to time Ray would dig in and rip a right that would make Maxim grunt. But Joey was heavier and he was strong. And he was not dissipating his strength throwing punches. He threw few and his principal form of attack was to get in close and lean on Ray, using his weight.

The rounds spun by. Ray was far ahead on points. It seemed obvious that Robinson was going to become the third man in ring history to win three major titles. Between rounds 9 and 10, there was an unexpected development. Referee Goldstein said he felt dizzy. Dr. Alexander Schiff, the official at ringside, administered emergency first aid to Goldstein. Ruby said he would continue. But at the end of round 10, he staggered to the ropes. Dr. Schiff again jumped into the ring. He examined Ruby and told him he was finished for the night because of heat exhaustion. Ray Miller took his place. The two fighters, resting on their stools with their handlers dousing them with water and fanning them with towels, watched the mini-drama with curious eyes.

Robinson was brilliant in the eleventh. He had Maxim holding. In the twelfth, however, Robinson suddenly showed the effects of the heat. His knees dipped, he was wild with his punches, he had no speed. Maxim continued to plod along, doing little or nothing in the way of punching.

The thirteenth round was a frantic one. Ray reeled about the ring, rubbery from fatigue. His swings were wild, easily avoided by the calm Maxim. On one occasion Robinson almost pitched right through the ropes. Then he brought up a right uppercut from down around his ankles, missed, and fell flat on his face. But just before the end of the round Ray summoned all his ebbing power and shot a hard right cross to Maxim's chin. Joey blinked but did not go down.

When the bell sounded to end the thirteenth, Robinson was holding onto the ropes in a neutral corner, his eyes glazed, his knees bent. Ray's handlers had to scramble across the ring to get him. They got him back to the stool and worked feverishly. Smelling salts were thrust under his nose, enough to send him back three feet under normal circumstances. Ice packs were pressed against face and neck. Dr. Schiff was there supervising everything. The bell rang for round 14. Ray could not get off his stool. Dr. Schiff informed referee Miller that Robinson could not continue. Maxim was declared the winner by a TKO in the fourteenth. The official diagnosis was heat prostration for Robinson.

The defeat and especially the frustrating circumstances under which it took place crushed the previously uncrushable Robinson for several months. He did not fight again in 1952. In December, he announced that he was retiring from the ring at the age of 31. He had been beaten only three times in 135 bouts. The Sugar Man announced a new career—he would be a cabaret performer, dancing and singing. Some big-time Broadway people put an act together for him. The asking price was $15,000 a week. For a while he got it, but the novelty wore thin. Bookings fell off. The asking price fell to $5,000 a week. Ray was running out of money. His Harlem investments were floundering. In November, 1954, he announced that he was returning to boxing.

He fought an exhibition with Gene Burton. Early in 1955, he beat Joe Rindone, and then he lost a 10-rounder to Tiger Jones in Chicago, of all places. Did it mean he was all through? Not quite. He won three fights in a row and earned another shot at the middleweight title, then held by Bobo Olson. The fight was scheduled for Chicago. Ray's luck held and his punch returned. He stopped Olson in two rounds.

That started the great juggling act with the 160-pound crown. In January, 1957, Ray lost it to Gene Fullmer, an awkward but aggressive fighter, in Madison Square Garden. On May 1, 1957, Ray took it back—in Chicago, of course. It was the fourth time he had won the title. At 36, he still had ring class, and he proved it against Fullmer. Gene mauled Ray for four rounds, elbowing, butting, digging to the body and keeping Sugar off balance. In the fifth, however, Ray rammed a right to the body. Fullmer dropped his hand instinctively. Ray started a hook from his left ear, and it was traveling fast when it exploded against Fullmer's chin. They counted Gene out. Ray was the champ once again.

In September, 1957, Ray lost the championship again. This time it was to the battle-scarred warrior from Canastota, New York, Carmen Basilio. It was a real war in New York, but the rematch was scheduled for Chicago. It was held in March, 1958, and Ray got the decision in 15 rounds. It was the fifth time he had won the middleweight crown. It was his sixth victory in a title fight in Chicago. It also was his last fight in Chicago.

Ray fought no more in 1958. In August, 1959, the National Boxing Association vacated Ray's title. Fullmer and Basilio were allowed to fight for the crown, and Gene won it on August 28, 1959. Robinson finally put on the gloves again in December of 1959 and knocked out Bob Young in two rounds in Boston. He then met Paul Pender in January, 1960. Pender won and was recognized as middleweight champ by the New York, Massachusetts and European commissions.

Robinson was nearing 40, an advanced age for a fighter. But he would not quit. He tried Pender again in June, 1960, and lost. In December, he went after Fullmer for the NBA title and managed to get a draw. In March, 1961, Gene whipped him in Las Vegas in another title match. Ray's speed was gone. His timing was terrible. His punches were at half-strength. Yet, something drove him on and on.

In 1962, he had six fights in such varied places as New York, Trinidad, Los Angeles,

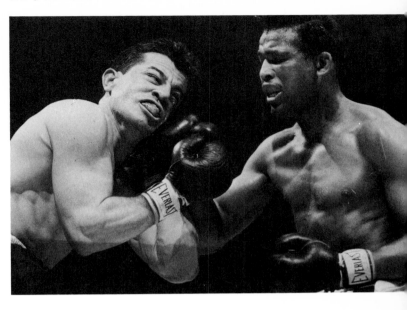

London, Vienna and Lyons, France. He won three and lost three. In 1963, he had 10 bouts, half of them in Europe, and won 8, drew one, and lost the other, in Philadelphia, to the only name fighter on the list, Joey Giardello.

In 1964, it was more of the same. Ten fights, most of them in Europe, none against top-flight opponents. Seven victories, two draw decisions and one loss. Ray's last year in the ring was 1965. He fought 15 times, but Young Joe Walcott was his opponent on 3 occasions and Stan Harrington on 2. Ray won nine fights, lost five and one was called no contest. On November 10, 1965, he lost to Joey Archer in Pittsburgh and was beaten so badly that he knew it was time to call it a day.

"When a light hitter like Joey Archer can drop me," Ray said, "I know it finally is time to quit."

The final scorecard on Sugar Ray Robinson was fantastic. He had 202 fights. He won 175—109 by knockouts. He lost 19 and had 6 draws. One fight was ruled no-decision and one no-contest. He was stopped just once, by a merciless thermometer at Yankee Stadium.

For one who engaged in so many bouts, the Sugar Man said something rather odd when he quit, "You know, I never liked fighting," he admitted, "although I guess I owe everything to the ring." That didn't stop him from being elected to the boxing Hall of Fame. No fighter has deserved it more.

CHARLES MOREY

221

The Age of Affluence

They called it "the Sports Explosion." It wasn't that it happened all of a sudden—it just seemed so. One spring morning one awakened to find himself smothered with sports events of high priority. Major league baseball was starting another season. Postseason play-offs in two rival professional basketball leagues, the National Basketball Association and the American Basketball Association, were vying for headlines and the spectator dollar. The battle for hockey's Stanley Cup was in full swing. The pro golf tour was featuring big money tournaments every weekend, and the tennis pros, contract and otherwise, were fudging in on weekend network television space. Pro football was arranging its preseason schedule, which was to begin in August.

Entering the 1970s, big-time sports hit on all cylinders. Across the country, old ball parks were being razed and replaced by glistening new multipurpose arenas of glass and stone. Houston's Astrodome, built in 1965, served as a model. The administrators of all sports—baseball, football, basketball and hockey, particularly—extended their seasons in an effort to milk the last dollar from the avid fan. The golf tour became a $7-million-plus enterprise, with a $60,000 first prize sometimes hanging on a single putt. Lamar Hunt, the Texas millionaire, bought up the contracts of leading tennis professionals and put them on a $1 million tour, rivaling the national associations, which in rebuttal set up their own $1 million circuit.

The seventies introduced the age of superstars with super-appetites. Athletes no longer were mere performers. They were conglomerates. Joe Namath, the widely hailed quarterback of the New York Jets, opened a string of cocktail lounges called the Bachelors III, one of which he was forced to separate from in New York by edict of National Football League commissioner Pete Rozelle. He and Yankee slugger Mickey Mantle shared an employment agency. Broadway Joe acted in movies, had his own television show and lent his name to a popular Christmas item—Joe Namath dolls.

His ancillary interests were rivaled only by those of Arnold Palmer, the first of the millionaire golfers. Arnie owned a chain of pitch 'n' putt courses, built his own golf company, manufactured golf carts, attached his name to several clothes manufacturers, owned a printing firm and even had a controlling interest in a bank. He made instruction records, wrote books, did TV commercials and also had bit parts in movies. Jack Nicklaus and Bill Casper followed suit on a smaller scale.

It got to a point that a topflight athlete felt undressed if he did not have a business manager, a tax lawyer and a public relations expert always at his elbow. Salaries skyrocketed. Outside interests mushroomed, turning athletes into business tycoons. Established banking firms turned their attention to a new and lucrative facet —that of the management of sports stars.

Nicklaus, Palmer and Lee Trevino, all were $200,000-plus winners in official golf earnings. Rod Laver, the tennis pro, won more than any of them—close to $300,000. Hank Aaron, the Atlanta Brave who became the main challenger for Babe Ruth's all-time home-run mark, in 1972 signed a three-year contract for a total of $600,000. Pele, the soccer player, claimed that he earned $500,000 a year in salary and bonuses. The war between the National Basketball Association and the American Basketball Association produced $1 million contracts for fuzz-faced kids. Most of the superstars drew salaries equivalent to that of a president of a leading corporation.

The dollar mark made its imprint on all big-time sports. Major league baseball players struck at the start of the 1972 season over demands for an increased pension fund. The rival basketball leagues went to Congress with a bill to merge, contending it was necessary to prevent dual suicide. Curt Flood's suit against baseball, seeking to throw out the reserve clause binding a player to one team for life or until traded or sold, went to the Supreme Court.

Meanwhile, the sportsmen themselves continued to grow in size and skills and brought forth the consensus: "Every year people become bigger and stronger—run faster, throw farther, jump higher and do things better. Records were made to be broken. Comparisons are odious but one thing is sure: The present-day athlete always is the best."

Willie Mays
Say Hey

Willie Mays turned down the champagne. He smiled through a mask of weariness in the San Francisco Giants' clubhouse after the 5–1 victory over the San Diego Padres that clinched the National League's Western Division title on the final night of the 1971 baseball season.

"That's not for me. I don't drink. That's for them; they deserve this moment so much," the 40-year-old center fielder explained as his younger teammates went through the cork-popping ritual of champions. "I'm excited the young kids are having such a ball."

Another play-off, the third in Mays's career, stood between the Giants and the World Series. The victory at San Diego left the Giants one game ahead of the Los Angeles Dodgers at the end of a wild pennant race. The Eastern champion Pittsburgh Pirates were rested and waiting.

"I just want to rest myself and get ready," said Mays, whose fourth-inning double drove in the first San Francisco run in the division-clinching victory.

The Giants won the opener of the best-of-five series with Pittsburgh but were beaten soundly, 9–4, in the second game on October 3. The Pirates went on to win the championship series in four games. Mays's final home run in a Giants uniform came in a losing cause on October 3, exactly 20 years after he watched the most famous home run in the team's history from the on-deck circle at New York's Polo Grounds.

He had had just four months' major league experience and was little more than a year out of high school in Fairfield, Alabama. The Giants, who signed him out of the Negro National League in early 1950, didn't intend to rush him to the Polo Grounds. It just happened that way.

Willie Howard Mays was born May 6, 1931, in Westfield, Alabama. His father, William Howard Mays, worked in the Birmingham steel mills and was a pretty good ballplayer—a center fielder—for black semipro teams in the area. Willie played with his father, usually in left field, before joining the Birmingham Black Barons of the Negro National League at 17.

"That was tough pro ball, let me tell you," Mays recalled about the league that produced most of organized baseball's early black stars, including Jackie Robinson, who broke the color barrier by signing with the Dodgers' organization in 1946. "I just played home games until the summer, when school was out. Then I was allowed to go on the trips."

Giants' scout Eddie Montague, assigned to scout another Barons' player, spotted Mays in the spring of 1950, and the Giants signed him for $5,000. Mays stayed with the Barons through May, until he finished high school, and then reported to Trenton of the Class B Interstate League, where in 81 games he batted .353. The Giants promoted him to Triple A ball the following spring. He joined the Minneapolis Millers of the American Association, and after 35 games he was batting .477 with eight homers and 30 RBIs.

Back in New York, the Giants were struggling. They opened the season with a loss, won a game and then collapsed into an 11-game losing streak. In late May, they were fifth in the standings. The Dodgers were on top, clearly the team that would have to be beaten. Giants' manager Leo Durocher thought they could be.

The call went out for Willie Mays.

"I was in Sioux City, Iowa, at a movie, and they flashed it on the screen," Mays recalled 21 years later. "It was a message telling me to go back to our hotel. Tommy Heath was my manager and he told me that the Giants had called me up."

Heath was left momentarily speechless by Mays's reaction. The 20-year-old center fielder, doubting he could handle big league pitching, didn't want to go. Heath and Mays then called Durocher, and the perturbed Giants' manager told Mays that the call-up was a command, not an invitation. Instead of playing an exhibition game in Sioux City, Mays left for New York. Giants' owner Horace Stoneham put an ad in Minneapolis newspapers, apologizing to Millers' fans for taking away their star.

Mays, in uniform number 24, joined the Giants on May 25. The solidly built 5-foot 11-inch athlete weighed 185 pounds, the same number of

Following a game-ending catch in Philadelphia in 1954, Mays rushes past young admirers. Willie has been one of baseball's most popular players since his debut in 1951.

pounds he would weigh some 20 years later.

His first three games were in Philadelphia, where the Giants won three straight. Mays had no hits in 12 at-bats.

Then the team returned to New York. The Giants' fans disregarded the out-of-town box scores and cheered Mays as if expecting something special. The rookie's first plate appearance was against the Boston Braves' Warren Spahn, the league's classiest left-hander. Mays knocked the first pitch over the left-field roof for the first of 646 regular season home runs he would hit as a Giant. The Giants lost that game, 4–1, but Mays would help beat Spahn several times later in the overlapping years of their careers. The great southpaw served him more home run pitches (18) than any other hurler.

After Mays's ice-breaking big league hit, his batting troubles resumed. One day Durocher found the rookie, batting .039, sitting by his locker in tears.

"I can't do it," the youngster told the manager and asked to be sent back to the minors. Durocher told him he was staying where he was, in center field for the Giants, so that he might as well stop worrying.

"That was what I needed. My problem was just a confidence thing," Mays said after two decades as the team's center fielder. He batted .274 in 121 games, hitting 20 homers and driving in 68 runs, and was voted National League Rookie of the Year in 1951.

By the time the Dodgers and Giants reached the most famous play-off in baseball history, Willie Mays was known as "the Say Hey Kid." In that rookie season, he couldn't always remember the names of his new teammates.

"You don't have to say something many times to get a nickname," Mays recalled as one of the game's most venerable veterans. "If I couldn't think of a fellow's name, I'd say, uh, 'Say Hey.' But it's been a long time since I didn't know the names of the fellows I play with."

Also, Mays said, "It used to take a long time before you were accepted. I was really lucky, but most rookies got a hard time. Everybody helped me. That's why I was lucky. Leo Durocher, Alvin Dark, Eddie Stanky, a lot of guys. I wanted to learn, and I'm still learning."

In Mays's case, the tendency to haze a rookie was tempered by recognition of talent.

Whether playing in Candlestick Park or in Ebbets Field, Willie was the same great fielder. Above: Missing a Drysdale hit. Right: Foiling Brooklyn.

"He didn't get any hits right at first," said Wes Westrum, the Giants' catcher and a .219 hitter in 1951, "but Willie hit line drives. We could see he was going to be a great one."

Durocher said, "Willie could do everything the day he joined the Giants, and the only other player who could do it all was Joe DiMaggio." Mays's first major league manager concluded, "Willie Mays can do the five things you look for in a player—run, catch, throw, hit for distance, hit for average—better than anybody I ever saw. So he never had to be taught a thing."

In the 1951 World Series, Mays managed only four singles in 22 at-bats. The New York Yankees, with DiMaggio playing his final games in center field and rookie Mickey Mantle in right, won in six games.

Despite the rookie honors and predictions of stardom ahead for Mays, his 1951 record reflected only great promise. In his first full major league season, the promise was realized. But the year was not 1952. Mays played only 34 games that season, before the army took baseball's best young center fielder and made him the center fielder for a service team at Camp Eustis, Virginia. Giants' fans found out how those Minneapolis people felt a year earlier. Uncle Sam didn't send any apologies for taking away Mays.

The Say Hey Kid returned to the Polo Grounds in 1954. He brought with him the "basket catch," something he picked up on his own. He now caught most fly balls with his hands cupped by his belt buckle, in a style so smooth there was nothing ostentatious about it. Pennant hopes began stirring again, although the 1953 Giants had finished 35 games behind the champion Dodgers.

Willie made up for lost time, particularly in the home run department. By the end of July, he had 36 homers, for a pace that no one in National League history had maintained before. Babe Ruth's record of 60 homers was within reach.

But Durocher asked Mays to concentrate on hitting for average. The pressure of keeping up with Ruth's 1927 pace disappeared and Mays's average went up as the Giants rolled to a pennant. On the last day of the season, he went three-for-four against Philadelphia's Robin Roberts and won the league batting title with a .345 average, beating teammate Don Mueller and Brooklyn's Duke Snider. Mays settled for just 5 home runs over the last two months, giving him 41 to go with his 110 RBIs.

He made his first All-Star Game appearance in 1954, getting a single that started him toward a record number of career hits in the midsummer classic. In October, he made one of the most famous fielding plays in World Series history.

The 1954 Cleveland Indians won 111 games, a major league record, and broke the Yankees' string of five straight American League championships. They were favored over the Giants when the Series opened in New York. "The catch broke our backs," Indians' manager Al Lopez said later of Mays's fielding gem in the eighth inning of the first game.

With the score tied 2–2, Cleveland runners on first and second bases and none out, Vic Wertz belted a 450-foot drive to center field. It was over Mays's head but he somehow got to it, catching it on the dead run with his back to home plate. He whirled—his cap flying off, another Mays's fielding trademark—and fired the ball back to the infield, a perfect throw that killed Larry Doby's chances of scoring from second after the catch.

Mays made another great fielding play in the tenth, one that he judged the tougher of the two, when he cut off a Wertz drive near the left-field wall and held the Indians' slugger to a double. The Giants won, 5–2, on Dusty Rhodes's pinch-hit homer in the bottom of the tenth and were on their way to a surprising four-game sweep of the Series.

The 23-year-old Mays was named Most Valuable Player in the National League. And he won the Associated Press's Athlete of the Year Award, beating out Dr. Roger Bannister, the British miler who broke the 4-minute barrier.

Willie Mays was the toast of New York, but the Giants had won their last pennant in the Big Town. He had to settle for personal achievements during the team's final three seasons at the Polo Grounds. In 1955, he hit 51 homers to win the first of four home-run titles. The team changed, with players like Thomson, Sal Maglie, Eddie Stanky and Monte Irvin leaving. Durocher also left. In 1957, the team finished sixth, 26 games behind the champion Milwaukee Braves. Attendance for the Giants' final two seasons in New York was the worst in the league, under 700,000 each year.

Stoneham decided to accompany the Los Angeles-bound Dodgers to the West Coast in 1958, and Mays said later, "The move cost me a million dollars, but I didn't say anything. There's nothing a ballplayer can do about things like that." Mays knew his immense popularity in New York could be turned into income off the field.

In San Francisco, Mays found, baseball fans already had a center field hero, Hall of Famer DiMaggio. "People wanted to compare me with Joe DiMaggio. He was my idol, too. I only had five years of major league baseball and I was proud to be compared with him, but they made it sound like we weren't friends," Mays said on his fortieth birthday, at a party attended by DiMaggio, one of his greatest admirers. "They said, 'Now show us,'" Mays recalled about his early San Francisco seasons.

He showed them with a .347 batting average, the best of his big league career, in 1958. He had 29 homers and 96 RBIs. The fans seemed more excited about Orlando Cepeda, the rookie first baseman who broke into the majors with 25 homers, 96 RBIs and a .312 average.

Mays remained the team's top attraction away from home. The Giants were consistently the league's best drawing team on the road, and Mays seemed to respond to the appreciative audiences. In 1959, for instance, Mays batted .339 in road games and only .287 in Seals Stadium. The next season, the Giants moved into Candlestick Park and Mays hit .338 on the road, .299 at home.

An inordinate number of his greatest plays and batting achievements also came on the road. On April 30, 1961, at Milwaukee he became the ninth player in major league history to hit four home runs in a game. All four drives carried at least 400 feet. "This is my biggest thrill," Mays said. "I knew the fans were pulling for me and it felt wonderful."

Mays hit three home runs in a game twice, both times on the road, in the early 1960s. In 1961, he found out how much he was missed in New York. A large crowd turned out on a rainy night at Yankee Stadium for a Giants–Yankees exhibition game and gave Mays a long, standing ovation when he was introduced.

The Giants' star made his off-season home in New York until 1962, when his first marriage ended in divorce after six years. Mays was married again in 1971, to San Francisco social worker Mae Louise Allen.

In 1962, the Giants gave San Francisco a National League championship. It was also the year that a new team, the Mets, moved into the Polo Grounds in New York. The Mets made a $650,000 offer to buy Mays, but Stoneham told them, "Mays isn't for sale or trade."

Mays once said he felt he had to show San Franciscans that "I loved the game of baseball and that all down the road I tried, I tried very hard." Late in 1962, with the Giants and Dodgers fighting for first place, it became evident to everyone how hard Mays played the game.

He collapsed in the Giants' dugout at Crosley Field on a hot, humid September night in Cincinnati. Doctors said it was just a case of nervous exhaustion. On Labor Day, 1963, he had a dizzy spell while batting at Candlestick Park and slumped to his knees at home plate. Dr. E. C. Sailer said that the baseball player was exhausted because he "plays so hard all the time. Some of the others take it a little easier sometimes, but not Willie."

Mays was out of the lineup four days after the incident in 1962. The Giants lost six straight games and appeared to be out of the race. With seven games to play, they were four games behind the Dodgers. But Mays and the Giants finished strong. The Dodgers couldn't hold their lead. On the last day of the season, Mays's eighth-inning home run off Houston's Dick Farrell gave the Giants a 2–1 victory. The Dodgers lost 1–0 to St. Louis, and it was play-off time again.

Willie did it all in the play-offs. He belted two homers, his forty-eighth and forty-ninth of the season, as the Giants won the opener, 8–0. The Dodgers won the second game—following the same pattern as 1951—and led, 4–2, going into the ninth inning of the rubber game. With the bases loaded and one out, Mays singled to drive in a run and make it 4–3. Cepeda tied the score with a sacrifice fly, two walks forced in the tie-breaking run and the final run in the 6–4 Giants' victory came home on an error.

The World Series, as in 1951, was somewhat of an anticlimax. The Yankees won in seven games, but Mays and Willie McCovey kept it interesting down to the final out.

Mays had a career-high 141 RBIs to go with his 49 homers, and he batted .304 in San Francisco's first championship season. He finished second in the Most Valuable Player balloting, behind Los Angeles's Maury Wills, who stole 104 bases that year for a major league record. Over the winter, the Giants' star signed a $100,000 contract, making him one of the highest-paid players in the game's history.

In the summer of 1963, in a game at Milwaukee, the Giants' center fielder threw out a runner at home plate to keep the score at 0–0. It remained that way until the sixteenth, when a Mays home run gave San Francisco a 1–0 victory. The pitcher: Warren Spahn. In 1964, Giants' manager Alvin Dark named Mays team captain, making him the first black player in major league history to hold such a job.

Mays hit 47 homers and totaled 111 RBIs in 1964 but batted only .296, dropping under .300 for the first time in eight years. One San Francisco columnist suggested that Mays's best days were behind. "I never did gain the respect of certain segments of the San Francisco press that I felt I deserved," Mays said several years later.

The 1965 season was perhaps Mays's greatest. He was the National League's Most Valuable Player, batting .317 with 52 home runs and 112 RBIs. He won his third home-run title in a four-year period. In August, he hit 17 four-baggers, the most any National Leaguer had ever hit in one month. But the Giants lost the pennant, overtaken by the Dodgers in the final weeks of the race.

"I'd rather have won the pennant than the award," Mays said. The Giants finished second, a spot they would occupy five frustrating years in a row.

Mays, at age 34, had 505 home runs. Everyone began asking him whether he thought he could break Ruth's major league record of 714. "I don't believe in goals," Mays said about the future. "You start worrying about goals and you don't do anything for the team. You play well and you get the records anyway."

There were several records in sight the following season, and Mays couldn't ignore the pressure as he approached them. Home run number 512, breaking Mel Ott's league record, came after a 10-day wait.

"It was a long time coming," Mays said, after hitting the milestone blast off the Dodgers' Claude Osteen in a 6–1 victory at Candlestick. A cake was waiting in the clubhouse. Mays didn't cut into it, remarking, "That thing must have been here a week."

On August 17, he passed Jimmy Foxx and became number two on the all-time homer list by belting number 535 off the St. Louis Cardinals' Ray Washburn in San Francisco.

Mays played in 152 games in 1966, establishing a major league record by appearing in 150 or more games a thirteenth consecutive season. He batted .288, with 37 homers and 103 RBIs.

But the baseball insiders admired most the things Mays continued to do that couldn't be summed up in cold statistics. "When it comes down to needing a run, he's the greatest," Dodgers' manager Walt Alston said after Mays's base-running beat his team one day late in the 1966 pennant race. In the twelfth inning of a game at Dodger Stadium, pitcher Joe Moeller had a count of three and nothing on Mays. There were two outs and no one on base. Alston told Moeller to walk Mays, believing that the 35-year-old star wasn't a threat to steal since he had a pulled groin muscle.

Rookie Frank Johnson followed with a single to right field and Mays scored from first. The veteran decided to go all the way after rounding third and noticing young second baseman Jim Lefebvre running the ball in after taking the throw from the outfield.

"It's hard to throw when you're running. I wanted to win the ball game," said Mays, whose hard slide knocked the ball out of the catcher's grasp at home plate and gave the Giants the winning run.

The defeated Alston said, "An ordinary guy doesn't try to score. Lefebvre hesitated just enough. I don't think he believed Mays would try to score."

An attack of flu put Mays in the hospital for a week in July of 1967, and he went without a home run that month. It was the first full month of his big league career that that had happened. Despite a good start for the season, he slumped to a .263 average and totaled only 22 homers and 70 RBIs in 141 games.

He came back in 1968 to play 148 games, with a .289 average, 23 homers and 79 RBIs. But in 1969, it appeared that his career was near its end. Sickness limited his playing time to 117 games, and he produced only 13 home runs and 58 RBIs while batting .283. His last homer of 1969 was number 600 of his career, a pinch-hit blast at San Diego that gave the Giants a victory.

The *Sporting News* named Mays baseball's Player of the Decade for the 1960s, and he started the 1970s with another comeback season. He had 28 homers, 83 RBIs and a .291 batting average for 139 games. On July 18, 1970, at Candlestick, he punched a single to

left field off the Montreal Expos' Mike Wegener to become the tenth player in baseball history to record 3,000 big league hits.

Another question he was tired of answering was how much longer he expected to play. "I'm not even thinking about next year. I'm thinking about now," he said. "Baseball wasn't fun last year. Maybe I'd lost interest in the game. This year, I decided to just go out and have fun. I'm feeling good."

Early in the 1971 season, Mays's fortieth birthday was celebrated at a party thrown by the Baseball Writers Association of America. One of the guest speakers, Joe DiMaggio, said this about Mays: "Too much emphasis is placed on his home run hitting. He is a hitter, all right, and one of the best that ever lived. But this man does it all. He fields, he runs, he studies, he hardly ever makes mistakes. . . . He is a very special person."

There was no need for DiMaggio to speak in the past tense about Mays's talents. The 40-year-old center fielder hit four home runs in the first four games of 1971. He was batting .406 when his birthday arrived and the team was in first place. "We're doing things together this year, in the clubhouse and on the field, things that win a pennant," Mays said.

The Giants held on to win the Western Division race, but Mays couldn't keep up his hot starting pace. He had 15 homers before the All-Star Game, in which he appeared for the twenty-second consecutive time, but only 3 after that.

"I know I'd have had more homers if I hadn't had to play so often. But I've had to play every day," said Mays, who filled in at first base for the ailing McCovey part of the season. He was in 136 games, batting a respectable .271.

"I was dead tired at the end of the season," he said the following spring. "But I wanted to get into the World Series. I thought it might be my last chance."

It was his last chance—with the Giants. They sent him to the New York Mets in a surprising 1972 trade, just after his forty-first birthday. "I'm very thankful I can come back to New York. I don't think I'm just on display here. There's no doubt in my mind that I can help the Mets," Mays said. He made his first appearance for the Mets on May 14. The Giants were visiting Shea Stadium and Mays's home run in the fifth inning broke up a tie game to give New York a 5–4 victory.

"There's no place to play like New York," Mr. Mays said. After one game, "the Amazing Mets" had a new nickname—"the Amaysings."

ERIC PREWITT

When, in 1972, Willie was traded from the Giants to the Mets, most fans felt that the reason for the trade was sentimental, but Mays pounded game-winning homers, as against the Phils (above).

233

Dick Butkus
"Animal"

During a game against the Miami Dolphins, Dick Butkus smashed into a pile of bodies. When the pile untangled, Butkus was accused of biting guard Larry Little and of trying to nip an official. Said Dolphins' center Bob De-Marco, "He's like a mule."

Throughout a game against the St. Louis Cardinals, Butkus ranged far afield and was charged with four personal fouls, one for trying to separate Willie Crenshaw's leg from the rest of his body. Said St. Louis coach Charley Winner, "I don't see why a player of his caliber has to do things like that."

During a game against the Detroit Lions, Butkus was accused of provoking three fights and indulging himself by poking his fingers through the face mask of tight end Charlie Sanders. Said Russ Thomas, the Detroit general manager, "That Butkus is an annihilating S.O.B."

"I guess," said Dick Butkus, in a rare moment of introspection, "people think the Bears keep me in a cage and let me out only on Sunday afternoons."

Dick Butkus, middle linebacker, Chicago Bears, became a prime source for research material; investigate his soul, check his heart, record his emotional polygraph. The reading was a synthesis of Gino Marchetti, Chuck Bednarik, Joe Schmidt and Deacon Jones—a prototype of every defensive player who ever went against an offensive player with premeditated mayhem in his mind.

The one word to describe such a prototype? Animal.

"It makes me sad sometimes," Butkus said. "Some people think I have to get down on all fours to eat my couple of pounds of raw meat every day. Nobody thinks I can talk, much less write my name. When I cut a record of Shakespeare quotes—a parody—the record company said it was too good. Not enough *deese, dems* and *doses*. What the hell is this society doing to people? I did what it told me I could do. I didn't have any identity crises. In the fifth grade, I knew what I was going to be—a professional football player. I worked hard at becoming one, just like society says you should. It said you

had to be fierce. I was fierce. Be tough. I was tough.

"I knew my trade. When I got to the Bears, I made it and I made it beyond the Bears. I made it to all-pro. And then what happened? They call me an animal."

Butkus never discouraged it, and what he did encouraged it. There was the incident against Miami. Against St. Louis. Against Detroit. His teammates added to the picture. "With the highest respect," said tight end Mike Ditka, "I've got to say Dick is an animal. He works himself up to such a competitive pitch that the day of the game he won't answer a direct question. He'll grunt. I saw Jim Taylor come around end on a power sweep for Green Bay and Butkus, getting over there from the middle, grab him by the throat with one hand and bring him down."

"He'll be all right," defensive back Ron Smith said once when it was pointed out that Butkus seemed somewhat out of sorts, "as soon as he has his couple of cups of blood. You know him—he chews cement and spits out sidewalk."

The opposition sharpened the image in similar language. "He plays the middle like a piranha," said Joe Walton, a scout for the New York Giants. "He gets himself so angry at the other team that he plays like a wild man."

"He's very foul-mouthed on the field," said Detroit center Ed Flanagan. "Foul-mouthed and insulting."

"If he doesn't tackle you," said Pittsburgh quarterback Terry Hanratty, "you can still hear him coming. You know he's going to be there eventually. It's savage."

The picture is undeniably animal. But the picture, like the cover of a book, doesn't necessarily reveal the whole story. The whole story reveals an athlete with the heft (245 pounds) to hurt the opposition, the agility required by the position and the dedication to his profession that has enabled him to rise above the rest; to rise so high that the image overshadows the man. "Dick Butkus is a legendary football player," said Los Angeles coach Tommy Prothro after he had spent his first year watching But-

"Some people think I'm kept in a cage and let out on Sundays."

kus. "I never thought any player could play as well as writers write that they play, but Butkus comes as close as any I've ever seen."

How close he actually came is reflected statistically. At the height of his career, from the day he became a rookie pro in 1965, to 1971, when his knees began to give way, he averaged some 200 tackles, unassisted and assisted, each season; totaled 19 interceptions and 20 fumble recoveries (just 2 under the National Football League record) and scored twice, on a safety and on a conversion pass. After studying Butkus's game films, in which defensive players are graded on four important areas—being at the point of attack, pursuit, performance on dropback passes and performance on play-action passes, Bears' coach Jim Dooley reflected on Butkus's achievements:

"It's impossible for a player to get a one hundred percent score in all four areas. Butkus consistently receives the highest grades among our defensive players. What Butkus does best is being at the point of attack. That's always his best grade. Butkus often has been scored between ninety and one hundred percent on all four general items. That makes him the NFL's Phi Beta Kappa of defensive football."

No one ever accused Butkus of being a Phi Beta Kappa in any other category, least of all Butkus himself. One of nine kids—and not the biggest—of a Lithuanian family growing up on Chicago's rough South Side, Butkus absorbed the lessons it had to offer. "You gotta be hungry," he always explained. "You see this in different neighborhoods, looking at the kids.

The well-off kid doesn't have the aggressiveness. He's got everything. But the kid on the other side of the tracks, he's going to fight you down to the last straw."

Butkus channeled his aggressiveness into football—actually became obsessed with the idea of a pro football career in grade school—and devoted his adolescent and teen-age years to reaching his goal. "Football is just what I always wanted to do," he explained. "Some guys' goals change many times. Mine never did. I didn't like school one bit. I wanted to quit at first, but I went through with it because I knew that was how I could get to my goal."

As soon as he arrived at the University of Illinois, coach Pete Elliott knew what he had. "Without any question," said Elliott, "we knew from the first day he reported that he was a great one. He moved well and he had a sure instinct to do the right things. I never saw him take a loafing step." The honors came —two-time all-America, Lineman of the Year, and number three in the Heisman trophy balloting. But the biggest reward was just around the college corner. The Bears made him a number-one draft choice and lured him into the NFL (the war with the American Football League still was on) for a contract reported to be $235,000.

It was different in the pros; he was accorded the same treatment as every rookie. A group of veterans, discovering that Butkus's shoe size was 11½ triple E, dubbed him "Paddles" and told him he "looked like an elephant on roller skates" when he attempted to do one of the Bears' balancing exercises. In addition, Butkus admitted to being confused by the mountain of material he had to absorb in order to handle the intricate middle-linebacking position. "It's all I can do to figure out where I'm supposed to be," Butkus said at one frustrating juncture.

What Elliott knew he had when Butkus came to Illinois, George Halas of the Bears quickly realized he had when Butkus came to the pros. When the 1965 season started, Butkus started it at middle linebacker. It wasn't long before everyone else knew what Elliott and Halas knew. The accolades poured in from the Baltimore Colts after they faced Butkus for the first time. "He's the best rookie I've ever seen in my time in the league," said tackle Jim Parker.

"Me, too," said running back Lenny Moore.

"He'll be all right as soon as he has his couple of cups of blood. . . he chews cement and spits out sidewalk." Right: New York Giant, Homer Jones, looks up as number 51 gets set to blast.

"Every time I saw daylight and made my break, there would be number fifty-one closing off the hole."

Butkus closed off so many holes, knocked down so many passes, knocked down so many people that even though he was a rookie, there was no way to keep him off the all-NFL team. He was there throughout the rest of the 1960s, the only question then being whether he was the best of all time—better than Bednarik, Schmidt, Huff, Nitschke.

Possibly the most amazing aspect of that question is that while the argument raged, the best record the Bears were able to put together after the 1965 season was the seven wins, six losses and one tie they managed in 1967. Nevertheless Butkus maintained his hold on the all-NFL middle-linebacking spot. Few people may have been watching the Bears at the time, but everyone was fully cognizant of Butkus's ability. The image never faded—the fearless defender, the ferocious tackler. When he hit, it hurt. When he didn't hit, you still looked for him. His very presence gave the Bears respectability. What Gale Sayers was to the Bears' offense, Butkus was to their defense. Each was a game-breaker, a guy who all by himself could win a game.

Nothing is more indicative of that fact than Butkus's performance in the Bears' 1971 opener against Pittsburgh. Making only his second start following off-season knee surgery, Butkus intercepted passes in the first and second quarters, then won the ball game for Chicago in the fading minutes of the final half. The Steelers led, 15–10, and had a first down on their own 19, needing only to run out the clock to win.

Abe Gibron, the Chicago assistant coach, and Butkus discussed strategy on the sidelines. It was decided to unleash Butkus on the "fumble blitz." Butkus was the acknowledged master of the strategy, in which the middle linebacker charges with the snap of the ball with the express purpose of getting the hand-off from the quarterback before the running back can take possession.

Steeler quarterback Terry Bradshaw spun to hand off to Warren Bankston—and there was Butkus. "He damn near took the hand-off," said Gibron. While Butkus didn't get the ball, he did jar it loose. Ed O'Bradovich recovered for the Bears, and Kent Nix's touchdown pass to George Farmer with 44 seconds left gave Chicago a 17–15 victory. Butkus, however, was the key—with just that one play—turning defeat into victory.

Still, with the general public, Butkus was more the animal let out of his cage on Sundays than the skilled performer doing his job as well as it ever has been done. Butkus studied Shakespeare to help his diction. While his diction improved, he continued to contribute to his image, because whenever he was called on to articulate, the words tumbled out with such honesty that diplomacy was forgotten.

Asked if he had actually bitten a Miami player, Butkus replied, "I was on the bottom of the pile. You think I'm dumb enough to start a fight when I'm on the bottom? Besides, I'm a football player, not a gourmet."

Does he ever have any feeling about the men playing opposite him? "I don't personally like anybody," Butkus answered. "I don't like to get involved with people on the field. If I can intimidate anyone, I will. It's part of the game. I want to get a good measure on a guy and strip him down. If I can strip him down and make him drop the ball, that takes it out of guys."

Is Dick Butkus really as mean as he sounds? "I wouldn't ever set out to hurt anybody," Butkus replied, "unless it was, you know, important—like a league game or something."

Those closest to him have attempted to explain. "It's his intensity," said O'Bradovich. "You can see it in his eyes. He has complete and total desire to win. I don't care if we're down forty points with a minute to go, he just has to get in there and hit."

"Dick is one of the last old-generation type of players," said Gibron. "He's one of the last of the great guys who play without asking or giving any quarter."

Those who have played against him agree. "You can say anything you want about Butkus," said the same Charlie Sanders who has had Butkus's fingers in his eyes, "but he's a great football player. You may hate him, but you've got to respect him."

"Dick doesn't like to be blocked and he gets a little overzealous sometimes," said the same Bob DeMarco who called Butkus a mule, "but he's a heck of a football player. No question about it—a rugged performer."

"Butkus," said Phil Bengtson, when he was coaching at Green Bay and owed his allegiance to Nitschke, "rates with any linebacker I've ever seen—Bulldog Turner, Joe Schmidt, Ray

"I wouldn't ever set out to hurt anyone." Father Dick with son.

Nitschke, George Connor. He has as much enthusiasm as any player I've ever known."

The enthusiasm, according to Butkus, was a product of the love of a man for what he was doing. "Ever since I was in the eighth grade, I've been nuts about this game," he explained. "I love to hit and I love to win. It has to be that way. You can never let yourself be embarrassed. I always keep in mind that any game could be my last. You never know in this business. I wouldn't ever want my last game to be a stinker."

Alex Karras, the Detroit defensive tackle who built his own reputation as a mean character, never saw Butkus play a stinker. But he was always certain that the Bears would have played plenty of them without Butkus. "He is the best all-around football player I've ever seen play the game as far as dominating the game and doing an individual job is concerned," said Karras. "He's very aggressive and brutal—very

brutal, and he'll beat you up. He's a wild, wild performer. If you had eleven like him going against you, you wouldn't get any points on the scoreboard. Ever.

"He's one of those rare superstars—like Wilt Chamberlain and Lew Alcindor in basketball or Gordie Howe in hockey in his great years, where just by being on the field the game changes. He has to be the best middle linebacker I've ever seen in my life. He absolutely keeps that defense together. He *is* their defense."

Maybe even more. At the end of the 1971 season, a young lady living in a Chicago suburb, an obvious fan of the Bears, wrote to a local newspaper to tell of an incident that had just occurred. The young lady had written to the Bears requesting a team picture.

The Bears sent her a photograph of Butkus.
MIKE RATHET

239

Wilt Chamberlain
The Champion Who Always Was

Cheers rolled down in waves from the Los Angeles Forum, a deafening crescendo that was music to Wilt Chamberlain. A smile cracked his usually expressionless, bearded face as he sat on the sidelines, work done, and waited for time to signal a new National Basketball Association champion for 1972—his Los Angeles Lakers.

The game-ending siren broadcast the death of the New York Knicks. The Lakers had won their first NBA championship with a 114–100 victory. Chamberlain was the man most responsible.

"The guy we could least afford to lose in these play-offs was Wilt," said teammate Jerry West. "He was simply the guy that got us here."

"I have never seen Wilt play as well over a sustained period as in these play-offs," said Bill Russell, an old friend but an NBA enemy when he was with the Boston Celtics.

The "Big Dipper," figuratively termed a fading star years before 1972, shone brightly at the age—ancient for basketball—of 35. Chamberlain was as good as ever—maybe better.

He played with pain throughout the season, a distressing hazard of his profession, but helped the Lakers set a spectacular modern sports record of 33 straight victories. The team wound up with 69 triumphs, also a record.

Broken fingers and stretched ligaments notwithstanding, the old man of the Lakers delivered his teammates to a surprisingly easy victory over the tough Chicago Bulls in the opening round of the play-offs. He then outfinessed the NBA's Most Valuable Player, Kareem Abdul-Jabbar, as the Lakers cut down the powerful defending champion Milwaukee Bucks in the Western Division finals.

The Knicks, then, remained the only hurdle left for the title-hungry Lakers, who had attended many of these play-off affairs through the years but had always gone home losers.

Swathed in bandages, cushioned against further injury, Chamberlain played his best basketball after the opening game, won by New York. He soared to block shots, swooped high to score and intensified his all-around talents as the individual situation happened to demand.

After three straight victories over the Eastern Division winners, the final contest was Chamberlain's most dramatic. A fall in the fourth game had sprained his right wrist, and Chamberlain was a doubtful starter for game number five in Los Angeles. The morning of the crucial match, the Laker center was reported to be in such great pain that he couldn't lift a spoon to eat.

Chamberlain had spent an uncomfortable night treating his wrists with ice packs and whirlpool baths at his fabulous $1.5 million Bel Air mansion. He reported to the Forum with the swelling in his wrist significantly reduced.

"We brought a ball into the locker room," said Dr. Robert Kerlan, the Lakers' physician, "and as soon as I saw him palm it, catch it and throw it, I knew enough flexibility had been restored so that he could play. But, believe me, this was a serious injury and an unexpectedly fast recovery."

He played that night—and gave a demonstration few will forget. The leading man of the Los Angeles cast scored 24 points, had 29 rebounds and harassed New York shooters no end. With a little more than a minute left and the game belonging to the Lakers, the big man strolled off the court to standing applause. The strength he showed in the play-offs was reminiscent of bygone glories.

He stole the scene wherever he went because of his Herculean proportions. At 7 feet 1 inch, Wilt Chamberlain did not tower over all his contemporaries in the National Basketball Association. With his mountainous height, however, he blended an almost supernatural strength. He was, in fact, a monster of a man who handled opponents on the basketball court as if they were pawns on a chessboard.

Chamberlain was self-conscious about his size and resentful of the curiosity he created in public life. He wanted to get lost in crowds, but this, for him, was impossible. A New York hotel had a special nine-foot, king-size bed built for him, and Wilt was invited to an unveiling that promised all the fanfare of the

Chamberlain blends mountainous height with Herculean strength.

launching of a battleship. He refused to show.

"What is it with people, anyway?" Chamberlain complained. "They see someone extra big and somehow all politeness is off. They seem to think nothing of just grabbing me or walking right up and breaking into a conversation. When I'm eating, they just stand there and watch me eat. I think they regard somebody unusual as public property."

If Chamberlain was unusual, it was in the most complimentary sense. If he was a freak, then he was a basketball freak—someone who was very special at what he did. He was called "the most perfect instrument that God made to play basketball." Certainly he revolutionized the professional game.

He unlocked ceilings on salaries as soon as he signed a contract with the old Philadelphia Warriors. He not only broke scoring records, he splintered them—and he stamped pro basketball as a big man's game. The graceful brute hyped attendance and transformed NBA franchises into money-makers. He changed the face of the game with one sweep of his backboard-rattling dunk shot that coaxed roaring responses from the crowd.

But for all his success as a single powerful force, the gentle giant was targeted for personal abuse, both on and off the court. "Whatever Wilt does is at once too much and not enough," said a sportswriter.

To chastise a player who scored 50 points and averaged 25 rebounds a game over the course of the long NBA season, as Wilt did in the 1961–62 season, seemed an incongruity. It happened to him, nevertheless. It was mainly charged that Chamberlain rarely gave 100 percent and wasn't a pure team player, the critics pointing to several barren years with no championships.

"The trouble is," said one of Chamberlain's former teammates, "that Wilt is so close to perfection, he's always being compared to the perfect. If he did everything better than anyone else, someone would say something like, 'He's all right, but he doesn't have a very good shot with his right foot.' "

Then there was his foul shooting—it was an obvious failing. Chamberlain admitted an all-too-human psychological barrier against the free throw. "Ridiculous—any high school player can shoot better than that," said Chamberlain's coach, Dolph Schayes, after a particularly galling defeat.

If people expected too much from the guy, it was a folkway indigenous to the American society. He was simply too big to be human in the eyes of many fans. This unreal figure had very human beginnings, however.

"I suppose it would make a better rags-to-something story if I could say that I was raised in those cotton fields far away and that some coach found me barefoot outside a backwater, one-room Georgia schoolhouse," said Chamberlain, revealing his droll brand of humor. "Actually, we were a pretty fine family from Philadelphia."

From West Philadelphia, it must be pointed out, since the boundaries of that city were clearly defined when Chamberlain came into the world on August 21, 1936. The section that bounded the Chamberlain home was not a rich area, to be sure, but it was at least a comfortable place of clean, well-lighted row homes, the trademark of old Philadelphia.

There was no immediate indication that Wilt would grow so tall. His father and mother were both of normal height, and the youngster was literally lost in a family of nine children until he was 10 years old. Then the genetic reach of his 7-foot grandfather touched him and the sky was the limit. Growing fast, he was soon knocking into things.

"I was always bumping my head in doorways and places where the ceiling was low," he recalled.

One day while playing in an empty house, he bumped into a pipe by accident and suffered a black eye. He was chided by friends and told that he should "dip under." They dubbed him "The Dipper," "Dippy" or "Dip." The tag later became a professional label.

His height soon became a problem for his father, Bill, a handyman at the Curtis Publishing Company. Not only was clothing expensive, but Bill Chamberlain spent half his off-hours raising all the chandeliers and light fixtures in his home. Wilt still had to sleep in a normal-size bed, however, uncomfortably curled into an S shape.

Basketball, never a passion with Wilt, entered his life in late boyhood when he and several thousand other Negro youths in Philadelphia realized that they could make a living out of it. Jackie Robinson had broken the color line in professional baseball late in the 1940s. The breakthrough had revolutionized the other major sports as well, and suddenly there was a reason for playing basketball—a college scholarship and, perhaps, a professional career.

Although Chamberlain had always thought it was a "sissy game," he decided to try it anyway. His first real taste of basketball came from Haddington Center, a recreational facility built by the city of Philadelphia. This center, just five minutes from Chamberlain's house, triggered a basketball boom in West Philadelphia. "Youngsters you round up on almost any street in Philadelphia would make high school all-Americans anywhere else," said Blinky Brown, recreation leader at Haddington and an early Chamberlain counsel.

Perhaps he was overstating the facts, but in Chamberlain's case it was so. And his talents grew with his height. By the time he was ready for Overbrook High School, he had exploded to nearly 6 feet 11 inches. "His legs were very thin and it didn't seem that they could carry him up and down a court," recalled. Brown. "In fact, I had a fellow once bet me that Wilt would never be strong enough to play college ball. One of the good things about him was that he'd always listen to his coaches. He'd listen carefully, but he'd always make up his mind about what he was going to do."

Most of his 202 pounds seemed to be resting atop two long stilts. A Philadelphia sportswriter immediately named him "Wilt the Stilt." "With that big torso atop those long, thin legs, he looked just like a man on stilts," said the writer. "The name came to me the first time I saw him."

Chamberlain never liked the name, but it stuck with him. "It sounds like some kind of an ugly bird," he said. "I prefer 'Dipper.'"

The gigantic teen-ager was also called "Hook and Ladder" and a dozen other nicknames as he displayed his "Dipper Dunk," a maneuver in which he'd rise high above the basket rim and drop the ball in while opponents stood around helplessly. The big fellow had lost most of his early awkwardness and now could shoot with the best of the pros.

"Wilt had unusual coordination," said Overbrook coach Cecil Mosenson. "He had great stamina, too. He could run all day."

As a sophomore, Chamberlain led Overbrook to the Public League title, even though the opposition threw triple-teaming defenses at him. In his junior year, he began attracting admiring glances from scouts as he broke scoring records by the basketful, taking his team first to the Public League title, then to the prestigious Inter-League championship against the city's Catholic school winner.

By the time he was a senior, Chamberlain was scoring at a point-a-minute pace. In each of two games he scored 90, and in another, 73. He blasted all Philadelphia's high school marks by a laughable margin as Overbrook again won both important city titles in his final year. In three seasons, Chamberlain had a record 2,252 points, an average of 37 per game. The team had lost only three times in three seasons under Wilt's omnipresent force. He had also led the Christian Street YMCA to the national YMCA title after his sophomore year, adding another dimension to his three-year accomplishments in Philadelphia.

He had grown to 7 feet, and people were continually asking him how the weather was up there. The youngster bore the jokes stoically and attempted to be polite most of the time. Other times, bored by thoughtless questions, he forgot the people were there. He became marked as a moody young man.

Chamberlain was romanced by several colleges during his senior year at Overbrook. He once counted more than 200 inquiries, many of them from major schools as far away as Hawaii. He spent weekends zigzagging around America on flying missions, courtesy of the various schools. After inspecting the school three times, he chose Kansas, mainly because he felt that Negroes were treated fairly there. Also, he liked the idea of playing under Forrest ("Phog") Allen, one of the country's most respected coaches.

There were reports about lavish offers that the highly publicized Chamberlain received for going to Kansas. "I had a full scholarship and a fifteen-dollar-a-month job, and that was it," said Chamberlain. "No one believed me."

Among the disbelievers were members of the NCAA, ruling body of collegiate sports. Chamberlain called them a "real ring-a-ding outfit" after several inquiring phone calls and an especially long interview session. They wanted to know what he had received for going to Kansas. After Wilt had told them, an NCAA member said, "It was nice talking to you, but I don't believe a word of it."

Coach Branch McCracken of Indiana, a school that Chamberlain had considered earlier, fanned the fires by saying, "We couldn't afford that boy Wilt. He's just too rich for our blood."

While McCracken squeezed the sour grapes

dry, Chamberlain officially became a Jayhawk. He got a royal welcome at the Kansas field house when 14,000 paid to see him perform as a freshman against the varsity. They liked what they saw. The towering youngster lived up to advance notices, scoring 42 points as the rookies beat the veterans, who were preseason favorites to win the Big Seven title.

More than a thousand miles away, in Syracuse, New York, the Warriors made Chamberlain their number-one pick at the NBA draft, expecting to collect him when his class was graduated four years later. It was quite a vote of confidence for a guy who had not yet played college basketball.

Hidden in relative obscurity his first year, since the freshmen didn't play an official schedule, Chamberlain managed to make news nevertheless. His amateur status was questioned by reports that he had played as a professional under an assumed name. He was arrested once on a charge of speeding. He missed some practice because of minor throat surgery. And an irate coach from an opposing school said he would sue whoever had written the story that said he had tried to reroute Chamberlain to his side.

With all the minor disturbances out of the way, the Jayhawks unveiled their fabulous Chamberlain as a varsity player in December,

1956. Playing under new coach Dick Harp, since Allen had been forced into retirement at the age of 70, Chamberlain scored 52 points and led Kansas to an 87–69 victory over Northwestern in his first game. The Jayhawks were ranked number one in the Associated Press's weekly poll, and by early in the season, they were given a better-than-even chance of winning the national championship.

Bill Strannigan, the Iowa State coach, scouted Kansas for an upcoming game and reported, "I'd enjoy the next few weeks if I hadn't seen Chamberlain. He's the greatest player I've ever seen. Why, once he even led a fast break. He was the middle man, and he passed off behind his back to set up a score. Who ever heard of a seven-foot player doing that? He's unbelievable."

"What can be done about him?" someone asked Strannigan.

"Just be patient—and he'll graduate," said the Iowa State coach.

"They'd set Wilt near the basket like the Statue of Liberty until the play developed," said a sportswriter. "He'd either shoot or pass out to an open man and then wait for a rebound. There was no give-and-go, no screens, few picks."

Wilt hankered to be a professional. That game, he said, was more wide open and suited to his varied talents. "The game I was forced to play at Kansas wasn't basketball," he said in a magazine article telling why he was quitting college. "It was hurting my chances of ever developing into a successful professional player." But he never knocked the school itself. "Kansas was great. I'll never regret the years I spent there."

Shortly after the article appeared, the big man signed a contract with the Harlem Globetrotters. "How in heaven's name will Wilt improve his professional talents with them?" somebody asked. The obvious answer was that he probably wouldn't, but he would get big money right away.

"I'm no comedy star," said Chamberlain, "but I started with a basic salary of sixty-five thousand dollars to go Globetrotting. By the end of the year I had added several bonuses. We were drawing great crowds, and the pay came out close to a hundred thousand dollars." By comparison, the top players in the NBA were getting about $25,000 to play a more-intense type of game. Chamberlain, always generous with his family, used some of the money to buy a spacious home for his parents in suburban Philadelphia.

He nostalgically called his year with the Globetrotters "the greatest time of my life." It wasn't all frolic, though. It was brutally wearing, physically and psychologically. It was a succession of one-night stands, long bus rides, poor food, sleepless nights and an overly long schedule. The Globetrotters' nonsensical brand of play never let them lose, of course, and they wound up with a 411–0 record in the 1958–59 season. Abe Saperstein, leader of the group, said that Chamberlain never shirked his responsibility as the leading attraction. He usually preceded the team into cities as a promotional gimmick, making special appearances, press conferences and hot dogs a daily diet.

In a way, Chamberlain was a revolutionary figure even before he made the NBA. The Globetrotters used him as a guard—probably the first and last 7-foot backcourtman in the history of basketball. But it added to the appeal of the team and improved Wilt's ball-handling techniques. The usual scheme was to feed the ball to him near the center line. "In two steps he'd be at the basket dunking it," said Saperstein. "The people went nuts."

The Globetrotters drew packed houses around the world and survived natural and un-

Left: Wilt in Kansas relays, performing in the hop, skip and jump. Above: Against Knicks. In 1972, Wilt achieved his ultimate goal, playing on team winning NBA championship.

natural elements—a riot in France, a bus strike in London and almost always terrible weather when they played outdoor games.

Armed with this crowd-pleasing charisma, the most publicized college player of his era sat down to talk contract with Eddie Gottleib of the Philadelphia Warriors. On May 30, 1959, he signed with the Warriors for an announced $30,000, plus "benefits" that were expected to put his name well above those of Bob Cousy and Bob Pettit, the big money-makers of the day at $25,000 per year.

From the moment Chamberlain stepped onto an NBA court, Gottleib never regretted the contract terms. Chamberlain's presence immediately gave the Warriors championship aspirations. They had finished in last place the year before. In his debut as a pro, Wilt scored 43 points, seized 28 rebounds and blocked many shots as Philadelphia beat the New York Knicks, 118–109, in Madison Square Garden.

Hardened professionals, such as perennial all-star Dolph Schayes, marveled at the rookie's excellence.

"He took a pass, backed into me and leaped high in the air as if he had been propelled off a launching pad," said Schayes. "When I jumped—and I'm six feet eight—my hands reached over the rim, but there was Wilt lookdown at me and stuffing the ball into the basket. At the same time, the Philadelphia public address system screamed, 'Another Dipper Dunk.' It was horrifying."

When Chamberlain had his long-awaited meeting, the start of a string of classic match-ups, with Boston's great Bill Russell, they played to a standstill. The Celtics won the game and it set a career-long pattern for the two close friends. Chamberlain was tired after the game and Russell was impressed.

"I've played against men as big," said Russell, "but never against anyone that good and big. You can't relax for a second against him. He's the best rookie I've ever seen. I wish I had been that good when I started."

Later that season, Chamberlain scored 58 points at Madison Square Garden to break the arena's record, one of many he'd rewrite. He scored 2,707 points in his rookie year—600 more than Bob Pettit's mark. He averaged 37.6 points a game—no one before had averaged as much as 30. He rebounded at the pace of 28 a game, also a new league high. He became the first player to score 50 points or more in

a game seven times in one season. He set league standards in field goals, shots attempted, foul shots attempted and minutes played. He helped the NBA boost attendance by 24 percent over the previous year. "Wilt is responsible for nineteen of that twenty-four percent," said an NBA official. Chamberlain was voted Most Valuable Player and Rookie of the Year, the first time that both awards had been given to one NBA player.

In fact, it was a perfect first season for Wilt the Stilt—other than the fact that his team couldn't catch the front-running Celtics and couldn't beat them in the play-offs. The terrible moment of defeat and the brutally taxing style of NBA ball had left Chamberlain drained, swearing to leave the game forever. "I quit," the rookie said. "I'll never play basketball in the NBA again."

He then came out of one of the shortest retirements in history to sign up for three years with the Warriors at an unprecedented salary. He was soon simultaneously acclaimed and disdained for being the best player in the league and for having the worst foul shot. While Philadelphia won its first nine games of the 1960–61 season, Chamberlain's misguided free throws were lost in the big winning margins. But when they began to lose close ones, the blame was often placed on the center's erratic charity throws. In one four-game losing streak, he hit only 24 of 63 from the foul line, an outrageous .379 average.

The situation became so severe that a private tutor was hired to give Chamberlain foul-shooting lessons. It didn't help much. "I kept saying, 'Don't let it bother you; don't let it bother you,' " Wilt reported. "But whenever you find yourself saying that, you know it is bothering you."

The gross inadequacies of his foul shooting, however, didn't prevent Wilt from having a sophomore year that was better, all-around, than his first. He became the first NBA player to score more than 3,000 points in a season. He built a stronghold of individual achievements—but still Boston finished first behind the less-spectacular Russell.

The departure of coach Neil Johnston, with whom Chamberlain had fiercely battled about playing style, and the arrival of Frank McGuire opened new scoring vistas for the star center in the 1961–62 season. The former college coach announced that he wanted his 7-foot wonder to "break every scoring record in the book." Wilt did just that. On March 2, 1962, he scored an incredible 100 points against the New York Knicks at Hershey, Pennsylvania, while the crowd chanted throughout: "Give it to Wilt! Give it to Wilt!" He had a fistful of league marks that year, but above them all he cherished his average of 50.4 points a game.

Once. again, the Warriors didn't win the championship, and Chamberlain's painful non-winning image grew heavier on his broad shoulders. They had come close to toppling the lordly Celtics, but McGuire said that close wasn't enough. "In this country when you finish second, nobody knows your name."

Critical abuse was now common to Wilt, who said he was sick and tired of the charges that he wasn't a championship player.

The next year the franchise was shifted to San Francisco and wound up playing second fiddle to the baseball Giants, not to mention the rest of the NBA's Western Division. Frustrations of that season boiled as the mild-mannered Chamberlain was involved in court brawls and was thumbed out of a game for the first time in his life. Under Alex Hannum the following season, the Chamberlain-led San Francisco team won the West but lost as usual to the Celtics.

The reasonably successful season, however, didn't ensure a money-maker in the Bay City. Although their star was a big gate attraction on the road, there was a distinct lack of fan support at home. So the Warriors, owned by Frank Mieuli, traded Chamberlain and his $65,000 salary to the Philadelphia 76ers in 1964 for three players distinctive only by their lack of distinction.

The agonizing search for basketball's championship ended two seasons later when Chamberlain finally caught up with Boston on April 11, 1967. It was "The Year the Celtics Lost the Pennant" by a crushing 140–116 score in the fifth and final game of the Eastern Division play-offs at Philadelphia's Convention Hall. The 13,000 fans chanted, "Boston is dead, Boston is dead" as time ran out on the defending champions.

When, with victory a certainty, Chamberlain was finally taken out of the game, the fans practically brought down the roof with their noisy enthusiasm. He had beaten back Boston with colossal blows: 36 rebounds, 29 points and 13 assists.

Wilt's college career began as a freshman at Kansas.

"I've been chasing them a long time," he said, "and it's hard to explain how I feel. But I'll really feel it in July and August. That's when people used to look at me as somebody seven feet one who couldn't be a winner."

Russell came into the raucous Philadelphia locker room looking for Chamberlain. He moved through the crowd, wearing his familiar black cape and a stoic expression. He reached Wilt and put out his hand. "Great," was all Russell would say.

"Right, baby," Wilt said, the face deadpan.

"Great," said Russell, then walked away.

The arch-enemies disposed of, four games to one, the 76ers then whipped San Francisco in six to claim the world title. It was almost anticlimactic after Boston, but Chamberlain had the championship ring this time, the one thing some said he would never have.

In later years, he took his $200,000-a-year salary to the Los Angeles Lakers in a three-for-one trade following exorbitant financial demands. He made a dramatic comeback from a knee injury that knocked him out of most of the 1969 season. Adding point number 30,000 to his career total and another NBA championship in 1972 were additional milestones. But more important, he could never again be called a loser.

KEN RAPPOPORT

Muhammad Ali
"Float Like a Butterfly—Sting Like a Bee"

"I am the king—I am the greatest," the young Cassius Marcellus Clay boasted when he was in his physical prime. "I float like a butterfly—sting like a bee. Rumble, man, rumble." He repeated the boast so often that it began to sound like a stuck phonograph record. At first, fight fans scoffed at him. "That Cassius," they said. "What a card!" They called him "Cassius the Gassius." They labeled him "Big Mouth" and "Blowhard."

Hardened ringsiders laughed at his poetry ("My shortest poem: 'Whee, Me!' "), indulged his assorted gimmickry and refused to be offended by his bombast. They regarded him as more or less a charlatan and a fake until that memorable night, February 25, 1964, in the auditorium at Miami Beach, Florida, when he scored an astounding seventh-round technical knockout over cold-eyed, awesome Sonny Liston. When he repeated the victory 13 months later in Lewiston, Maine—this time with his fabled "phantom punch" in the first round—no one dared laugh at the copper-colored destroyer from Dixie, who in the interim had adopted the Black Muslim name of Muhammad Ali.

Ali became more than a mere fist fighter. He became a social symbol. As a Muslim, he espoused peace and refused to take up arms for the United States. As a conscientious objector, he declined to take the step for military service. He was stripped of his title. Black militants and civil-rights groups rallied to his defense. Convicted on a charge of draft evasion, Muhammad took his case to the higher courts and scored perhaps his greatest triumph in the highest tribunal in the land, the Supreme Court.

In Chicago, the door of a South Side store swung open and the storekeeper, a small black man, rushed out after the customer who had just left after purchasing an orange. He grabbed the man, hugged him and shouted, "I'm so happy for you. You're free. You're freed."

"Thanks to Allah," said Muhammad Ali in his first reaction to the news the little man had heard on the radio that morning of June 28, 1971—that the U.S. Supreme Court had overturned Ali's conviction for draft evasion. Ten months later, Ali rested on a bed in a darkened hotel room in Oklahoma City the night after an exhibition fight and said in a voice husky with sleep, "I just want to sit one day and be an ordinary citizen, go to the hardware store, cut the grass. Don't talk to nobody, no more lectures."

But nothing was ordinary for Muhammad Ali from the very first stirrings of a career that carried him to the heavyweight championship of the world and to the brink of prison. He made people laugh and he made them curse; he earned their adulation and he was a target of their hate. But he was never ordinary, not in the ring as Cassius Clay–Muhammad Ali, the heavyweight champion, or out of the ring as Muhammad Ali, the Black Muslim.

Even after he lost to Joe Frazier on March 8, 1971, in the so-called Fight of the Century—his first professional defeat after a string of 31 victories—the garrulous Clay refused to be gagged. "I whupped him," he insisted in his rich Kentucky dialect. "I hit him more than he hit me. Look at his face. It looks like it's been through a meat grinder."

It did, too. The big, tough Frazier was so sensitive about the damage done to his profile that he refused to be photographed and remained closeted in his hotel room for two days afterward.

The two of them then began taking on set-up opponents while negotiations continued in the back rooms for a return bout, which hit a temporary snag when Ali reportedly demanded a $5 million guarantee.

Muhammad, while toning down his aging figure and seeking the punching sharpness of his younger years against a wide range of non-descript foes, continued in the public eye. He was a frequent guest on television shows. He was in wide demand on the college campuses. He stopped traffic in New York, Chicago and wherever else he elected to take a stroll on the streets.

There is no telling what majestic heights Muhammad might have reached had his battle with the U.S. government not taken three-and-a-half years out of his life at a period when his

"I am the king—I am the greatest." Muhammad Ali crashes a right to the body of Floyd Patterson in tenth round of their Las Vegas title fight, won by Ali in the twelfth round.

body and mind were at their absolute peak.

He was a superb athlete—6 feet 3 inches tall and weighing 210 pounds at his fighting best. His bronze skin, the color of coffee with plenty of cream, rippled with long, sinewy muscles that had an animalistic quality. He moved with the grace of a ballet dancer and punched with a speed that could not be followed by the naked eye. He had a fine, strong face— boyish and pleasant with big brown eyes. There was a boyish quality also about his personality. He was always on stage. He always was putting his audience on. But, on occasion, he could be aloof and fiercely cold.

Cassius Marcellus Clay was born January 17, 1942, son of a Louisville house painter and grandson of a Kentucky slave, who was first in the line to carry the name of Cassius Marcellus. "He was born with a noble name," said his father, Cassius Marcellus Clay, Sr. "He came into the world with a good body and a big head."

Young Cassius earned the reputation as a good rock fighter and a deadly marble player on the Louisville playgrounds. He took up boxing, fought in the gymnasiums and finally became good enough to compete in the Golden Gloves amateur tournaments. By 1960, when he was 18, Cassius had piled up 108 amateur victories with only eight defeats ·on his record. He won six Kentucky Golden Gloves titles, two National Golden Gloves and two National Amateur Athletic Union championships.

He represented the United States in the 1960 Olympics at Rome. Fighting as a light heavyweight, he knocked out a befuddled Belgian, a Russian, an Australian and a Pole en route to the title. "I was so proud of that gold medal I even wore it to bed," Clay said later. At the time he was a pleasant, outgoing youngster who had not yet taken the blustering, bragging role that marked him later as a professional.

As Olympic champion, he naturally attracted the eyes of professional promoters. Many made grabs at him, but he finally put himself in the hands of 11 captains of finance in his hometown of Louisville. The group was headed by Billy Reynolds, wealthy Kentucky businessman. The syndicate's arrangement was to pay all expenses and to give Clay $500 in cash each month and 50 percent of his earnings. Fifteen percent of the remainder was to be put into a pension fund, which was to start accruing when he reached 35. Clay received

$10,000 for signing and a guarantee of $4,000 the first two years. One of the country's leading trainers, Angelo Dundee, was hired to handle him.

Cassius was blessed with exceptional speed, fast hands and supreme confidence. Dundee taught him how to snap punches. Clay won his first six fights, five by knockouts and most of them before the fourth round. He was ragged but cocky. The more he won, the cockier he became and the louder he got.

As Clay's knockout record climbed to 9, then 10, then 11, Cassius started spouting poetry and naming the round in which his victims would fall:

> They all must fall,
> In the round I call.

He fought the veteran Archie Moore, who was on his forty-fifth knockout when Clay was born. Said Clay:

> Archie's been living off the fat of the land,
> I'm here to give him his pension plan.
> When you come to the fight, don't block
>   the door.
> You will go home after round four.

Archie went down in 1:35 of the fourth. Cassius went on to stretch his string of victories to 19 with a controversial decision over Doug Jones at Madison Square Garden on March 13, 1963, and a fifth-round knockout of Britain's Henry Cooper in London, June 18, of the same year. Now he was ready for a shot at the title, but no one gave him hope against Liston, the brute of a man who twice had mauled Floyd Patterson into insensibility in the first round.

This notion was magnified on the day of the fight at the weighing-in ceremonies. Clay entered the ring in a state of frenzy—feigned or genuine, no one was ever to know. He yelled. He screamed. He brandished his fists and stomped around the ring as if crazed. The chief physician, Dr. Alex Robbins, assigned to perform the physical examinations for the Miami Beach Athletic Commission, reported that Clay's pulse was pounding at a runaway speed. "He is scared to death," the doctor said, and commissioners went into a frantic huddle with the idea of calling off the fight on the grounds that Clay was unable to fight.

However, cooler heads prevailed. The fight

went on as scheduled. That evening, Clay, perfectly relaxed, came out of his dressing room to watch his brother fight in one of the preliminaries. He was the picture of poise and confidence.

The crowd watched and waited in the early rounds, expecting any minute for Cassius to fall. He didn't. While his aides in the corner chanted, "Float like a butterfly—sting like a bee," Cassius dodged, pedaled and punched. His fists darted like a cobra's tongue. The bearish Liston was stunned and confused. The bell rang for the seventh round, but Liston remained seated on a stool in his corner, saying he had hurt a shoulder. Cassius Clay was the new heavyweight champion of the world. But he barely made it. The former Olympic light-heavyweight champion, a seven-to-one underdog to the powerful Liston, was shoved into action at the start of the fifth round by trainer Dundee. In the fourth round Clay had gotten something into his eyes and had trouble seeing. "I can't see," he told Dundee as he returned to the corner, but Dundee calmly washed out the fighter's eyes and shoved him toward the title.

"I don't have to be what you want me to be," Clay said the next day in announcing that he was a Black Muslim. "I'm free to be who I want," he added, emphasizing that from then on he wanted to be known as Muhammad Ali. There were no other fights that year for Ali, but he still made news.

He married Sonji Roi, a Chicago model, whom he later divorced because she refused to abide by Muslim customs. And the Louisville draft board classified him 1-Y, stating that he didn't qualify on mental grounds for military service. "I never said I was the smartest; I said I was the greatest," quipped Ali.

Ali's first defense of the title was May 25, 1965, when he knocked out Liston in one round at Lewiston, Maine, and his last defense before boxing's governing bodies stripped him of the championship because of his draft trouble was a seventh-round knockout of Zora Folley in New York's Madison Square Garden on March 22, 1967. In between, he stopped Floyd Patterson in 12, outpointed George Chuvalo in 15, knocked out Henry Cooper in 6, knocked out Brian London in 3, knocked out Karl Mildenberger in 12, knocked out Cleveland Williams in 3 and outpointed Ernie Terrell in 15.

The fight with Chuvalo March 29, 1966, was routine, not nearly as significant to Ali's career as something that had happened six weeks earlier. On February 16, Ali was notified that the draft board had changed his classification to 1-A, making him eligible for induction. "How can they do this," Ali asked, "without another test to see if I'm wiser or worser than last time? Why are they gunning for me?"

He talked freely about the war in Vietnam, stressing, "I got no quarrel with them Vietcong." It was statements such as these at a time when American casualties were high, plus his Muslim affiliation, that forced Ali to fight Chuvalo in Toronto, Cooper and Brian London in England and Mildenberger in West Germany.

Ali fought again in the United States when he met Williams in Houston. He also fought Terrell in Houston and then had the Folley fight in New York. Then the city of Houston came into Ali's life again, for after the Folley bout, he was ordered to report to Texas on April 28, 1967, for induction into the army. Ali went to Houston, but he refused to take the traditional step forward that signifies induction into the military service. He was a Muslim minister and should be exempt on the grounds that he was a conscientious objector, he claimed. On June 20, he was convicted of draft evasion, fined $10,000 and sentenced to five years in prison. "If I was going to jail for stealing or hitting somebody, that would be bad," he said, "but when you're standing up for your beliefs, it's not bad—it is honorable."

Then began the numerous appeals of Ali's conviction. He wasn't put into prison, but he also didn't enter the ring. He was a fighter who couldn't get a fight, because promoters would not risk confrontation with public opinion. One by one the important governing bodies of the sport withdrew their recognition of him as the champion.

During his banishment from boxing, Ali got married again and kept busy in many ways. He got involved in a few business ventures; he made some television appearances; he lectured at colleges, something he enjoyed and continued to do even after he returned to the ring, and he even appeared as the star in a short-lived Broadway musical called *Big Time Buck White*. Meanwhile, Joe Frazier and Jimmy Ellis shared the heavyweight crown, and Frazier had it all after stopping Ellis in Madison Square Garden February 16, 1970.

In the summer of 1970, Ali got his chance to return to boxing when the Supreme Court

Ali finally goes down against Frazier in March of 1971. Each fighter was paid $2.5 million. Afterwards Ali's manager said, "Don't worry, we'll be back."

ruled that an individual seeking military deferment on the grounds of conscientious objection could be motivated by a powerful moral conviction and couldn't be kept from fighting. On October 26 of that year, Muhammad Ali made his celebrated comeback. Ali's most avid fans turned out in the 5,000-seat auditorium in Atlanta, Georgia. They came in hand-painted limousines, dressed in jewels and furs, men and women alike, and they watched him stop Jerry Quarry on a cut eye after three rounds.

"He was so close to being the Ali of three-and-a-half years ago, it was scary," said Angelo Dundee. There were those who agreed with the little trainer's opinion. Others, although they agreed it was a remarkable performance for a man who hadn't fought for so long, felt Ali would have encountered difficulty if the fight had gone the scheduled 10 rounds. So, the contract for Ali's next fight called for 15 rounds against Oscar Bonavena, who had gone a total of 25 rounds with Frazier in two fights without being knocked down and had knocked Frazier down twice. The fight in Madison Square Garden, less than two months after the Quarry bout, fell on December 7, Pearl Harbor Day, a fact that brought cries of outrage from some veterans organizations.

"In nine, he'll be mine," chimed Ali in predicting he would knock the Argentine out in nine rounds. It was the talk of a younger Ali, of an exuberant Cassius Clay. But the Ali who fought Bonavena was a man of almost 29 who had lost something during his enforced layoff. The ninth round passed, and so did five more, and it was a weary and desperate Ali who was trying to hold off the bullish Bonavena. Ali knocked Bonavena down three times in the last round and won by a knockout.

"There's been a lot of talk about ring rust and coming back and having trouble in the late rounds," Ali said after the fight. "But in the late rounds, it was my skill and stamina that pulled me through. I ended up with more stamina than he did and more than Joe Frazier. He [Bonavena] said, 'You are the champion.' He said, 'You are stronger than Joe Frazier.'" Ali had come back but he had not come all the way back. There was still Frazier who held the title Ali felt belonged to him—and there still was the draft-evasion conviction and the accompanying five-year prison sentence.

The door of Toots Shor's restaurant in New York City opened on a cold day less than two weeks after Ali had beaten Bonavena, and through it strode Ali. He walked past the hat-check girl and down some stairs and began to shout, "I'm the greatest, I'm the greatest. Who's Joe Frazier? Float like a butterfly—sting like a bee." Across the room at the foot of the stairs, in a room jammed with reporters and photographers, sat Joe Frazier.

The time had come to announce the fight between Ali and Frazier to settle who was the real heavyweight champion of the world. It would take place March 8, 1971, in Madison Square Garden, would be witnessed by more than 300 million people throughout the world and the participants would receive a record guarantee of $2.5 million each.

Never did Ali display the showmanship, which set him apart from many other sports heroes and champions, to better advantage than he did at the signing of his fight with Frazier. He made himself the focal point. "Joe Frazier is too ugly to be champion," he shouted. "It's a big fight because of me," he hollered. "It's not big because of Joe Frazier. Joe Frazier never did no predictin'." Ali's prediction, disclosed on closed-circuit television shortly before the fight, was "Frazier falls in six."

The day of the fight arrived and was officially launched with the weigh-in. Ali climbed into the ring and was introduced as "the former heavyweight champion." He grabbed the microphone and snapped, "I'm sick and tired of all of this 'former champion' business. I'm gonna straighten this mess out tonight." He was noticeably irritated, but he was a far cry from the hysterical young man called Cassius Clay who weighed in seven years before for a shot at the title held by Sonny Liston.

The next morning in a hotel near the Garden, members of the news media were crowded into a room. The room was dark and at one end of it in an easy chair sat Ali. His voice was low. He seemed to be emotionally drained, detached from what he was talking about, and the right side of his face was swollen from a Frazier left hook. He talked of Frazier's pressure tactics and of his power and he said that he had hurt himself by clowning, but that he had outhit Frazier three punches to one and he felt that he had won nine rounds.

"Ain't no way I lost eleven rounds," he said, referring to one judge's card that had it in Frazier's favor 11 rounds to 4. One of Ali's aides moved through the room toward him, telling people to leave, to let Ali alone. But Ali nodded to him and said, "No, don't do that. I talk when I win, so I gotta talk when I lose."

He lost to Joe Frazier; he fought and lost like a champion. He had gone into the fight with 31 straight pro victories, and, in seeking to add to that string, he had jabbed, danced, punched in combinations and tried to buy time for his aching legs—clowning he later called it. But before a worldwide audience of 300 million, the "people's champion," as Ali called himself, could not stop Frazier and could not beat him. He fought back after being almost out on his feet in the eleventh round, and he got off the floor after being knocked down in the final round by Frazier's face-swelling hook. But at the final bell the faces of Ali and his cornermen showed that they knew the result even before the ring announcer declared Frazier the winner by a unanimous decision.

Ali did not go to the postfight news conference but to a hospital to have X rays of the swollen right side of his face. The X rays were negative. Drew ("Bundini") Brown, an Ali aide, went to the news conference and said, "Muhammad Ali will not be here. But don't worry about it, we'll be back. We ain't through yet. It was one of the greatest fights ever held. The people got their money's worth. Muhammad was out for three years. He's not complaining. We're not complaining."

A few days after the fight, Ali was telling anyone who would listen that he actually had won and he was talking about a rematch. But he was thinking about the U.S. Supreme Court and what it would do about his draft-evasion conviction. The Court, in an unsigned opinion, overturned the conviction, ruling that the Justice Department had misled Selective Service authorities by advising them that Ali's claim as a conscientious objector was neither sincere nor based on religious tenets. The vote was eight to zero, with Justice Thurgood Marshall abstaining.

"Life is full of pressures," Ali said after the Supreme Court decision. "I still got a lot of work to do."

ED SCHUYLER, JR.

Jack Nicklaus
The Golden Bear

Jack William Nicklaus attacks golf courses with a delicate power that ranges from howitzers off the tee to a near-surgical magic within sight of the cup. Few tame "the Golden Bear."

Even as a teen-ager, Nicklaus idolized golfing perfection, extracting traits from the winning methods of men such as Ben Hogan, Bob Jones, Byron Nelson and Sam Snead. Playing at full bore, he seemed to be a composite of greatness.

Jack bankrolled $1.5 million in his first 10 years as a pro, but while enjoying the pleasures of wealth, money was never the premier measuring stick in the mind of the solid thinker from Ohio State University.

"My goal is to win more major championships than any other man," he always said. "That is the true test. People twenty years from now won't be impressed that I earned two hundred fifty thousand dollars playing golf in one year. But they might recall who won the most big ones."

Jones, who never played golf for money, established the target of 13 major victories, and only Walter Hagen, who played golf always for money, had ever challenged that figure—he won 11.

Big Jack pulled even with Jones by winning his third U.S. Open—his thirteenth major—in the blustery winds on Pebble Beach's seaside links in 1972. Then he looked to new horizons.

Nicklaus began by capturing the 1959 and 1961 U.S. Amateur championships. Turning professional in 1962, he quickly bagged the U.S. Open and the following year added a Masters crown and a triumph in the PGA championship. He won the Masters again in 1965 and 1966, the British Open in 1966 and a second U.S. Open in 1967.

"At twenty-seven, I had won nine major championships. Maybe it had been too easy, because I began to have trouble. Three years went by and I was beginning to wonder if I'd ever win my tenth. When I finally did, it fired me up again to surpass Bob Jones's total and,

with some incredible luck, perhaps win the U.S. Open, Masters, British Open and PGA all in the same year."

Jack got number 10 at the 1970 British Open, made it 11 by running away with the 1971 PGA and hit a dozen at the 1972 Masters, his fourth success on the wide, rolling fairways at Augusta National Club. Still in his early thirties, Nicklaus seemed destined to become the greatest golfer the world had ever known.

Following a glittering amateur and collegiate career, Nicklaus began immediately to make money from his golfing talents. He debuted at the Los Angeles Open amid much fanfare and pocketed his first check—$33.33 for dead last. Ten years later, the Golden Bear was a millionaire with 40 tour victories and outside revenue to match the $1.5 million he won swinging a club.

The 1971 PGA victory at Palm Beach Gardens, Florida, made him the first man ever to capture the "Big Four" professional titles twice, an accomplishment that Nicklaus only mildly relished while in pursuit of major championships that would allow him to catch and surpass Jones.

It began January 21, 1940, when Jack was born into the family of well-to-do Columbus pharmacist Charles Nicklaus, an athletic fellow himself who played football, baseball and basketball at Ohio State, won the city tennis championship of Columbus and set a couple of municipal golf course records.

Jack's first sports loves were, as with most teen-agers, baseball, football and basketball. He played endlessly at local playgrounds. All that became secondary, however, the day Charlie Nicklaus took his boy to play golf.

Jack and his dad went nine holes, and the 10-year-old shot 51. It was to be the highest score of his life. Jack Grout, resident pro at Scioto Country Club in Columbus, was more than impressed with the raw power in Nicklaus's swing and enrolled him in junior golf classes. "Hit the ball with all you've got," ad-

The Golden Bear watches a putt drop in the Walt Disney World Open in 1971. More than earning money, Jack's desire is to win more major championships than any other golfer.

vised Grout, "and worry about style later." The approach was perfect for a boy who could belt drives completely off the driving range—in one direction or the other.

Jack was shooting 90 by age 12 and dipped to 81 a year later. As his game became smoother, scores plunged into the 70s by age 14, and Nicklaus qualified for the National Amateur championship when he was 15. It was decision time. Jack was a standout high school football prospect, but the grid schedule conflicted with the National Amateur. Golf won out, and young Nicklaus was on his way.

Jack was paired against a youngster named Bob Gardner in the first round of the 1955 National Amateur at Richmond, Virginia, near the banks of the James River. It was a day Nicklaus will never forget, no matter if he captures 30 major championships and two Grand Slams. Bob Jones, who had also once qualified for the National Amateur at the age of 15 and went on to become a golfing legend, was in Richmond and made a special trip to the course to see this young powerhouse from Ohio.

Even the sight of Jones stunned young Jack.

"I was getting ready to drive off the eleventh tee when I saw Mr. Jones. I was one over par for ten holes, but I became so excited, I hooked my drive into the woods. On the twelfth, I sculled my approach over the green. On the thirteenth, I really blew. By then I was so nervous I could hardly hold the club. I felt miserable. Then, I saw Mr. Jones, who had apparently seen enough, take off for the clubhouse."

Jones knew, though, that he hadn't seen the kid at his best. In later years, in his role as a founder of Augusta National Club, Robert Tyre Jones became one of the Golden Bear's greatest boosters. He even wrote a letter trying to convince Nicklaus not to become a professional. But the money had ballooned since Jones's heyday in the 1920s and Nicklaus really had little choice when the time came.

Jack won the Ohio Open at 16, and his reputation began to mature among the amateur golfing set. In 1959, he won his first National Amateur at Broadmoor in Colorado Springs, beating tough veteran Charles Coe on the thirty-sixth hole and went on to lead the United States' Walker Cup team to a 9–3 triumph over Great Britain at Muirfield, Scotland.

Nicklaus showed his promise among pro-fessionals in the 1960 United States Open at Cherry Hills Club in Denver, shooting an amateur record total of 282 to finish second, two strokes behind Arnold Palmer, the man who was to become his great rival on the pro circuit in the 1960s. Nicklaus was upset that year in defending his National Amateur crown, losing a four and three match in the fourth round to Charles Lewis of Little Rock, Arkansas.

Later in 1960, Nicklaus again stamped himself as a future great by chewing up the fabled Merion course near Philadelphia with a 269 total in the World Amateur Team championships—the Eisenhower Cup matches—beating everybody in sight by at least 20 strokes in one of the finest four-day exhibitions in golfing history.

Before tucking away his second National Amateur, Nicklaus made another nonprofessional run at the U.S. Open in 1961 and again came razor close, losing by three shots to Gene Littler at Birmingham, Michigan. Jack struggled through a 75 the first day and then, for the closing 54 holes, was the field's hottest performer, finishing with 69, 70 and 70. As he entered the National Amateur that year, the pressure was mounting for the 21-year-old superboy to turn pro.

In the Amateur at Pebble Beach, California, Jack was an impossible target for the other entries. He was 20 under par for the week on the tough seaside course and smashed Dudley Wysong 8 and 6 in the finals.

Pro golf offered almost certain wealth, but Jack enjoyed being the world's greatest amateur. He kept reading that letter from Bobby Jones and thinking about his wife of one year, the former Barbara Bash. They wanted a family and he worried about the gypsy life on tour. "I was in a stew, but something had to give. I was doing three jobs at once, trying to get my degree at Ohio State, trying to keep up a little insurance business and trying to play golf. I wasn't doing justice to any, so I chose to turn pro."

Starting with that $33.33 payday at the 1962 Los Angeles Open, Nicklaus struggled to live up to his billing as the next Arnold Palmer of the tour. He came close in the $100,000 Thunderbird Classic at Upper Montclair, New Jersey, finishing second to Gene Littler, who was to defend his Open title the following week at Oakmont, Pennsylvania.

Littler was ablaze in the first round of the

Open and took the lead—but not for long. The smooth stroker from California began to falter, and the first of the Palmer–Nicklaus dogfights emerged. Arnold was a national hero who could excite the female portion of the gallery with a hitch of the trousers and impress the working-man with his tough background in a small Pennsylvania mining town. In contrast, Nicklaus's sex appeal was buried under excess poundage, and he seemed to wear a half-smile, half-sneer that turned off the crowd. Immediately, Jack was the villain, magnified by the fact that Oakmont was only a few miles from Arnold's hometown of Latrobe.

Arnie and Jack were knotted at 283 after the regulation 72 holes, and while other competitors headed down the road, they prepared for an 18-hole showdown. "I wish I were playing anybody but that big, strong, happy dude," Palmer was heard to say.

On play-off day, the "home field" advantage increased for Palmer. Arnie's army was unbearable, cheering for their idol as well as being hostile to Nicklaus. They ran as he putted and whispered, "Miss it, Jack," as Nicklaus lined up fairway shots. Palmer became embarrassed and tried to help control the mob that loved him.

All the clatter didn't faze Nicklaus. He never cracked and was four strokes ahead after eight holes. The gallery became restive. Palmer began one of his famed charges, putting his way to a one-shot deficit after 12 holes. But Jack stood over putts like a man about to cut a diamond, a trait for which he was to become noted, and hung on tenaciously to take a three-stroke victory with a round of 71.

"I never got scared," Nicklaus said afterward. "I just told myself not to be an idiot. When Palmer starts moving, most players get flustered and start making bogeys. I told myself to keep playing my own game—and I did."

He went on to win the Seattle and Portland Opens on the regular tour that year and pocketed $61,868 as a rookie professional, winning money in each of the 26 tournaments he entered. Nicklaus had also become the youngest man ever to win the U.S. Open and was named the top first-year golfer by the Professional Golfers Association. The Open was worth $15,000 and the Thunderbird runner-up check was $10,000, but the Seattle triumph was good for only $4,300 and the Portland Open paid $3,500 in a leaner era on the circuit.

The so-called sophomore jinx didn't bother Jack as he roared into 1963. He held off Sam Snead's fourth-round surge to take the Masters, later won the PGA championship along with the Tournament of Champions, Sahara Invitational and Palm Springs Classic. His earnings were $100,040, second on the tour. That total didn't include the TV-promoted "World Series of Golf," good for $50,000. The year's major disappointment came at the British Open at St. Anne's-on-the-Sea when he came into the final two holes needing par golf to win. He stumbled home with two bogeys, and New Zealand's left-hander Bob Charles eked out a one-shot victory.

Major titles escaped the roly-poly power-house in 1964, but money poured in nonetheless. He earned official tour cash of $113,284, which made him the number-one money-winner for the first time. He took the Tournament of Champions for the second straight year and was just a hair off an incredible season with second-place windups in the Masters (to Palmer), the PGA and the British Open.

Nicklaus won his second Masters crown in 1965 and began to chisel away at Palmer's reputation as the king of Augusta National. The score this time was a dazzling 271, shattering Ben Hogan's 1953 record by three blows. Jack's stroke average continued to drop—his 70.1 was

257

best on the tour a second straight year. Earnings jumped ahead to $140,752 and he was again number one.

Another year, another Masters title—that was 1966, It took a three-way play-off to do it, as Nicklaus edged Tommy Jacobs by two strokes with a 70, while Gay Brewer tagged along with 78. It was the first time a man had conquered the Masters field in back-to-back years, and was only the beginning to another great year.

Jack took the British Open at Muirfield, Scotland, and became only the fourth man to have won all the "Big Four" championships. Jack teamed with Palmer in the World Cup at Tokyo, and they established a team record of 32 under par for 72 holes. After five years as a pro, Nicklaus had reached $527,364 in official earnings, and the pots on the tour were just beginning to blossom with events on the horizon to offer up to $300,000.

Jack won his ninth major title in nine years at the 1967 U.S. Open, dropping a 22-foot putt on the final hole at Baltusrol in New Jersey to shatter Hogan's 1948 mark with a 275 total. He also was first in the Westchester Classic, good for $50,000, then the tour's richest payoff. He wound up the season with $188,998 to be the top money-winner for the third time in four years.

Nicklaus endured another year of second bests in 1968. Much like four years earlier, he finished second in the U.S. Open and British Open and fifth in the Masters. Most memorable from a $155,285 year was a five-hole play-off victory over Lee Elder in the American Golf Classic at Akron, Ohio. Jack was the year's number-two money man.

The lack of a major championship was the story again in 1969, and it required a late-season charge by Nicklaus—$62,300 in three events—to pump up his winnings to $140,167, third among the tour dollar gang.

There was something else about 1969. Jack, never bothered by his excess weight before, began to puff around courses and found himself low on energy. His doctor had always said, "As long as you're comfortable and you don't get tired, the weight won't bother you."

"I was getting tired and knew it was the time to act," said Nicklaus. He embarked on a diet with the same vigor he would use in facing a 10-foot putt to win the Open. Twenty pounds of fat came off his 5-foot 11-inch frame in three

weeks. As Christmas neared, the outside world knew little of the weight change and found it hard to believe even after reading an off-season Associated Press feature story.

When the 1970 tour began at Los Angeles, everyone noticed. The 20 pounds he had lost seemed more like 50. Nicklaus's once-bulging thighs were trimmed by six inches. He wore new, flashier clothes and soon began to let his formerly slicked-down hair grow into a fluffy, mod style.

Nicklaus obviously enjoyed the attention as well as the new image. Writers portrayed him as a sex symbol, a fellow beginning to grab the female galleryites away from Palmer and tour playboys, such as Doug Sanders.

"When people say I am more attractive, certainly it makes me happy," he said. "Nobody likes to be called fat or a slob. I never liked reading such things about myself and now it's nice to see what adjectives writers can think up for me. The words leave a much more pleasant taste, as I'm certain anyone can understand. Especially anyone who has been over-weight and called all the names that go with it."

Golf columnists wondered in print whether the thinner Nicklaus could hit the ball as far as the guy they once called Ohio Fats. Would it change his swing? Ruin his tempo?

Jack answered such critics the way he answered Sam Snead once when the Slammer suggested that Nicklaus was burning out at an early age because of his slow, meticulous play. He answered by playing spectacular golf. He won the British Open for a second time, in an 18-hole play-off with Sanders at St. Andrews in Scotland, shared the National Team championship with Palmer and then beat Arnold in a sudden-death play-off in the Byron Nelson Classic at Dallas. Jack's official money was $142,148, fourth best, but a third $50,000 victory in the World Series of Golf helped kick his total to $218,548.

The slim man did even better in 1971, bagging his second PGA title—to complete the "Double Grand Slam"—in his backyard at PGA National Club in Palm Beach Gardens, Florida, along with another Tournament of Champions and another National Team championship with Palmer. He tied for the U.S. Open title at Merion and lost in the play-off to Lee Trevino. Five tournament victories in all produced a $244,490 year, and early in 1972, Nicklaus zoomed past Palmer, 10 years his senior, as

the top money earner of all time in pro golf.

With all that money, Jack had looked through the years to find the best man possible to manage his personal finances and businesses. Shortly after dropping weight, Nicklaus found the man—himself. He broke away from Cleveland sports lawyer Mark McCormack, who had handled his affairs along with those of Palmer, Gary Player and many other athletes. Golden Bear Enterprises, Incorporated, set up an office across the lake from Jack's huge home in Florida, and money rolled in as never before.

The combination of excellent golf and a new, attractive appearance made Nicklaus a business blockbuster. He began appearing in scads of clothing ads and pitched other items ranging from lawn mowers to Pontiac automobiles. He opened his own Pontiac agency with a friend from Palm Beach.

"I find handling my businesses just about as challenging as playing golf," he said. "Among other things, we build golf courses, and I find it stimulating to eliminate what I think are bad things and put in some new twists that I believe make them better courses. I enjoy going to the office and keeping a finger on what's going on. It's fun, not really work, for me. When it starts being work, I'll quit it."

As for golf, Nicklaus looked ahead and planned "to play as long as I can compete. Golf is still fun for me, especially since I can control my career and not have to play each week. I have a rule: never be away from home more than fourteen straight days. Only once have I not kept the rule, and that was when I was in Australia and gone fifteen days. Golf has been a great and rewarding thing in my life, but it's not everything and never will be."

HUBERT MIZELL

Nicklaus tees off during the 1972 Masters at Augusta, which he won for the fourth time. That victory, combined with the 1972 Open, put him two legs up on golf's Grand Slam.

259

Bobby Hull
The Golden Jet

The date was March 14, 1966, a Saturday night, traditionally a night to howl, but on Chicago's dreary West Madison Street, pandemonium broke loose inside and outside monstrous Chicago Stadium when Hull scored his fifty-first goal of the campaign, breaking the mark he had shared with Montreal's Maurice Richard and Bernie ("Boom Boom") Geoffrion.

It happened at 5:34 of the third period in a game against the New York Rangers. Lou Angotti, a speedy Chicago forward, had knocked the puck from the stick of the Rangers' Reg Fleming and kicked it ahead to Hull. Bobby swooped into the attacking zone with his strong, fluid skating strokes and let fly with a shot. Flashing in front of New York's lanky goaltender Cesare Maniago was big Eric Nesterenko of the Hawks. He lifted Maniago's stick off the ice at the last split second. There was a momentary hush. Had Hull scored number 51, the record breaker, or had Nesterenko tipped in the goal?

It was Hull's! Pandemonium! A giant firecracker exploded, casting a large, white cloud over a jam-packed crowd estimated at 20,000. The air fluttered with hats, newspapers, popcorn, programs. A seven-minute ovation ensued. Hull, grinning broadly, skated to the sideboards and pressed a kiss through the glass barrier to his attractive wife, Joanne. He discovered a top hat among the mounting pile of debris on the ice and placed it on his head at a jaunty angle. The crowd cheered lustily again.

A Chicago society-page columnist once told her readers about Bobby Hull in these glowing words: "He's a statue come alive from the Golden Age of Greece, incredibly handsome even without his front teeth. A man who inspires sighs in every maiden and envy in the blood of every man."

Conn Smythe told it differently. The founder of the Toronto Maple Leafs, who had seen almost every player since the National Hockey League was formed in 1917, observed, "He's as fast and stronger than almost anyone who's ever played this game. The hockey fans of today are lucky to see him play. Not many of his kind come along."

Goalies described the Chicago Black Hawks' star from still another angle. "It's Chicago roulette," said Denis DeJordy after attempting to stop a number of Hull drives. "Compared to his shots, others are tennis balls." Johnny Bower explained after being struck on the forearm by Hull's powerful 60-foot slap shot, "It felt like I had been seared by a branding iron." Jacques Plante related, "His shot once paralyzed my arm for five minutes. It's unbelievable!"

When Bobby Hull was hot during the 1960s, he came on like the Chicago fire. His bull-like strength, unmatched speed and power, wavy blond hair and muscled torso prompted the nickname "the Golden Jet." Some called him "Golden Boy," the title of a Clifford Odets play. And the brilliant left wing put his name right in the book, too. He broke the all-time goal-scoring record for one season with 54 in 1965–66 and then shattered it again with 58 in 1968–69. He led the league in point scoring three times and twice was named the league's Most Valuable Player. He was also named by the Associated Press the hockey player of the decade. It was an exciting decade for Hull, a native of Point Anne, Ontario, who, in 1957, moved up to the big league of hockey when he was only 18 years of age. Two years later, he was to become the second-youngest player ever to win an NHL scoring title.

Hull wore two hats during his term in the National Hockey League, which totaled 15 seasons after the 1971–72 campaign. For the first 12 years, he concentrated almost solely on offense until club management forced him to pay attention to his defensive assignments. To the public he appeared to be easygoing and affable, smiling virtually all the time while leading the league in signing autographs. He was all of these, but also intelligent, a deep thinker, a complex man who seemed in later years to have become bored with success. His story ran the gamut of promising young star

Bobby Hull slides for puck in 1959 game against the Canadiens. It was Hull's third year as a pro. Later he would change his number to 9, the same as Gordie Howe's and Maurice Richard's.

to maturing superstar to aging, cynical presence.

It began in 1942 when Bobby got his first pair of skates a week before his third birthday. He raced downstairs on Christmas morning where he found them waiting for him underneath the tree. The skates had been bought for him by Robert Hull, Sr., who worked in a cement plant in Point Anne in southeastern Ontario. Bobby's father had once hoped to play professional hockey, but he forgot about it when he married and started a family that grew to 11 children. Young Bobby, supported by two older sisters, went across the road on skates to the Bay of Quinte, 50 yards from the front door of their home.

"I looked out the window a couple of hours later," his mother recalled, "and I could hardly believe it. Here was this little gaffer skating by himself. He fell down often, but he would always get back up, brush off the snow and keep on skating. In a little while he could skate by himself without any help from his sisters."

The elder Hull remembers sneaking down to the rink one night when his boy was five. "I couldn't believe what I saw," he said. "The boy was making plays as well as kids twice his age. I said to myself, if ever I've seen an NHL player, this is it."

"When I was eight years old," Bobby Hull reminisced, "I started going out into the woods with my grandfather. I chopped down trees with an ax and that helped develop my arm and back muscles. I also walked to and from school four miles a day, and during the winter I shoveled snow from morning till night." The work paid off as Bobby developed into a rock-hard, 5-foot 10-inch, 195 pounder. "I once saw him in a dressing room at an All-Star Game," Gordie Howe recounts. "He looked bigger every time he took off more clothes." And a teammate once noted, "He's got muscles on muscles."

Hull was 14 when he was playing with a group of other youngsters on a frozen pond in Belleville, Ontario. During one game he caught the attention of Bob Wilson, an Eastern Canadian Scout for the Black Hawks. Wilson persuaded Bobby to sign a form that made him the property of the Chicago organization. He was sent to Hespeler, a junior B club, where he received five dollars a week. The following season

he moved to Woodstock, Ontario, where he helped his team win the Junior B Ontario Hockey Association championship. His performance merited promotion to St. Catherines of the Junior A Ontario Hockey Association.

In 1957, general manager Tommy Ivan of the Black Hawks invited Bobby to the major league team's training camp, although his intention was to return the youngster to St. Catherines for his final year of junior eligibility. Bobby, however, had other ideas. He was so outstanding in the practices and early exhibition games that the Hawks retained him. "It was quite obvious," Ivan explained, "that Hull was too good for the junior league. He would have been wasting a season. He looked so good we had to turn him pro."

The handsome blond scored only 13 goals his first year with Chicago and 18 the second. After the second season he found himself in Europe and probably found himself as a player. The New York Rangers and Boston Bruins had scheduled a series of exhibition games overseas. Hull was picked by the Rangers to replace a player who couldn't make the trip. He was put on a line with Eddie Shack, an aggressive puck carrier. Bobby had been accustomed to carrying the puck most of the time he was on the ice. "It was in the games overseas," he explained, "that I learned to pace myself. Up until then I only knew one way to play—all out all the time. In Europe I started to lay back and let Shack carry the puck. It seemed to work because I scored fifteen goals in twenty-one games."

Bobby was still pacing himself in the 1959–60 NHL season and it worked. He scored 39 goals and captured his first scoring crown. "I had an awful lot to learn those first two seasons," he said. "In junior hockey, you pick up bad habits. I was trying to do too much by myself. I had to learn to pass the puck and to team up with the other fellows."

Bobby was given a thorough physical beating in his early years in the NHL. Because he skated with his head down, he was an easy target for body checks. He learned the hard way to keep his head up, to elude an onrushing defenseman, to fend off a defender with one arm and control the puck with the other.

"Hull," said Lynn Patrick, then general manager of the Bruins, "is worth a million dollars. I don't think you could buy him at any price. A player of his skill comes along maybe once every ten or twenty years—if you're lucky."

Toe Blake, Montreal's coach, compared Bobby with Howie Morenz, a great Canadian forward of the 1920s and early 1930s. "As a youngster," Blake noted, "Morenz fairly flew down the ice and had a powerful shot. Hull skates just as fast as Morenz and is built as solidly as Howie."

In his first year in the NHL, Bobby wore uniform number 16 but switched later to number 9 because two all-time greats, Howe of Detroit and Maurice Richard of the Canadiens, wore the same uniform number.

It didn't take Hull long to get the numbers of the NHL goalies. "Someday, Hull will kill somebody," predicted Maniago in a magazine article featuring Hull's hard shot, which traveled an estimated 119 miles an hour. The story was titled, "Why Goalies Fear for Their Lives." Related Ed Johnston, the Bruins' netminder, "One time Bobby took a shot at me. I never even saw the puck, but I sure heard it." Gerry Desjardins admitted, "I am frightened by him. There isn't one goaltender around who isn't. Even if you stop the shot, you're apt to get a bruise." Doug Favell of the Philadelphia Flyers pointed out, "When the average player shoots the puck, you can follow it. With Hull you don't see it leave his stick. That's the difference. It's gone! Faster than a speeding bullet. Like Superman."

Superman flew by himself in the air, but when Bobby Hull sped down the ice, he was constantly harassed by opposing players assigned to impede his effectiveness. They earned the nickname "Bobby Hull's Shadows." Wherever Bobby went, they were sure to follow. Those "shadows" were anything but lambs, though. They elbowed, kneed, held and impeded Bobby every way they could—legal or illegal. The most flagrant violator of checking etiquette was Bryan Watson, a pugnacious performer whose harassment of Hull in a Stanley Cup play-off series in 1966 earned him the nickname "Superpest." In that series, Watson held Hull to two goals and scored two himself as Detroit eliminated the Hawks.

Bobby couldn't eliminate those developments from his mind during the off-season. He bristled when he recalled Watson's tactics. Early the following season, Detroit met the Hawks in Chicago Stadium, and Coach Sid Abel of the Red Wings announced that Watson would again be shadowing Hull. In the open-

Puck slides by Toronto netminder as Hull raises his stick.

ing minutes of the game, Watson was on Hull like a cloak. The play shifted to the front of the Detroit goal while Phil Esposito, then with Chicago, battled for the puck behind the cage. Esposito got the disk on the blade of his stick and whipped it to the front of the net for Hull while Watson attempted to crowd the Chicago star out of position. The puck glanced off Watson's knee and into the net. The red goal light was on and the public address system blared, "Scoring for Chicago . . . Bobby Hull."

Watson, talkative and persistent, continued shadowing Hull. He began taunting him about the fluke goal. "You don't intend to take that goal, Bobby? Be a man and give it to Esposito. It belongs to him," Watson said. Later in the first period the two players crunched against the boards, and when they bounced off, they were swinging. Both were penalized for five minutes.

When the second period started, play shifted to the Detroit zone and suddenly there was a flash of sticks and Watson was down on the ice. Watson was helped to the first-aid room, bleeding from a cut above his right eye. The 18-stitch wound had been opened by Hull's stick. However, Bobby was not penalized. The players then moved into position for a face-off in front of the Detroit bench. At this point, Coach Abel leaned over the railing and spoke to Hull. "I've always admired you, Bobby, until now," he said. "There was no reason for you to give the kid the stick. He was only doing his job."

Hull replied, "I've had enough of your Detroit hatchet men. They've been on me for the ten years I've been in this league and I don't intend to take it anymore." At the end of the second period, Hull went to the first-aid room where Watson was being treated and apologized to the Detroit player. "I'm sorry Bryan . . . I meant to hit you, but I didn't mean to hurt you."

After the game, Hull sat for a long time in his cubicle in the Hawks' dressing room. He was visibly upset. He had been wracked with pain from bursitis in a hip, an ailment that had tormented him for two months. He seemed to be struggling while dressing. "There are times when I hate this game," he said. "Look what it does to you. It is not in my makeup to do something like what happened out on the ice tonight. This game changes a man."

It didn't change Bobby's penchant for scoring even in the face of considerable hardship. He still sought to break records—even while playing with a broken jaw. Nobody—not even Hull himself—is sure exactly how the fracture occurred. He remembered coming away from a rough game in Detroit on December 19, 1969, with soreness in his jaw, but nothing serious enough, he thought, to require X rays. He played the next game against Pittsburgh, and then, on Christmas night, he caught an elbow from Toronto's Mike Pelyk flush in the mouth and backed away in excruciating pain. There were X rays this time, and they revealed a fracture below Hull's right ear. The doctors wired his jaw together. He missed only one game. However, underweight from taking his meals through a straw and his eyes obscured by a makeshift helmet and a football face guard, the Hawks' ace appeared to have lost some of his speed. Still, he maintained a remarkable scoring pace, eight goals in the eight games following his injury.

"I've got to be careful," he explained. "I don't go blasting into the corners the way I usually do, and I've got to keep my elbows up. I've got to keep people away from my face. Trouble is, I can feel myself getting weaker—especially when we've been playing four games in five nights. I've lost fifteen pounds already."

His condition reminded some people then of the 1963 Cup play-offs, during which he played with a nose so severely smashed that the fracture extended into his skull. With the Hawks one game away from being eliminated, Hull ignored the orders of his doctors, checked out of a Chicago hospital and flew by himself to Detroit. That night—with both eyes blackened, his nose encased in tape and blood draining into his throat—Bobby played against the Red Wings. He scored three goals and an assist in a heroic effort, although Chicago still lost, 7–4.

Hull's jaw was unwired after six weeks during that 1968–69 season. He began scoring even more consistently. His strength returned. His rink-long rushes returned. And his shadows returned. In addition to the pesky Watson, they included Claude Provost of Montreal and Ed Westfall of Boston. "He's the only one that really bothers me," said Hull, referring to Watson. "If you have a lot of idiots playing against just one player, if you want to see that kind of hockey, it becomes a gladiator sport and you'll need a different set of rules."

264

Bobby started to swing back—within the rules. He had two fights with John Ferguson of the Canadiens, one of the league's toughest forwards. "We don't exactly leave Bobby alone, but we don't want to make him mad either," revealed Scotty Bowman, coach of the St. Louis Blues. "Sometimes I'm almost tempted to tell my guys to hum to him, sing to him if they have to—just don't make him mad. You make a guy like him mad and he'll kill you."

Despite the strength-sapping jaw injury, the Hawks left wing moved close to his record of 54 goals set in 1965–66. He broke it on March 20 in Boston. He had entered the game with 53, and with three minutes left in the game, he fired a 45-foot shot past Gerry Cheevers of the Bruins for the record-tying score. Only 13 seconds later, he drilled a 40-footer home. The Boston Garden fans gave him a standing ovation. "That ovation was really wonderful," Hull said. "When you consider that it came in a visitors' rink, it was awfully impressive."

Hull had signed an impressive contract with the Hawks just before the start of that 1968–69 season. He had held out and had even announced his retirement, but he finally agreed to terms for an estimated $70,000. Despite his record-breaking campaign, however, the Black Hawks finished in last place in the East Division. The following September he told reporters that Black Hawk officials had made promises to him before the previous season and were reneging on those promises. On the eve of the 1969–70 season opener, he again announced his retirement. He changed his mind, however, and returned after having missed a dozen games.

While he was away, Ivan, the general manager, and Billy Reay, the coach, concluded that the team needed more consistent goaltending and more attention to defense. Reay began to insist on more checking by his forward lines, urging the wings to come back when the puck was lost. When he was ready to take over his left wing position, Hull complained to the coach about not being allowed to chase after the puck in his old freewheeling style. However, he followed orders. He scored 38 goals that 1969–70 season, as Chicago moved from last to first in the East Division, and 44 in 1970–71 when the league increased its number of teams to 14, 8 more than it had had in 1966. In 1971–72, Hull reached the 50-goal mark for the fourth time in his career, although he finished 6 goals behind his former center, Phil Esposito, who had been traded to the Bruins, scoring an incredible 76.

In the overall 1971–72 point standing, Hull placed a solid seventh with 93 points. His career goals totaled 604, second on the all-time list. The Golden Boy, though, had become a 33-year-old veteran. Much of his blond hair was gone, and he invested in a transplant to fill in some of the bare spots on his increasingly high forehead. But those shadows were still there.

"I'd love to play one season—just one season—as an ordinary left wing," he said. "I sit on the bench and see all the other left wings. When they get the puck, there's no one within fifty feet of them. When I get it, there's always someone right next to me. As far as I'm concerned, it's absolutely senseless for an expansion team to check me like that. Here they are trying to sell tickets, and they advertise that, well, Bobby Hull is coming to town. Then the people come out to see what they advertise, and when do they see instead? Some guy out there preventing you from doing what people came to see."

What Reay saw was a changed Bobby Hull. "I can remember when he was a bull out there when he had two goals," he said. "You knew he wanted me to send him out there to get another goal, another hat trick. Now he gets two and he couldn't care less if he got the third."

"Every day the game loses some of its appeal," Hull insisted. "Expansion has diluted the old pride that gave such prestige to playing in a six-team, one-hundred-twenty-man league, and I'm afraid that pride may never be regained. The game is big business now, run by money men, not sportsmen. They are in the game so that they can tell their wives and friends, 'Come on. I'll take you down so you can meet the boys.' Fortunately, the longer part of my career was the good part—before expansion."

But, for all his idealistic views, Hull found himself not averse to the monetary lures. In June, 1972, he signed a $2.5 million contract as player–coach for the Winnipeg team in the new World Hockey Association. A new life began at the age of 33.

BEN OLAN

265

Willie Shoemaker
Six Feet Tall in the Saddle

The field flashed by the quarter pole in the 1959 Kentucky Derby and headed for the final two furlongs, the run through the stretch, past the thousands jammed into the ancient stands at Churchill Downs and the thousands more pushing against the outer edges of the infield. A racy bay colt named Tomy Lee, stung by the whip of jockey Bill Shoemaker, had his head in front—barely. Coming hard on the outside with a bristling bid was Brookmeade Stable's Sword Dancer with jockey Bill Boland hunched over his neck pumping on the reins—"scrubbing" for all he was worth.

As Sword Dancer ranged up alongside him, the always calm and friendly Shoemaker called out: "Hope you win it, Bill." Having said that, he proceeded to ride the ears off Boland in one of the most bitter battles through the stretch the one-mile oval has seen. Sword Dancer seemed to have it won. His head was in front 20 yards from the wire. But in the last few strides, Shoemaker moved the reins with his own brand of special magic. Tomy Lee changed leads, a matter of choosing which leg a horse will stride with first, and won by the width of a race-track pencil. There had been some bumping. Boland claimed foul. It was not allowed.

Shoemaker had pulled off another patented instant miracle. It was his second Derby winner, Swaps in 1955 having been his first, and later he posted another, Lucky Debonair in 1965. His superb saddle job on Tomy Lee atoned for his boner in 1957, the year he misjudged the finish line, let up on his mount, Gallant Man, for a split second at the sixteenth pole and lost the race in a photo finish with Iron Liege, ridden by the moody but brilliant Bill Hartack.

Shoemaker is the Little Giant of the sports world and has been for a quarter of a century. At 4 feet 11 inches and 103 pounds, he stands hip-high to basketball player Wilt Chamberlain. Baseball fungo bats are almost as tall as he is. A pro football team would consider Willie too light for the job of water boy. But he almost certainly has earned as much money as anybody else in sports.

Everytime the Shoe rode a winner in even an ordinary claiming race, he added to his record of most victories by a jockey, which went over the 6,300 mark in 1972 and kept on climbing. Each triumph in a stakes race added to his record in that category. It went past 560 in 1972 and continued upward. His winning ride on Cougar II in the $106,600 Century Handicap on April 28, 1972, was his ninety-fourth in a race with added money of $100,000 or more. There was nobody close to him in money earned by his mounts. In 1972, it went by the $46 million mark and was still rising. Since Willie was paid the rider's fee of 10 percent on all of that, he earned $5 million in less than a quarter of a century.

It was an incredible record for the tiny Texan, who was born in 1931, a premature baby, on a cotton farm near Fabens. Bill weighed in at two-and-a-half pounds, and he was so frail that the attending doctor doubted that he would live. His grandmother paid no heed to the doctor's words. She put the tiny infant in a padded shoebox and set it on the door of a warm oven, in effect a homemade incubator.

Bill survived, and by the time he was in high school in El Monte, California, he was up to 85 pounds—all bone and whipcord muscle. He won an amateur boxing championship, competing against boys 20 pounds heavier. It was about that time that he began to listen to broadcasts of races from Santa Anita and Hollywood Park.

"Around the race track," he explained to his father, "I'd only have to compete against guys my own size." He went to work as a groom and exercise boy at a local ranch. Two years later he had learned enough to catch on as a regular exercise rider at a California track. Finally, trainer George Reeves was impressed enough to let Bill have his first ride in a race

Willie stands under 5 feet tall, weighs in at 103 pounds.

at Golden Gate Fields. His first victory came in only his third race, very soon for an apprentice rider, on a horse which Shoe said "was a lot smarter than I was."

After one full year of riding, he had 219 winners. In his first full season, he tied for the jockey title with 388 victories. But in 1953 at the age of 22, he rode 485 winners, an all-time record. Nobody doubted that he could have gone over the 500 mark if he wanted. But he quit 10 days before the end of the season with the laughing explanation, "Some of the other jockeys have to make a living, too."

The trademark of a Shoemaker ride was smoothness. He was in perfect rhythm with his mount. There were times when his horse seemed to glide on air. No motion was wasted. The whip was used sparingly, but the Shoe could sting when necessary. He would not use a horse unduly in the first half of a race, but he was a menacing shadow coming ever closer as the field drove toward the stretch. Bill was a student of racing. He made a habit of going over a horse's past performances before a race, searching for the key to his top effort. If there was one, the Shoe would find it.

There never was even a pinch of a swollen head in Bill, despite all his success. He was frequently found exercising horses the morning after a $100,000 victory, exchanging banter with the exercise riders who never got into even a cheap race.

On the eve of the 1965 Kentucky Derby, a prerace banquet roared on into the small hours of the morning. There a friend laughingly told Bill he would not be able to make it to the track for a dawn workout. Shoe chuckled, nursed two cups of coffee, remained awake while others lurched home and shortly after 5 A.M., he rode a horse around Churchill Downs while still wearing his tuxedo. He grabbed a few hours sleep and then guided Lucky Debonair to victory in the Derby, winning by a shrinking neck against the furious late rush of Dapper Dan.

Like any jockey, Bill has been injured. His upper right leg was broken by a fall in 1968. It sidelined him for 13 months. Twice the leg was reportedly mending badly. Once it had to be reset. Not too long after his return to the track, a filly in the Hollywood Park paddock rolled backward on his slight body, damaging his pelvis and bladder. But once again he returned to action.

It was on Labor Day, 1970, that he booted Dares J, a juvenile filly, home in front in the fourth race at Del Mar in California. It was win number 6,033 of his career and it broke the previous record of 6,032 set by Johnny Longden. Longden, by then a trainer, was on hand in the winner's circle to congratulate the Shoe. The following year a bronze bust of Shoemaker was unveiled at the Santa Anita track alongside the one of Longden.

"The thing about Shoemaker," commented Longden, "is that he never seems to be trying hard. But he wants to beat you at anything. He simply wants to win a lot, something like me." Longden rode for 40 seasons and got his 6,032 winners in 32,000 rides. The Shoe topped him in half the time and about 25,000 rides.

The competitive drive Bill had in high school that enabled him to outbox much heavier boys remained very much a part of him in early middle age. Observers were fascinated to see Shoemaker playing head to head with the burly Vince Edwards, television's Dr. Ben Casey, in a pick-up game of basketball at the beach. Bill frequently went around a golf course in the high 70s. He was versatile enough to have danced and joked across a television screen with the Hollywood music man Burt Bacharach, a horse owner.

"The wonderful thing about Willie is his innate modesty," Bacharach observed. "I love the guy. He's so straight down the pipe, such a gem in every way. It's the only thing he knows and it's what made him the man that he is."

Willie Shoemaker in two familiar positions.
Above: Studying prerace charts with fellow
professional. Right: Atop the victor after a stakes
race, one of a record number of wins.

Another close friend of the Shoe's, the highly successful trainer Charlie Whittingham, said, "His intelligence and general sense are just what they always were. Shoe always knows where he is. He can sit there with a hundred grand laying on the finish line and wait until you want to shout at him. Then he comes flying when the others are wobbling and gets the job done."

On March 2, 1972, Shoemaker set another towering race track record, breaking the previous one set by his golfing companion and long time friend Eddie Arcaro, who retired in 1961 with 554 stakes wins. When the Shoe got Royal Owl home in front in the San Jacinto Stakes at Santa Anita, it was his win number 555. It was only natural that Shoe would be asked how it felt to break Arcaro's mark.

"Before the race Eddie wished me the best of luck," Shoemaker said. "Of course, I must say I had a big edge over Eddie. There are more stakes races now than when he was riding. And I know some day someone will break all my records. I'll be the first to cheer when he does."

The Shoe rode most of the great horses of the American turf for a quarter of a century, and never was much for trying to rate them. But he went so far as to call Swaps the first great horse he ever rode. "I won my first Kentucky Derby with him," he said, "and, in 1956, he was Horse of the Year." Bill was also the regular rider for the 1971 Horse of the Year, Ack Ack, but he would not draw a comparison between the two. He may have given a not too oblique hint on how he felt though, by commenting, "Ack Ack was a great horse, too, but he wasn't running against the kind of horses the others did."

Bill obviously had a soft spot in his heart for Gallant Man, the horse on which he blew the 1957 Derby. He later rode Gallant Man to the easiest kind of victory in the Belmont Stakes in 2:26.6 for a mile and a half, a new track and American record for that demanding distance. Looking back at the race, he chuckled, and said, "Gallant Man was a much better horse than people realized. In the Belmont we went by Bold Ruler, a great colt, like he was standing still."

The Shoe's first victory in a $100,000 race came aboard Great Circle in the 1951 Santa Anita Maturity. Great Circle was not a great horse. But that same year Bill handled a Calu-

met comet, Coaltown, and in 1953, he handled Determine, who was headed for a 1954 Kentucky Derby victory—but without the Shoe. In 1955, of course, it was Swaps. In 1956, it was Clem. Gallant Man came along in 1957 and so did the grass-loving Round Table. In 1958, it was Tomy Lee, a juvenile, and Shoe also had an exciting trip on Silky Sullivan to win the 1958 Santa Anita Derby. He came from what seemed like Baja, California, to get there with the late-running Silky. Bill won the 1959 Belmont on tough little Sword Dancer. He was superb on Jaipur to take the 1962 Belmont in a finish much like Tomy Lee's Derby and did it again on that colt in the Travers.

The list runs on with Candy Spots and the quick Never Bend, the blazing Gun Bow, tough-timbered Northern Dancer, hard-running Tom Rolfe, the brilliant Buckpasser and the explosive Damascus. There also was a Cowdin Stakes win on Dr. Fager, possibly the fastest horse of the last quarter of a century and one

The date was February 11, 1969 (above), his first race in a year.
Willie accepted three mounts and won with all three. "My
greatest thrill in racing," he said. Right: Leaving hospital.

of the few Shoemaker failures. Bill handled the good Doctor in the Champagne and had trouble rating the headstrong colt. He lost the race to Successor, and trainer Johnny Nerud found another jockey for Fager.

One of the axioms of the equestrian art, whether on the race track, the horse-show world or the bridle path is to always follow the rhythm of the horse's movement. Shoemaker agreed with the quote completely.

"To always be with the horse, to be in equilibrium with its center of gravity, describes it well," Bill said. "Some horses are easier to get with than others. I've ridden some pretty good horses that were rough and hard to get with. But the very best ones are smooth and easy. And the good ones, somehow they seem longer in the body."

A rival jockey once said that all riders talk to their horses but that Shoemaker was the only one the horses talked back to. Arcaro more or less said the same thing about Bill: "Horses run for Bill. He gets more out of a horse with his hands than he does with a whip, which is the mark of a great rider."

Traditionally, there is a lot of feuding among jockeys and also considerable jealousy, but Shoemaker, always polite and friendly, avoided it. Eddie Belmonte, a star rider from Puerto Rico, thought enough of the Shoe to name one of his sons after him. Another star from Puerto Rico, Angel Cordero, Jr., summed it up this way: "Shoemaker is a gentleman. Everybody likes him."

Kenny Church, a superb horseman although not a big name among the country's jockeys, studied Shoemaker at close range both on and off the track. Church once saved another jockey from serious injury during the running of a race by sacrificing his own chance of winning. The other boy's equipment snapped and he was in real danger of being thrown in the middle of the pack. Church came alongside and gave him a hand.

"Nobody could ever dislike Bill Shoemaker," Church commented. "He does things he doesn't have to do for other people and he never shuts the door on anyone. Where some riders may tell a trainer off or snub an owner, Shoe's always nice to them. It's not his style to be any other way. But when it comes to competition, you name it and the Shoe will beat you at it. I don't care if it's golf or tennis, Ping-Pong or pool. He's just a natural athlete and a tough competitor. He likes to be a winner."

Shoe matured into a stylish dresser. His tailored clothes fit his pony frame perfectly. His hair, flecked with gray in his later years, was always groomed immaculately. He established residence in Beverly Hills, the fabled movie star community, with his wife, Barb, and their adopted son, Mitchell. There was inevitably in that milieu a constant social whirl, and the Shoemakers became part of it.

Bill played tennis with Burt Bacharach, whose horses the Shoe rode whenever possible. Bill made himself available for charity functions and, on one memorable evening at the University of Southern California, even went so far as to hold a class in how to handicap horses.

As he entered his early forties, Shoemaker said he had no plans for retirement. Many jockeys rode well into their fifties. Longden was almost 60 when he put away his tack. Bill indicated that as long as he felt good, he would ride. Keeping his weight down, a big problem for aging jockeys, did not trouble him. He ate most anything he wanted, although he avoided desserts. He indicated a desire to do some work in television when he finally quit the saddle. "I've done some TV work and I like it," Bill said. "I think that if I worked at it, devoted more time to it, I could become better."

There was one more record the Shoe coveted, the Kentucky Derby mark of five winners for a jockey. It was shared by Arcaro and Bill Hartack. In 1972, after winning the San Jacinto at Santa Anita aboard Royal Owl, a three-year-old, Bill thought he had a shot at number four. Royal Owl never even got to the post at Churchill Downs.

Despite his many victories on great horses and in great races, the biggest thrill for the Shoe came on an ordinary program at Santa Anita on February 11, 1969. It was the day the Shoe returned to the races after having been out for slightly more than one year because of injuries. He accepted only three mounts that day, not wanting to overtire himself, and he won with all three. They were ordinary horses, Princess Endeavour, Racing Room and Jay's Double, the first two having been saddled by trainer Charlie Whittingham, a close friend of the Shoe's.

"I would have to say that that was my biggest thrill in racing," Shoemaker said. "I'll never forget that day. For me it topped anything I had ever done in racing—winning the Kentucky Derby or any other big race and breaking riding records."

The Shoe rode with a steel rod in a bone in his leg, the result of one of his accidents. It was supposed to be a temporary thing, but well into 1972, it was still there. "It doesn't bother me," Bill said, "I just haven't found the time to have it taken out. I will someday."

If one had to single out one facet that made Bill Shoemaker a great race rider, besides his matchless natural talent, it would be his enthusiasm for the sport. "I love what I do," the Shoe said. "I'm not hungry any more. I've made enough money. But as long as I do my job well, there is no real reason to stop."

It's for that reason that on many mornings in Beverly Hills when the other celebrities were still asleep or perhaps even just getting home, the Shoe was up at dawn. He would dress swiftly and silently, grab a cup of coffee, climb into his car and drive to Santa Anita or Hollywood Park. There he would work out three or four horses, a fair morning's chore. Then he would treat himself to a big breakfast—ham and eggs—scrutinize the racing form to examine his mounts for the day's card and scout the opposition. Sometimes there would be a card game with some of the other riders in the usual neighborly Shoemaker style. But once the day's racing would start the Little Giant would grow taller and taller. There were people who swore he grew six feet upon the call "riders up."

CHARLES MOREY

Rod Laver
The Millionaire of Tennis

Rod Laver was always ranked high wherever he played his magnificent game of tennis, but no one ever accused him of being a successful prophet.

In 1962, when on his way to winning his first Grand Slam—the sweep of the Australian, French, British and United States Opens—Laver reflected that he probably had another five years as a top tennis player. After that, he said, he might turn to golf and maybe even attempt to enter that sport's professional ranks.

Seven years later, in 1969, two years past his predicted demise, Laver again won the Grand Slam. He was the first man to win it twice. He was not just another good tennis player — he was the best.

If the fans who cheered him at Wimbledon and Forest Hills had been shown pictures of the young Laver in his home of Queensland, Australia, perhaps the only features they would have easily recognized would have been his thin reddish hair and his sharp, beaklike nose. Nothing about the young Laver made him look like an athlete, much less a champion.

His sunken chest, bandy legs and slight build made Rod appear even smaller against his older brothers, Trevor and Bob. The three received their first tennis instruction from their father, Roy, whose occupation was cattle rancher but whose avocation was tennis.

Great promise was held for the two older Laver boys because of their strong athletic builds and steady strokes. But Rod, a left-hander, had something that an early tennis coach noted might prove more valuable than classic form—Rod had determination.

"Trevor's got beautiful strokes," Charlie Hollis, a Rockhampton coach told the boy's father. "They're better strokes than Rodney's, but Trevor's got an explosive temper like you. He's never going to be a champion. Rodney's like his mother, quiet and determined. He'll make it."

The Queensland lad grew, but not much. He stood 5 feet 8 inches with a weight of about 150 pounds. Still, his strong service, powerful returns and developing steady strokes earned him notice and a place on the Australian Davis Cup team by the time he had reached the age of 18.

From the Australian outback to the Davis Cup was a journey that Rod Laver had begun in his own backyard when he was 10. Roy Laver had rolled the clay surface smooth and strung up a net and lights so that the older boys would be able to practice at any time.

One night, young Rodney slipped out of the house to watch his father and brothers hit balls with Charlie Hollis, who, when he spotted the youngster, invited him to join them.

It wasn't long before Rod was getting up before sunrise to travel with his brothers to the Rockhampton Tennis Association to take instruction from Hollis. It was two hours of practice before school and then back to the courts for more practice when classes were over. Charlie Hollis was not only Rod's teacher, he was his friend. And Rod became Charlie's favorite pupil.

Rod would help around the coach's shop, stringing rackets and doing odd chores. In return, Charlie spent long hours working with Rod on his grip and strokes, on building up his forearm and wrist and, most importantly, on developing a winning temperament.

According to Hollis, a player should demolish his opponent 6–0, 6–0 in every match. He insisted that Rod follow his advice and not be disturbed by mistakes on the court, teaching that the mind is what makes champions..

Laver's adherence to the theory of a winning attitude began to reap dividends before he was 12. He reached the final match of the Queensland Junior Tournament for players 16 and under. Although he lost to his brother Bob, he later won the doubles competition. Two years later, he won the under-14 state championships at Brisbane, playing for the first time on grass courts.

When Aussie Davis Cup coach Harry Hopman first saw the 16-year-old Laver at a tennis clinic in Brisbane, he was shocked at the boy's skinny appearance. However, he was impressed with his movements on the tennis court and he tagged Laver with the nickname that followed him throughout his career: "the Rocket."

Hopman later traveled with Laver and

"The Rocket" in an opening match on the grass at Wimbledon.

Bob Mark, another promising young Aussie, on a world tour financed by Australian millionaire Arthur Drysdale. The trip was to give the two 18-year-olds some experience playing outside their home country. The tour lasted five months, beginning in Paris and ending in California.

Rod began to gain attention. He won a couple of matches in the singles at Wimbledon; he and Mark gained the round of 16 in the doubles. Rod reached the final of the junior world championships, losing to ·America's Ron Holmberg. He then won the Canadian and American junior titles.

When Laver was chosen as the sixth man on the Davis Cup squad, he was put under Hopman's tough conditioning program but he wasn't able to play in any of the international matches because of the strength of the first five players on the Aussie team.

He returned to the team the next year, but that squad fell before the United States in a series at Brisbane. Australia then defeated the Americans at Forest Hills in the 1959 Challenge Round, with Laver dropping, to more experienced players, the only pair of matches his team lost.

But Laver, despite his losses, was showing an aggressiveness that was attractive to the fans. He first attacked with a spinning, left-handed service that, while not powerful, was devastating because of the difficulty of returning it. He would follow up by whipping drives off both forehand and backhand with remarkable accuracy. He also moved rapidly to the net after return of service, often hitting for winners. His method was to attack, attack, attack.

He returned to Australia after the rugged 1959 schedule, having lost five tough finals. He didn't appear ready for world-class competition.

But Laver's game and luck turned in the Australian Nationals in Brisbane in 1960. He defeated Aussie Neale Fraser, 5–7, 3–6, 6–3, 8–6, 8–6, for his first major title. The victory gave him added confidence because Fraser had won the U.S. title the year before.

The excitement of his victory soon turned to frustration, though, as he lost in the finals at both Wimbledon and Forest Hills. He was having trouble holding his temper, and he was attempting to make every shot a winner.

Laver lost the 1961 Australian final to Roy Emerson, then won Wimbledon over American Chuck McKinley. Emerson was unmatchable in

Rod on his way in 1962 to winning the first of his Grand Slams: Serving with his left-handed power thrust. Right: Racing to hit a low forehand return.

the U.S. Open as he won in straight sets over Laver.

Rod Laver had thought about winning the Grand Slam, the dream of every tennis player. American Don Budge had won the Slam in 1938, the year Laver was born, but no one since had been able to tack down the four titles in one year. Laver thought he might pull it off in 1960 or 1961, but both years he fell far short.

With counseling from Charlie Hollis and Adrian Quist, a former Davis Cupper, Laver had worked his game to near perfection by the start of the 1962 tournament season. He defeated Emerson in four sets for the Australian title, then moved on to take the French Open, again topping Emerson, this time in five sets. At Wimbledon, it was Australian Marty Mulligan who was Laver's victim in the straight-set final.

As expected, it was Laver and Emerson in the final at Forest Hills. Laver began aggressively by winning the first two sets. Emerson rallied to win the third. In the tenth game of the fourth set, Laver, leading 5–4, made three slashing serves Emerson was unable to return. Laver won the set, the match—6–2, 6–4, 5–7, 6–4—and the Grand Slam.

Laver's Grand Slam was hailed as one of

the great sports achievements of the century, especially since he also captured the Italian, Netherlands, Norwegian and Swiss championships in 1962. He was the world's greatest amateur tennis player.

He was by far the best of the amateurs, but there were many professionals willing and anxious to teach him a few tricks.

Laver became a tennis professional in 1963. The professional Laver looked no different from the amateur Laver. Both were red-haired and freckle-faced with a long nose. On the court they played in the same manner. But the amateur Laver won; the pro Laver lost.

The Rocket began his pro career in Sydney against a master, Lew Hoad, who defeated him in a match that lasted almost three hours. The following day pro veteran Ken Rosewall dropped Laver in straight sets. In all, Laver lost eight straight games to Hoad and eleven of thirteen to Rosewall.

"I didn't know what to expect in pro play," Laver said. "But I figured my tennis education was just beginning."

Laver lost 14 of his first 16 pro matches. It was astounding that a player who could sweep through the amateur ranks so handily could do so poorly against a group of players not long removed from the amateur ranks themselves. If the tennis crowd was unnerved, Laver wasn't.

"I'm definitely not going to change my game because I lost a few," he said. "I'm going to play my game as I see it."

Those were gutsy words for a new player who was being embarrassed in almost every performance. But Laver's logic was that pro players such as Hoad, Rosewall, MacKay and Andres Gimeno of Spain had years of experience on him. He felt he would soon catch up and boost both his tennis and bank account. He didn't plan to keep losing.

Laver's determination and personal pride carried him the next year as he at first struggled, then glided through the pro events. He soon emerged from the shadows with the winning attitude and confidence that had marked his amateur career. Laver's game was together again as the no-style stylist mowed down his opponents just as Charlie Hollis had urged him to do years before.

Within two years, Rod Laver was the top professional player, often going through the last rounds of major international tournaments without ever dropping a set to his opponent.

His timing and steellike wrist made his game fearsome. He swung at everything hard and fast. True to his training, he still used his spinning service rather than an overpowering one. But once service was returned, Laver's opponents faced a variety of shots that all came with speed and accuracy. He took a full round-house-loop on both his forehand and backhand, considered by many tennis observers the best in the history of the game.

Even after Rod had been winning in the amateur and pro tournaments, there were coaches who tried to convince him that he was not big enough to hit the ball hard. He simply ignored them and concentrated on hitting and attacking on every shot.

Laver moved well in the professional setting, earning large purses for his victories, money for endorsements and acknowledgment as the world's top tennis player. But for Rod and his fellow pros there was no Wimbledon, no Forest Hills. Their status as professionals barred them from competing in the world's prestige tournaments. They were considered part athletes, part showmen in their privately sponsored events.

But while the pros were battling each other in closed competition, a change was taking place in the attitude of the International Lawn Tennis Federation. In 1968, it was finally decided that Wimbledon would open to the professionals.

It was somehow fitting that Laver, who had won Wimbledon in his last appearance there as an amateur, should blast his way through to winning the first open title there as a professional.

The following year, with open tennis a reality, Laver once again began pursuing the Grand Slam. At Milton Courts in Brisbane, he whisked through five opponents, including Gimeno, in the final—6–3, 6–4, 7–5—to take the Aussie title. Then he topped his old nemesis, Rosewall, in the French Open final, 6–4, 6–3, 6–4.

At both Wimbledon and Forest Hills, Rod again proved he was the master of world tennis, defeating John Newcombe, 6–4, 5–7, 6–4, 6–4, for the British title and Tony Roche, 7–9, 6–1, 6–2, 6–2, for the U.S. honors.

With a number of professional circuits in operation, Laver found that he could make money almost anywhere he wanted. In 1971,

he won eleven straight $10,000 winner-take-all Tennis Champions Classics. Earlier, he had captured four U.S. pro championships in five years.

Still, the Rocket could not top his countryman Rosewall in the richest of tournaments, the World Championship Tennis finals worth $50,000 to the winner. In 1971, Rosewall beat Rod, 6–4, 1–6, 7–6, 7–6. The following year, in a match almost four hours long, the 38-year-old Rosewall was again the winner, 4–6, 6–0, 6–3, 6–7, 7–6.

"I know Kenny's over the hill," Laver said wryly about his losses. "I've been hearing that since 1963 when I played him, and lost, in my second pro match."

Despite Rosewall, Laver's tennis earnings were records. In 1970, he won $210,453 and then increased it the next year to $292,717. He was tennis's first million-dollar performer, accruing winnings of $1,006,947 in his first nine years as a professional.

Rod Laver failed to lose a step as he aged. His experience and his study of the game enabled him to keep an edge on younger players who sought to topple him from his lofty position as the best in tennis. His prophecy of spending five years at the top faded before his second Grand Slam, and the game of golf was deprived of Rod Laver.

TOM EMORY

Ten years later (above right) at Houston, his backhand as lethal as ever. Note apparent aging—contrast youthfulness of young player (left) at Wimbledon in 1961.

A.J. Foyt
Hard-Nosed Demon of the Ovals

On a small, dingy racing car oval somewhere in the Midwest, in a year in the mid-1960s, it was nearly time for the 40-lap feature race for the small, fast and extremely dangerous midgets. The drivers were mostly local boys, the 2,000 spectators made up of friends and relatives who peered through a haze of smoke and fumes that blanketed the pit area.

Suddenly, there was a buzz of excitement and someone yelled, "Foyt!" The bleacherites already had spotted the late-model station wagon pulling into the infield, drawing behind it a trailer on which was mounted a shiny maroon racer with the numeral 1 on its nose and the initials *A. J.* near the cockpit. The incomparable Foyt, a legend in his own time, had arrived—without prior notice, without the fanfare of local press, to do battle with the locals for a purse that, should he win, would hardly pay the expense of his being there.

Race officials, awed by the unexpected presence of the king of auto racing drivers, three-time winner of the hallowed Indianapolis 500, by then a four-time national champion, gathered around quickly to help with the unloading.

"What in the hell is he doing here?" one official asked. "He doesn't have to run the little ones anymore; he doesn't need the money. Why does he do it?"

"Obsession," replied the other. "Obsession is driving him."

Foyt overheard the remark. "Look," he snorted truculently, "ole A. J. is driving this race car. Obsession can find his own ride."

It had rained earlier. The dust on the pint-sized oval had turned to slick, slimy mud. Foyt, ignoring the attention he was receiving, hustled his little racer off the trailer, warmed it up briefly, then headed out to make his qualifying run for a starting position. It wasn't a good effort for the national champion. The mud, the ruts in the track and the haze that hung over it like a blanket cut his speed. The other drivers, more familiar with the conditions, went out later, after the track had dried a bit, and turned faster times. Foyt was bumped from the field. The national champion failed to make

a local show that any other driver of his stature would have passed up completely. There were a few catcalls from the bleachers, which Foyt heard. Grim-faced, he approached the last-place starter and offered him $100 for his ride. The driver accepted eagerly because the show paid only $400 to win. Foyt hopped into the car and, during the next 45 minutes, drove through and around the field to win it going away. Satisfied with his effort, he packed his own gear and left.

Obsession? Yes!—to be a true champion, to be the best race driver in the world, to win them all, anywhere, anytime, against all comers. Sheer guts. A few weeks after the midget race, Foyt went to a small track in Missouri for a stock car race. He broke his engine in practice, couldn't qualify for a spot in the lineup and again bought a seat in the last-place car and again won going away.

Said an associate: "Never has there been a driver with such absolute urge to excel, the absolute need to win, fairly and honestly, gut against gut, skill against skill, flat out and belly to the ground. The total race driver, that's Foyt."

Anthony Joseph Foyt, Jr., was his official handle, but he was just plain "Tex" to his friends, "A. J." to the media, Tony to those who didn't know him, "Super Tex" to others, "Tough Tony" to those he had beaten or something less flattering to a few.

Hard-nosed, sometimes violent, often truculent, always intense, sometimes boisterous, many times gentle, impetuous, rough, forceful, vehement, self-made, never vengeful, Foyt was the original "fish or put away the pole" man of auto racing. He would laugh with you one minute, completely ignore you the next. He was deliberately articulate one hour, purposely unresponsive the next. He could be moody, surly, happy, smiling, taut as a banjo string under stress, a model in charm when things were going "according to Foyt."

Five times a national driving champion, winner of more events on more tracks in the United States Auto Club than any other driver, Foyt scored at Daytona, Le Mans, Sebring, Nassau, Ascot, Wentzville, Rolling Plains,

A. J., determined to win, anytime, anywhere, against anyone.

Podunk, Tri-City and Double Oaks X-Roads. He won in midgets, sprint cars, coupes, sedans, stock cars, championship cars, in sports cars, open-wheelers. He was even holder of the speed record for turbine-powered trucks.

He was a man of many facets and contradictions—gentleman rancher, breeder of fine horses and cattle, businessman, husband, father, auto salesman, penny pitcher at the county fair, high-stakes thrower at Vegas; practical joker, story-teller, patriotic flag-waver, handsome, alert, a mechanical genius.

There are those who say good race drivers are born, not made. Anthony Joseph Foyt, Jr., was born a driver. Otherwise, he couldn't have learned so much from the time he was born January 16, 1935, to the time he got into his first race car just five years later. His father, A. J., Sr., built the car for him. The kid went out that same year and, in a match race at a local track, beat an adult driver who had more to lose from a tarnished reputation than from the money at stake. If Foyt ever saw his winnings, he never remembered it, but they were the first of a cascade of dollars that were to bring him untold wealth, more than $2.5 million in prize money, race triumphs that he quit counting long before his name became legend.

The competitive urge was planted early in life. His father had been a sometime race driver, but mainly he was a genius with tools, a master at the art of tuning engines. There was a race car somewhere around the premises all the time. A. J. quit school in the tenth grade to drive full time—midgets, sprints, hot-rod stockers. Grease, grime, hamburgers, soft drinks, sleeping in the rear of a truck or on the ground, Foyt quickly became the leading driver at most of the tracks he could get to.

"Those were the days," he recalled once at a victory dinner. "There were times when the dust was so thick that the only way you could get around the track was to keep your eye on the rear fender of the car just ahead. It was brutal, but it was thrilling, satisfying."

He had conquered Texas by the time he was 18—a sturdy, 5-foot 11-inch, 185-pounder, hard as nails, clear gray eyes, fair skin as yet unmarked by the burns and breaks that were to come later. There were new fields to conquer, particularly in that Midwest section of the nation that seemed to be the major pipe line for drivers seeking fame and fortune and sometimes death at Indianapolis, the home of the famed Indy 500 and the shrine of auto racing.

Foyt entered the pipe line in the Midwest, racing against better-known and established stars of the early 1950s. He did well, so well that by 1956 he already was being watched from Indianapolis by those who control the destiny of the richest, most prestigious auto race in the world. He joined the United States Auto Club, sanctioning body for Indianapolis and one of the leading employment agencies for drivers who desire the full cycle of stocks, midgets, sprints and "big cars."

He was 21 when he made his first USAC start, a midget feature at a small oval just across the street from the big Speedway. That night, May 29, 1956, the hard Texan finished fourth in his qualifying heat and thirteenth in the main event for a take-home check of $68. He paid homage to no one.

"Some of the drivers I had heard about all my life were in the race or in the stands," Foyt said later. "Was I impressed? Naw, not one bit. They were regular guys, but no better than I was. Anyway, I already had made up my mind I could do just as well as most of them at the old track across the street."

Foyt had been to Indianapolis before. He had paid his way in for three years, walking Gasoline Alley, ogling the racing cars, sometimes hustling from garage to garage meeting drivers and mechanics, always listening, storing information. His reputation as a driver already was known in the garages, but he had no friends among the drivers.

The Texan, though, was ready for the big time. He knew it, and others knew it, particularly the people who owned the famed Dean Van Lines specials that had roared around Indy for years. Foyt was invited to drive one of the cars, the one formerly assigned to the great Jimmy Bryan, in the 1958 Indianapolis 500. The brilliant Clint Brawner was to be his chief mechanic.

"It was a ride far beyond anything I had hoped for as a starter, a rookie at Indy," Foyt said. "Rookies normally don't get equipment like that and a mechanic like Brawner."

Foyt qualified the front-engined roadster twelfth in the field at 143.130 miles per hour, the fastest he had ever gone in a race car, even in the rookie tests he had cleared with ease two weeks before. On race day the rookie got his first taste of the fury that constitutes high-speed racing at the old Brickyard.

Winning the Indy 500 in a Sheraton-Thompson-Watson Offenhauser.

He was riding easily in the middle of the pack, feeling his way around while the hot-shots battled for position, watching the cars in front of him and in back, as a rookie is supposed to do in his first start. But he wasn't too far in the rear when suddenly, ahead of him, 14 cars became involved in a grinding, awesome crash in the third turn before even the first lap was completed. Foyt skidded around the carnage that cost the veteran Pat O'Connor his life. He gradually moved up again but lost control during lap 148 and spun out in the southwest turn. He was credited with a sixteenth-place finish, worth $2,962. He had made it to Indy and he would be back.

Foyt "arrived" as a race driver in 1959. He returned to Indianapolis in the Dean Van Lines Special, starting seventeenth and coming home tenth. But more importantly, he had a good ride for the rest of the championship trail and he made the most of it. He locked horns with the great Rodger Ward in many races, winning some and losing some, but when he won the final battle of the season at Phoenix, Arizona, he captured his first national driving title. Ward finished second.

Foyt changed sponsors in 1960, driving for the first time for the Bowes Seal Fast team. He could do no better than a sixteenth-place start at Indianapolis and could make only 90 laps before being sidelined with clutch failure. And, though he went on to win the driving title again, his mind already was on the 1961 Indy. That race was a classic.

The old Speedway was celebrating its fiftieth anniversary. The vociferous Eddie Sachs, the clown prince of racing, had won the pole and promised all who would listen that if he won, it would be his last race. And it was a supreme Indiana day; the age of sellout crowds had begun. Foyt earned a starting berth on the inside of the third row. There was big money ahead. His carefully laid plans jelled, and by the two-thirds point, it had boiled down to a duel between Sachs and himself.

The two swapped the lead several times, battling furiously in the turns, neither giving an inch. Foyt, however, found himself running low on fuel with 15 circuits of the 2.5-mile oval to go—almost-certain defeat would result if he were forced into a pit stop then. His crew waved him in, Foyt muttering a few well-chosen words under his breath as he watched Sachs streak by and head for the first turn. Back in action, Foyt roared after Sachs, who appeared a sure bet to collect retirement benefits before the day was over. Then with three laps remaining, Foyt realized that Sachs was slowing down, the white fabric showing on his right rear tire. Foyt sailed triumphantly by as his rival went to his pit for a replacement and the Texan was home free.

Foyt had made his first visit to the victory circle at Indianapolis in just four tries, and his payoff of $77,625 plus lap money was the biggest for any Indy winner until then. His take for the year, including championship bonus money, totaled $117,975.

Sachs, meanwhile, made two other trips to Indianapolis in quest of his retirement fund. On his last visit, in 1964, when Foyt won again, the portly Sachs was killed in a first-lap crash that also claimed the life of Dave McDonald, one of the few drivers who could claim to be really close to Foyt.

Foyt now was king. Regardless of car ownership, he was the boss of his garage and pit area and he made no bones about it. His temper, his all-consuming drive for perfection, both for himself and his crew, his inability to lose easily and with grace, his frequent periods of depression and desperation when things weren't going right, particularly in 1965 and 1966 when Mario Andretti tumbled him from the top rung of the ladder, were the subjects of many conversations in garage and pit areas. Many of the tales about Foyt's troubles with his crews were true, notably his falling out with George Bignotti, one of the great chief mechanics of all time, and later with another mechanical genius, Johnny Pouelson. But other tales, some without foundation, were embellished by members of the media, some of whom had got short shrift from Foyt at one time or another, probably after mechanical breakdowns had cost him a victory. Foyt later brought out his own line of race cars, which he called Coyotes, and his father assumed the role of crew chief.

Foyt won the driving title again in 1963, which included a third-place finish at Indianapolis. He won it all again in 1964, and his wealth began to accumulate. He bought a sumptuous ranch house near Houston for his wife, Lucy, and his two sons and daughter. He began stocking it with cattle and horses, and he made the house a castle. He ruled it, and his guests, as the baron he had become—firmly and selectively. He was gone much of the time, to Nassau, to California, to Florida, to whistle-stops. But the ranch was home, and Foyt was always glad to get back to it to walk among the cattle, to ride his walking horses. There also were three direct telephone lines in the house, two of them listed publicly, and they were always busy.

The low point in Foyt's career encompassed the 1965 and 1966 seasons. He won the pole at Indianapolis in 1965 but was eliminated from the race by a broken gearbox after 115 laps. He went on to capture five championship events, but Andretti ousted him from the driver championship. His greatest satisfaction that year came when he won the Firecracker 400 stock car race at Daytona, beating Richard Petty, Bobby Isaacs, David Pearson, Buck and Buddy Baker and Fred Lorenzen. He was to make other forays into the Dixie lair of the "good ole boys" in later years, and he won more than his share of their races, including the Daytona 500.

In 1966, his Sheraton-Thompson Special was destroyed in a first lap pile-up of cars at Indianapolis, and Foyt escaped injury by bailing out and climbing the fence in front of the main grandstand. That, he said later, hurt him more than had he been injured. His career reached rock bottom with only a 25-mile midget win and a 15-mile sprint victory.

In 1967, Foyt bounced back. He won his third Indianapolis race and two weeks later hooked up with Dan Gurney in a Ford Mark IV to win another of auto racing's great races, the 24 hours of Le Mans in France. His fifth driving title that year was icing on the cake. Indeed, it took the pressure off his determination to be the best driver in auto racing. He was voted the race driver of the decade, he had banked more than $2 million in prize money and he could afford to assume the role of gentleman driver and devote more time to his business ventures. He bought a car agency in Houston. He took over Ford's engine project at Indianapolis and became parts distributor for it. He designed and raced his own cars, maintained lucrative ties with the Goodyear Tire and Rubber Company and a long list of sponsors. He also mellowed somewhat. He smiled and joked a lot.

Foyt had an obsession during his climb to the top. To him, racing was a profession and his employer was any race track for big money or little money. Obscure dirt tracks were his "fun outings," and he frequently showed up without filing an entry blank—thus depriving the promoter of a chance to use the champion's name to overpack the house. Yet he probably collected more "deal money"—under the table guarantees—than any other driver in history. He was worth it. His name was a sure ticket seller for any promoter. And he always gave his best. He drove to win, and he savored a victory over the local hotshots just as much as if he had beaten the bigger names in the business.

Foyt loved stock car racing. He won the USAC driving title for stock cars twice, but his stomping grounds were the big stock car ovals of the South, where he was accepted as a "half-Yankee" who asked no quarter and gave none. It was in one of the stock car events that Foyt came closest to losing his life.

He had won Indy and the national driving title in 1964, was at his peak physically and mentally and was a prime favorite in a 500-mile race for stockers on a road course at Riverside, California. A Ford man most of his life, Foyt was to drive one of that make engineered by the famed Holman and Moody firm. Early in the race, however, the machine lost its brakes going into a sharp corner and, rather than risk ramming two other cars just ahead, Foyt looped the car over a 35-foot embankment. It was one of those spectacular flips from which drivers are not expected to escape. Foyt didn't; he was pulled from the wreckage broken and bent, his vertebrae smashed.

He recalled later, "My insides were all out of shape, the pieces being where they shouldn't be. I was hurt so bad I couldn't enjoy the hospital nurses." He survived, though his long period of recuperation contributed to his bad 1966 season. He had another narrow miss the next season, receiving second- and third-degree burns over his face and much of his body in a bad spill at Milwaukee. The scar tissue left on his face did little, however, to mar his handsome countenance, and the broad, sometimes impish, smile returned with his big year in 1967.

There had been other close shaves with death in other years, and Foyt could regale his listeners for hours on end as he recounted them. There was the time at Daytona when old friend Jim Hurtubise blew the engine in his stock car at 175 miles an hour, and Foyt had to take instant action to avoid a crash. He was riding Hurtubise's rear bumper waiting for an opportunity to pass.

"Son of a gun," Foyt told Hurtubise later, "you damned near did me in that time. Least you could have done, if you were determined to put me out, would have been to wait until we were playing before five thousand people instead of a hundred thousand."

Foyt hadn't always been that kind to drivers who found themselves in Hurtubise's situation. He was loud in his denunciation of drivers he figured were responsible for the multicar crash that put him out of action in the 1966 Indianapolis 500. And there were times when he almost came to blows with drivers he claimed had cut him off by refusing to yield to his faster car or had caused him to spin out. It was known that he and Andretti, never close, were at odds at times over one another's driving tactics and habits.

Whatever tactics Foyt used had emanated from a burning thirst to be the best. Record-winning years quenched the thirst.

BLOYS BRITT

Hank Aaron
"Records Are Made to Be Broken"

"For sixteen years no one knew I was playing baseball. Then suddenly last year everybody began to wonder where I came from." Henry Aaron spoke those words in March, 1970, while sitting in front of his cubicle in the Atlanta Braves' clubhouse at their spring training site in West Palm Beach, Florida. His candid assessment of the amount of publicity he had received up to that point was not very far from the truth.

It was the slugging outfielder's misfortune to perform unobtrusively, even though brilliantly, during an era in which Roger Maris eclipsed Babe Ruth's one-season home run record, Sandy Koufax pitched a record four no-hit games, Mickey Mantle caught the fancy of baseball fans with scores of gigantic home runs and Willie Mays caught everything in sight with a flair in center field while maintaining a fair distance between himself and Aaron in career home runs.

It wasn't until Henry had moved past Mantle in career homers by hitting home run number 537 and advanced into third place behind Mays and Babe Ruth in 1969 that people began to sit up and take notice and stand up and cheer this steady, noncontroversial player who had achieved unprecedented success with little fanfare. And the trumpets blared with increasing volume in 1970, 1971 and 1972 as Aaron became the eighth player to reach 3,000 career hits, climbed past Mays in career homers and advanced enough to threaten Ruth's legendary 714. The Internal Revenue Service also sat up and took notice early in 1972 when Aaron became the highest-paid player in baseball history by signing a three-year contract for an annual baseball income of $200,000. It was a long way away from his taxing situation when, as a member of the Indianapolis Clowns in the Negro League, he'd play a doubleheader in Washington, a single game in Baltimore the same night and then climb back on a bus to try to sleep on the way to Buffalo. His salary then, in the early 1950s, was $200 monthly.

Henry Aaron was born in Down the Bay, a Negro district of Mobile, Alabama. There was no bay in sight and nobody knew why the area was called that. Thus no one knew exactly why the youngsters of Down the Bay considered themselves superior to those of Toulminville, another Mobile district to which Henry's father moved his wife and eight children. This was the first discrimination Henry had known. "It wasn't white to black," he once said. "It was black to black. The Down the Bay kids just thought they were better than we were. Anyway, it cost me my first chance at a big league try-out." Neither Central High School, where Henry went for a while, nor Josephine Allen, the private school where he finished, had a baseball team. The emphasis was on football, so he played halfback and end. He did play on the schools' softball teams, and by the time he was 15 years old, he was playing the infield and hitting cross-handed for the Mobile Bears, a sandlot team. "Sometimes on Sunday," he recounted, "I'd make five or six dollars."

In 1951, at 17, Hank began playing for the Indianapolis Clowns. At the end of the season, he was purchased by the Braves for $10,000 on the recommendation of Dewey Griggs, a scout. In his first season in organized baseball, he was voted Rookie of the Year in the Northern League. In 1953, he came away with Most Valuable Player honors in the South Atlantic League after pacing the circuit in batting average with .362, hitting 22 homers and accumulating 125 runs batted in for Jacksonville. He was at the time already a solid 6-footer weighing 175 pounds. He had heavy sloping shoulders and thick, powerful wrists. Although a right-handed batter, he could hit with almost equal power to all fields. He played shortstop for Jacksonville, but in the winter of 1954, he was shifted to the outfield at the Braves' request while playing for Caguas of the Puerto Rican League. He hit .324 in 68 games for Caguas, tied teammate Jim Rivera for the home run lead, placed second in runs batted in and helped his club capture the Caribbean World Series.

When he appeared in spring training with the Braves for the first time in March, 1954, he impressed all who saw him hit. Joe Adcock, a first baseman who had been one of the few ever to hit four home runs in one game, commented, "Everything the kid hits is a line drive.

Aaron goes high for 1963 smash hit by Johnny Callison. Said Braves' manager Fred Haney, "He always seems to get the fly ball ... when there's any chance of making it."

And he hits more drives through the box than anybody I ever saw. He's already come close to flattening a couple of pitchers with his screamers through the middle of the diamond. Those fellows had better watch out." Despite his excellent showing, however, the 20-year-old Aaron was ticketed to play for Toledo of the American Association, still not the big leagues but a jump of two notches over the South Atlantic League, a Class A circuit.

In mid-March, though, Henry Aaron got a break. It came in the form of a fractured leg suffered in a Braves' exhibition game by Bobby Thomson, an outfielder who only two-and-a-half years before had fired the shot heard 'round the world by hitting a pennant-winning home run for the New York Giants in a play-off game against the Dodgers. The injury sidelined Thomson for six weeks, and Aaron got a chance to play regularly in the spring practice games. He made the most of it. When the regular campaign opened, he was in the starting outfield. Hank himself suffered a severe leg injury late in his rookie season, but even so, he played in 122 games, finishing with a .280 average, 13 homers and 69 runs batted in. By the end of his second year, he was already an established major leaguer. He walloped 27 home runs, drove in 106 runs and hit .314 in that 1955 campaign.

He had no special theories on batting. "I just leave the dugout swinging," he explained. "The secret of hitting is to keep swinging."

Because Hank was quiet on and off the field, some people questioned his intelligence. He had to deny one story that said that after he had tagged Robin Roberts, an outstanding pitcher, for four consecutive hits, he had asked who the opposing pitcher had been. When someone answered, "Ford Frick," who was then the baseball commissioner, he was alleged to have asked, "Who's he?" Someone else said that when Hank was asked what he looked for when he had two strikes on him, his answer was "the baseball."

"A lot of people think I'm a dummy," he said. "I'm not dumb when it comes to hitting. I do a lot of thinking about it. I keep it up in my head. I study the pitchers all the time, and when I find one giving me trouble, I study him extra hard. I want to know why he's getting me out and what I can do about it. Don Drysdale of the Dodgers used to get me out with a change-of-pace pitch. In fact, all the Dodgers used to

kill me with that pitch. So, after my first year, when I got home to Mobile, I got my brother Tommy to throw change-ups to me all the time. After that they didn't throw me that pitch very often. I wait for the pitcher to make a mistake. You got to think with pitchers and I'm thinking with them all the time."

Henry had opposing pitchers thinking constantly. In 1956, his third year with the Braves, he led the National League in batting with a .328 average. The following season he paced the loop in homers with 44 and in RBIs with 132. He was selected the National League's Most Valuable Player.

And he was indeed valuable—never more so than on September 23, 1957. The score was 2–2 in the eleventh inning at Milwaukee—and the magic number for Milwaukee's first pennant (the Braves had moved from Boston to Milwaukee in 1953) was one. Billy Muffett, a curve baller, was pitching for the St. Louis Cardinals. He hadn't served a home run ball all season. He threw a curve. Aaron swung. Wally Moon went back to the 402-foot sign in center field and jumped. The ball landed in the seats and a cast of thousands burst into tears of joy.

For several seconds of Milwaukee's finest hour, Henry Aaron wasn't there. Running between second and third base, he was back on Edwards Avenue in Mobile, on his way home from school. The day was October 3, 1951. Henry had just heard on somebody's radio that Bobby Thomson had homered to win a pennant, and he ran the rest of the way giving a little leap every few steps as Thomson did. The Negro sandlotter from Toulminville was Bobby Thomson that day until he rounded third base, saw the reception committee and knew it was at least as much fun to be Henry Aaron.

It wasn't all fun and games. Some people accused him of being lazy. He argued, "Just because I don't jump and holler and run to and from the outfield doesn't mean that I don't go all out. Maybe I don't look like I'm hustling but that's just my way. It's the only way I know. I couldn't change if I wanted to. If I did, I'd probably foul myself up."

"Aaron's loping style is deceptive," explained Fred Haney, who took over as Braves' manager from Grimm in 1956. "You'd almost get the impression he wasn't hustling at times. But he's about the last player you'd accuse of that. He just runs as fast as he has to and he always seems to get the fly ball or to a base in time when there's any chance of making it."

Henry continued to make it big as a batter. After the Braves' pennant-winning year in 1957, he hit .322 and .326 and then captured his second batting crown in 1959 with a .355 mark, collecting a resounding 223 hits. His career home run aggregate accumulated by leaps and bounds with 44, 30, 39, 40, 34, 45 and 44.

Henry wore uniform number 5 in his rookie campaign with the Braves but requested that he be given what was to become a familiar number , 44 , when he came to training camp the following spring. "I tried to talk him out of it," Donald Davidson, the club's veteran executive, was to recall many years later. "I pointed out that most of the superstars, people like Babe Ruth, Lou Gehrig and Joe DiMaggio, all had low numbers—but Hank insisted on the change. We gave him number forty-four when he got to camp. He's hit exactly forty-four homers in four seasons since, and I sometimes wonder what might have happened if we had given him number seventy-seven."

For at least his first decade and a half in the majors, however, the pitchers talked about him more than the sportswriters wrote about him. "He not only knows what the pitch will be but where it will be," said relief pitcher Ron Perranoski of the Dodgers. "He hit one home run off me and he went after that pitch as if he'd called for it." Said infielder Gene Oliver, a teammate, "Pitchers don't set Henry up. He sets them up. I honestly believe he intentionally looks bad on a certain pitch so that he'll get it again."

"Certain players are cut out for being recognized," Henry said. "There would be more recognition if I played in New York or Los Angeles, but I have no regrets. I was fond of Milwaukee for twelve years and I grew to like Atlanta after the Braves moved there in 1966." Atlanta gave him a day in 1968. Hank Aaron buttons were sold. The usual gifts of a car and a diamond ring were appreciated sincerely by Aaron, but the money raised for the YMCA made him beam. "I didn't dream as a boy in Mobile that I would be making so much money playing baseball and that thousands of people would stand and cheer me," Hank told that crowd in Atlanta.

They began cheering Hank Aaron more often. The 1970 issue of *One for the Book*, a records compendium published by the *Sporting News*, was put out with Aaron's picture on the front cover. The first name listed among the players who had batted .300 or better for 10 or more years was Henry L. Aaron, who had done it 12 times and carried a .313 lifetime mark into the 1970 season. On May 17, 1970, in the second game of a doubleheader against the Reds in Cincinnati, he hit an inside fastball from pitcher Wayne Simpson in the first inning. Reds' shortstop Woody Woodward managed to knock down the ground ball, but Hank beat it out for a single. It was career hit number 3,000 for Hank. The Braves lost both ends of the twin bill, and later Aaron said characteristically, "Sure, I feel good about the three thousand hits, but I don't feel too good about the losses. I'm relieved to get number three thousand and I'm glad it's all over." Asked what his next baseball goal was, he quickly proclaimed, "To win a ball game."

More milestones followed. On April 27, 1971, he slammed his career home run number 600. It came in the third inning off Gaylord Perry of San Francisco, who had said earlier in the day, "If he gets number 600 off me, he's going to earn it."

The advancing years threw him a few curves. He developed back trouble in 1970. In 1971, he developed fluid in a knee that had to be drained periodically. In May, 1972, he disclosed that he was suffering from an arthritic condition in his neck. Still, at the age of 37 in 1971, he compiled a personal one-season high of 47 homers, drove in 118 runs and batted .327. At that time, after 18 years with the Braves, he had played in 2,715 games; totaled 10,447 official at-bats; scored 1,901 runs; collected 3,272 hits, among which were 562 doubles, 95 triples and 639 homers; driven in 1,960 runs and stolen 234 bases. His lifetime batting average was .313.

Although his baseball statistics changed from year to year, his personality remained relatively unaltered. He did have one fight on a team plane with teammate Rico Carty in 1967, but the turbulence was quelled quickly. "Actually," Eddie Mathews, an all-time great slugger who had become a Braves' coach, said in the spring of 1972, "Hank really hasn't changed much from those early days. He looks about the same, maybe a couple of pounds heavier, and he still has that quick stroke. He just waits on the ball and whacks it. He's the same in the clubhouse as he always was. You can kid him and he can take a joke and he can needle you

back but he doesn't tell funny stories. He just goes out every day and plays like hell. That's really what's made him a great player—consistency. Year in and year out, his average is always about the same. Until now, he was pretty much ignored in the press. All of a sudden, he's getting close to Ruth's record and people are discovering him. Hell, he's been doing this for eighteen years."

"My hitting style has changed since we moved to Atlanta," Aaron pointed out. "The park was built for home runs and now I look for a pitch I can pull. When I first started, I hit most of the balls hard to right center field. One year in Milwaukee, I had forty-four homers and twenty-two of them went to right field."

Although he maintained that Willie Mays was one of the best friends he had in baseball, there were times when Aaron appeared annoyed because he took a back seat to Willie in the press. While speaking before the Houston chapter of the Baseball Writers Association in January, 1972, he said, "I think Willie is a great player, but if he had played in Milwaukee and Atlanta like I did, he wouldn't have gotten the publicity he did."

And it was to Hammerin' Hank's further annoyance in May of that year that Mays again grabbed the headlines when he returned to New York as a member of the colorful Mets following a trade that sent pitcher Charlie Williams to San Francisco in exchange. Mays slammed a home run in his first game for the Mets, and as the campaign passed the Memorial Day weekend, it was virtually unnoticed that Aaron had eight homers and had climbed to within one of Mays's record, 647 to 648, in the career home run race behind Ruth.

Actually, Aaron and Mays could have been playing in the same outfield. "We almost lost Hank," Donald Davidson, the Braves' executive, once recounted. "When Dewey Griggs scouted him the time Hank played for the Indianapolis Clowns, he was so impressed that he said he'd pay the ten thousand dollars out of his own pocket to get him. That convinced John Mullen, our farm director, and we got Hank five minutes before a set deadline. Otherwise the Giants would have gotten him. At the time, the Giants already had Mays. Imagine one club with Mays and Aaron. Heck, you wouldn't need another outfielder."

When he was a very young man, Henry gave little thought to Babe Ruth. "I really wasn't much of a fan," he admitted. "I just wanted to play. The thing I remember most about seeing his pictures is how fat he was. He must have been some hitter to hit like that with that body." However, as he drew closer to Ruth's 714, Aaron confessed, "I'd be telling a lie if I didn't say I was thinking about it. After eighteen seasons, it's nice to know that I can look forward to such a target, that it's within my reach. It would mean something to the black race. It probably would mean something to every kid, black or white, but a little more to the black race. It was such a long time before we were accepted into the game. But I hope both blacks and whites are pulling for me."

Hank revealed in the spring of 1972 that he had been made aware that there were people who were pulling for him to fail in his pursuit of the Babe's 714. "I have begun to get quite a few pieces of mail about the record," Aaron said. "The letters are not vicious. But there have been some that said I wouldn't have been able to hold Ruth's jacket when he played. I realize that if I ever break his record, people may not accept me as being a better hitter than Ruth was. But records are made to be broken."

He has always been accepted, though, as a great batter by some of the game's greatest pitchers. "Aaron is the last guy I want to see coming up there to the plate," Koufax once said. "Some guys give me more trouble one year than another, but Aaron is always the same. He's 'Bad Henry.'"

Bad Henry was being discussed in the Montreal Expos' training camp on February 28, 1972. Denny Lemaster, a veteran pitcher, was throwing in batting practice and Gary Sutherland, an infielder, was at the plate. "Okay," Gene Mauch, the Montreal manager, said to Lemaster, "pretend you've got two strikes on Aaron. Just drop that slow curve on the outside corner." Lemaster complied, and Sutherland swung and hit a pop fly. "Let's try that two-strike pitch again," Mauch said, motioning to Lemaster.

At that point, catcher John Boccabella stood up and peered through his sweat-stained mask at Mauch. "There's only one problem, as I see it, skipper," Boccabella said.

"What's that?" asked Mauch.

Answered the catcher, "How do we get the first two strikes on Aaron?"

GEORGE VECSEY

Hammerin' Hank connects for his five-hundredth career home run. He had more than 3,000 hits, was closing in on Ruth's career home run record and was the highest-paid ballplayer in history.

Joe Namath
Crises Quarterback

It was in the winter of 1969 that the people of Beaver Falls, Pennsylvania, decided to do something for Joe Namath, who had managed to put the soot-soiled steel town on the map. The pride in their product resulted in the usual welcome-home parade and a green-and-white banner that long after the festivities were over, remained suspended high above Seventh Avenue and Eighth Street near the Club Naturale. The sign announced:

Beaver Falls, Pa. The Home Of
Joe Willie Namath
Super Quarterback

There is the suggestion in that banner that Joe Willie Namath would not have been a superquarterback had Beaver Falls not spawned him. Imagine: No $427,000 contract. No satin sheets and llama rugs. No Johnny Walker Scotch. No Bachelors III. No Raquel Welch to escort to the Oscar ceremonies. None of the accouterments that have become accessories to the player many believe is the best passer in the history of professional football.

A visitor to Beaver Falls quickly found that the suggestion made by the banner was supported by the Namath worshippers, including an instructor at Beaver Falls Area High School, Bob McClain, Jr., who recalled growing up on the other side of Eighth Street.

Eighth Street split Beaver Falls into two sections. Those above Eighth Street, like McClain, were the "haves" of the little town set in the Allegheny foothills 30 miles northwest of Pittsburgh. Below Eighth Street, down a steep grade, was the Lower End, the grimy section occupied by the "have-nots." Joe Namath was born at 802 Sixth Street. "Fortunately," McClain explained on a number of occasions, "we both got lucky. I had a father who made me get a college degree. Joe had a football."

The scouts who scouted Namath, the coaches who coached him and the players who played with and against him almost unanimously agreed that Namath threw that football better than anyone else they had ever seen. Beaver Falls insisted that Namath developed his arm because of Beaver Falls, its geography and the fact that he lived at 802 Sixth Street. Those kids whose families were better off than the five children of John and Rose Namath ran with the Dead-End Gang. Those kids who lived on the Namaths' side of town ran with the Lower-Enders. When they ran into each other, there were the inevitable clashes of youth.

"We would sometimes fight by throwing scrap from the mill—old tube castings, and junk," McClain recalled. "We had the edge. The Lower-Enders had to throw uphill." The folklore of Beaver Falls claims that throwing uphill gave Namath his strong right arm—an arm strong enough to bring 100 colleges to his doorstep, clamoring for him to rescue their football programs, an arm strong enough to bring about a bidding battle between the New York Jets and St. Louis Cardinals that brought Namath his $427,000 contract, an arm strong enough to enable him to lead the Jets to a stunning Super Bowl victory over Baltimore and back to Beaver Falls for the big parade of 1969.

The Joe Namath story remained a local Beaver Falls story until the beginning of the sixties when the swarthy young man, christened Joseph Alexander Namath in St. Mary's Catholic Church in 1943, moved south to the University of Alabama, replaced Alexander with Willie, came under the tutelage of coach Bear Bryant and began throwing the football for the Crimson Tide under the spotlight that always falls on Bryant's teams. By 1964, Namath was a national figure, destined to become a pawn in the war between pro football's two leagues, the American and the National.

The main figure on the chessboard at the time was Sonny Werblin, the show-business-oriented president of the Jets who was looking not only for a passer but a personality as well. He saw what he wanted in Namath. "I needed to build a franchise with somebody who could do more than just play," Werblin said. "So we went down to Birmingham, and the minute Joe walked into the room, it lit up. At that moment, I knew he was our man." The bidding then began between the NFL's Cardinals and the AFL's Jets, and when it ended, Sonny Werblin

This superb throwing arm led AFL football into the big time.

had his man and Joe Namath had his $427,000.

The image was created. What Namath did and said only enhanced it. What he did was to move into an East Side bachelor's pad and fill it with an oval bed, a llama rug, a $5,000 mink coat, a crystal chandelier and a full wardrobe of the latest in male threads, including bell-bottom pants and Edwardian jackets. What Namath said was "I wish I'd been born rich. I'd know how to spend money. Boats. Planes. Cars. Clothes. Blondes. Brunettes. Redheads. All so pretty. I love them all. What's there in life but to relax and have some fun. Man, if you don't have it, you're not living and I like to live."

Fortunately for Werblin, the Jets and the American Football League, Namath also loved football the way he loved money and the color of hair. And history shows that Namath has been equally successful at both his loves—females and football. He threw for as many as 26 touchdowns in one season and gained as much as 4,000 yards in one year. He did it with a fast dropback that gave him an extra split second, a quick release that enabled him to throw the ball even with a defender inches from his body and a strong and accurate arm that enabled him to throw short or long with startling results. He did it despite ailing, painful knees. And praise came from all quarters.

"I remember seeing a picture of him against us on one play when I hit him a terrific shot," said Oakland defensive tackle Tom Keating. "He had both feet off the ground. But somehow he still threw forty yards for a completion. It doesn't seem to matter whether he's throwing off his right foot, his left foot—or neither one."

Coaches declined to have their names used with their comments since their selecting Namath as the best quarterback invariably reflected on the abilities of their own quarterbacks. But, in a collection of comment about Namath from rival coaches in 1971, the following underscored the unbelievable respect Namath was accorded: "Joe Namath," said one coach, "has more talent than anybody in life." "He's got a great arm, he's football-wise, he knows the game," said another. A third waxed more analytical, noting, "There are two factors in judging a quarterback—preparing for him and playing him. Joe Namath scares you both times. When you play the Jets, your whole approach to the game involves him. You're so conscious of him it disrupts your planning, more so

than against any other quarterback. And in the game, no matter what the down or distance, he's capable of hitting a big play on you."

The lasting proof of that was Super Bowl III, played in Miami January 12, 1969, a battle between Namath's Jets, 18-point underdogs, and the Baltimore Colts of the NFL, supposedly an invincible team that was expected to add NFL Super Bowl victory number three—despite the presence of the guy whose shaggy hair curled up over the bottom of his helmet and whose football cleats were painted an outlandish white. But the shaggy-haired, white-shoed Namath didn't buy the odds and even said so before the game, creating headlines all over the nation when he stood up publicly at an awards dinner the week of the heralded game and announced: "The Jets will win Sunday. I guarantee it."

It was unprecedented verbal bravado, but Namath knew what he was doing. "If I seemed to have more faith than anybody else, it was because of what I saw in the films of the Colt games—and what I knew I could do to them if I was on my game," Namath explained, but only afterward. "They used a lot of various safety blitzes. I was absolutely confident that if they tried that stuff against us—and they had to because it was their game—we could move the ball on them, score on them."

The waiting world, however, didn't know that. All it knew was that the Colts had a supposedly impregnable pass defense and that Namath would get the comeuppance due him. The only thing Namath got on Sunday, however, was the open-mouthed admiration of every football fan everywhere for both the brilliance of his passing and his astounding play-calling, play after play succeeding against the Colts as Namath barked out the signals. The result was 17 completions in 28 passing attempts for 206 yards and a 16–7 victory that stunned the Colts and amazed the country.

Returning to New York City, Namath received a hero's welcome and the key to the city. He reveled in the limelight, holding court almost nightly at a club in which he had a share —Bachelors III, an East Side night spot. The euphoria lasted only until June, and suddenly Namath was holding a press conference at the rear of the restaurant, announcing that he had been ordered by commissioner Pete Rozelle to sell his interest in the watering spa, that he would not do so and that, therefore, he was announcing his retirement. It was the first of

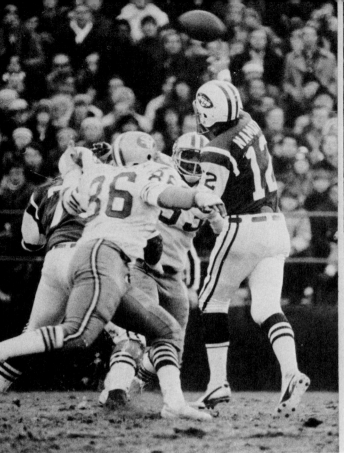

a series of crises that plagued Namath almost from the day of his greatest triumph and his ascendancy to the number-one spot among the sport's quarterbacks.

Namath ultimately sold his interest in Bachelors III, returned to the Jets and led them into the 1969 season. But he couldn't get them back to the Super Bowl. They lost to Kansas City in a play-off game at Shea Stadium on a wind-swept day that left Namath with little desire to return to the same stage.

"Football used to be number one with me, but at this stage it's not my main concern," he said. "I honestly don't know what I'm going to do. I'm working to get my problems solved. Some of them are business problems, a lot are personal."

A cause célèbre ensued—not because of what Namath was doing but because of what his teammates were saying. What they were saying wasn't very complimentary. Middle linebacker Al Atkinson censured Namath for not caring about his teammates. "What really disgusts me," said Atkinson, "is this quarterback not thinking for a minute about the married guys on this club, the little guys who have families to worry about." Defensive end Gerry Philbin acknowledged that the Jets operated under a double standard—"one set of rules for Joe and one for the rest of the club." Again, Namath returned to the club. No one knew it, but despite the fact Namath had solved all his problems, fate in the form of injuries now was going to deprive him of doing what he finally had realized meant the most to him— playing football.

Five games into the 1970 season, Namath broke a bone in his wrist attempting to throw a pass against the Colts. He played no more that season. When he returned to the team for 1971, he was a changed Namath. "Last year, I didn't want to play," he pointed out. "Other people quit jobs and people say nothing about it. An athlete's different. There's all that publicity. But when I got hurt, I found I didn't want to be away from the game. It's hard to have something taken away from you when you can't do anything about it. You really begin to miss it."

It was, Namath said, like something that had happened to his mother. "Her dog was run over and killed," Namath explained. "You live with something for eleven years and then you lose it and it hits you hard."

Good quarterbacks are fair game. Above: 49ers get to Joe.

He remained in that frame of mind for just one game—the opening exhibition against Detroit. But, late in the first half, he had a pass intercepted and ran over to make the tackle. He didn't make the tackle, but he did rip up his knee. Even as he headed for his fourth operation, Namath guaranteed he would return, despite the pleas of teammates such as Emerson Boozer and even his father, John, not to. "Joe should never play again," said Boozer. "If he gets hurt again, he could become a wheelchair victim."

"I want him to quit," said his father. "We don't want him coming home without his legs."

Namath, however, never worried about his legs, although he readily admitted to the pain they caused. "I'm not looking for sympathy," he said, "but they sure do hurt. Going up and down stairs is a problem for me once the season is under way and even walking bothers me. But it's something you accept; that's the way it is. You're lucky if you have legs at all, and if they hurt, they hurt. I know that by the time I'm fifty, I'm really going to have problems walking, but since there isn't anything I can do about it, there's no sense in tying up my mind with stuff like that. Of course, I have a definite weakness—if I were to get hit with a direct shot to the knee, then I would be out of the game for good."

So Namath went through the process of getting his knees ready again, finally appearing in the Jets' lineup in the eleventh game of the 1971 season against San Francisco and just missing pulling off an upset of the team that went on to win the Western Division title in the National Conference. Despite a performance that drew raves from the critics who watched him on his return to action, Namath was not satisfied with his performance. He ended the season that way, happy to have returned but feeling that only the future could determine whether he had made it all the way back after two years during which he had played just nine games.

Why did he come back in 1970? In 1971? "I love the game," he explained. "Basically, it's my whole life. So I ended up playing again. I realize how much football means to me. And, when you think you're the best at your position, you want to prove it." Oddly enough, for most, he already had proved it.

MIKE RATHET

Joe Namath in huddle during Jets-San Francisco game in New York.

Namath, out of action from early-season hurt, with Unitas.

Kareem Abdul-Jabbar
Standing Tall

In college, he was "Mount Alcindor" and "Big A." He turned UCLA into "Lew-CLA" and the "University of California at Lew Alcindor." After he led the Bruins to another national basketball championship, one writer datelined the story, "Lewisville, Kentucky."

He later played under the Islamic name of Kareem Abdul-Jabbar with the Milwaukee Bucks of the National Basketball Association. Only his name and the places he played changed. He remained the same dominant force.

He was saluted as the best player in the game, but off the court he was icily aloof. He was a peaceful, religious person. Yet, when he felt it was warranted, he came to blows with opposing players.

Despite his success, his life wasn't always serene and uncomplicated. He felt the painful pressure of having to live up to advance billing. He was jeered by the fans. His 7-foot 2-inch frame cast him in an unpopular role.

"Nobody ever likes Goliath," he said repeatedly, echoing the thoughts of dozens of ultratall sports figures who were considered villains because of their dominating appearance. "Nobody likes a dominating person," Abdul-Jabbar said.

He was ruler of every basketball realm he surveyed. Not since Wilt Chamberlain started his NBA career had any rookie received as much fanfare as Abdul-Jabbar. He was a superstar on paper long before he had put on a Milwaukee uniform. Then he had to earn his stars by battling—literally.

After three stunning seasons at UCLA, during which he had been the tower of strength on the nation's dominating college team, he was expected to produce more magic in the pros. He was expected to turn a loser into a winner overnight—and he did. But before moving the expansion-poor Bucks into the NBA play-offs as a freshman and to the heights of a league title his second year, Abdul-Jabbar made an adjustment to the punishing style of professional play.

"Muscle is not my game. I'm not interested in tag-team wrestling, I'm a basketball player," he said, wearing soulful dark brown eyes in an expressionless, peaceful mask of a face.

Finesse was his strength, but he nevertheless met muscle with muscle because he deemed respect more important than anything. He retaliated in a swirl of punches when Darrall Imhoff pushed him too hard. After he decked the Philadelphia 76er center, he heard boos for the first time in the pros and answered with a V sign in one hand and a raised fist in the other.

Abdul-Jabbar and New York center Willis Reed almost went at it after the Milwaukee rookie struck his adversary's head in a fierce rebounding battle. The brawny Reed whirled and cocked his fists, but the hot-tempered youngster held back.

"I was getting pushed and I guess I hit him and he got mad," said Abdul-Jabbar. "I didn't hit him on purpose. . . . I told him it wasn't on purpose."

It happened again with John Block of San Diego, when the two exchanged fiery words. In Seattle, he threw his weight at John Tresvant and Bob Rule.

"Tresvant hit me a couple of times and Rule got a finger in my eye," recalled Jabbar. "Man, I went for Rule. And I spit. And there was a kid, some bad-mouthed teen-ager—I gave him a shove."

It wasn't what the sensitive Milwaukee star had wanted at all. He wished to stand for something else. He said, "I always tried to represent something positive for the people in the community, because kids idolize people. It's not good if these idols are something you wouldn't want your kids to be. So, if you take the responsibility on yourself to give them something to look up to, maybe that's one way to encourage them. I just want people to respect me. If you get respect and you earn it, you're doing yourself justice."

This gifted athlete, one of the best centers ever to crash the talent-rich NBA, still wasn't convinced that basketball was really important. He found it mundane and looked to future pursuits—writing, music, social work. But he believed he had a job to do as player, and he stuck to it tenaciously. He was never satisfied

Kareem Abdul-Jabbar dominates game against the Knicks.

with his game, a quality of the perfectionist that had been drummed into him from childhood, when he was called Lew Alcindor.

Although his parents, Ferdinand Lewis Alcindor, Sr., and Cora, were both strikingly big people, the new baby of the household—Ferdinand Lewis Alcindor, Jr.—appeared to have inherited his size from his grandfather, an imposing, bearded giant of 6 feet 8 inches from Trinidad. In the year of Alcindor's birth in New York City, 1947, the delivering doctor noted the baby's size—12 pounds 11 ounces and 22½ inches long—and said, "Here's a basketball player."

When it came time to attend school, Lew was made a pupil at St. Jude's, a Catholic grammar school run by the Presentation Sisters. It was an auspicious debut. A teacher spotted Lew in the back of the room and said:

"You, there, sit down."

"But I am sitting down," responded Alcindor in that subdued, unemotional manner that would remain a lifelong trademark.

For several years, he never gave basketball a thought. He was active in other sports, such as swimming, skating and Little League baseball. But finally his height was simply too good to be true—and so, in the fourth grade, he had his very first basketball game. He was 5 feet 4 inches tall and learned from scratch—the pushing, pulling and tugging of that peculiarly indigenous New York style. He was nine.

Alcindor soon guaranteed success for St. Jude's in New York's Catholic Youth Organization grammar school program. Farrell Hopkins, his first coach, put him on a program of weight lifting for strength and rope-skipping for speed, coordination and reflexes. His father played handball with him to further build up the youngster. "Lew," his father said, "it's up to a man to improve himself."

Alcindor entered the fifth grade and his world became a basketball calendar, summer and winter. The practice sessions were arduous. He stayed overtime to learn. At first, although he worked one or two hours more every day than any of his teammates, he couldn't shoot lay-ups.

Said Hopkins, "Look, Lewie. Making lay-ups is just a matter of practice. If you miss a lay-up at your height, you look ridiculous. You only give people something to laugh at."

He had struck a sensitive chord. Most of all, Alcindor didn't want people to laugh. They were already snickering at his height, which had leaped to 6 feet 6 inches in the seventh grade and to 6 feet 8 inches in the eighth. By the time he was ready to go to high school, he was 6 feet 10 inches tall.

The decision to go to Power Memorial High School wasn't made in a moment. At age 14, Lew could dunk a basketball with professional authority and was besieged by offers from prep schools, whose hard-sell recruiting matched that of any college. He finally decided on Power because it was just a 20-minute train ride from his house and—more importantly—because his friends went there. He was still unsure and afraid to break away from familiar surroundings.

His next coach, Jack Donohue, probably extended the most powerful influence on Alcindor's life style. The steel-willed Donohue, who had been turning out winners at the midtown Manhattan Catholic school long before he knew Alcindor, at once put a "no-talk" ban on his newest player. Nobody was able to reach the boy without the coach's permission, including the most vital of publicity outlets—the newspapers.

"It wasn't something that started with Lewie," insisted Donohue. "I always had the rule, but nobody realized it until Lewie came along. It wasn't so much for newspapers as it was for colleges. Without being imposed upon, he got as much publicity as he was going to get.

Rookie-of-the-Year Jabbar stuffs ball in game with Seattle. Kareem averaged 28.8 points a game his first year. "Wilt is stronger, Alcindor more versatile," said one player.

I couldn't let him be subjected to all the scouts that wanted to talk to him."

And how they wanted to talk. After an inauspicious first year, the young giant made big news as a sophomore. An opposing coach recalled the first time he saw Alcindor, who had grown to 7 feet at the tender age of 15: "I watched him walk out for warm-up, chewing a lollipop. Then he began striding down the court with those giant steps, flicking the ball into the basket, first with one hand, then the other—and I realized what we were up against. By game time, half my team was in a state of shock."

"He could run and he could catch the ball," said Donohue, pointing out the first two qualities that caught his attention immediately. "Running and catching well are very important for a big man. The one thing he always had was this tremendous pride, which was the big difference between him and a lot of other kids. He didn't mind hard work and long hours of practice."

Power went through an unbeaten season as Alcindor stirred wide reaction in his second year of high school. He improved tremendously from his freshman season in all facets of the game, using his exceptional 220-pound body to better advantage under Donohue's stern tutelage. He leaned closer to the basket to utilize his height and perfected a hook shot, delivered beautifully with either hand. He totaled 444 rebounds, about 16 a game, and scored 515 points, an average of 19.1 an outing. He made 53 percent of his shots from the field, and Power won 27 games, including the New York City Catholic high school championship.

Hundreds of schools wrote to the boy wonder after he led his team to another city championship. "The rule is this," Donohue said firmly, holding the line. "No talking to Lew until his senior year."

In his senior year, the school winning streak reached 71 victories before losing a close one to DeMatha in another battle between two of the country's most powerful high school clubs. When DeMatha beat Power 46–43, it broke Alcindor's heart. The youngster sat near his locker, his head bowed. He blamed himself for the defeat because he scored only 16 points.

"Now wait a minute," Donohue admonished. "It's very selfish of you to say that you lost this game. What you're implying is that you won all the other games. If you want to take the blame for losing this game, then you have to take the credit for winning the other seventy-one. Are you willing to take the credit? Yes or no?"

"No," said Lew.

In his last game as a high school player, Alcindor scored 32 points, had 22 rebounds and set the New York City record for career points (2,067) and career rebounds (2,002), as Power defeated Rice High 73–41 for another Catholic league championship. "I'll trade two first-round draft choices for him right now," said Gene Shue of the Baltimore Bullets.

But the pros would have to wait four more years to barter for his services. First, Alcindor had to go to college. The importance of that decision was reflected in the number of newsmen (80) that on May 4, 1965, appeared for his press conference in the Power gym, where the superstar was to announce his decision. It was the first time in anyone's recollection that a high school basketball player had held a press conference.

"This fall, I'll be attending UCLA," said Alcindor succinctly. "That's the decision I came to. It has everything I want in a school."

Ignoring the pressure of his first game in UCLA togs while several thousand looked on in Pauley Pavilion, Alcindor scored 31 points to lead the freshmen over the varsity, 75–60, in a warm-up game for the 1965–66 season. This was the same varsity, incidentally, that had won two straight national championships.

"UCLA is number one in the country and number two on its own campus," wrote one newsman.

While maintaining high academic standards, the same that put him near the top in his high school class, Alcindor waited restlessly for his sophomore year when he would be a varsity player. "I just want to go out there and be able to do my thing and see whether it is good enough," he said.

When he got his chance, he not only did *his* thing, he did everything. In his first game as a full-fledged Bruin, Alcindor ruined Southern California with 56 points, a school record. UCLA routed its cross-town rival, 105–90.

Wooden, always sparing in praise, shocked some by calling Alcindor "awesome." "At times," Wooden said, "he frightens me."

Alcindor accepted his responsibility without vanity. There was no egotism at work—he was a realist who knew his potential and used it to full advantage in the scheme of team play. He helped UCLA knock down opponents right and left, frustrating every defense—double-teaming, triple-teaming and pressing. And he shrugged off the illegal maneuvers, too—elbowing, gouging, bumping and stepping on his feet. His raillike appearance was deceptive.

"He plays his best when it gets tough," said Wooden. "I'm amazed that he can take that kind of play in there and still keep his poise. I don't think there's anyone who can handle him legally."

At the end of the season, UCLA had won 30 games without a loss, including another NCAA title with a 79–64 victory over Dayton in the finals at Louisville. Alcindor was the architect, collecting all-America recognition and the Most Valuable Player trophy in the NCAA play-offs. During the season he averaged 29.7 points and 15.5 rebounds a game.

The following year, they banned the dunk shot, Alcindor's favorite weapon. The rule, which later came to be known as the Lew Alcindor rule, only fired the big man to greater accomplishment in his junior and senior years. Alcindor was sold on fundamental basketball, not individual achievement, and he wanted passionately to become the consummate player.

"I want to improve my game," said Alcindor, who sometimes had trouble with his foul shooting, "and it will be a challenge for us now that we've won a national title. Everyone will be shooting for us."

The Bruins ran their winning streak to 47 during Alcindor s junior year. Then "the Big A" met "the Big E," Elvin Hayes, when UCLA. played Houston in a natural rivalry of ranked teams. Alcindor gave no excuses, although he played with double vision because of a scratched eyeball. Hayes outplayed Alcindor, and Houston won, 71–69, before an appreciative home crowd in the Astrodome. The next time they met was in the NCAA semifinal play-offs in the Los Angeles Sports Arena. UCLA gained a measure of revenge and a big chunk of respectability, beating Houston into submission by the outrageous score of 101–69.

Victory over Houston was exquisitely satisfying for Alcindor. "They had a lot to say about us and I didn't think they were correct," said Alcindor. "They were annoying and insulting. We wanted to teach them some manners."

He referred specifically to Hayes, who had downgraded the UCLA center after the first meeting. Alcindor's pride was showing again. After "teaching Houston manners," UCLA taught North Carolina basketball with a 78–55 whipping in the NCAA title game of 1968. Alcindor scored 34 points.

"This is the best team of all time," said North Carolina coach Dean Smith, "and Alcindor is the best player who ever played college basketball."

Alcindor was not only a great player, he was also a concerned black athlete. He worked with children in New York's ghettos during his summer vacation, and in the summer of 1968, after his junior year, he became especially interested in the movement for Negro athletes to boycott the Olympics. The movement proposed to point up racial injustices in America.

"If you live in a racist society and you want to express yourself about racism, there's a lot of things you can do . . . and a boycott is one of them," said Alcindor. The proposed boycott wasn't successful, and the United States continued its basketball domination in the Olympics without Alcindor's services.

At this point in his life, he began studying the world of Malcolm X and Islam. Although born and raised a Roman Catholic, he soon became a Muslim. Just before his senior year, he had his baptism into Islam. He was a Sunnite Muslim with a new name—Kareem Abdul-Jabbar, which loosely translates into "Generous," "Servant of Allah" and "Powerful." His new holy book, the Quran, replaced the Bible. He was literally at peace with the world.

"The genuine Muslim bears witness that there is one God—Allah—and that all men, black or white, are brothers," he said. "There is no room in Islam for racial hatred of any sort."

During his last year at UCLA, Alcindor had the attention of both the NBA and rival American Basketball Association. He liked it: "That attention makes me feel pretty good. I don't want to sound money-hungry . . . but I can use that to assure what I'm worth. I can see six figures immediately."

Coming back to New York for a basketball game, Alcindor played magnificently in the Holiday Festival Tournament at Madison Square Garden. But his personal Olympic ban had touched off a furor, and some fans responded to his appearance with boos. The new Kareem Abdul-Jabbar suffered through it.

"I can see the light at the end of the tunnel," he said. "I'll get my degree soon and be finished with this whole academic scene."

It turned out that the six-figure salary estimates by the young star were a bit modest. "Start at a million and go from there," was the general feeling.

But there was no bidding war between the leagues. Abdul-Jabbar insisted that he receive one offer only from each of the teams involved —the highest would win his services. The New York Nets of the ABA laid a $1 million check on the table for him. The Milwaukee Bucks of the NBA offered him $1.4 million. He signed with Milwaukee, although it later came out that the ABA was willing to boost the kitty by a considerable sum and that Alcindor actually preferred playing in New York.

"It's a dream come true," said Wes Pavalon, chairman of the board of the Bucks.

Milwaukee, which had had one of the worst records the year before, thus opened its second season in the NBA with a new outlook and a new center—number 33. The club statistician measured him in bare feet as 7 feet 1⅝ inches. Opponents swore he looked more like 7 feet 6 inches with his semi-Afro hairdo, two thick pairs of socks and heavy-soled sneakers.

Abdul-Jabbar scoffed at reports that he would be torn apart by more-muscled NBA players. Hayes, his old adversary and now a pro star, didn't miss a chance to needle. "I really feel sorry for the guy. Whenever he goes into a town, players will be keying on him. The big thing for Lew will be how he reacts to physical punishment. If he says, 'You can't get away with that, I'll show you,' then he's in trouble."

The new kid on the block had to prove himself all over again. In his first game on October 18, 1969, he scored 14 points in the first period against the Detroit Pistons. He wound up with 29 in the game, took 12 rebounds, blocked three shots, had six assists and three steals and handled the ball like a guard.

Along with his varied talents, Abdul-Jabbar was especially applauded for his ability to hit the open man. "He ought to," said Detroit coach Butch van Breda Kolff after the rookie's debut. "He's looking down on everyone."

Milwaukee built up winning streaks, a new-found euphoria for last year's losers, and Abdul-Jabbar got most of the credit, even though he wasn't looking for it. "Chamberlain is stronger, but Alcindor is more versatile," said teammate Guy Rogers, who played with both of the men.

Some said he'd make the NBA all-star team on name alone. He made it on merit. Others said he'd be too frail to play the arduous 82-game schedule. He averaged 43 minutes a game. There were some who said he'd find rebounding in the pros tough. He averaged 14.5 a game, third in the league, in his first year. He led all NBA centers with 337 assists, finished second in scoring with 28.8 points a game, was a near-unanimous choice as Rookie of the Year and finished third in the Most Valuable Player balloting. The Bucks won 56 of 82 games, more than doubling their victory output of the previous year, and wound up in the play-offs in only their second year of existence.

After beating the Philadelphia 76ers in the semifinals, the Bucks lost the NBA Eastern Division title to the New York Knicks while some raucous fans in New York serenaded the star rookie with: "Goodbye, Lewie, goodbye, Lewie, good-bye, Lewie, we hate to see you go."

"They sang because they were scared," Kareem stated. "I can't feel bad about it, it's their problem. If they want to act that way, that's their business. But we've got nothing to be ashamed of."

In his second year as a pro, Abdul-Jabbar coupled with newly acquired Oscar Robertson to lead the Bucks to their first world championship. It had taken the New York Knicks almost a quarter of a century to do the same thing the year before. Milwaukee did it in three years.

The big fellow came loping down the corridor inside Baltimore's Civic Center after the Bucks had disposed of the Bullets in four straight for the NBA title. His oversized fists were tucked into his sides as he moved along, smiling.

"Just like UCLA?" someone asked him.

"No, no," said the man who had led the NBA in scoring with a 31.7 average in his sophomore season and had been named Most Valuable Player. "That was college. Here you're playing against the very best in the world."

It was a new plateau, but not the last by any means. He won the MVP award again in 1972, when the Bucks placed first in their division, but were eliminated by Los Angeles in the play-off semifinal. Despite the defeat, Kareem Abdul-Jabbar stood tall.

KEN RAPPOPORT

Joe Frazier
Street Fighter

Members of the South Carolina legislature rose to their feet early in April, 1971, and applauded the high school dropout who, during a 12-minute address, had told them, "You can do anything you want to do if you really put your heart and soul and mind into it."

Thirty days earlier the feelings of a far different gathering had rolled in waves of sound over Joe Frazier after he had put his heart, soul, mind and body into 45 minutes of fighting against Muhammad Ali. The record book notes that Frazier became the heavyweight champion of the world the night of February 16, 1970, when he beat Jimmy Ellis in New York's Madison Square Garden. Joe, recognized as champion by six states, twice knocked down Ellis, the World Boxing Association champion, and when Ellis was unable to leave his corner for the fifth round, Joe leaped into the arms of manager Yank Durham, shouting, "Free, I'm free at last." But he was not free of the shadow of Ali.

Ali had been stripped of the world title and banned from the ring by the various governing bodies of boxing because of his refusal to be drafted into the army. But in the minds of many people throughout the world, Ali was still the champion and would be until he lost the title in the ring. Joe Frazier, some people said, was a pretender who wouldn't have a title if Ali's hadn't been taken away.

"I didn't hear them," Joe said.

But he did hear the voiced doubts that he really would beat Ali in the ring and he heard the taunts of Ali and other blacks that he was a white man's champ. "I'm no Uncle Tom," he once snapped. "I'm black, I'm blacker than him. Next time I see Clay [Joe always referred to Ali as Cassius Clay], I'm gonna ask him to show me one black spot on his brown body."

On the night of March 8, 1971, Frazier got the chance to answer his critics and Ali's taunts —he got the chance to answer with his fists. On that night he stood in a corner of the ring in Madison Square Garden and looked across at Ali. Ali, his draft-evasion conviction earlier overturned by the U.S. Supreme Court, had returned to the ring the previous October. On December 30, he and Frazier had signed, for purses of $2.5 million each, to decide the true heavyweight champion of the world.

After the fight, Frazier said, "Let me go clean up my face. I'm not this ugly." His face was badly swollen, but Joe had just scored a unanimous 15-round decision over Ali before a roaring crowd of 20,455 that paid $1,352,951— both indoor boxing records—and a worldwide television audience of 300 million that would swell the total receipts to the neighborhood of $20 million.

For 15 grueling rounds, with the Garden crowd knifing the tension with shouts of "Ah-lee, Ah-lee" and "Joe, Joe, Joe," Frazier had moved toward Ali, slamming at his body, shooting hooks and short right-hand punches to the head and catching uncountable punches with his own head. He bobbed and weaved, snarled through his mouthpiece and even exchanged taunts with the former champion. In the fifth round Joe spent most of the three minutes with his hands at his sides, moving forward, daring Ali to hit him and laughing when he did. At the end of the round, as Ali turned to go to his corner, Joe waved at him. He didn't wave or laugh in the eleventh round. In that round he almost ended the fight. Growling, "Let go of me," as referee Arthur Mercante pulled the fighters apart, Frazier went after Ali, staggered him twice and had him reeling around the ring with glassy eyes as the round ended.

Clang! The bell announced through the din of the crowd the start of the fifteenth round, with Ali going out for a knockout and Joe there to meet him. Then about a minute into the round, the crowd came to its feet as a long left hook by Joe sent Ali over backwards and to the floor for a count of four. "I brought it from the country," Joe said of the punch that ballooned the right side of Ali's face and sent him to a hospital instead of to the postfight news conference. "Frazier is not a great boxer," Ali said later. "He is a great street fighter." Joe later went into a hospital for a week, leading to rumors that he was dying and prompting Ali to say he had given Joe a bad beating and should have been given the decision. But doctors said that the champion was all right and that he was just

Joe Frazier sends a left hook to the head of Muhammad Ali in their "Fight of the Century" at Madison Square Garden. Frazier handed Ali his first heavyweight defeat.

suffering from "athlete's kidney," an ailment caused by physical and psychological pressure.

Joe didn't fight again until January 15, 1972, when he knocked out little-known Terry Daniels, and during his 10-month absence from the ring, he once again was overshadowed publicly by Ali. But now Joe was content in the knowledge that he was the unbeaten heavyweight champion of the world.

After leaving the hospital, Joe turned his energy toward his other profession, music, which he seemed to enjoy at least as much as boxing but with which he had anything but championship success. After the big fight, Joe took his rock-and-roll group, the Knockouts, on a European and South American tour—a financial failure. But Joe was not about to admit defeat outside the ring any more than he would quit in it.

Joe told the South Carolina legislature, "Every time I see a black person taking a step forward, I feel proud." The first big step the youngest of 13 children born to a field worker took on the road through a Philadelphia slaughterhouse, to an Olympic heavyweight title and on to the professional championship of the world was to leave Beaufort, South Carolina, where he was born January 12, 1944. "I left school at fifteen, because I wasn't learning and I was just taking up space," said Joe. "I guess I had the mind of a man early and I mean about everything."

The same year Joe quit school he got married, and the next year, 1960, he became the father of a boy. So, Joe went north to New York where he lived with a brother, Tom, for a year. Then he moved to Philadelphia, got a job in a slaughterhouse stripping sides of beef for $105 a week and brought his wife and son from Beaufort. He also decided to lose weight and went to the Twenty-third Police Athletic League gym where he began to fool around with boxing and where he met Durham. However, Yank didn't handle Joe until he got to the trials for the 1964 Olympics in Tokyo.

Joe lost to Buster Mathis in the heavyweight final of the trials, but arrangements were made for Joe to get time off from his job and accompany the team to Japan as an alternate and sparring partner. But he ended up as the U.S. representative in the heavyweight division because Mathis broke a finger on his right hand while sparring with Frazier in an exhibition. Given his chance, Joe went all the way to an Olympic gold medal, winning his final match while fighting with a broken left thumb, an injury he had kept secret. Then he returned to Philadelphia with his gold medal.

His broken thumb prevented him from training and from working in the slaughterhouse, so he got a job as a janitor in the Bright Hope Baptist Church. Later, when his thumb had healed, he turned professional under the management of Durham. On August 16, 1965, Joe knocked out Woody Gross in one round in his first pro start. He had three more fights that year and won them all.

After Joe's fourth straight knockout, Durham decided that he would need financial backers for a drive to the heavyweight championship. Cloverlay, Incorporated, was formed. Cloverlay was comprised of a group of highly respected Pennsylvanians and was to be the guiding light in the handling of Joe's affairs. Cloverlay began with capital of $22,000 on 88 shares of stock selling for $250 per share. Before the Ali fight, Cloverlay had expanded to include ownership of several other fighters, several apartment buildings and a gymnasium. A share of its stock was valued at $14,000.

From the start, Frazier's style consisted of putting constant pressure on an opponent. He was compared to another heavyweight champion whose style also was pressure and power underscored by superb stamina—Rocky Marciano. Joe and Rocky, each about an inch under 6 feet, were among the smallest men ever to win boxing's biggest prize, although Joe's best fighting weight was about 205 pounds, while Rocky fought at about 185. However, Durham liked to compare Frazier with another famous fighter.

"People compare him to Marciano," said Yank, "but Marciano never slipped punches the way Frazier does. Joe's a big Henry Armstrong."

And, indeed, Joe often did resemble Armstrong, the tireless puncher who held the featherweight, lightweight and welterweight championships simultaneously. "My corner told me after the first round to wait for my spots," Foster said after being knocked out in the second round of the fight in Detroit, "but he won't let you wait."

Both Foster and Ellis can attest to the numbing power of Frazier's punches. Ellis went down twice from left hooks, spraining an ankle the second time as his descent to the canvas imitated the movement of a corkscrew. Ellis got up after each of the two knockdowns and was sitting on his stool when the fight was stopped. But just how hard Jimmy had been hit was revealed at the postfight news conference. "When did you first pick up the count?" someone asked.

"At eight," Ellis replied.

"Both times?" shot the questioner.

"I was only down once," said Ellis. The next day he could not remember being down twice.

"Who's the greatest fighter you've ever seen?" was the question put to Frazier at a luncheon several weeks before the Ali fight. Joe stared at the questioner for a moment and said matter-of-factly, his face revealing nothing, "The greatest fighter today is myself."

This poise and confidence in his ability was tested early in Joe's pro career, and he passed the test. On September 20, 1965, Mike Bruce floored Joe with a punch to the chin. Joe got up, went after Bruce and knocked him out in the third round. However, the big test was yet to come for the future champion, and when it did, it came in the form of a hulking, square-jawed Argentine named Oscar Bonavena.

Cloverlay stock came very close to taking a nose dive the night of September 21, 1966, in Madison Square Garden in what was Joe's twelfth pro fight. The crowd had just got nicely settled and the Cloverlay stockholders were admiring their asset when Bonavena connected with a right hand to the jaw in the second round, sending Joe to the canvas. He got to his feet at the count of five, took the mandatory eight-count, wobbled toward Bonavena and was met with a left hook that put him down again. Once more Joe got to his feet, this time with about two minutes left in the round and a chance of losing on the rule that ends a fight when one fighter goes down three times in a round. Joe not only withstood Bonavena's desperate bid for another knockdown, he went on to win a 10-round decision.

Joe ended 1966 with a tenth-round knockout over Eddie Machen, a clever fighter who some boxing buffs thought would have too much experience for Frazier. He opened 1967 with a sixth-round knockout of Doug Jones and won his other five fights of the year, stopping rugged George Chuvalo in four rounds in one of them. His last 1967 bout was a third-round knockout of Marion Connor, and his first 1968 match was on March 4 against Buster Mathis, who had beaten Joe twice in the amateur ranks. During the time between these two fights, Ali was stripped of his title, and the World Boxing Association set up an elimination tournament, eventually won by Ellis, to find a successor, but Durham declined to enter Frazier.

So Joe and Buster got together in Madison Square Garden for the heavyweight championship of the world according to the states of New York, Illinois, Pennsylvania, Maine, Texas and Massachusetts. In the eleventh round, Frazier, in complete control of the fight, landed a right hand to the chin and a left to the side of the head and Mathis landed on his back, blood streaming from his nose. He got up, but the referee halted the fight and Joe Frazier was a champion of sorts. He defended his share of the title by knocking out Manuel Ramos in 2 rounds, outpointing Bonavena in 15, knocking out Dave Zyglewicz in 1 and stopping Jerry Quarry in 7. Then came Ellis and finally Ali, and Joe Frazier had stepped to the top of his profession, overcoming many obstacles, truly free at last.

ED SCHUYLER, JR.

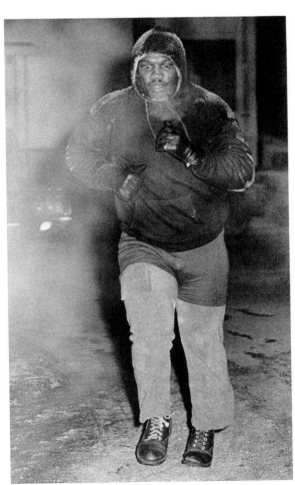

Joe jogs in frost in preparation for another fight.

Arnold Palmer
Charged by an Army

It was a balmy day in the early spring of 1960, and Ken Venturi was comfortably settled into the white, colonial style clubhouse of the Augusta National Golf Club, leisurely trying on green jackets for the proper size.

Venturi had just finished his final round over the flower-bedecked layout and was listening to a briefing for a television appearance as he shrugged in and out of a series of jackets. The Californian appeared a sure winner of the Masters with a score of 283. Although a handful of players—including a powerful, magnetic young man named Arnold Palmer—still were out fighting the famed course, none seemed to have any chance of depriving Venturi of the title and the highly prized green coat.

Palmer failed to get needed birdies on the thirteenth and fifteenth holes, parred the sixteenth and came to the seventeenth tee needing one birdie on the final two holes to gain a tie and force a playoff. His chances were remote. They were two of the toughest finishing holes in golf, and the pressure was tremendous.

Palmer's drive was long and down the middle on the par-four seventeenth, a 400-yard downwind hole. He punched an eight iron to the green, where the ball sat down too quickly and left him a 25-foot putt. Twice he lined it up and took his stance only to step away when he was distracted by a movement in the crowd. Finally, he tapped the ball firmly. It rolled toward the cup, seemed to hesitate on the lip just a heart-stopping moment, then fell in. A birdie. Now he needed only par on the final hole for a tie.

The eighteenth was a 420-yard par four, uphill and into the wind. Palmer hitched at his britches with a gesture that was to become one of the most familiar in sports and decided to go for it boldly—to go for the victory and ignore the tie. He waggled the driver, the muscles in his forearms tensing, then boomed his shot down the left side of the fairway. The position gave him a straight shot at the pin, set to the right and on the lower deck of the big, two-level green. He quickly stroked a six iron low into the wind. The ball came to rest five feet from the cup as the gallery gasped, then howled in glee. With the eyes of millions watching on television, Arnold studied the putt carefully, dropped a half-smoked cigarette and crouched over the ball in a knock-kneed stance. He stroked it. The ball hit the left side of the cup and dropped in. He had his birdie—a second Masters championship—and a legend was born.

It was the legend of Arnold the miracle maker; of Palmer the bold, go-for-broke gambler; of the man with the riverboat dash, odds-defying flamboyance; constructor of breath-taking fairway drama.

He became an instant hero, a national figure with an incredible following, one of the most popular players ever to compete in the game—or in any other form of sports.

And the phenomenon that was Palmer occurred, for golf, at precisely the right moment.

Television was just moving into the game. The public loved it. A flick of the dial could and did bring the world's finest courses and greatest players into millions of living rooms. The channels quickly became clogged with live and taped golf competition, particularly on weekends.

To sustain and prolong this interest—which produced purses for the players that doubled, redoubled and doubled again in value—it was necessary for the game to produce a giant, a Ruthian figure. It did.

He was a rugged, strong-faced son of a greenskeeper and professional in the little town of Latrobe, Pennsylvania, about 30 miles from Pittsburgh. A sturdy 170 pounds, he was built like a middleweight fighter, with a trim waist and powerful, sloping shoulders. He had hands like hams and arms like pistons. His boyish, deeply tanned face ran the gamut of expressions. When concentrating, his brow became furrowed and his jaw tightened like a vise. When he rolled in a long birdie putt—which, his opponents grumbled, happened distractingly often—his face broke into a wide, joyous grin. He carried on a running conversation with the gallery.

Personal magnetism, however, was only a fraction of Palmer's amazing appeal. It was his ability to manufacture miracle finishes—dramatic dashes down the stretch holes when he turned defeat into impossible victory—that

1958 and Palmer on his way at Augusta to first Masters win.

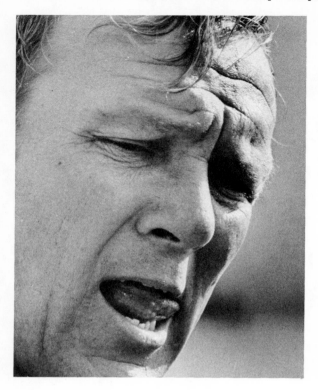

really captured the enthusiasim of the public.

It got to a point that fans flocked to the big tournaments in mushrooming thousands, and millions more hugged their television sets just to see another Palmer miracle. No matter how far he fell behind, these disciples were convinced Arnie could putt it out. Fantastically, he often did—usually in the big championships where the money stakes and prestige values were high and everybody was watching.

His following was not restricted to golf fans, people who admired him for the power of his swing or the precision of his putting. Housewives addicted to cliff-hanging soap operas, teen-agers and others knowing little or nothing about the game joined his legion of fans which became known as "Arnie's Army."

"It's very distracting," one prominent player said. "These people have a regard for no one but Palmer. If he putts first, they break and run, stampeding for the next hole. They don't care how much they bother the other players."

At one point Palmer was forced to putt last —even though out of turn—in deference to his playing companions. He often raised his hands and admonished the crowd, "Let the other players putt out, please." It did little good.

Arnie's Army operated under its own rules. It needled Palmer's rivals, particularly the feared Jack Nicklaus. It ran and yelled and hollered.

Palmer, appreciative of this intense loyalty, sought to harness his wild fan club. He copyrighted the name "Arnie's Army." He sent letters and official buttons to the members. But their sometimes rowdy behavior and enthusiasm continued unabated.

Arnold Palmer won the National Amateur in 1954 and his first Masters in 1958, but he didn't really fire the public imagination until that charging Masters triumph over Venturi in 1960. The blazing finish in a tournament famous for the spectacular made Palmer the game's golden boy. He had the golf world at his feet. Then, as ever, the man with that intense competitive drive was not satisfied.

"I won't be content," he said at the time, "until I score a professional Grand Slam. My ambition is to win the Masters, the U.S. and British Opens and the PGA, all in a single year. I think it would be a greater achievement than Bobby Jones's Grand Slam in 1930."

The second leg was the U.S. Open at Cherry Hills in Denver, and it appeared that the flame of Palmer's lofty golfing goal was destined to flicker away almost before it was fully lighted. Mike Souchak got off to a blistering start with rounds of 68 and 67, while Palmer was scrambling around in 72 and 71. His prospects were little brighter after a third-round 72. He was seven shots back of Souchak, and there were 14 players between him and the top spot going into the final round.

It appeared to be an impossible situation— the kind of spot that challenged Palmer and thrilled his army. "Go, Arnie, go," they shouted as the players teed off for the final round.

Palmer tugged at his trousers and responded.

He drove the first hole, a 346-yard par four with an elevated tee, and two-putted from 20 feet for an opening birdie. On the 410-yard second he holed out a 30-foot chip shot from off the green. He hit a wedge to within a foot of the hole on the third and dropped a 20-foot birdie putt on the fourth.

Four birds in a row and the gallery literally was going wild. They cooled off a bit when Palmer had to settle for a par five on the long fifth hole after running into sand trouble, but ignited again on the sixth where he holed a 25-foot putt. A wedge shot to within six feet on the seventh hole brought Arnie still another birdie.

At this stage, Palmer had played seven holes and birdied six of them. It was one of the most amazing spurts under pressure the game had ever seen.

At the 230-yard eighth, Arnold dumped his tee shot in a trap, blasted out to within three feet but missed the putt. It was a bogey. He had to scramble for his par on the ninth. He hit a six iron over the green, chipped back long and had to sink an eight-foot putt. But he turned in 30, matching the lowest nine ever played in the Open, and he was back in contention. He played the back nine in one under par for a stunning 65, the lowest round ever shot on a final round by a winner.

And he was that, posting a 72-hole total of 280, two strokes in front of then-amateur Jack Nicklaus, second at 282. He had two legs on the Slam.

From Denver, Palmer flew to the Centennial Anniversary British Open at historic St. Andrews in Scotland, where he missed by a slender stroke in his bid to add a third jewel to pro golf's Quadruple Crown. He was making one of his patented rallies when a heavy rain forced postponement of the last round. The charge expired in the downpour, and he finished as runner-up to Kel Nagle of Australia. Back home, he led the first round of the PGA at Akron, Ohio, but fell off the pace and the title went to Jay Hebert. He'd missed the Slam by two eyelashes.

But the reputation was established. He was the comeback man. The miracle maker. They called him "the King," "the Charger." Every time he teed up the ball his fans came to expect the impossible.

He fell three strokes back of Gary Player of South Africa after nine holes of a playoff for the Masters crown in 1962, then birdied five of the first seven holes on the incoming side to win by three strokes. But he had his moments of despair and defeat. He had the 1961 Masters in his pocket only to blow up on the last hole, taking a double-bogey six and losing by a stroke to Player. A year later he lost in a play-off to Nicklaus for the U.S. Open crown.

He won some and lost some, yet he went on to become the greatest money-winner in the sport's history. He was the first to go past the $1 million mark in career winnings. He set a single season mark of more than $125,000 in 1963 when he didn't win a major title. Through other enterprises related to golf, he pushed his yearly income well beyond $1 million.

He became the outstanding sports personality of his day—as well as the richest. He was writer, actor, teacher, business tycoon. Five lawyers, working for him almost exclusively, were needed to handle his business and financial interests. Two secretaries were hired full-time just to answer his fan mail.

He set up his own company, which manufactured golf clubs, balls, shirts, slacks, shoes and gloves. He headed 11 clothing companies with branches in Australia, Japan and Europe. He was the largest stockholder in a chain of putting courses, had an interest in driving ranges. He owned his own printing company, insurance agency, investment firm and several golf courses. He had a string of instructional schools. He produced golf carts, driving nets and table-top golf games.

He acted in the movies, took bit roles on television, produced and played in his own television golf show, sometimes hosted talk shows, cut records and endorsed dozens of items.

Palmer acknowledged that the pressure of his business enterprises often affected his golf, but he refused to let them become his principal interest or dedication.

"When I feel myself getting burdened with business, I just knock off, go back home and play with Pap," he said. "I think it's important to make money while you can, but my chief aim is to be the best golfer in the world. I won't let anything interfere with that aim."

"Pap" was Milfred ("Deac") Palmer, Arnold's father, teacher and severest critic, who started as greenskeeper and later became professional of the little nine-hole course in Latrobe where Arnold swung his first club shortly after he was old enough to walk.

"I don't think Deac ever once told Arnie that he thought he had made it," Arnold's mother once said. "He's told me, but he would never tell Arnie. He wouldn't give him that much satisfaction."

Arnold was given his first golf club by his father when he was four. By the time he was eight, he was playing regularly with some of the older boys who served as caddies at his dad's course. He became a caddie himself when he was 11.

"I couldn't wait to get out of school and get on the golf course," Palmer later recalled. "I hated to study, but nobody had to force me to work on my golf. I loved every minute of it. And even in those days I hated to hit a bad shot. It made me feel awful."

He shot a 71 and won a local tournament while in the seventh grade. He played in his first national tournament, a junior event, in 1946. He later entered Wake Forest but quit midway through the senior year when Bud Worsham, his closest friend, was killed in a highway accident. He signed up for three years in the Coast Guard and for several months played hardly at all. His interest was rekindled by a group of friends when he transferred to Cleveland.

He was 24 when he got out of the Coast Guard. He obtained a job as a manufacturer's agent in Cleveland and, at that time, had no intention of turning professional. In 1954 he won the National Amateur, and shortly after that, playing in a tournament in Pennsylvania, he met Winnie Walzer. Within less than a week he had proposed and the two were planning a honeymoon in England during the Walker Cup matches the following spring.

The more he thought about it, the more Palmer became convinced that if he planned to play golf, he should do it for money. He talked it over with his father and his bride-to-be. Late in the year he turned professional and signed a contract with a sporting goods company. He and Winnie were married during the Christmas holidays.

Under rules of the Professional Golfers Association, he was not eligible to receive prize money from PGA-sponsored tournaments for six months. But he won some $2,000 in a pro—amateur event in Florida and another tournament in Panama and had a stake.

He and Winnie borrowed $600 from his father and bought a secondhand house trailer. He continued to make enough in nonsanctioned events to keep going until his probationary period was over. Success came soon after that. He was the leading money-winner in 1958 with $42,607 and big paydays began to come regularly.

While his last-gasp, high-drama finishes thrilled the public, they took their toll on the man who made them.

"People are always accusing me of purposely getting behind so that I can do something spectacular," Palmer once said. "That's ridiculous. I bleed a little bit on those tight finishes. If I had my way, I'd win every tournament by at least twelve or thirteen strokes."

One of the best insights into the playing character of Palmer was offered by his long-time caddie at the Masters, affectionately known as Ironman.

"It's let it go or blow it, all or nothing," Ironman said. "This man don't know what it is to play safe." The caddie said he could tell when Palmer was ready to make one of his charges. "He tugs at his glove, jerks on his trousers and starts walking fast and then he turns to me and says, 'The game is on.' "

But there was a limit to the miracles even Palmer could fashion. He started running into mild slumps beginning in 1962. Then they got bigger and longer. Finally, in advancing years, Palmer began fighting his nerves.

"It's my putting," he lamented time and again. "I'm hitting the ball better from tee to green than ever . But I just can't get in the hole."

Usually, he went home to Latrobe to work on his clubs and play a few rounds with his father. Then he'd come back, good as ever. Eventually, that formula failed, too.

He won his last major championship in the Masters in 1964, took another title a month later and then went 18 frustrating months with only a single victory.

One of his biggest disappointments came in the 1965 PGA National Championship, played on his home course, the Laurel Valley Country Club. It was the only major title he had never won. Now, on his home course and before thousands of friends, he was ready to make the big effort. Disaster struck quickly. He drew a two-stroke penalty in the first round for allowing the removal of some wooden bridge railings that obstructed a shot. He took another two-stroke penalty the second round for grounding his club in a hazard. He was out of it.

But his biggest collapse came in the 1966 U.S. Open in San Francisco. He had divested himself of many of his business interests to concentrate on golf. He was on a determined comeback and he forged a seven-stroke lead with nine holes to play over the Olympic Club course.

Ben Hogan's Open scoring record was within sight and he kept his eyes trained on that goal—a mistake. Playing in bold, gambling fashion—the only fashion he knew—he began to encounter trouble, going into the woods, hitting traps, putting too boldly. The lead dwindled, then vanished as Billy Casper caught him on the final hole—then beat him in an 18-hole play-off the next day.

The slumps continued to come and go. His golfing obituary was written scores of times. His biggest trial came when he was forced to withdraw from the 1969 PGA championship at Dayton, Ohio. Suffering from bursitis in the hip, he failed to break 80 in the first round, then pulled out, announced he wouldn't play again until he was healthy and went home.

Many thought the game's most fabulous career was over.

He came back again, fired by that indomitable competitive drive. He scored consecutive victories in the last two events of the year—then went 18 months before winning again. But his victory in the 1971 Bob Hope Desert Classic was the first of four titles that season. He went past the $200,000 mark in earnings that year and was named Athlete of the Decade.

The money was important only as a measure of his golfing success to the man who traveled to business and golf in a private jet.

"Golf is my life," he said. "I like to win. I am determined to win. I'll play as long as I think I am capable of winning."

BOB GREEN

Crowds love to see Arnie give vent to disgust with bad shots.

311

Bobby Orr
Two Trophies for One

In 1962, when Robert Gordon Orr was a crew-cut 14-year-old playing hockey in Oshawa, Ontario, in Canada, the Boston Bruins' chances of winning the Stanley Cup were dead almost from the start of the National Hockey League season. They came alive only after the young defenseman joined them four years later.

In between the Bruins' enthusiastic supporters suffered . . . and how they suffered! The team ran to five a string of last-place finishes, extending even into Orr's first big league campaign. For eight consecutive seasons they failed to qualify for postseason competition.

In 1972, ten years after joining the Boston organization, the brilliant defenseman led the team to its second championship in three years while playing with a penny-sized chunk of cartilage loose in his left knee. "He's better on one leg than most other players are with two," said one opponent.

When Bruins' executives saw him play for the first time, Bobby had two good legs. They discovered him playing a peewee hockey game. It didn't take them long to realize that they had stumbled onto something special. Bobby Orr was only 12 years old then, but he stood out as much as he did among the big leaguers almost a decade later.

The Bruin representatives fanned out over the building as is routine for hockey scouts who want to see players from all angles. Wren Blair, Boston's superscout at the time, sat in one section. Weston Adams, president of the club, moved into another area. Lynn Patrick, at that time the Bruins' general manager, and Milt Schmidt, then the coach, sat together in a third section. They agreed to huddle after the first period.

Management decided that they had to obtain the young man. Blair was given the task of securing Bobby for Boston. It was no simple job. Fortunately for the Bruins, no other NHL team was sponsoring the Parry Sound minor hockey program. That meant Orr was a free agent, so Boston quickly invested $1,000 in the small Ontario town's program, making Bobby something of a Bruins' chattel. Next, Blair had to convince the Orr family that Bobby should

sign a "C" form—a document that would formalize the young man's relationship with the Bruins. The Orrs were in no hurry.

"He's too young," argued Arva Orr, Bobby's mother. "Wait a few years." But time was the last thing the Bruins had. In Boston, the team was losing regularly and needed a hope to maintain the fans' enthusiasm. Orr was that hope, and after two years of negotiating with the Orrs, Blair got Bobby's parents to agree to sign the form that would move the young man into junior hockey, the next step to the NHL.

There was one vital stipulation to the agreement. Bobby would be allowed to sign the form and play for Boston's Oshawa, Ontario, farm club, but he would continue to live at home in Parry Sound, some 150 miles north of Oshawa. He would commute to the games. There would be no practice with the team. On the day of the game, Orr would be chauffeured to Oshawa, play for the team and then return home. If that was the only way they could get Orr, then that was the way the Bruins would take him. What was important was that Bobby would be playing in the organization and that in four years he would be 18, eligible to turn pro and play in the NHL for the Bruins.

The commuting defenseman was named to the Ontario Hockey Association's second all-star team that year and Blair grinned at the honor. "Imagine," he said, "if he had been able to practice with the team."

The next year Orr's parents gave Bobby the green light to board at Oshawa. Young Bobby scored a record-shattering 30 goals that season, increased it to 34 the next season and finally to 38 in his final year of junior hockey.

His apprenticeship complete, Bobby was ready for Boston and was Boston ever ready for Bobby! The Bruins had been selling the arrival of Orr to their fans for four years, simply because it took their minds off the home team's dreary performances in Boston Garden. With his junior hockey career over, Orr was set for delivery. There was one small matter to settle beforehand. It was his contract. Just how much were the Bruins willing to pay this 18-year-old prodigy? The answer was not enough—at least

"He was a star from the moment they played the national anthem." At right, Bobby contends with the Rangers' Walt Tkaczuk in '72 Stanley Cup finals. Orr played with torn cartilage in knee.

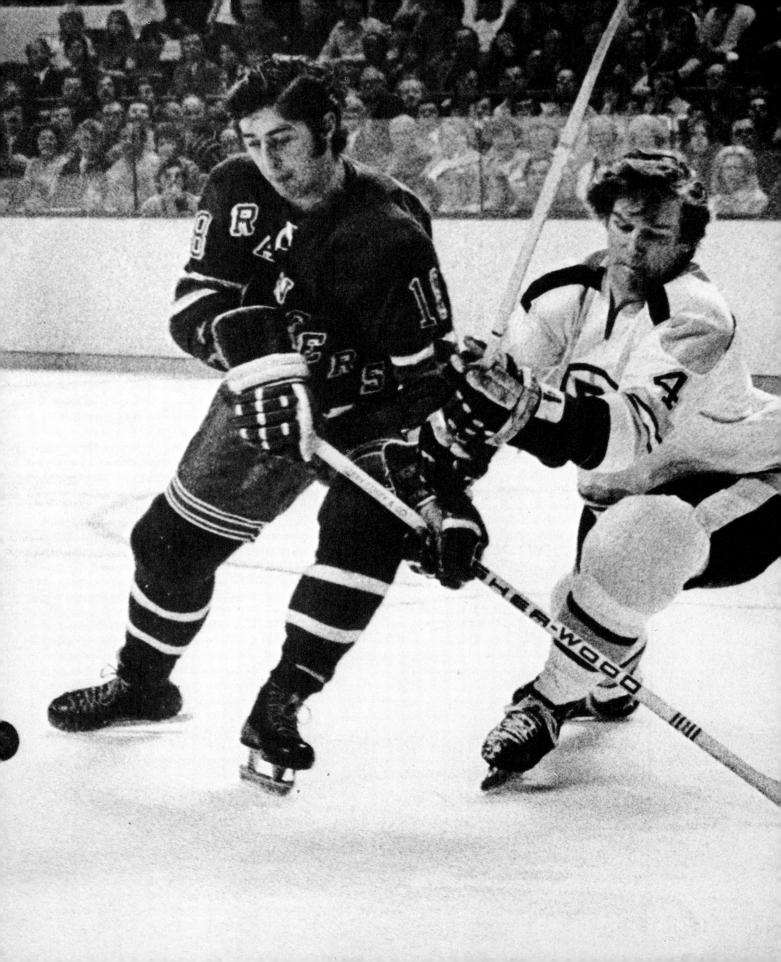

not enough to satisfy Alan Eagleson, the Toronto lawyer hired by the Orrs to handle that first signing.

Two decades earlier, when the Detroit Red Wings signed Gordie Howe, they used a club warm-up jacket and $400 as a bonus. But times had changed and Eagleson made the most of it. "The National Hockey League isn't the only place Bobby Orr can play hockey," warned Eagleson. "There is the Canadian National team too."

The Canadian Nationals offered a different set of benefits for Bobby. There was scholarship help to support Orr's education and the pride of representing his country in the Olympics and world championships. The idea appealed somewhat to Orr but gave Boston management heartburn. Eventually the contract negotiations went the way Eagleson wanted them to. The threat of the National team was dropped, and Orr agreed to a two-year contract estimated to be between $50,000 and $70,000. No hockey rookie had ever signed for so much cold cash. And few, if any, players on the Bruins were doing as well financially. Bobby would have to prove to the veterans that he was worth the price.

"I was a little nervous about the reaction among the Bruins," said Orr, recalling his first training camp. But instead of resentment, Bobby found a warm welcome. The Boston players accepted Orr quickly as a member of the team. The suspicion was that this young man with the pockets full of money would soon be putting money in his teammates' pockets as well. And those suspicions were well founded.

Orr flew up and down the rink like a motorized defenseman. He displayed moves that left observers wide-eyed in admiration. After one impressive practice session, veteran Boston defenseman Ted Green skated over to Orr and whispered in his ear. "I don't know what you're getting, kid," said Green, "but it isn't enough."

"I've never been so nervous in my life," said Orr, recalling his Boston debut. "This was my big night. This was what I was waiting for. The NHL." And the NHL was waiting for him. Tough guys such as Reg Fleming, Orland Kurtenbach, Ted Harris and others were anxious to test the young man. Would he hit back or could he be intimidated?

He was tendered the customary welcome to the NHL from Detroit's Gordie Howe—a wicked two-handed rap with the stick across the gloves.

Toronto defenseman Kent Douglas left him with a purple welt across his midsection. Then Harris, a rugged defenseman, decided to test, and that's when Orr started hitting back. He decked the heavyweight Harris twice in a single confrontation, and when word of the scrap filtered back to Kurtenbach, hockey's uncrowned heavyweight king, the big forward was impressed.

"Did he really knock Harris down?" asked Kurtenbach. Assured that he had, Kurt shook his head. "He's got good balance. He's hard to knock off his pins."

"I don't look for fights," said Orr, "but I don't back down from them either."

The Bruins' 6–2 opening game victory in Orr's rookie season started things off right. Bobby assisted on one of the goals after a misplay. He had intended to shoot the puck but almost fanned on it, sliding it instead weakly over to teammate John Bucyk, who scored. "I guess it looked like I was passing the puck," said Orr. "But I wasn't. I just missed it."

The Bruins played at home against Montreal in their next game, and the faithful fans turned out in force to see their wonder boy in person for the first time. Orr didn't disappoint them. He unloaded a slap shot that whipped past goalie Gump Worsley for his first NHL score. It very nearly brought Boston Garden down. The thunderous cheers seemed to shake the ancient building at its very foundations. "I never heard anything like it," said Toe Blake, coach of the Canadiens.

Orr's rookie season continued that way. The youngster scored well, accumulating 13 goals and assisting on 28 others for a respectable 41 points. He was voted Rookie of the Year and awarded the Calder Trophy in recognition of his accomplishment. When New York's Harry Howell, then 36, was voted the Norris Trophy as the league's top defenseman the same year, the veteran Ranger was thrilled.

"I'm glad I won this award now," said Howell, eyeing the Norris award, "because I've got a feeling from now on it's going to belong to Bobby Orr."

Despite the presence of Orr, the Bruins still finished last in the standings. But there seemed to be a light at the end of the tunnel, provided by the crew-cut defenseman who looked like the kid next door but who played hockey as though he'd been in the NHL for 15 years. "Bobby Orr was a star from the moment they played the national anthem in the opening game of the season," said his coach, Harry Sinden.

"I looked for the opening," said Orr. "If it's there, I take it. If it's not, I get rid of the puck." But when he got rid of the puck, it was because he chose to. Rarely would he lose the rubber to an enemy checker. And when he spotted his opening, he would shoot for it, using what his teammates often called "18 speeds of fast." Like a hot rodder, Orr seemed able to shift gears in midice, throwing his muscled legs into high speed with a thrust that sent him flying into the attacking zone. An Orr assault left heads spinning and often ended with the puck in the net.

Orr ran into injury problems in his second year and was limited to 46 games. But a measure of what he did in those games can be appreciated by the fact that he captured the Norris Trophy as the league's outstanding defenseman and the Bruins qualified for the play-offs for the first time in nine seasons. Orr had been better in 46 games than any other defender had been in 74. And the only NHL observer who didn't think so was Orr himself.

"They gave me the Norris Trophy," said Orr, "but I didn't deserve it. I only played, what, forty-six games? I had a bad play-off and, all in all, I thought I had a terrible year." Orr might have thought that for the 1967–68 year but he couldn't think it after that. The next year he scored 21 goals—only the second defenseman in history to hit that plateau—and 64 points, a record for a defenseman. It was a record that didn't stand up long.

Orr started the 1969–70 season as though he were a man with a mission. Defenseman Green had been cut down in a violent preseason incident, suffering a skull fracture and leaving the Bruins without a leader on the ice. Orr moved into the role. Time after time, he led the Boston rushes up ice, and time after time, the Bruins scored. Orr piled up goals and assists at a record pace. He became the first defenseman in league history to lead the scoring race after one month of play, and, incredibly, he maintained that margin as the season moved past the first of the year.

"You think you've got him lined up for a check," said Ranger defenseman Jim Neilson, "and . . . whoosh . . . he's gone again." When the subject of the scoring title was brought up to Orr, he laughed off the suggestion. "We're only a little more than halfway through the season," Bobby said, "and some guys haven't started scoring the way they can." The key was that Orr was scoring the way he could.

With Orr setting the pace, the Bruins soared to the top of the NHL's East Division and stayed there through the final weeks of the torrid race. On the final night of the season, Chicago squeezed past Boston by the slimmest of margins—a matter of five more victories—even though both teams finished tied in points. Orr was the scoring champion with an incredible 33 goals, 87 assists and 120 points—nearly twice his own previous point record for defensemen.

Next came the play-offs and Orr was at it again. Bobby scored 9 goals and assisted on 11 others, setting another record. His final goal came in overtime of Boston's fourth game victory over St. Louis and clinched the Stanley Cup for the Bruins—their first Cup since 1941.

Twenty-eight years between Stanley Cups was a long time to wait. But Orr had ended the drought. And one sip of that Cup champagne could become addictive. That's the reason the disappointment was so deep when Orr and the Bruins were eliminated from the play-offs in the opening round of the 1971 Stanley Cup.

Orr, his arms full of his usual award hardware, accepted the Norris Trophy as best defenseman and the Hart Trophy as Most Valuable Player at a May luncheon. He stared longingly at the Stanley Cup and asked, "Would anybody like to trade two trophies for one?"

Bobby had no takers, but a year later, in May, 1972, he needed none. Once again, he led the Bruins to the treasured Stanley Cup, and once again, he scored the winning goal in the deciding game. With three consecutive Hart Trophies as MVP and five straight Norris awards as the top defenseman, Orr had established himself as one of hockey's greatest all-time performers. He also had won the Calder Trophy as Rookie of the Year, the Ross Trophy for his scoring championship and two Conn Smythe Trophies as play-off MVP. But the one that counted most with Bobby was the battered but beautiful Stanley Cup.

"I feel great," he said, after the Bruins clinched the 1972 play-off title. "Winning does that to you. Winning . . . that's the only thing."

HAL BOCK

Edson Arantes do Nascimento
Pele: The World's Most Famous Athlete

It happened in 1959 in a São Paulo State League game between Santos and Juventus. Perhaps 60,000 fans were on hand. But, as in all moments of sporting magnitude, a million will claim to have seen it.

Santos was on the way to recording another of the lopsided victories it was to score for many years to come. One man stood in front of the goal, waiting for the ball. When it came, he deftly flicked the ball over one defender and dashed around him. As two more approached, he gathered the ball in, then once again booted it skyward, where it seemed almost to pause in midair. After feinting to the left, he suddenly dashed between the converging opponents. And as the bewildered goaltender stood rooted to the spot, looking on in disbelief, the attacker intercepted the descending ball and rocketed it into the net with his head. One Santos sports announcer exclaimed, "It was the greatest goal he ever scored."

The man who scored it seemed to agree. "I guess it was my best goal from a technical standpoint. I can't say it was my biggest thrill because it wasn't important enough. We were ahead four to nothing at the time and we didn't need a goal that much. But I must admit, it was something special."

The man who scored it was named Edson Arantes do Nascimento. That, at least, is the name on his birth certificate, his marriage license and various other legal documents. But as long as there are fans of the sport of soccer, it will be "Pele." Pele put the ball in the net. He put it there an incredible 1,086 times in his incomparable 16-year professional career, before he retired from international competition on July 18, 1971.

If that inconsequential goal is the best Pele ever scored, it is not too difficult to call it the best goal anyone ever scored in the game that is soccer in the United States but football in the rest of the world, for, without question, Pele is the best the sport has ever known. He is the world's most famous athlete. To any youngster who has ever booted or headed a ball toward a net, he is an idol. And to the countrymen and countrywomen of his native Brazil,

he is a demigod. He is Pele—"the Black Pearl."

It actually began with his father's career. Joao Ramos do Nascimento was a relatively unknown soccer player in the small town of Tres Coracoes when his son Edson was born. He played, as all Brazilian players do, under a nickname, his being Dondinho. And when Pele was five, Dondinho was promoted to a slightly better team in Bauru, to which city he moved his wife, Celeste, and their three children.

Soon Pele became a familiar sight in the street, practicing with a makeshift ball, a stocking stuffed with rags. By the time he was 10, he had quit school because of poor grades and disputes with classmates and had begun making a name for himself in neighborhood soccer games, some against construction workers three times his age. "Football was the only career I ever thought of," he said. "I wanted to follow my father's path. I was convinced he was the best player who ever lived but that he never got a chance to prove it."

At 11, Pele got his own chance, thanks to his father's friend Waldemar de Brito, a former São Paulo player. Three years of diligent training paid off as Pele became a star with Bauru. But Bauru was still the minor leagues, and so off they went in search of the big time in São Paulo. But the richer, prouder, more glamorous teams were impressed neither by his reputation nor by what they saw in tryouts. They turned Pele down—a decision they obviously regretted as evidenced by their later offers of as much as $500,000 for his contract. "I was very naïve," Pele recalled, "but I really thought I could make some team."

Rejected by the elite of São Paulo, de Brito turned to his own former team in the seacoast city of Santos. Its coach, Luiz Alonso Perez, known as "Lula," agreed to take a look at Pele. And after one practice session and over the objections of team officials, Lula hired Pele on a trial basis for $75 a month. "I felt as if I was lost," the once-confident but now shaken youngster said. "I was only fifteen and suddenly I had to live with strange people in a strange place. I was scared of failing."

He needn't have been. Lula remembered

Before retiring from his country's national team in 1971, Pele, "the Black Pearl," scored 1,086 goals during his 16-year career. He earned as much as $500,000 yearly.

that at first, Pele was "just an errand boy for the older players. He would buy soda for them —things like that. Then, before they knew it, they were looking up to him." He was quickly promoted from the junior team to the reserves of the first squad and his salary leaped to $600 a month. Santos club officials were so exuberant that they even awarded a $1,000 bonus to de Brito.

"My first real chance," Pele said of those early days, "came when four of us were loaned by Santos to the Vasco da Gama team in Rio when they were shorthanded for a tournament. We won and I scored some goals. When I got back to Santos, everyone was saying I was great and I was put on our first team. But I still wasn't sure I had made it. I was only sixteen and I needed my coach to keep teaching me and giving me confidence."

If he wasn't sure of his own ability then, he was a year later when, in 1958, he exploded onto the international scene in the World Cup matches in Stockholm, Sweden, with the Brazilian national team. After less-than-impressive games against Austria and England, Pele was inserted into the lineup for the team's crucial qualification game against the Soviet Union, and although he didn't score against the Russians, his performance was paramount in Brazil's 2–0 victory. It was only a glimpse of what was to follow.

His place in the lineup secure, Pele booted in three goals against France in the semifinals and then scored two more in the victory against Sweden that gave Brazil its first championship. "I still think that winning that World Cup was my biggest thrill because I was so young. I wasn't prepared for it psychologically," he said after having been toasted with champagne by Brazilian president Juscelino Kubitschek and declared, for the first time, his nation's king of soccer.

Then it was back to Santos, the club that had won just two major state-league titles before Pele's arrival. It was to win the next six in a row. And in 1962, Brazil was back in the quadrennial World Cup competition—but Pele was not. In the second game of the series in Chile, he was injured and sat out the remainder of the games. "But, thank God, Brazil won," he exclaimed after his team had captured its second straight championship.

Six years earlier he had met Rosemarie Cholby and had become secretly engaged. They had never appeared together publicly and she had never watched him play in all those years. Pele said that this was to protect her from waves of fans and jealous girls. His friends said that it was also to assure himself that a girl friend might not merely be seeking publicity. Now he was convinced and the wedding plans were announced.

The reaction was not unexpected. A collective moan arose from Brazil's single females, and as they pored over fan magazines with stories of Pele's love life, society pondered the protocol of such a major event. But Pele put an end to those matters. Dismissing suggestions that the wedding be given the attention accorded to ceremonies of state—one fan proposed that the ceremony be conducted in Santos's 35,000-seat stadium—Pele and Rosemarie were wed simply and quietly in his parents' home.

Insisting upon keeping his soccer stardom separate from his personal life, he refused to take the marriage vows unless he was addressed as Edson. The honeymoon, a tour of Europe, proceeded smoothly as well, with friends appearing everywhere to help the couple avoid the expected crowds. They might have gathered not solely because of his exploits on the playing field. "Don't you think," he was asked, "a Negro with a white wife might have had some trouble in some parts of Europe if the Negro's name wasn't Pele."

The groom seemed a bit puzzled. "I don't know—I never even thought about it," he replied. "I've never been faced with any kind of race trouble. Here in Brazil we hardly think about race. I know that Cassius Clay is always talking about fighting for his race. I wouldn't criticize him because I don't know the situation where he comes from. But in Brazil no one thinks that way. I could fight for my country or my friends but not for one color."

There were other goals yet to be reached. In 1966, at age 25, he was already thinking of retirement. "Perhaps, if I'm able," he said, "I might stay another two or three years, until I am twenty-eight. . . . Maybe, if I was needed badly, I might play in the World Cup in Mexico in 1970, but I don't think so." When Brazil failed to win its third World Cup, though, he changed his mind and continued to blaze along toward what was to become his most magnificent individual achievement.

In the low-scoring game of soccer—score-

Pele in action in 1969 against Venezuela.

less ties are not uncommon—a goal is to a soccer player what a home run is to a baseball player. Babe Ruth holds the baseball record at 714. By 1969, Pele had long since passed that figure and was approaching the millennium. He was approaching it by doing things with a ball that many would have called impossible. Gliding along the field, the 5-foot 8-inch, 160-pounder dribbled as though the ball were somehow connected to his feet by invisible strings. As defenders approached, he could feint and then pass the ball between his opponent's legs. Or he could deliberately boot it against their shins and then sweep by with the rebound. Then, facing the goal, he could unleash a shot equally devastating with either foot, head it in or, in a move that seemed to defy the very laws of gravity, flip the ball in the air, whirl with his back to the goal, hurl his body into the air and, while almost upside down, smash the ball netward.

The momentous goal number 1,000 finally came on November 19, 1969, at Rio's Maracana National Stadium before more than 100,000 fans. Newspapers had been blanketed with stories as the countdown reached its climax, giving Pele even more coverage than another countdown event, the lunar landing of Apollo 12. "This is more important than anything that's going on on the moon," one delirious fan shrieked. And a Brazilian reporter understated: "The government ought to contract Pele as a cabinet minister. He knows how to get people enthusiastic."

Then it was 1970 and once again Brazil was battling for the World Cup, this time against Italy, another two-time winner seeking to retire the Jules Rimet Trophy with a third triumph. The clash was played before a sellout crowd of 112,000 in Mexico City's Azteca Stadium. In the eighteenth minute, Pele took a pass and fired in a header that gave Brazil a 1–0 lead. But a mix-up in its defense gave the Italians a goal and a halftime tie. Then about 20 minutes into the second half, Brazil went ahead to stay and Pele sealed Italy's doom—and brought Brazil the trophy for good—by setting up two more goals in the following 7 minutes. It was "the greatest excitement I ever had as a player," he said after the 4–1 victory.

After that, there was but one more step—the step down. On May 31, 1971, he announced: "There is nothing that can change my mind. I must think about my family, my business and my private life. I've done enough for the selection of my country and I think that it is now time for the officials to start thinking about a replacement."

The end came in Rio on July 18. It was an international event, televised not only throughout Brazil but across Europe and North America as well. In Seville, Spain, bullfights were canceled. "With Pele on live TV," one bullfight expert explained, "we doubt that one-tenth of the ring could be filled." A week earlier in São Paulo, he had scored what was to be his final goal in international competition—goal number 1,086—as Brazil had tied Austria 1–1. The Austrian goalkeeper, when he saw he was beaten, had made a sweeping bow after the ball on its way into the net.

The last game with the Brazilian national team was played against Yugoslavia. Officials in Belgrade called it a great honor. Pele played the first half and then broke into tears as hundreds of admirers mobbed him. After a short stay in the referee's tunnel, he trotted around the field to the beat of his nation's anthem and "Obrigado Pele"—Thank you, Pele—a national hit. Tears still running down his cheeks, he stripped off his shirt and twirled it in the air as he jogged around the field before a record 130,000 fans. He watched the second half from the official box as Brazil fought back from a 1–0 deficit to finish in a 2–2 tie.

"It is all too overwhelming," he said, his voice choked with emotion. "I had tried to imagine what this would be like, but it surpassed anything I could think."

Then it was over. He was no longer Pele. Once again he was Edson Arantes do Nascimento, except for his appearances with Santos, and after stepping down from the pinnacle, he said he would miss it. "There is nothing like soccer," he said. "Full stadium, thousands of banners, the ball, shining white, ahead. A sure kick. Goal!"

BRUCE LOWITT